THE NEW ECONOMIC DIPLOMACY

Global Finance Series

Edited by
John Kirton, Munk Centre for International Studies, Trinity College, Canada,
Michele Fratianni, Indiana University, USA and Paolo Savona, LUISS University,
Italy

The intensifying globalisation of the twenty-first century has brought a myriad of
new managerial and political challenges for governing international finance. The
return of synchronous global slowdown, mounting developed country debt, and new
economy volatility have overturned established economic certainties. Proliferating
financial crises, transnational terrorism, currency consolidation, and increasing
demands that international finance should better serve public goods such as social
and environmental security have all arisen to compound the problem.

The new public and private international institutions that are emerging to govern
global finance have only just begun to comprehend and respond to this new world.
Embracing international financial flows and foreign direct investment, in both
the private and public sector dimensions, this series focuses on the challenges and
opportunities faced by firms, national governments, and international institutions,
and their roles in creating a new system of global finance.

Also in the series

The New Economic Diplomacy
Decision-Making and Negotiation in International Economic Relations
Second Edition

Edited by

NICHOLAS BAYNE
and
STEPHEN WOOLCOCK
The London School of Economics and Political Science, UK

ASHGATE

Published by
Ashgate Publishing Limited
Gower House
Croft Road
Aldershot
Hampshire GU11 3HR
England

Ashgate Publishing Company
Suite 420
101 Cherry Street
Burlington, VT 05401-4405
USA

Ashgate website: http://www.ashgate.com

British Library Cataloguing in Publication Data
The new economic diplomacy : decision-making and
   negotiation in international economic relations. - Rev. ed.
   – (Global finance series)
   1. International economic relations 2. International
   cooperation 3. Commercial policy 4. Negotiation in business
   I. Bayne, Nicholas, 1937- II. Woolcock, Stephen
   337

Library of Congress Cataloging-in-Publication Data
The new economic diplomacy : decision-making and negotiation in international eco-
nomic relations / [edited] by Nicholas Bayne and Stephen Woolcock.
      p. cm. -- (Global finance)
   Includes bibliographical references and index.
   ISBN 978-0-7546-7047-6 -- ISBN 978-0-7546-7048-3 1.
International economic relations. 2. International cooperation. 3. Commercial policy.
4. Negotiation in business. 5. Decision making. 6. International economic
relations--Case studies. I. Bayne, Nicholas, 1937- II. Woolcock, Stephen.

   HF1359.N4685 2007
   337--dc22

                                                             2007020566

ISBN: 978-0-7546-7047-6 (hardback)
ISBN: 978-0-7546-7048-3 (pbk.)

Printed and bound in Great Britain by TJ International Ltd, Padstow, Cornwall.

Contents

List of Figures and Tables

Figures

Tables

Notes on Contributors

Sir Nicholas Bayne, KCMG, is a Fellow of the International Trade Policy Unit of the London School of Economics and Political Science (LSE). While a member of the British Diplomatic Service from 1961 to 1996, he served as High Commissioner to Canada, Economic Director at the Foreign and Commonwealth Office (FCO) and UK Representative to the OECD.

Dr Stephen Woolcock is a Lecturer in the International Relations Department of the LSE and Visiting Fellow at UNU CRIS Brugge.

Kate Macdonald is currently based in the Government Department of the LSE. She has previously worked as a Research Fellow at the Centre for Applied Philosophy and Public Ethics at the Australian National University and as Research Officer at the Department of Politics and International Relations at Oxford University.

Martin Donnelly, CMG, is Director General Europe and Globalisation at the Foreign and Commonwealth Office (FCO) and UK Foreign Affairs Sous-Sherpa for G8 summit preparations.

Professor Dr Reinhard Quick, LL.M, is Director of the Brussels office of the German Chemical Industry Association (Verband der Chemischen Industrie e.V.). He teaches international economic law at Saarland University, Saarbrücken.

Phil Evans is Head of Consumer Policy at Fipra, a specialist public affairs consultancy. From 1996 to 2005 he was Principal Policy Adviser to the Consumers Association. He contributed a chapter to the first edition of this book.

Matthew Goodman is Managing Director of Stonebridge International. From 2002 to 2004 he was responsible for US economic policy towards Asia in the National Security Council, after being Head of Government Affairs at Goldman Sachs International, London (1999–2002) and Financial Attaché and Treasury Representative at the US Embassy in Tokyo (1992–1997). He contributed a chapter to the first edition.

Kishan S. Rana is Professor Emeritus of the Foreign Service Institute, New Delhi, and Senior Fellow at DiploFoundation. As a member of the Indian Foreign Service (1960–1995), he was Ambassador/High Commissioner to Algeria, Czechoslovakia, Kenya, Mauritius and Germany, as well as serving in Prime Minister Indira Gandhi's office and as Consul General in San Francisco. He retains the copyright of his chapter.

Matthias Buck is a Policy Officer in the International Environmental Agreements and Trade Unit of the Environment Directorate General of the European Commission. Before joining the Commission in 2005, he worked as a researcher and policy advisor with a focus on linkages between environmental, economic and development issues.

Joan MacNaughton, CB, is Senior Research Fellow at the Oxford Institute of Energy Studies (OIES). From 2002 to 2006 she was Director General for Energy at the Department of Trade and Industry and UK representative on the Governing Board of the International Energy Agency, chairing the Board in 2004 and 2005. She retains the copyright of her chapter.

Sir Nigel Wicks, GCB, CVO, CBE, is Chairman of Euroclear, the European system for securities settlement. From 1988 to 2000 he was Second Permanent Secretary (Finance) at HM Treasury, after being Principal Private Secretary to the Prime Minister (1985–1988) and UK Executive Director to the IMF and World Bank (1983–1985). He contributed a chapter to the first edition.

Roderick Abbott is a Visiting Fellow at the LSE and a member of the Advisory Board of the European Centre for International Political Economy (ECIPE). From 2002 to 2005 he was Deputy Director General of the World Trade Organization (WTO), after being Deputy Director General for Trade in the European Commission (2000–2002) and Permanent Representative of the European Union to the WTO, the United Nations and other international organisations in Geneva (1996–2000).

Preface to the Revised Edition

Economic diplomacy, as presented in this book, is the brainchild of the late Mike Hodges, Senior Lecturer in the International Relations Department at the LSE. In 1997 he had the idea of bringing together the analytical skills of academics with the experience of policy practitioners, to examine how states organise and conduct their international economic relations. He approached Nicholas Bayne, then recently retired from the British Diplomatic Service, and they planned a series of graduate seminars in Economic Diplomacy at the LSE in 1998–1999, at which pairs of academics and practitioners would share the platform. This was intended to be the forerunner to a full graduate course, to begin the following year. But tragically Mike died in June 1998, before he could bring his plan to fruition.

Stephen Woolcock had then just become a Lecturer at the LSE's International Relations Department. He joined forces with Nicholas Bayne to continue what Mike Hodges had begun. The seminar series went out as planned. It was followed, in 1999–2000, by a full graduate course, in which academic lectures, by Bayne and Woolcock, provided the framework for a sequence of lectures by practitioners, drawn from government, international institutions and the private sector. These practitioner lectures formed an integral part of the course.

The Economic Diplomacy course became established and will soon complete its first decade. Early on, we decided to make the lectures the foundation for a book. This first edition of *The New Economic Diplomacy* appeared early in 2003, with each chapter corresponding to an academic or practitioner lecture. This revised and updated edition follows the same structure. It is entirely free-standing and does not require reference back to its predecessor. Nevertheless, it may be worth recording the main differences from the first edition. These are:

- we have simplified the analysis in the academic chapters, especially in Chapter 1;
- we have cut back on narrative and on historical background. The previous case studies on the International Trade Organisation and the early G7 summits have disappeared and an earlier chapter ('Current Challenges in Economic Diplomacy') has been absorbed into Chapter 1;
- a new academic chapter provides deeper examination of multi-level economic diplomacy, with a special study of investment;
- among practitioner chapters, we have provided a new one on business in economic diplomacy, to complement the studies of government and civil society;
- we have given more attention throughout to the growing influence of major developing countries. This especially appears in Chapters 11 and 12, which feature China and India, among others;

- we have added a case study on the International Energy Agency, to recognise the greater salience of energy issues;
- the references to each chapter and the Bibliography make more use of material from electronic sources and include lists of useful websites.

We believe these changes make our book more accessible and definitive and reflect the most recent shifts in economic diplomacy.

In producing this revised edition, we have incurred many debts and take this opportunity to express our thanks to the many people who have helped us both with this book and its predecessor and with the course itself. Our first debt of gratitude is to those who have shared the burden of teaching and running the course. These are: Mathias Koenig-Archibugi, our third academic lecturer; Phil Evans and Kate Macdonald, who have contributed chapters to the book; Jeff Chwieroth, Manfred Elsig, Olu Fasan, Ken Heydon and Heidi Ullrich. We are also indebted to our other colleagues at the LSE who have welcomed and encouraged this innovation, spoken at lectures and helped us in manifold ways. They include Christopher Alden, Christopher Brown, Robert Falkner, Charles Goodhart, Christopher Hill, Graham Ingham, Daphne Josselin, Richard Layard, Margot Light, Hilary Parker, Razeen Sally, Julius Sen, David Stasavage, Paul Taylor, Andrew Walter, William Wallace, Sarah Wenban and Michael Yahuda.

Second, we thank most warmly all the practitioners who have agreed to speak for us in the lecture programme over the years. Our greatest debt is to those who, in addition to lecturing, have written chapters to this updated volume, as listed in the Notes on Contributors. In addition, we are most grateful to all the other speakers, both practitioners and non-LSE academics, who have contributed to the programme from the beginning: Colin Budd, Richard Carden, Ivan Mbirimi and Patrick Rabe (who all wrote chapters for the first edition of the book); Celso Amorim, Michael Arthur, Matthew Baldwin, Bryan Carsberg, Robert Chote, Stephen Cristina, Matthias Duwe, David Earnshaw, the late Huw Evans, David Fisk, Andrew Fraser, Graham Fry, Duncan Green, Michael Grubb, Charles Hay, Sebastian Herreros, Tony Hutton, Noe van Hulst, Sylvia Jay, Emyr Jones-Parry, Edwini Kessie, Julian Lob-Levyt, Matthew Lockwood, Gustavo Martin-Prada, Ann Pettifor, Stephen Pickford, Marithza Ruiz de Vielman, Joakim Reiter, Alan Rugman, Garry Sampson, Tom Scholar, George Staple, Nicholas Stern and Gunnar Wiegand.

Third, we are indebted to everyone who has taken part in the lectures and seminars and contributed to the development of our ideas on economic diplomacy. These have included not only LSE students, but also members of British government departments, thanks to the encouragement of the Foreign and Commonwealth Office, the Department of Trade and Industry, HM Treasury and the Department for International Development.

Finally, we would like to thank Kirstin Howgate for her initiative in commissioning this updated edition and all those at Ashgate involved with bringing this book into its published state. The first edition also owed much to John Kirton and Madeline Koch, from the G8 Research Group of the University of Toronto, and to our four anonymous reviewers. Thanks to them, the ideas that we have been developing and testing in the laboratory of the LSE can continue to reach out to a wider audience.

Nicholas Bayne
Stephen Woolcock

Hampton Court, Brussels and London
April 2007

List of Abbreviations

ACC	American Chemistry Council
ACP	African, Caribbean and Pacific associates of the EU
AFTA	ASEAN Free Trade Area
AIDS	Acquired Immune Deficiency Syndrome
APEC	Asia-Pacific Economic Cooperation
APR	Africa Personal Representative in G8
ASEAN	Association of South-East Asian Nations
ASEM	Asia-Europe Meeting
ASP	American Selling Price for chemicals
ASSOCHAM	Associated Chambers of Commerce of India
Bank	Short for World Bank
BATNA	Best Alternative To a Negotiated Agreement
BCIM	Bangladesh China India Myanmar
BDA	Bundesverband der Deutschen Arbeitsgeber
BDI	Bundesverband der Deutschen Industrie
BIAC	Business and Industry Advisory Committee of the OECD
BIMSTEC	Bangladesh India Myanmar Sri Lanka Thailand Economic Community
BIS	Bank for International Settlements
BIT	Bilateral Investment Treaty
BSE	Bovine Spongiform Encephalopathy – mad-cow disease
CAFOD	Catholic Fund for Overseas Development
CAFTA	Central American Free Trade Agreement
CAP	Common Agricultural Policy of the EU
Caricom	Caribbean Community
CBC	Commonwealth Business Council
CBI	Confederation of British Industry
CEFIC	European Chemical Industry Council
CfA	Commission for Africa
CFCs	Chlorofluorocarbons
CHOGM	Commonwealth Heads of Government Meeting
CTHA	Chemical Tariff Harmonization Agreement in the WTO
CIA	Chemical Industries Association of the UK
CII	Confederation of Indian Industry
CIME	Committee on International Investment and Multinational Enterprises of the OECD
CITES	Convention on International Trade in Endangered Species
COP	Conference of the Parties to Environmental Treaties
COREPER	Committee of Permanent Representatives of the EU
DATA	Debt AIDS Trade Africa

DDA	Doha Development Agenda
DEFRA	Department of the Environment, Food and Rural Affairs of the UK
DFID	Department for International Development of the UK
DG	Directorate General of the European Commission
DM	DeutscheMark
DSB	Dispute Settlement Body of the WTO
DTI	Department of Trade and Industry of the UK
DTIE	Division of Technology, Industry and Economics of UNEP
EBRD	European Bank for Reconstruction and Development
EDB	Economic Development Board of Singapore
EEC	European Economic Community
EC	European Community
ECB	European Central Bank
ECJ	European Court of Justice
ECOFIN	Economic and Finance Council of the EU
ECSC	European Coal and Steel Community
ECU	European Currency Unit
ED	Executive Director of Fund or Bank
EFTA	European Free Trade Area
EMS	European Monetary System
EMU	Economic and Monetary Union
EP	European Parliament
ERM	Exchange Rate Mechanism of the EMS
EU	European Union
FAO	Food and Agriculture Organisation
FASS	Foreign Affairs Sous-Sherpa in G8 summit preparation
FCC	Federal Communications Commission of the US
FCO	Foreign and Commonwealth Office of the UK
FDI	Foreign Direct Investment
FICCI	Federation of Indian Chambers of Commerce and Industry
FSS	Finance Sous-Sherpa in G8 summit preparation
FTA	Free Trade Agreement
FTAA	Free Trade Area of the Americas
FTAAP	Free Trade Area of the Asia-Pacific
Fund	Short for International Monetary Fund (see also IMF)
GATS	General Agreement on Trade in Services in the WTO
GATT	General Agreement on Tariffs and Trade
GCAP	Global Campaign Against Poverty
GDP	Gross Domestic Product
GFAC	General and Foreign Affairs Council of the EU
GM	Genetically Modified
GMS	Greater Mekong Sub-region
GNP	Gross National Product
GOM	Gulf of Mexico
GSP	General Scheme of Preferences

G6	Group of Six leading negotiators in WTO
G7	Group of Seven – summit, finance ministers and other groups
G8	Group of Eight – summit and other groups
G10	Group of Ten countries protecting agriculture in WTO
G20	Group of 20 finance ministers on new architecture in IMF *or*
	Group of 20 major developing countries in WTO
G24	Group of 24 developing countries in the IMF
G33	Group of 33 developing agricultural importers in WTO
HIPC	Heavily Indebted Poor Countries
IBSA	India Brazil South Africa
ICC	International Chamber of Commerce
ICCA	International Council of Chemical Associations
ICCM	International Conference on Chemicals Management
ICFTU	International Confederation of Free Trade Unions
ICITO	Interim Committee of the ITO
ICSID	International Centre for the Settlement of Investment Disputes
IEA	International Energy Agency
IEP	International Energy Programme of the IEA
IES	International Enterprise Singapore
IFCS	Intergovernmental Forum on Chemical Safety
ILO	International Labour Organisation
IMF	International Monetary Fund, also known as the Fund
IMFC	International Monetary and Financial Committee of the IMF
IOMC	Inter-Organization Programme for the Sound Management of Chemicals
IPCC	Intergovernmental Panel on Climate Change
IPE	International Political Economy
ITA	International Tin Agreement
ITC	International Trade Commission of the US
ITO	International Trade Organisation
ITUC	International Trade Union Confederation
JCIA	Japan Chemical Industry Association
JODI	Joint Oil Data Initiative
LOOP	Louisiana Offshore Oil Port
LSE	London School of Economics and Political Science
MAI	Multilateral Agreement on Investment in the OECD
MEA	Ministry of External Affairs of India *or*
	Multilateral Environmental Agreement
METI	Ministry of Economics, Trade and Industry of Japan
MFN	Most-Favoured-Nation treatment in GATT and WTO
MNC	Multi-National Company
MOFTEC	Ministry of Foreign Trade and Economic Cooperation of China
MOP	Meeting of the Parties to Environmental Agreements
MTMOMR	Medium Term Oil Market Report of the IEA

NAFTA	North American Free Trade Agreement
NAMA	Non-Agricultural Market Access
NATO	North Atlantic Treaty Organisation
NEPAD	New Partnership for Africa's Development
NIC	Newly Industrialising Country
NGO	Non-Governmental Organisation
NTB	Non-Tariff Barrier
NTI	National Treatment Instrument of the OECD
OECD	Organisation for Economic Cooperation and Development
OEEC	Organisation for European Economic Reconstruction
OFTEL	Office of the Telecommunications Regulator in the UK
OPEC	Organisation of Petroleum Exporting Countries
OPS	Overarching Policy Strategy of SAICM
POPs	Persistent Organic Pollutants
PD	Political Director in G8 summit preparation
Quad	Quadrilateral of trade ministers (US, EC, Japan, Canada) in GATT
REIO	Regional Economic Integration Organisation
SACU	Southern Africa Customs Union
SAICM	Strategic Approach to International Chemicals Management
SEM	Single European Market
SPD	Social Democratic Party of Germany
TABD	Trans-Atlantic Business Dialogue
TEC	Treaty establishing the European Community
TNC	Trade Negotiations Committee of the WTO
TRIMS	Trade-Related Investment Measures agreement of WTO
TRIPS	Trade-Related Intellectual Property Rights agreement of WTO
TPRB	Trade Policy Review Body of the WTO
TUAC	Trade Union Advisory Committee of the OECD
UIC	Union des Industries Chimiques of France
UK	United Kingdom
UN	United Nations
UNCED	United Nations Conference on Environment and Development
UNCSD	United Nations Commission on Sustainable Development
UNCITRAL	United Nations Centre for Investment and Trade Law
UNCTAD	United Nations Conference on Trade and Development
UNEP	United Nations Environment Programme
UNFCCC	United Nations Framework Convention on Climate Change
UNGA	United Nations General Assembly
UNICE	Union of European Industry and Employers' Confederations (now renamed BusinessEurope)
UNIDO	United Nations Industrial Development Organisation
UNITAR	United Nations Institute for Training and Research
US	United States of America

USSR	Union of Soviet Socialist Republics
USTR	United States Trade Representative
VCI	Verband der Chemischen Industrie, e. V. of Germany
WBSCD	World Business Council for Sustainable Development
WEF	World Economic Forum
WGTI	Working Group on Trade and Investment of the WTO
WHO	World Health Organisation
WMO	World Meteorological Organisation
WSSD	World Summit on Sustainable Development
WTO	World Trade Organization
WWF	World-Wide Fund for Nature

Chapter 1

What is Economic Diplomacy?

Nicholas Bayne and Stephen Woolcock

This is a book about how states conduct their international economic relations at the start of the twenty-first century: how they make decisions domestically; how they negotiate with each other internationally; and how these two processes interact. While states are at the centre of this study, it also includes non-state actors, whose influence on decision-making is growing. This book focuses on the methods and process of decision-making and negotiation, rather than the content of policy. It is not intended to be a manual for negotiators, but rather to explain why governments and other actors in economic diplomacy behave in the way they do.

We call this book *The New Economic Diplomacy* to emphasise how much this activity has changed in the 1990s and early 2000s. Through most of the period since World War II, economic diplomacy was dominated by permanent officials from the governments of a limited number of countries.[1] It was shaped by the constraints of the Cold War. Now, with the end of the Cold War and the advance of globalisation, there are far more non-government players; ministers and heads of government are active alongside their officials; and a single economic system covers the entire world, with many more countries active in it. Economic diplomacy, originally concerned only with measures taken at the border, increasingly operates 'within the frontier' and influences domestic policy. Cold War political impulses have been replaced by worries about globalisation and, since 11 September 2001, the fight against terrorism. All these trends will shape this book. They have gathered pace since it first came out in 2003 and we have updated this new edition to reflect this.

There are several reasons why economic diplomacy, that is, the process of international economic decision-making, is worthy of attention. First of all, it fills a gap in current academic studies. The discipline of International Political Economy (IPE) focuses on structural factors, such as the relative power of states or the structures of influence within national economies, rather than on process. But where power relationships are balanced, the process of decision-making and negotiation can determine outcomes, as Professor John Odell points out in his book *Negotiating the World Economy* (Odell 2000). The examination of economic decision-making also illuminates how governments try to make their

---

1   In this book we normally follow the European usage of 'ministers' and 'officials', rather than the American terms 'politicians' and 'bureaucrats'.

policies more efficient and how they respond to pressures for greater democratic accountability. Since the end of the Cold War economic diplomacy, to enhance prosperity, has been the main priority for states in most regions of the world. Though security concerns have revived since the terrorist attacks of 11 September 2001, economic diplomacy also contributes to the efforts to address the root causes of terrorism.

Economic diplomacy is not just a subject for academic study. It is an activity pursued by state and non-state actors in the real world of today. In some respects economic diplomacy is like sex: easier to describe if you have practised it yourself. So while much of this book is written by Nicholas Bayne and Steve Woolcock of the LSE, with the help of our colleague Kate Macdonald, an integral part of it is contributed by experienced practitioners of economic diplomacy. The practitioner chapters, starting at Chapter 6, provide case studies and illustrations of how economic diplomacy works.

This opening chapter covers the following:

- it begins with a broad definition of the scope and content of economic diplomacy;
- it briefly identifies the relevant theoretical approaches;
- it sets out the analytical framework used throughout the book, based on three tensions of economic diplomacy;
- it picks out the new trends of the 1990s and early 2000s and the responses to them.

The chapter concludes with a brief review of the structure of the book, showing how the academic and practitioner chapters fit together.

Defining Economic Diplomacy

'Economic diplomacy' is the term chosen to describe the subject of this study. This has the advantage that 'diplomacy' is a broad and elastic term. But precisely because it admits of wide interpretation, some further definition is needed, to make clear what is and is not included in this book.[2]

The classical concept of diplomacy defines it as: 'the conduct of relations between states and other entities with standing in world politics by official agents and by peaceful means' (Bull 1977/1995, 156). A more recent definition says that: 'Diplomacy is concerned with the management of relations between states and between states and other actors' (Barston 2006, 1). To do justice to *economic*

---

2   Marshall 1999, 7–8, distinguishes six different meanings of diplomacy. Berridge and James 2003 offer two definitions of 'economic diplomacy', which they rightly distinguish from 'commercial diplomacy'. We are closest to their first definition; for the second – the use of economic sanctions – we prefer the term 'economic statecraft', as noted below.

diplomacy, it will be necessary to stretch these definitions and dispose of some misleading stereotypes associated with the term diplomacy.

According to these stereotypes, diplomacy is conducted only by diplomats, that is, by people from foreign ministries; it applies to informal negotiation and voluntary cooperation, not to rule-based systems and legal commitments; it is a weak and imprecise activity, where conciliation leads only to meaningless compromises; it is elitist, conducted by an establishment of privileged officials; and it is secretive and opaque, with diplomats striking deals in secret conclaves and emerging only to announce agreement. None of these stereotypes apply to economic diplomacy, as covered by this book. As the following sections will show, the scope and content of economic diplomacy is much broader and more purposeful.

International and Domestic

Economic diplomacy is concerned with *international* economic issues. In principle, this should simplify the analysis. The Bretton Woods system of international economic institutions created after World War II was based on what John Ruggie has called 'embedded liberalism' (Ruggie 1982). This meant that the system developed rules for economic relations between states, but left national economic autonomy largely untouched. As long as *domestic* policies did not have negative impacts on others, governments could pursue whatever employment, tax or industrial policy they wished.[3] But the increase in economic interdependence over the last 60 years has put an end to such tidy distinctions between what is domestic and what is international policy. The advance of globalisation since 1990 obliges economic diplomacy to go deep into domestic decision-making. This makes economic diplomacy much more complex, bringing in more issues and more actors.

State and Non-State Actors

Economic diplomacy is mainly concerned with what *governments* do, in the broadest definition. It goes much wider than foreign ministries or any closed circle of bureaucrats. All government agencies that have economic responsibilities and operate internationally are engaging in economic diplomacy, though they might not describe it as such. Ministers and heads of government, parliaments, independent public agencies and sub-national bodies are all making their influence felt.

A great variety of *non-state* actors also engage in economic diplomacy, both by shaping government policies and as independent players in their own right.

---

3   For example, when the General Agreement on Tariffs and Trade (GATT) was formed in 1948, there was a clear understanding of what was a trade issue, and thus potentially subject to GATT rules, and what was a non-trade issue. Provided domestic regulation or policies did not discriminate between imported and local national goods, GATT rules provided no constraint on national policy autonomy.

In the past, business tended to be the most active interest group. Now non-governmental organisations (NGOs), grouped as civil society, have assumed centre stage. International organisations are important as a forum for negotiations. But this book does not treat them as independent actors. Instead it focuses on how governments make use of these organisations and integrate them into their own decision-making processes.

Instruments and Issues

Economic diplomacy uses a full range of *instruments*. It embraces the whole spectrum of measures from informal negotiation and voluntary cooperation, through soft types of regulation (such as codes of conduct), to the creation and enforcement of binding rules. Progress in usually made by persuasion and mutual agreement. Economic diplomacy can be confrontational and include punitive economic measures taken in the pursuit of political goals, such as sanctions. But we prefer the term 'economic statecraft' for sanctions and related policies; they are well analysed elsewhere (Baldwin 1985; Hanson 1988) and are only covered in passing in this book.

Economic diplomacy is best defined not by its instruments but by the economic *issues* that provide its content. We follow the same categories as used by Odell in determining the scope of economic negotiation: 'policies relating to production, movement or exchange of goods, services, investments (including official development assistance), money, information and their regulation' (Odell 2000, 11). This is a very wide range of issues. A single volume could not cover them all and, of necessity, this book is selective. It concentrates on the central issues of trade, finance, energy and the global environment. These are topics of high political profile, which arouse strong popular concern and bring out well the interplay between different actors in economic diplomacy

This book also has to make choices between the countries studied. Much of it is about economic diplomacy as practised by the major powers of Europe, North America and Japan. These have been the most influential countries in the international system and their decision-making practices are relatively open and easy to study. But this offers only an incomplete picture of the world, where developing and ex-communist countries are becoming more active internationally and the problems of the poorest countries attract growing concern. So this revised edition gives more space to developing countries, especially rising powers like China, India and Brazil.

The Impact of Markets

A distinctive feature of economic diplomacy is that it is sensitive to *market developments*. This sets economic diplomacy apart from political diplomacy and its study through foreign policy analysis. Increased economic integration has created global markets for production and investment. National regulatory policies can change the competitiveness of different locations, so that markets can punish national policies which are not in line with expectations. Market developments will shape the actors involved in any issue, influence their negotiating positions and possibly offer alternatives to a negotiated solution. This means economic diplomacy will not succeed if the market offers a more attractive alternative. As Odell puts it, markets can be endogenous to economic diplomacy, in that they form an integral part of the process (Odell 2000, 47–69).

Is There a Theory of Economic Diplomacy?

Theoretical aspects of economic diplomacy are the subject of Chapter 2 of this book. But it is important to make clear at the outset that there is no single theory of economic diplomacy that can provide answers on how states, under given circumstances, will conduct policy. Such theories are concerned with the prediction of outcomes: they make significant simplifications, for example, by regarding states as unitary actors with clearly defined and stable policy preferences; and it must be possible to test whether they are correct or not. Theories of this kind are not much help in economic diplomacy, which is concerned with the interaction between international and domestic factors and between economic and political concerns. It makes no sense to assume that states are unitary actors, that negotiators have full knowledge of national policy preferences or that these preferences will be steady and not affected by market developments.

The alternative use of theory is to underpin an analytical framework that will help to identify which questions to ask. A framework of this kind will help in sorting out the complex factors that shape the decision-making process. The aim is to identify the main explanatory factors and then consider which of these are most important in a range of case studies. This will enable some generalisations to be made on the nature of economic diplomacy

The development of this framework draws on the existing literature on international economic cooperation and IPE in general, which considers the systemic, societal and state-centred factors shaping national policy preferences. This literature, as noted, looks predominantly at structures of interest and power and allows for different levels of analysis of economic relations between states, as follows:

- *Systemic* In systemic theories, the international system is regarded as decisive in explaining events. Realist theories, for example, put much weight on the relative economic power of states. Hegemonic stability theory, which has been much used in IPE, argues that economic cooperation only comes about when there is a dominant state able to ensure that it happens. Regime theory provides insights into how and why states cooperate, whether this takes the form of formal institutions or more informal processes, in which shared values and norms help develop confidence in the mutual benefit of cooperation. There are other 'structural theories' which see national economic policies as dependent on the wider global capitalist system; these include dependency theory.
- *Domestic* In contrast to systemic theories, which concentrate on relations between states as single entities, domestic theories look within the state for

explanations of international behaviour. At the national domestic level there are societal and state-centred theories, which divide as follows:

o   societal theories see policy as the outcome of interaction between different interest groups, with government officials acting as agents in negotiations. Societal forces such as interest groups can also operate across borders as transnational actors;

o   state-centred theories focus more on the role of institutional structures and the interplay of interests between different government departments. Here the interaction between national parliaments and the executive branches of government is seen as important, as is the role of the bureaucracy.

•   *Ideas and individuals* Some theories argue that ideas, like political ideologies, or individuals have a determining impact on policy. This impact can be felt both domestically and internationally.

In addition to the mainstream international relations and IPE literature, there are approaches that can be directly applied to negotiation and are thus useful for economic diplomacy. These include:

•   *Rationalist and constructivist models* Rationalist models have built on societal theories by viewing governments as rational actors in international negotiations that seek to maximise their utility function. Maximising utility has normally been defined as retaining power. The rationalist theories therefore seek to model the interaction between interest groups and government. In recent years there has been more emphasis on constructivist theories that stress how the expectations and views of negotiators can be changed through persuasion.

•   *Two-level games* The two-level game model developed by Professor Robert Putnam seeks to capture the interaction between different levels of analysis. It is of particular value for economic diplomacy, because it explains the interaction between international and domestic and puts the negotiation process at the core of analysis (Putnam 1988).

•   *Economic negotiation and markets* Professor John Odell has applied theories of negotiation between private parties, as in industrial relations, to international economic negotiations between governments. His approach is useful for economic diplomacy in providing valuable insights into negotiating strategies and integrating the role of markets into the analysis (Odell 2000).

To recapitulate the discussion of theory, the aim is not to identify a parsimonious theory that could be used to predict the outcome of domestic decision-making or international negotiations. This might be an interesting academic study, but would not be able to interpret what happens in practice. Instead, the objective is to formulate a middle range framework of analysis that will help in understanding the factors at work in economic diplomacy and reaching some broad conclusions consistent with the evidence provided by practitioners.

The Analytical Framework of this Book

The main analytical framework adopted in this book draws on the theoretical strands identified in the last section. But it combines these with observation of how economic diplomats themselves behave, as illustrated in the later case studies. The main argument of this book is that governments are trying to reconcile three types of tension, so that policies become mutually reinforcing rather than conflicting with each other. These tensions are:

- first, the tension between politics and economics;
- second, the tension between international and domestic pressures;
- third, the tension between governments and other actors, such as private business and civil society.

Taken together, these three tensions provide the principal lines of enquiry for this book.

Tension between Economics and Politics

The first major tension is between international economics and international politics. In an ideal world, states would be able to keep politics and economics apart. But states are political entities rather than economic ones, so that politics constantly encroaches on economics in the pursuit of international objectives. Governments strive to reconcile politics and economics, both in the objectives chosen and the methods used, so that they do not conflict but mutually reinforce their preferred policies. Systemic theories are most relevant in analysing this process.

The impact of this first tension has varied over the last 60 years, but is always present. In the period following World War II, the United States launched major initiatives that combined political and economic objectives. The Bretton Woods institutions and the Marshall Plan had the essentially political aims of deterring future wars and helping Western Europe to resist communist encroachment. To achieve these political objectives the Americans adjusted their economic policies accordingly, so that politics and economics strongly reinforced each other.[4] Later in the Cold War, however, Americans and Europeans disagreed over economic diplomacy towards the Soviet Union: the United States wanted to impose economic restrictions to weaken the USSR politically, while the Europeans wanted to use economic relations to open up the closed Soviet system. Today the focus on terrorism since 11 September 2001 has reshaped this tension, as discussed later in this chapter.

Governments have developed a variety of methods for reconciling this tension. For example, most economists argue that countries gain economic benefit by removing barriers to external competition, whatever other countries may do. But this meets political obstacles, when governments think that others will take advantage

---

4 For a good analysis of the origins of the Bretton Woods institutions, see Gardner 1980. For a vivid practitioner's account of the Marshall Plan, see Marjolin 1989.

of the reforms they are adopting. One technique to overcome this obstacle is to negotiate away trade barriers by reciprocity.[5] Countries find this politically easier, if economically sub-optimal, because they visibly get something in return for whatever they may put on the table. Since the political obstacles here derive as much from domestic pressures, this brings us to the second tension of economic diplomacy.

Tension between Domestic and International Pressures

The second major tension is between domestic and international pressures in economic policy-making. This fundamental tension underlies all economic diplomacy today. The international penetration of domestic economies, by trade, direct investment and financial flows, has been growing steadily since the end of World War II. It has accelerated since the Cold War ended, so that interdependence has become globalisation. In this context domestic, state-centred theories are most relevant, combined with those models like Putnam's that explain the interaction between the domestic and the international.

This tension, first of all, complicates domestic decision-making. In political diplomacy, foreign ministries are clearly dominant. In economic diplomacy other departments usually have the lead and foreign ministries may struggle to get their word in. As more economic issues get international exposure, more government agencies become involved. As a result, bargaining to achieve a common agreed view within a national government is the first step in economic diplomacy. All the different interests need to be reconciled in a way that still enables the government to act decisively.

Every government then sits down in international negotiations with interlocutors that have gone through internal bargaining that is parallel to its own. Each will want an international outcome that meshes with its domestic process. But in the course of negotiations domestic positions will generally have to be modified to reach an internationally agreed result. Linkages in international negotiations often mean that concessions in one area are needed to achieve objectives in others. The national negotiator must decide whether the new position still advances the country's objectives and, if so, win over the varied domestic interests. Governments need an *efficient* process for doing this, to establish how far the various domestic interests should have a say in the redefinition of international negotiating objectives. This process will be shaped by domestic institutional arrangements, which may be laid down in law or in national constitutions, or may be the result of precedent.

However much governments may be convinced of the economic benefits of international agreement, their legitimacy depends on the support of their electorates. They therefore have to win over their legislatures, and through them their electorates, who may have instinctive anxieties about being vulnerable to forces outside their control. The advance of globalisation and the growing number of constituencies touched by developments in the international economy

---

5   Reciprocity is one of the basic principles on which the GATT was founded in 1948 and it survives in the WTO – see Chapter 18 below.

has generated growing pressure for greater *accountability* of decision-makers. In short, economic diplomacy has to be made democratic. But this can lead to a conflict between efficiency and accountability. Greater accountability may argue for including the legislative branch of government in the redefinition of national interest. But if so, the politicisation of the process may lead to deadlock.

Finally, this tension affects the choice to be made between formal rules and 'softer' voluntary cooperation. Rule-based systems appear more predictable, more durable and a better protection against abuses. If markets are global, that argues that the rules governing markets should also be internationally agreed. Rule-based systems require governments to surrender some of their sovereignty, but the international penetration of their economies may have undermined their sovereignty anyway. However, the articulation of national policy preferences is still primarily a domestic function. If domestic policy preferences change, international rules may not be able to accommodate this, so that they are no longer regarded as legitimate. In such circumstances the less demanding but more flexible technique of voluntary cooperation appears preferable.

Tension between Government and Other Forces

The analysis so far has focused on governments, defined to include both executive and legislature. The third major tension in economic diplomacy, which has greatly advanced since 1990, is between governments and other forces. The penetration of international factors into domestic economies is led not by governments but by private sector agents – traders, investors and financiers. As globalisation advances, other groups and social movements become involved in economic diplomacy. Their activities can go beyond seeking to influence national governments; they can combine so as to operate transnationally. In consequence, some argue that globalisation is removing any role for the nation state.[6] This book does not endorse that view, but it argues that governments have to operate in a different context than before. For this tension, domestic societal theories are relevant, as well as analyses like Odell's that incorporate the role of markets.

Economic activity has been stimulated by government giving more opportunities to private firms and by transferring power to them: by the removal of trade barriers, deregulation and privatisation. This transfer of powers has profound consequences for economic diplomacy. It opens the question of what responsibilities governments should keep, what private business should undertake and how government and business can work together. This is linked to the issue of how governments deal with market pressures. Decisions taken by a government, in fiscal, monetary or regulatory policies, will affect how markets view the credibility of that government. Effective market regulation is considered

---

6   Held and others 1999 divides attitudes to globalisation between 'hyper-globalisers', 'sceptics' and 'transformationalists'. Examples of hyper-globalisers who believe that globalisation undermines the state are Ohmae 1992 and 1995 and Strange 1996. Hirst and Thompson 1999 are sceptics. The authors belong to the transformationalist school. See also note 7.

a prerequisite for attracting foreign investment and ensuring that the domestic economy is internationally competitive.

Many issues in economic diplomacy, like the environment and world poverty, stimulate highly motivated and articulate non-governmental organisations (NGOs). Some of these are constructive and well informed and have a lot of expertise to offer government. But others are destructive and anarchistic, gathering hostile crowds at international economic meetings. Some aspects of the growth of civil society represent efforts of interest groups to bypass national governments, because the interests concerned no longer have confidence in the formal lines of democratic accountability. This leads NGOs to argue for more transparency and to claim that their involvement makes the process more democratic. Governments, while answering their negative critics, seek to cooperate with constructive NGOs in ways that allow each side to retain their independence.

New Trends in Economic Diplomacy

The developments of the 1990s and early 2000s shifted the balance of the first tension of economic diplomacy, greatly intensified the second and raised the third to equal terms with the other two. This has obliged governments to develop a range of new strategies to confront them. These trends and responses are analysed in the following sections of this chapter.

The Legacy of the 1990s and Early 2000s

The shape of economic diplomacy changed profoundly during the 1990s, initiating movements that have persisted into the new century:

- First, the Cold War ended and the communist empire of the Soviet Union collapsed. All the countries of Central and Eastern Europe, including Russia, wanted to integrate into the international economic system. This now became truly global and there was no longer a real alternative to the open competitive regime favoured by the West. But the end of the security threat from a hostile super-power removed a political incentive for settling economic disputes.
- Second, the interdependence that had hitherto prevailed between Western developed countries mutated towards globalisation, encompassing the whole world. Countries increasingly opened their economies to external competition, so that trade grew faster than output and investment faster than trade. Governments adopted policies that would take advantage of this and often shifted power to the private sector. Globalisation brought increased prosperity to those states that could take benefit from it – conspicuously the United States, the countries of East Asia and, more recently, India. But many other countries found it harder to adapt and fell further behind the leaders.[7]

---

7   An excellent compact account of the advance of globalisation in the 1990s is in Cable 1999. For later analyses, see Bhagwati 2004, Wolf 2004 and Stiglitz 2006.

- Third, there was growing resistance to the way globalisation was being managed. Domestically, civil society groups argued that social values were being sacrificed to the search for economic advantage. Internationally, developing countries complained that the system still operated in ways that benefited the rich industrial countries. There was concern that the poorest countries, especially in Africa, were being marginalised by globalisation, as flows in development aid shrank in real terms during the 1990s. A movement developed in civil society that questioned the merits of globalisation and organised mass demonstrations, often destructive, at international meetings that were seen as symbolic of it.

During the 1990s global economic regimes were agreed that would have been impossible while the Cold War was on, but often the initial momentum has slackened later:

- *Trade* The World Trade Organization (WTO), created by the Uruguay Round agreements adopted in 1994, encompassed all trade, involved almost all countries and went deep into domestic policies.[8] But the WTO ministerial at Seattle, late in 1999, failed to launch a new round of multilateral negotiations. Though NGOs had campaigned against this, the real cause of failure was the discontent of developing countries over what was on offer (Bayne 2000; Bhagwati 2001). The WTO did succeed in launching the 'Doha Development Agenda' (DDA) late in 2001, with the aim of redressing the balance in favour of developing countries. These countries have become better organised and more engaged in the negotiating process, but they are still dissatisfied with what the rich countries have put on the table.
- *Finance* After serious financial crises, in Mexico in 1994, East Asia in 1997 and Russia in 1998, the International Monetary Fund (IMF) and World Bank put in place new international financial architecture (Eichengreen 1999; Evans 2000; Kenen 2001). Financial markets have avoided contagious crises since then, even after the collapse of Argentina late in 2001. The buoyancy of the world economy in the early 2000s has removed the pressure for further radical reform. But the system has not yet been severely tested.
- *Environment* The United Nations Conference on the Environment and Development (UNCED) in Rio in 1992 created new global instruments to protect the environment. But progress after Rio was frustrated by emerging differences between Europe (where consumers drive policy) and in North America (where producers are more influential). This inhibited agreement, especially on climate change and biodiversity, while developing countries were reluctant to make commitments.

---

8   The official history of the Uruguay Round is in Croome 1999. Preeg 1995 gives a more reflective analysis. Ostry 1997 sets the results in a historical context and looks forward.

The terrorist attacks on the United States on 11 September 2001 generated a new set of political pressures to which economic diplomacy has had to adapt. Some have had less impact than expected: extra security controls on the transport of goods and people have not held back trade; new measures to track the financing of terrorism have produced meagre results. Some of the pressures were benign, in that the initial reaction of the US was to not only to attack the symptoms of terrorism but also its causes, including poverty and economic marginalisation. This gave fresh impetus to meeting targets that were endorsed by the UN in 2000 as the Millennium Development Goals: halving the numbers living in extreme poverty (that is, on less than $1 a day), getting all children into primary education and lowering child and maternity mortality rates, all by 2015 (DFID 2000). There were new initiatives to increase aid flows to poor countries, especially at the Monterrey Conference on Financing for Development in 2002; to tackle specific problems like excessive debt or infectious diseases; and to support both political and economic advance in Africa, through the New Partnership for Africa's Development (NEPAD).

But many of these initiatives, once launched, lacked proper follow-up and needed constant high-level pressure, as at the Gleneagles G8 summit of 2005 (see Chapter 6 below). While rich countries worried about corruption and misgovernment, developing countries wanted to have 'ownership' of their own programmes. There were other less favourable consequences, especially after the United States decided to invade Iraq in 2003. Worries about the vulnerability of energy supplies, combined with strong demand for oil imports in China and elsewhere, led to a surge in the oil price, from $20 a barrel in 2001 to over $75 in the summer of 2006, though it then dropped back to around $60 in early 2007. The world economy absorbed these high prices without undue loss of growth. But they led to assertive policies by major consumers (like China) and producers (like Iran, Russia and Venezuela). Concerns about energy security reinforced pressure for stronger action on climate change, to implement the Kyoto Protocol and to agree on a tougher successor regime. This was advocated by NGOs, epistemic communities (notably the Intergovernmental Panel on Climate Change – IPCC), most developed governments and a growing share of the business community. But the US government resisted any firm commitment, so that developing countries continued to hold back.

Globalisation: Demands and Responses

The advance of globalisation makes heavy demands on governments in economic diplomacy, as indicated earlier:

- The range and variety of economic diplomacy has greatly increased. Many new subjects have become active, including issues which arouse strong popular concern, like international crime and world poverty.

- Economic diplomacy penetrates deep into domestic policies, and is no longer limited to measures applied at the border. It involves many more actors inside and outside government.
- The range of countries active in economic diplomacy spans the entire globe. Leading developing countries like China, India, Brazil and South Africa have such economic weight that they must be involved in major decisions. International institutions have to operate for the benefit of the entire membership, not just the richer ones.
- The relative power of governments to shape events is shrinking and so are the resources available to them. This decline in power and resources means that governments are often trying to do more with less.

Four New Strategies

Governments have therefore searched for new ways to improve decision-making and negotiation in economic diplomacy. The aim is to compensate for their relative loss of power; to address international economic issues which touch their domestic interests ever more closely; and to manage a global system in which all countries participate. From this search four strategies have emerged:

- involving ministers;
- bringing in non-state actors;
- greater transparency;
- using international institutions.

Each will be examined in turn.

Involving Ministers

The first strategy is the greater involvement of ministers – politicians of cabinet rank – both at home and abroad, thus raising the political profile. Up to the 1980s, international economic negotiation was largely in the hands of bureaucrats. Ministers held rare, formal sessions. But the WTO has a regular cycle of ministerial meetings, while informal groups of ministers meet in the run-up to them. Ministerial Committees at the IMF and World Bank have become more purposeful and are flanked by meetings of smaller groups like the G7. The heads of international institutions used to be former officials. Now they all have had ministerial experience: Pascal Lamy at the WTO, Rodrigo Rato at the IMF and Angel Gurria at the Organisation for Economic Cooperation and Development (OECD).[9]

Ministers make their contribution not only at international meetings but also by their impact on the domestic decision-making process:

---

9   Robert Zoellick, President of the World Bank, at first looks like an exception. But he held very senior political appointments – US Trade Representative and Deputy Secretary of State – in the first Administration of US President George W. Bush.

- First, as they are usually elected themselves or otherwise linked to the electoral process, ministers are closer to the people. They have more domestic political authority and their involvement enhances accountability.
- Second, officials prefer continuity; their instinct is to adapt an existing technique or institution. But ministers are innovative; they put a premium on change and new ideas.
- Third, officials like to strike deals behind closed doors. Ministers put a lot of weight on public presentation. They advocate greater transparency (see below) but may sometimes settle for show rather than substance.
- Fourth, ministers tend to be impatient: they want quick, visible results. They are more used to taking positions that resonate domestically, than they are to negotiating.

Agreements reached between ministers thus have strong authority and legitimacy. But ministers' impatience increases the risk of failing to agree and, when they do, the consequences are more serious.

Heads of government – prime ministers and presidents – have even more to contribute, with their supreme authority and capacity to reconcile international and domestic pressures. When the G7 summit and the European Council were founded in the 1970s, they were almost alone of their kind, but now international economic summit meetings happen constantly. The European Union and other regional groupings have regular summits, not only of their own members, but also more widely. The United Nations holds special summits on economic issues, like UNCED and the World Summit on Sustainable Development a decade later. Even between summits, heads of government increasingly intervene in economic diplomacy.

Bringing in Non-State Actors

The second strategy is to involve players from outside government in the decision-making process. Non-state actors, as we have seen, are already much more engaged in economic diplomacy. Now, as governments' own powers and resources shrink, they try to get the private sector to share their burdens. In development they encourage the use of private capital for investment; and they work with charities like Oxfam and Médécins sans Frontières. In financial crises they do not want IMF money simply to bail out private banks – they want the banks themselves to contribute. Many governments of developed countries include representatives from business, trade unions and NGOs in their delegations to international conferences.

In this, the challenge for the government is to spread the load while remaining in control of the agenda. Governments seek help with inputs to economic diplomacy and with spreading the results, but they want to keep responsibility for negotiation. They have so far found it easier to deal with private business than with the NGO community. There are now established parallel business channels for economic diplomacy aimed at facilitating agreement between governments. These can operate at regional level, as in Asia-Pacific Economic Cooperation

(APEC), plurilaterally, for example, through the OECD, or multilaterally. With NGOs, the picture is more complex. The mass demonstrations, often violent, which started at Seattle in 1999 and led to a death in Genoa at the 2001 G8 summit, make the headlines (Green and Griffith 2002). But the street protests are only the visible part of the iceberg and do not fully reflect the *positive* influence of the NGOs. In fact, NGOs make much more impact on decision-making when their public demonstrations are complemented by direct contacts with governments and with institutions, such as the UN on the environment and the World Bank on development issues (O'Brien and others 2000).

Greater Transparency

The third strategy in economic diplomacy is the drive for greater transparency – for better information, greater clarity and more publicity. The pressure for this comes both from the greater involvement of ministers and from the participation of NGOs, since both seek and use publicity to mobilise support for their objectives. Business may also argue for transparency as an alternative to formal rules, on the grounds that if everything is in the open, the market can be relied on to produce an efficient outcome.

NGOs in their campaigns give high priority to transparency. They complain about the secrecy of negotiations and want more public scrutiny of governments and transnational companies. Governments and firms alike seek to respond to this, so as to counter popular anxieties about globalisation. Institutions like the IMF and the WTO are responding to pressure to become more accessible and to explain their activities better.

Transparency is a useful strategy, but it can on occasion be the enemy of fruitful negotiation. In many ways, negotiation is like courtship: there is usually a period of private exploration and preparation before the parties are ready for public commitment. Governments make tentative proposals to see what responses they produce – and may later withdraw or modify them. All this is harder if conducted in public. Chinese Premier Zhu Rongji, when in Washington in April 1999, made proposals on trade policy going well beyond what had been authorised before he left Beijing. He was damaged back home not only because Clinton turned him down but because the Americans made his proposals public, via the internet.

Using Institutions

The fourth strategy is the greater use of international institutions. Where governments' individual powers are shrinking, it makes sense to act collectively whenever possible. The 1990s were as active in institution building as the years after World War II, both in creating new institutions and transforming old ones.

Among global institutions, the WTO replaced the GATT. The Rio process produced a network of new environmental bodies linked to the UN. In finance, the 'new architecture' left the IMF and World Bank largely unaltered in their basic structure. But there was innovation round the edges and the process of change is not complete.

Among plurilateral institutions, the G7, now the G8, mutated during the 1990s from an annual summit meeting into an apparatus of distinct groups in finance, environment, energy, crime and many other things. The OECD took on new members and the Commonwealth found an economic vocation, centred on the poorest and the smallest countries.

But it is at regional level that the institutional growth was most striking in the 1990s: the North American Free Trade Area (NAFTA), Mercosur in South America, the ASEAN Free Trade Area (AFTA) in South-East Asia and comparable groups in South Asia, Southern Africa and the Caribbean. Some of the new regional groups have a very wide geographical scope: APEC goes all round the Pacific; the Free Trade Area of the Americas (FTAA) would cover the whole Western Hemisphere. This growth has continued into the 2000s, with new initiatives in Asia and the launching of NEPAD in Africa, though bilateral agreements have been gaining ground.

In Europe, the European Union deepened its economic integration in ways which had strong international impact, completing its single market, and launching economic and monetary union (EMU). As well as absorbing twelve new members, mainly from Central Europe, the EU reached out to its neighbours in the Mediterranean and developed new systematic links with North and South America and with Asia.

The change is not just in the number and range of institutions. It is also in the way governments make use of them in support of their domestic objectives. They do not just use the institutions to extend their reach internationally, but also to endorse and justify their domestic actions and to share the burden of politically difficult decisions. As governments reduce their ability to intervene nationally, through privatisation and deregulation, they become keener on international disciplines, for example in telecommunications or financial regulation or even in agriculture. However, when governments give higher priority to domestic interests than to international agreement, negotiations are more likely to fail or lose momentum, as has happened in both the WTO and in regional groupings.

The Structure of this Book

After this introductory chapter, the first part of the book – Chapters 2 to 8 – examines the nature of economic diplomacy. Chapter 2 reviews the relevant theoretical approaches. Chapter 3 considers how governments organise domestic decision-making and how that fits into international negotiation. Chapters 4 and 5 analyse the growing ranks of state and non-state actors in economic diplomacy. These academic chapters are supported by three chapters by practitioners, who write from their direct experience of the role of government, business and civil society in economic diplomacy. In Chapter 6 Martin Donnelly of the British Foreign and Commonwealth Office shows how government policy is made, using the G8 summit process as a case study. Reinhard Quick of the German Chemical Industry Association explains in Chapter 7 how private business organises and conducts its lobbying operations. Phil Evans, formerly of the Consumers

Association, analyses the questions facing NGOs in trade and competition policy in Chapter 8.

The second part of the book examines multi-level economic diplomacy, depending on whether it is pursued bilaterally; through regional groupings; or through plurilateral or multilateral institutions. This provides an analytical framework for this part of the book, which is explained in Chapter 9 and illustrated by the case of international investment. Thereafter the book moves through the different levels, with academic chapters illustrated by practitioner case studies. Chapter 10 looks at bilateral economic diplomacy, arguing that bilateralism is particularly attractive to the United States. This is illustrated by the case study in Chapter 11, by Matthew Goodman from Stonebridge International (formerly of the US Treasury and the White House), on the complex economic diplomacy pursued by the United States with East Asia, including China and Japan. Chapter 12, by Kishan Rana of DiPLO Foundation and formerly the Indian Foreign Service, analyses the way in which major developing countries organise and conduct their economic diplomacy. Chapter 13 examines regional economic diplomacy, as practised by the European Union in trade and monetary relations. Matthias Buck of the European Commission complements this with Chapter 14, explaining how the EU constructs and deploys its international environment policy.

Economic diplomacy through international institutions, both plurilateral (like the OECD) and multilateral (like the World Bank), is the subject of Chapter 15. This is supported by three case studies: Joan MacNaughton writes in Chapter 16 on how countries cooperate in energy policy through the International Energy Agency (a plurilateral body), whose Governing Board she chaired; Nigel Wicks, late of the British Treasury, reflects in Chapter 17 on international financial institutions; and Roderick Abbott, from his experience in both the European Commission and the WTO Secretariat, examines the world trading system in Chapter 18. While these chapters analyse international institutions such as the IMF and the WTO, they focus not so much on the institutions themselves, as on the use which states make of them in pursuing their national objectives.

Conclusion

Economic diplomacy is an elusive subject. New questions are always coming to the surface and the context can change abruptly. As the 1990s ended, the world financial system was in turmoil, after the Asian, Russian and Brazilian crises, while the trading system looked robust. But the 2000s began with calm returning to the financial system, while the trading system was reeling from the disastrous WTO meeting at Seattle. The terrorist attacks of 11 September 2001 raised fresh uncertainties about the likely direction of economic diplomacy. Despite this volatility, however, some trends have become established in the first decade of the 2000s, while others are emerging. Thus the final chapter of this book, Chapter 19, draws some conclusions about where economic diplomacy is going in the future.

References

Baldwin, D.A. (1985), *Economic Statecraft*, Princeton University Press, Princeton, NJ.

Barston, R.P. (2006), *Modern Diplomacy*, 3rd edition, Longmans, London.

Bayne, N. (2000), 'Why Did Seattle Fail: Globalisation and the Politics of Trade', *Government and Opposition*, Vol. 35, No. 2, pp. 131–51.

Berridge, G.R. and James, A. (2003), *A Dictionary of Diplomacy*, 2nd edition, Palgrave Macmillan, London.

Bhagwati, J. (2001), 'After Seattle: Free Trade and the WTO', *International Affairs*, Vol. 77, No. 1, pp. 15–30.

Bhagwati, J. (2004), *In Defense of Globalization*, Oxford University Press, Oxford.

Bull, H. (1977/1995), *The Anarchical Society: A Study of Order in World Politics*, 1st edition 1977, 2nd edition 1995, Macmillan, London.

Cable, V. (1999), *Globalisation and Global Governance*, Royal Institute for International Affairs, London.

Croome, J. (1999), *Reshaping the World Trading System: A History of the Uruguay Round*, 2nd edition, World Trade Organization, Geneva.

DFID (2000), *Eliminating World Poverty: Making Globalisation Work for the Poor*, White Paper on International Development Presented to Parliament by the Secretary of State for International Development, Stationery Office, London.

Eichengreen, B. (1999), *Towards a New International Financial Architecture*, Institute for International Economics, Washington.

Evans, H. (2000), *Plumbers and Architects*, FSA Occasional Papers, Financial Services Authority, London.

Gardner, R.N. (1980), *Sterling-Dollar Diplomacy in Current Perspective*, Columbia University Press, New York.

Green, D. and Griffith, M. (2002), 'Globalisation and its Discontents', *International Affairs*, Vol. 78, No. 1, pp. 49–68.

Hanson, P. (1988), *Western Economic Statecraft in East-West Relations: Embargoes, Sanctions, Linkage, Economic Warfare and Détente*, Royal Institute of International Affairs, London.

Held, D., McGrew, A., Goldblatt, D. and Perraton, J. (1999), *Global Transformations: Politics, Economics and Culture*, Polity Press, Cambridge.

Hirst, P. and Thompson, G. (1999), *Globalisation in Question*, 2nd edition, Polity Press, Cambridge.

Kenen, P. (2001), *The International Financial Architecture: What's New? What's Missing?*, Institute for International Economics, Washington.

Marjolin, R. (1989), *Architect of European Unity: Memoirs 1911-1986,* Weidenfield and Nicholson, London, translated by William Hall from *Le Travail d'une Vie*, Robert Laffont, Paris 1986.

Marshall, P. (1999), *Positive Diplomacy*, Palgrave, Basingstoke.

O'Brien, R., Goetz, A.M., Scholte, J.A. and Williams, M. (2000), *Contesting Global Governance: Multilateral Economic Institutions and Global Social Movements*, Cambridge University Press, Cambridge.

Odell, J. (2000), *Negotiating the World Economy*, Cornell University Press, Ithaca, NY.

Ohmae, K. (1992), *The Borderless World: Power and Strategy in the Interlinked Economy*, Routledge, London.

Ohmae, K. (1995), *The End of the Nation State*, HarperCollins, London.

Ostry, S. (1997), *The Post-Cold War Trading System: Who's On First?*, University of Chicago Press, Chicago.

Preeg, E. (1995), *Traders in a Brave New World,*, Chicago University Press, Chicago.

Putnam, R.D. (1988), 'Diplomacy and Domestic Politics: the Logic of Two-Level Games', *International Organization*, Vol. 42, No. 4, pp. 427–60.

Putnam, R.D. and Henning, C.R. (1989), 'The Bonn Summit of 1978: A Case Study in Coordination', in Cooper, R.N. and others (eds), *Can Nations Agree? Issues in International Economic Cooperation*, The Brookings Institution, Washington, pp. 12–140.

Ruggie, J.G. (1982), 'International Regimes, Transactions and Change; Embedded Liberalism in the Postwar Economic Order', *International Organization*, Vol. 36, pp. 379–415.

Stiglitz, J. (2006), *Making Globalization Work*, Penguin/Allen Lane, London.

Strange, S. (1996), *The Retreat of the State: the Diffusion of Power in the World Economy*, Cambridge University Press, Cambridge.

Wolf, M. (2004), *Why Globalisation Works*, Yale University Press, New Haven and London.

Chapter 2

Theoretical Analysis of Economic Diplomacy

Stephen Woolcock

Introduction

The aim of this chapter is to provide an introduction to the various theoretical approaches that can be used in the study of economic diplomacy. It provides a discussion of the various existing approaches offered by the general international relations literature and international political economy in particular, before discussing two approaches of particular value to students of economic diplomacy. In a short chapter is it not possible to provide a detailed account of these various models, but students are directed to further reading on each area. The aim of this chapter and indeed of the book is to help students *apply* the various approaches rather than attempt to develop an all embracing theory of economic diplomacy. In order to analyse a given episode in economic diplomacy in more than a superficial fashion it is necessary to have a good knowledge of the substantive interests and the conduct of negotiations. In order to illustrate how the various approaches can be applied in practice the chapter therefore makes reference to a concrete case. The case chosen is that of the Doha Development Agenda negotiations in the World Trade Organization.

Theory can be used for a number of purposes. This chapter discusses theoretical frameworks that can be used to understand why things have happened, rather than predict outcomes. Such frameworks can then serve as a point of reference for case studies. Through empirical work on case studies it may then be possible to derive some hypothesis regarding the importance of the different factors in specific circumstances (Odell 2000).

Economic diplomacy is about the process of decision-making and negotiation. It is this focus on process rather than the structure of power or interests shaping any given outcome that distinguishes the study of economic diplomacy from the rest of international political economy. The argument made here is that process matters. It is not claimed that process is more important than other factors. As will be discussed below, the structural and institutional factors can often provide quite comprehensive explanations of outcomes. But as noted in Chapter 1 there are instances in which outcomes differ between two negotiations even when the power and interest structures are essentially unchanged. In the trade case used in this chapter, the Cancun WTO Ministerial meeting of September 2003 broke down in failure (WTO 2003). A few months later negotiations in Geneva among essentially the same parties were able to achieve a measure of agreement, at least enough to enable the negotiations in the DDA to continue (WTO 2004). The outcomes of the negotiations differed, but the relative balance of economic power and the interests of the parties had not changed in the short period between the two meetings. The European Union was still defending its interests in agriculture and pushing an offensive position in manufactured products (non-agricultural market access – NAMA) and services. Brazil and other members of the G20 were still pushing for the EU to open its agricultural markets and the United States to reduce its farm subsidies. The relative power of the US, the EU and the G20 had not changed significantly and there had been no change of government in any of the major actors. The different outcomes of the two meetings must therefore have been due to differences in the way the negotiations were conducted, the negotiating strategies or expectations of the parties.

Process is becoming relatively more important. Deeper integration of the world economy means that there are now more actors involved in economic negotiations. Gone are the days when a small policy elite could determine the outcome of negotiations. In 1947 30 or so people sitting around a table in Geneva over a long summer more or less determined the shape of the General Agreement on Tariffs and Trade (GATT) and thus the trading regime for the next couple of decades. The WTO Ministerial in Cancun involved 149 WTO members and a cast of thousands. Negotiations are more complex. With deeper integration domestic preferences are often based on well established policies and practices. As trade policy is no longer simply a question of trading a tariff reduction in one sector for a reduction in another, but involves modification or reform of these deep seated preferences, negotiators must work much harder to reconcile domestic and international interests.

Process has also become more important in the sense that the power structure in economic diplomacy has become more heterogeneous. Rather than a system led by a benign hegemon in the shape of the United States, or even a system of hegemonic leadership in which the Quad (US, EU, Japan and Canada) represented a 'club model', international economic negotiations today include far more states.[1] The leadership of the OECD countries is again challenged by much of the developing world, as it was in the 1970s, and major emerging markets such as China and India now have an increased say in the outcomes of negotiations. Negotiators must therefore be able to find solutions that serve the interests of a larger number of active players and work to build broader coalitions among groups of countries. It is no longer sufficient to find an agreement among OECD countries and then extend this multilaterally to other countries, as was the practice in trade policy until the 1990s.

The denser web of institutions that exists in the 2000s gives negotiators more options and makes decisions on process, such as on the forum for negotiation or

---

1   Keohane and Nye 2001 argue that the breakdown of the club model affects 'input' legitimacy in terms of procedures and accountability as well as the 'output' legitimacy in terms of the effectiveness of cooperation in bodies like the WTO.

the type of agreement, more important. As Chapter 9 shows the choice between different levels or fora gives negotiators more options, but inevitably adds to complexity (Landau 2000; Princen 2005). A denser network of institutions means a choice between them. In the case of trade this means a choice, for example, between bilateral free trade agreements (FTAs) and the multilateral level of negotiations. This need not mean that the norms and expectations of negotiators in both differ (Woolcock 2006). But conducting negotiations on varied levels at the same time clearly means that how they interact counts a good deal and this is essentially a process issue.

Systemic Theories

Structures of Power

Process is but one factor shaping outcomes so any theoretical approach must first be aware of the structure of power. Relative power clearly influences policy outcomes including those in economic diplomacy. Indeed realists would argue that relative power is *the* determining factor. Realists see the desire to maximise the power of one's own state compared to that of others as a central explanatory variable in international relations. Realists do not discount economic or domestic interests but tend to see them as constraints on the pursuit of known national interests or preferences. In essence realists expect the relative power of nation states to shape the outcomes of negotiations and that negotiators will be motivated by relative economic benefits rather than the absolute gains.

Systemic theories based on realist assumptions therefore see the structure of the international economy as shaped by relative power relations. Hegemonic stability theory (HST) seeks to apply realist views on the influence of power to develop a predictive theory of international relations and international political economy. HST argues that a hegemon – a leading power able to shape outcomes – is needed if international economic cooperation is to succeed. Without the coercive power of a hegemon it would not be possible to ensure effective compliance with any regime that were established. The theory can also envisage a benign hegemon, that is not concerned about relative power gains, so that others may benefit more from the economic order than the hegemon responsible for providing it. HST has in particular been applied to help explain how the international economic order was established after World War II under US hegemony. This was in contrast to the chaos of the inter-war period, when Britain was no longer able to fulfil the role of a hegemon and the United States was not willing to provide such a role.

In the case of the trade regime HST would argue that the GATT and the open multilateral trading system it reflected was established thanks to US hegemony. The decline in US power then explains why multilateralism is being questioned. The United States has moved away from multilateralism, because it can no longer shape outcomes at this level. It prefers to pursue bilateral free trade agreements in which it is still able to benefit from an asymmetric power relationship in its favour. Realist interpretations of the trading regime also suggest that other countries move towards regionalism and FTAs in response to the anticipated weakening of multilateralism in the post-hegemony period (Gilpin 1987).

Like many theories of cooperation in the international economy, HST focuses on the establishment of a single international order. If one sets aside the role of 'a' single hegemon maintaining 'the' international economic order, it is possible to see how major economic powers still fulfill functions similar to hegemons within regional settings. Thus it is possible to argue that the United States has shaped the regional economies in the Western Hemisphere and beyond, as the European Union has in Europe.[2] HST provided a reference for studying the international economy but has a number of weaknesses, such as the difficulty determining when a hegemon exists or more to the point when it ceases to exist? There is also the problem that the international economy did not collapse as US hegemony declined in the 1970s as HST predicted. Hegemonic stability theory was transformed into the theory of hegemonic leadership, in which others supported the US in maintaining the international regimes established under US hegemony. This could be used to explain the 'club model' of the OECD in the 1970s and 1980s.

One does not need to subscribe to any predictive systemic theory to recognise that relative power can have a direct bearing on the negotiation process. There can be little doubt that the United States, and the OECD countries in general, have shaped the agenda in economic diplomacy through their leadership of the international institutions such as the WTO and IMF and through their initiatives in the G7 and G8.

So power-based analysis working on the realist assumption that relative power and relative economic benefit will shape outcomes is important, but it has some weaknesses. A general criticism is that power it is hard to measure. Indeed, it may only be possible to assess the relative power of parties on the basis of outcomes, which is no help if the aim is to try and predict outcomes. In the case of economic diplomacy it may be easier to measure power, or at least to find proxies for relative power, than is the case in international relations in general. In the trade case study relative market size provides a fairly good proxy for power, especially when reciprocity is one of the basic tenets of trade negotiations. The bigger your market the more leverage you have in negotiations. The practice of trade negotiations provides support for the view that relative gains are important. The whole trade regime has been built on the concept of reciprocity. In other words countries have been reluctant to liberalise unless they have been confident that other countries do so in equal measure. This is a mercantilist concept, but one that more accurately describes the world trading system than the free trade image that is currently presented as the character of the WTO regime. Strange has suggested that power can be broken down into four main components finance, production, knowledge and information. This can also help to assess relative power in economic negotiations (Strange 1988). The real difficulty comes when

---

2　Kindelberger (1973) listed a number of key functions that a hegemon needs to fulfil, including the maintenance of an open trade regime, stable exchange rates and a market for distressed goods. The EU provides all these across Europe – or at least in the eurozone.

negotiations are shaped by other elements of power, such as military power. For example, assessing the degree to which trade negotiations are shaped by national security considerations is a much more difficult endeavour.

Dependency theory is another systemic theory with predictive aspirations. This argues that the South will remain underdeveloped because the rich core countries including former colonial powers, will always gain more from a liberal trading order. There is certainly evidence that some developing countries are not much better off now than they were in the 1970s when they pushed for a New International Economic Order (NIEO) (Spero and Hart 2003). So there would seem to be some support for the dependency theory. The weakness is that dependency theory cannot explain why some developing countries have been able to develop and industrialise while others have not.

This brings us to the fundamental weaknesses in the realist view of economic diplomacy, namely that it does not pay sufficient attention to the role of international institutions and the role of domestic factors. In international relations but particularly in international economics there is now, as mentioned above, a dense network of institutions and regimes that attenuate the use of raw economic power. These must also be factored into our discussion, as economic diplomacy includes negotiation on the international regimes and rules shaping international economic relations. In more general terms economic diplomacy is about the interaction between international and domestic interests, so that we must pay adequate attention to domestic factors

International Institutions and Regimes

Systemic factors are not exclusively realist in nature but may also take the form of international institutions and regimes that reflect cooperation between states or anchor such cooperation in regimes and rules. Regime theory argues that states cooperate when there are cross border economic activities that require rules or norms of behaviour. For this reason the first regimes were identified in policy areas such as transport and telecommunications. Regimes encompass both formal cooperation in institutions but also less formal forms of cooperation based on shared interests, values and expectations (Krasner 1983).

In economic diplomacy today international institutions play a more important role than in the past. Since the creation of the Bretton Woods institutions and the GATT in the 1940s the main international economic institutions have evolved and some, such as in the field of trade, have been considerably strengthened. The World Trade Organization is a rules-based organisation in which national governments have accepted real constraints on their freedom to act. The liberal paradigm established in the 1980s and 1990s remains strong and within this order relations between states are not simply shaped by relative power relationships but by a complex interdependence that calls for cooperation, especially in the field of international economic relations (Bayliss and Smith 1997). Theoretical literature, such as neo-liberal institutionalism, explains this cooperation between states by pointing to the reduced transaction costs resulting from international regimes, by the enhanced trust they engender and by the improved compliance. This can be illustrated by the trade regime. A rules-based WTO means that there is no longer any debate about non-discrimination as the basis for the international trading system. This is a given, so that negotiations are on how to apply principles of non-discrimination to, for example, the services sector. With binding commitments within the WTO countries can be confident that they will not face arbitrary tariff policies or quantitative restrictions, although there remain of course some areas in which states can take arbitrary action. The WTO dispute settlement mechanism also ensures very high, although not 100 per cent, compliance with the agreed rules.

International institutions and regimes now reach beyond trade, monetary relations and development in the shape of the WTO, IMF and World Bank, to include a wide and ever growing number of specialist institutions such as in the field of international environmental policy, and a range of standards making bodies from the International Telecommunication Union through to the Codex Alimentarius for food safety issues. It is also necessary to include regional and bilateral regimes in this ever denser network of institutions. When counties commit to binding obligations within a regional or bilateral setting they also limit the range of policy options open to them.

In virtually every field of economic diplomacy therefore, whether trade, investment, monetary relations or the environment, there will be international regimes and rules that will have a greater or lesser degree of binding on national negotiators. The rules and standards set in international agreements will also represent important precedents that will shape agendas and expectations.

Domestic Theories

Societal Factors

The literature has distinguished between societal and state-centred domestic factors (Ikenberry, Lake and Mastandano 1988). Societal factors include primarily different interests that compete to shape national policy preferences in any negotiation. Analysis of such sector interests and how they interact in international negotiations provides valuable insights into the forces shaping negotiations. The balance between these different interests can be made at different levels of analysis. The analysis can be made at the level of factors, such as labour, land and capital, as in Garrett's use of the Stolper-Samuelson theorem to explain how interests are likely to respond to globalisation (Garrett 1988). This type of approach can also accommodate new interests such as the civil society movement that emerged in the 1990s. The analysis can also take place at the levels of specific sectors of the economy, such as in the case of protectionist agricultural interests in the EU against the liberal interests of the manufacturing sector and services. For example, the broad EU trade policy position over the past couple of decades can be summarised as the defensive interests of agriculture competing against the offensive market opening interests of manufacturing and services. These interests reflect the competitive positions of the respective sectors.

The national position or preference of any government in a negotiation can be identified, sometimes in fairly precise fashion, by looking at the positions of the major interests. For example, the EU position in terms of trade liberalisation in agriculture is more or less determined by the existing commitments under the Common Agricultural Policy. More liberalisation would mean more imports and a reduction in agricultural prices in the EU. This would in turn require increased subsidies to maintain farm revenue, but the European Council set a ceiling for the CAP budget in 2005.

State-Centred Factors

While the nature of domestic (sector) interests provides a powerful explanatory tool, one cannot ignore the institutional framework within which national positions or preferences are aggregated and defined. State-centred approaches to international relations therefore tend to focus on the institutional framework within which policies are made. These approaches stress that the institutional setting within which decisions are taken will have an important bearing on outcomes. Domestic institutional structures will in effect determine who decides on national policy preferences. Will it be elected representatives in the legislature or civil servants in the administrative branch of government? In practice, of course, it is both. The legislature gives political support or a mandate for the executive branch to negotiate. As Chapter 3 illustrates this is often an iterative process.

'Divided government' in which the legislature and executive are controlled by different parties will therefore influence policy outcomes or stymie the policy process (Milner 1997, 135–58). If you have a Democrat controlled Congress, but a Republican Administration or vice versa there are likely to be important differences between them. In the early 2000s such differences prevented the US administration getting Trade Promotion Authority. This in turn held back new trade negotiations in the WTO as well as bilateral negotiations between the US and other countries. Parliamentary systems (except in France) and stronger party discipline mean this kind of experience is rare in Europe. But another form of divided government is common in European countries, like Germany and Italy, where the administration regularly consists of a coalition of different parties.[3] In the context of the European Union one could say that 'government' is divided between the 27 Member States of the EU in that the Member States and European Commission both shape the day-to-day negotiations in European economic diplomacy.

Institutional approaches also consider the intra-governmental policy coordination process in which different departmental interests compete in shaping national policy. The institutional structure of policy-making determines the degree

---

3 Some American scholars (Aberbach and others 1981) have also argued that there are likely to be greater differences between ministries in Europe because there are fewer political appointees at the top of each ministry, as in the US, to ensure coherence across departments. But recent observation shows that the opposite is true – see Chapter 3 below.

of 'agent slack' or autonomy of negotiators. Indeed in principal–agent models of negotiations the domestic institutional structure effectively determines who are the principals, in other words who will authorise the agent – usually an agency in the executive branch of government – to negotiate on behalf of the country or other entity. The provisions for these principals to scrutinise or control the agents then determines how much flexibility the negotiators have. Finally, institutional arrangements affect the adoption or ratification of the results of any negotiation, such as whether these require the approval of the legislative branch of government and what sort of majority is needed for any given issue.

The case of trade policy can be used to illustrate this point. The US Congress (the principal) has competence for commercial policy under the constitution and delegates this to the executive branch (the agent) at regular intervals. In granting negotiating authority for a limited period the Congress sets out the aims for any negotiation. As Congress must ratify whatever agreement is reached by the US negotiators it clearly decides on the degree of flexibility available to negotiators. The executive must follow the negotiation mandate (authority) from Congress or it will not be able to get the agreement ratified. In these circumstances more agent slack will provide more scope for US negotiators to reach an agreement with the US's trading partners, but this could mean no ratification if negotiators misjudge the position in Congress. As negotiating authority is only delegated for a limited period of time in the case of the United States and the US is a key trading nation, Congress has in the past effectively determined the timing of trade negotiations.

The EU has a more complex institutional structure as a result of the need to find a common position among all 27 Member States. The European Commission is 'the agent' and the Member States in the Council of Ministers are 'the principals' who decide on the formal mandate and thus grant negotiating authority and adopt the final agreement. Institutional structures regarding ratification or adoption of agreements can spill back into negotiations. For example, if the adoption of trade negotiations in the EU is to be determined by a qualified majority of the Member States, the European Commission will have somewhat more agent slack than when the adoption of an agreement requires unanimity. With qualified majority decisions Member States fall into line rather than hold out against results they dislike. When the adoption of an agreement is by unanimity the EU negotiator has less flexibility (Woolcock 2000).

In developing countries government negotiators can be under less intense pressure from national legislative bodies or other institutional factors. But this agent slack often comes as a result of a lack of capacity within the developing country to monitor negotiations. In such circumstances there may be little understanding of the issues and little commitment to ratify and implement the final agreement. There is also a general point on ratification and implementation. If those negotiating an agreement do not expect the agreement to be ratified or not fully and effectively implemented, this will shape their willingness to conclude the agreement. Strong implementation commitments will make it harder to reach agreement as each party will double check that the letter and spirit of the agreement conforms to what can be implemented back home (Goldstein 2000).

Ideology and Ideas

In the extensive literature on international relations there has been a recognition that underlying ideological positions can have an influence on policy outcomes. For example Goldstein argues that the continued support for liberal trade policies in the United States during the 1980s was due to an ideological support for free trade, even though the balance of societal forces was tipping in favour of protection. (Goldstein 1988).

Underlying shifts in our view of the world can also influence negotiations. In the 1940s there was a broad Keynesian consensus among the western capitalist countries on the role of governments in domestic economic policy. There was also a belief in many countries that state intervention was a legitimate tool of economic development. During the 1970s and especially during the 1980s such Keynesian orthodoxies and interventionist industrial/development strategies gave way to a liberal paradigm. The shift towards liberal policies became a global trend with the end of the Cold War and the ideological competition between liberal capitalism and central planning. These shifts in the prevailing orthodoxy shape the general background against which policy is made and negotiations take place. Without some understanding of such paradigm shifts it would be difficult to provide a full explanation the switch to liberalisation, privatisation and liberal trade and investment policies, which has done so much to advance globalisation.

Individuals

The role of individuals and their preferences and prejudices has been included in the study of foreign policy, but it is seldom given much importance in international political economy. In the past individuals probably played a more important role in economic diplomacy, because the number of people involved was smaller and the issues less complex, so that an individual might be expected to have mastery of the issues and some sway over negotiations. Cordell Hull, the US Secretary of State in the 1940s with a firm conviction of the need for a liberal trading system certainly had some influence. Negotiation on the Bretton Woods institutions – the IMF, IBRD and ITO – were also shaped by a relatively small group of individuals, and some of these, such as Keynes, played a decisive role. There have been a number of negotiators since who, because of their political influence and personal negotiating skill, have been able to reconcile domestic and international levels in key negotiations.

In economic diplomacy in the twenty-first century one must expect individuals to play a smaller role because of the larger number of actors involved and the complexity of the issues. However, individuals can still have an impact. For example, heads of state and government come together in G8 and other summits and can, in the right circumstances, take policy initiatives or make progress on issues that have become blocked at lower levels of government. Even at quite low levels individuals who are dealing with a detailed policy brief can often have influence because they may be one of the relatively few people who understand the full implications of detailed changes in an agreement. When individuals have an ability to shape outcomes their motivations must then also be taken into consideration.

Models of Negotiation

Having discussed the main stream international relations and IPE literature it is now necessary to look at those theoretical approaches that relate more directly to negotiation.

Rationalist Models

Rationalist models have provided a valuable contribution to understanding the dynamics of negotiation. These can integrate realist and societal approaches, but are generally based on the assumption of a unitary state aggregating domestic interests in order to maximise utility in the shape of retaining power (Tollison and Willet 1979). Rationalist models of negotiation essentially build on the concept of the 'principal-agent' model, in that the government is seen as the actor and a set of national interests as the principals. Governments maximise their utility by serving the most powerful interests (defined as 'the national interest') who will determine their re-election.

Rationalist models often draw heavily on concepts borrowed from economics. Thus models of negotiation can be constructed in which the parties seek to maximise their mutual gains by moving towards a pareto optimum beyond which it is no longer possible for one party to improve its benefits without the other parties being worse off (Sibenius 1983). As single issue negotiations tend to be more zero-sum games, negotiators are expected to add issues in order to ensure that all parties can benefit from the negotiation. This adding of issues or linking of negotiations then provides scope for integrative negotiations in which all parties gain and reduces the distributive element in any a negotiation. Most authors have argued that economic diplomacy is generally a mixture of distributive and integrative strategies, or using the terms borrowed from negotiation theory, a mixture of value claiming and value creating strategies (Odell 2000).

One does not have to look very hard to find the use of policy linkage or adding issues in negotiations. This is reflected in the well established rationale for multilateral rounds as a means of promoting trade liberalisation, such as the DDA. The rationale is that linkage enables each party to come away with something and for the trading system as a whole to move towards the pareto frontier. If only agricultural trade were on the agenda in the DDA the EU would have to make extensive concessions, getting little in return. EU trade negotiators would be unwilling and probably unable to do this, given the expectation that trade negotiations are based on reciprocity. By adding more issues to the so called 'in-built agenda' of the WTO that emerged from the Uruguay Round, to form a 'comprehensive' trade agenda, the strategy of the EU at the time of the Seattle ministerial was to provide scope for trade-offs.

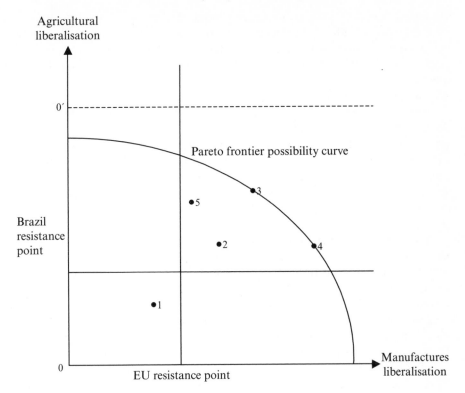

Figure 2.1 The pareto frontier

Figure 2.1 provides a simple illustration of the way linkage of policies can offer a range of possible outcomes. The case taken is that of the European Union–Brazil negotiations in the Doha Development Agenda, in which the EU wants liberalisation of manufactures in the NAMA negotiations, the horizontal axis, and Brazil wants an opening of the EU's agricultural markets, the vertical axis. Point 1 in the diagram is below the 'resistance points' for both the EU and Brazil. In other words at this point neither the EU nor Brazil are willing to accept the outcome of negotiations, as it is less than they 'need' in order to satisfy their domestic constituencies. If value creating negotiations enable the parties to reach point 2 this offers benefits for both, but this point is still below the pareto frontier. Assuming more give and take by the parties allows them to reach a point on the pareto frontier.

But the mixed nature of economic diplomacy can be expressed in that there are still a range of possible outcomes even on the pareto frontier. Point 3 represents an outcome that benefits Brazil more than the EU (relatively more agricultural liberalisation than manufactures). Realist interpretations would then expect the EU to try to move along the pareto frontier to 4 where it gains more than Brazil, if it is pursuing a mixed strategy. Alternatively the EU could opt for an outcome at point 2 and Brazil one at 5 even though both of these points are well below the pareto frontier, if they are concerned about relative gains. At point 2 the EU gains less than it could at 3 but ensures that Brazil does not make relative gains. At point 5 Brazil gains less than it could at 3 but ensures that it makes relative gains on the EU. While it has been argued that relative gains are always a factor (Grieco 1990), in practice economic diplomacy generally involves a mix of distributional and integrative approaches.

In terms of negotiation strategies the powerful might be expected to pursue value claiming strategies as they have less to lose from failure. For example, the EU is less dependent on exports of manufactures to Brazil than Brazil is on exports to the EU. If there is no agreement in the DDA, the EU can also negotiate bilateral free trade agreements with the major emerging markets, such as India or ASEAN and in this fashion open these markets for European manufactured goods but exclude agriculture. With a smaller domestic market Brazil has less leverage in such negotiations.

Rationalist theoretical models based on a sound understanding of the sector interests involved in any negotiation therefore constitute a powerful tool with which to analysis decision-making processes. But there are some weaknesses. First, the rationalist model depicted in Figure 2.1 is of course a simple two-dimensional one. Adding issues to negotiations may facilitate trade-offs but it also makes for complexity. Most negotiations have far more than two issues so that most rationalist models tend to involve a considerable degree of simplification (Eichengreen 1998). In the case of the Doha Development Agenda there is a long list of issues on the agenda, although in practice negotiators reduced the number of core issues to three: agriculture, non-agricultural market access (NAMA) and services. Assessing the linkages between the three main issues therefore provides a reasonable approximation of the central negotiating issues. A range of other issues were under discussion in the DDA, but progress on the second order issues depended on political decisions on these core issues.

A further weakness of rationalist approaches is that they tend to assume the state is a unitary actor (Milner 1998). In reality governments that negotiate are seldom unitary actors. As discussed above there are often different views within governments. But again this need not diminish the value of rationalist approaches in explaining the factors shaping negotiations. Such approaches can capture the economic and political factors shaping policy. For example, in our trade case rural voters dependent on agriculture are more likely to be swing voters due to the larger number of rural constituencies in many countries. Again one does not need to look very hard to find evidence of this in practice in France, where rural voters have this role. France in turn has a stranglehold over issues relating to agriculture in the European Council of Ministers (see Chapter 13). Much the same applies in other European countries as well as with rice farmers in Japan, farmers in general in Korea and the cotton, sugar or citrus producing states in the United States.

Nor can most negotiations be characterised as pure principal–agent models. Most governments have their own political or ideological preferences that influence how they aggregate the various national sector interests. They do not simply aggregate the various domestic interests in order to determine the national preference; they have preferences of their own. In cases where governments need to consider the election prospects at regular intervals such as in the United States, where there are mid-term elections every two years, decision-making may approximate to a utility optimising rational actor model. But in many countries the ideology of governments has a significant impact on policy. In the case of the European Union much trade policy is formulated and conducted by officials whose interests are not shaped by the prospects of re-election. It is European Commission officials who lead for the EU in most trade negotiations and the Commission's own agenda is also shaped by its role as guardian of the European Treaties and promoter of European integration. The Article 133 Committee of the European Union, in which much of the work on trade is carried out, includes representatives from the Member States that have held that position for a number of years and are not subject to the same sort of short term pressures emanating from the political cycle as political appointees.

One final weakness of rationalist models is that they assume preferences are fixed or immutable, whereas in practice the preferences of negotiators tend to change over time.

Constructivist Approaches

Constructivist approaches to international relations stress how interests and identities can change over time through discussion and dialogue. As negotiators bring together parties from either side over what can sometimes be extended periods, it would be surprising if discussion and dialogue had no impact on the opinion and views of the negotiators. In time the chief negotiators of various parties may come to share the common aim of concluding an agreement and seek ways of helping one another find answers to the domestic constraints under which they must work. Much of what has been discussed above concerns what might be called bargaining. In other words, negotiators offer inducements in order to get what they want, such as in the example of more liberalisation in agriculture but only if the other party liberalises manufactures or services. Bargaining can also take the form of threats. For example, if there is no progress in multilateral trade negotiations a major player may threaten to negotiate bilateral trade agreements in order to get what it wants, thus enhancing its alternative or fall back position and decreasing that of its negotiating partner.

Constructivist approaches stress the role of dialogue or persuasion, not just bargaining (Ulbert and Risse 2005). In other words when negotiators put forward a particular position they support this with reasoned argument not just self-serving arguments. In the case discussed here trade liberalisation is put forward as the optimal approach to increasing welfare and thus beneficial for all. Those favouring liberalisation therefore try to persuade more protectionist countries of the benefits of liberalisation. This is often done through the provision of information or studies that suggest that an agreement will enhance welfare of all the countries concerned. There may also be a sharing of information.

This kind of persuasion mostly takes place out of the glare of publicity in exploratory meetings or working groups set up to consider a particular issue.

Technical working groups are usually established once the negotiations have been launched. In the trade example, the DDA includes Working Groups or Committees on all the issues involved in the negotiation. These working or specialist groups are used to sound out the position of the other parties or to explore potential deals or value creation moves. But they also provide a forum in which persuasion and credible argument are used to get the negotiating partner to shift position. The same can of course occur at the higher, political level in negotiations, but these meetings are usually much shorter in duration and the ministers involved tend to arrive with a brief to defend. Having said this, meetings of heads of state or government in the G8 or other summit settings sometimes involve the use of persuasion and argument. This can be especially effective when the people concerned have been in power for some time and know their colleagues from other states (Bayne 2000).

Persuasion has the advantage over bargaining or coercion in that the negotiating partner 'buys in' to the agreement. This is important when it comes to implementation. For example, obliging developing countries to sign up to high standards of protection for intellectual property rights in the Uruguay Round by using inducements and threats may not have paid off in the end, since many countries have not felt committed to implementing the agreement. If, on the other hand, governments can be persuaded that the reform involved in implementing a trade agreement is beneficial, they will be more committed to full implementation of the agreement (Fasan 2006).

Information plays an important role in persuasion or argument. How it is handled can therefore be important. For example, should reports commissioned to promote the position of a negotiator be published in the country of the negotiating partner, the target country? The provision of credible information can shape domestic public opinion in the target country. Information may also be directed at the key 'principals' such as legislators in the target country. But engaging in public diplomacy can be unpredictable. On the one hand, making information public tends to improve the quality of discussion and argument, since parties have to make the case for a given policy in terms of a wider public good rather than their own narrow vested interests. On the other hand, governments may be unwilling to concede arguments made in public when they are willing to do so in private, especially when something is offered in return.

Theoretical Approaches Especially Valuable for Economic Diplomacy

In addition to the relevant international relations and international political economy literature and models of negotiation, there are some theoretical approaches that are of special value for economic diplomacy. These are the Putnam two-level game metaphor and the approach suggested by Odell.

The Two-Level Game Approach

Professor Robert Putnam (then attached to the White House) developed his two-level game metaphor from observing the complex negotiations on macroeconomic policy, trade and energy linked to the Bonn G7 summit of 1978 (Putnam 1988; Putnam and Henning 1989). His metaphor thus fits economic diplomacy very well, though it can also be applied to non-economic contexts (Evans and others 1993). The value of the Putnam metaphor is that it addresses directly the dynamic interaction between the domestic and international levels involved in any negotiation. Its central concern is to explain how this interaction shapes the negotiation process. In common with the constructivist approaches, the Putnam model assumes that preferences are mutable, although it does not stress the role of persuasion in bringing about change. Change is rather brought about through the strategic use of linkage by negotiators seeking to find an outcome that will satisfy both their international partners (the level I game) and their domestic principals (the level II game). This means changing the preference or the 'win-set' of the other party, by a variety of means. It can also mean using the pressure to find agreement in international negotiations to change the domestic win-set. Clearly governments are not going to do this unless they also seek the domestic reform. In cases where there is divided government or splits within the government, negotiators might use international negotiations strategically to promote their cause in preference to that of other departments or branches of government. This was the kind of process that Putnam observed at work in the G7 (Putnam and Bayne 1987).

Putnam's 'win-set' defines the range of outcomes that each party will accept. Negotiators can seek to manipulate the size of their own win-set or that of their negotiating partner. By narrowing the domestic win-set, such as by encouraging action by key actors (principals) that forecloses certain options, a negotiator might be said to strengthen his or her position, because a narrower win-set limits the scope for concessions and forces the other party to move towards the negotiator's own win-set. Negotiators will of course always stress the limited scope they have for making concessions because Congress or the EU Council of Ministers will not accept this or that outcome. In doing so they are trying to give the impression that they have a narrower win-set than they really have, in order to strengthen their position. This is something that trade negotiators habitually do and can give rise to the 'negotiators dilemma' (see below). If a negotiator has a wide win-set then they are, by definition, in a weak negotiating position because their negotiating partners will seek to make full use of any scope for concessions or compromise.

The Putnam metaphor seems to almost assume that negotiators are working together to find a mutually agreeable solution. This need not mean that they are necessarily persuading one another of the merits of their positions as a constructivist approach might suggest. But many economic diplomacy negotiations involve potential mutual gains, so that negotiators may seek to widen the domestic win-set in order to ensure an overlap with the other parties' win-set and thus facilitate an agreement. This can be done, for example, through side payments. In the context of our example, one could argue that the Commissioner for Trade (Lamy) and the Commissioner for Agriculture (Fishler) in the Prodi Commission did this at the time of the 2003 mid term review of the Common Agricultural Policy. By providing more income support for European farmers these two Commissioners, who were the EU's chief negotiators in the DDA at the time, were able to widen the EU's win-set so as to put a joint agriculture offer on the table with the US. As it turned out this did not prove sufficient to satisfy the G20 at Cancun, so there was no immediate breakthrough in the WTO negotiations, but it facilitated the deal later struck in Geneva.

Negotiators may also seek to influence the size of another country's win-set by engaging in the domestic debate in other countries. This can be done by commissioning reports to show that the stated policy aims of the other country are counter productive and clearly pointing out that those interests in the other country are carrying a disproportionate cost. As noted above in the discussion of constructivist approaches, this kind of public diplomacy can have unpredictable results. It is however, something that goes on a lot in trade policy. At regular intervals there are reports quantifying the costs of agricultural support programmes in an effort to shift the balance of opinion (further) against continued support for farming. Developing countries have also begun to make common cause with development ministries in the OECD countries, in their effort to moderate the pressure from trade ministries in these countries that typically work on the principle of reciprocity in trade.

Negotiators, if they have the capacity to do so, will also want to monitor closely the domestic level II debate in their negotiating partner's country. This can be done by engaging the diplomatic services to report on developments or again through commissioning studies. The information gathered then helps the negotiator get a clearer view of the nature of the win-set or preferences shaping the level II game of the person sitting across the table in negotiations and thus get a more objective view of the constraints under which they are really working.

The Putnam approach, like other approaches, acknowledges that negotiators are working in bounded rationality. In other words they do not have perfect knowledge of the win-sets of their opposite numbers or for that matter of their own win-set. In terms of identifying the national win-set, negotiators with the capacity to do so undertake consultations with a wide range of interests and throughout all government departments, in order to get as clear a view as possible of the various positions. In the case of trade policy the USTR has a whole network of Trade Advisory Committees to advise it on the views of the various interest groups. In developing countries this kind of a network seldom exists. For both developed and developing country negotiators, there will always remain a measure of subjective judgment in defining the national preference.

As mentioned above negotiators may provide misinformation in a conscious effort to give their opposite number a false impression of their bottom line. This raises the issue of the 'negotiator's dilemma'. In order to reach an agreement it is often important that negotiators retain the trust of their opposite number. Integrity in negotiations will also strengthen the credibility of a negotiator and thus their ability to make persuasive arguments. On the other hand, there remains the issue of relative gains. Even if negotiators are focused on absolute gains and are not concerned that the other parties make relative gains, they may still wish to push for 'a better deal'. In order to do so negotiators will be tempted to provide misinformation, in other words to claim that their win-set is narrower than it really is. But to do so can undermine trust and thus the chances of reaching an agreement. Mutual trust may well be needed to break a deadlock in negotiations such as the one that brought the DDA to a halt during much of 2006.

The Putnam metaphor builds on the various approaches developed in the literature and summarised above. For example, interest groups or societal factors shape the size of the win-set. It suggests that a heterogeneous structure to domestic interests will give the negotiator more opportunities to build domestic alliances in favour of agreement, or at least enough support to get the necessary votes in the relevant institution that has to adopt and ratify any agreement. At the same time a heterogeneous structure will also make it harder to define the scope of the win-set. In our trade case one could argue that, even with the limited agenda in the DDA in 2006, the EU negotiators could not be sure what combination of moves in agriculture, tariffs and services would be within the win-set of all 27 Member States.

The Putnam metaphor also incorporates the state-centred approach of institutional structure. For example it argues that the larger the autonomy of the negotiator the larger the win-set, because negotiators have the flexibility to find compromise positions with their opposite numbers or pursue value creating strategies in trade negotiations. As discussed above the domestic institutions determine the degree of autonomy of negotiators and the prospects for ratification, something that features strongly in the level II game. Developing country trade negotiators tend to have more autonomy by virtue of the fact that the negotiators are often foreign ministers or diplomats who also consider wider political issues. The relative weakness of national trade policy capacity also means that the degree of control by national parliaments or the private sector is limited. This would suggest that most developing country negotiators, already penalised by having smaller domestic markets, are in a weaker position than their EU or US counterparts in this area as well. Whether the EU or the US has a smaller win-set will vary from case to case, but it can be argued that the EU win-set in trade tends to be narrower. The EU institutional arrangements mean that the EU's negotiator, the European Commission, has even less policy autonomy than the USTR – see Chapter 13.

In sum the Putnam two-level game metaphor provides a useful framework for assessing negotiations. Its main strength is that it models the dynamic interaction between the domestic and international levels in any negotiation. A difficulty with the Putnam approach is that it can be very difficult to define the win-sets. For example, what are the upper and lower limits of Brazil's win-set in agricultural negotiations? In practice the win-set will be shaped by a range of factors and by the perceptions of the negotiator.

Odell's Approach to International Economic Negotiation

There is a body of literature on negotiation derived from study of business negotiations. (Breslin and Rubin 1991) This has been applied to foreign policy and international economic negotiations and provides some valuable additional insights into the process of negotiation. Putnam has drawn on this literature, but Odell has taken it rather further in his book *Negotiating the World Economy* (Odell 2000). The Odell approach is of particular interest because it is developed with international economic negotiations in mind.

Odell builds a framework in which resistance points – see Figure 2.1 – determine the range of possible agreements within what he terms the possibility frontier, which is analogous to but not the same as a pareto frontier. At the resistance point the negotiator reaches the point at which it is better to have no agreement than an agreement on the terms offered at this point. This is what Odell, drawing on the negotiation literature, calls the Best Alternative To a Negotiated Agreement point or BATNA. For example, if Brazil's resistance point in agriculture is O' there would be no agreement, because the possibility curve lies inside it. Equally point 1 lies below the resistance point for both Brazil and the EU, so both consider non-agreement better than agreeing to such modest results. Odell argues that the BATNA is easier to determine than a national preference or a win-set, in the sense that it is easier to determine the point at which parties prefer no agreement to what is on the table.

In practice the resistance point or BATNA may be difficult to pin down exactly. As discussed above the scope for further concessions, such as by the EU on agricultural market access, can be defined fairly precisely. But other factors still intervene, such as the wider costs of a failure in the DDA in terms of economic losses and damage to the trading system. The EU also needs to consider the political costs of being seen to be responsible for the failure of the negotiations. This latter concern drives negotiators to spend almost as much time explaining why they are not responsible for the lack of progress as they do on negotiations themselves. These wider considerations will vary in importance over time. In 1999 the US Administration felt that the political costs of facing the domestic opposition to a new round at the Seattle WTO Ministerial outweighed the international political costs of the failure to launch a round, but by 2001 the climate had changed because of 9/11.

Odell draws on negotiating theory to develop a number of hypotheses that he then applies to case studies. Odell suggests that markets should be seen as endogenous factors in any negotiation. In other words markets may offer alternatives to a negotiated outcome, or can be used to influence the BATNA of one's negotiating partner. The first point is also illustrated by the case of investment. Investment was one of the so called Singapore issues in the DDA, but was dropped because of developing country opposition to including common rules to facilitate investment flows. But investment flows happened anyway without any international agreement, because of market opportunities already available for investment in the larger emerging markets. In other words the market offered the BATNA for foreign investors interested in liberalisation and diminished the need for an agreement in the WTO. Negotiators can also seek to harness market forces in their efforts to shape their opponents BATNA. An example of this would be 'talking down' a national exchange rate when bargaining with a country on the revaluation of that country's currency such as in the yen-dollar diplomacy of the 1980s or the renminbi-dollar diplomacy of the 2000s.

Investment negotiations also illustrates a comparable technique to the BATNA, which is discussed in Chapter 9 below, in the context of multi-level economic diplomacy. Here negotiators put pressure on the other parties not by accepting a non-negotiated solution (Odell's pure BATNA) but by shifting to a different level of negotiation. The high standard, comprehensive investment provisions offered in bilateral free trade agreements provided a clear alternative to a multilateral investment agreement with lower standards. Because such agreements were more readily available for US investors after the NAFTA had been signed, the US negotiators felt able to drive a hard bargain in the Multilateral Agreement on Investment negotiations in the OECD, thus worsening the prospects of agreement.

A second hypothesis put forward by Odell is that an increase in agent slack will increase the risk of non-ratification. Odell derives this from some historical case studies, but examples can be found today. In our trade example, as noted above, developing countries, which generally have more agent slack have often had difficulties ratifying and implementing agreements. The delays in implementing the Uruguay Round agreement in many developing countries is a case in point.

Another hypothesis is that mixed strategies which combine value creating and value claiming are likely to be more productive. This is in line with the general argument favouring trade rounds. In the DDA value claiming has been pursued by the G20. This has been effective in retaining the cohesion of the coalition, but it has contributed to the difficulties concluding the round. Finally, Odell suggests that negotiators are less likely to choose a value creating strategy when they expect their negotiating partner to adopt tough or value claiming strategies. In other words expectations of the other negotiator are a factor.

Conclusions

This chapter has shown that any analysis of economic diplomacy can draw on a rich literature. The aim is to apply this literature to the specific case of economic diplomacy. How relevant are the various contributions from international relations in general and international political economy more specifically to the study of the process of decision-making and negotiation?

The systemic theories, in particular the realist view, are important in that they ensure that relative power is incorporated in our analysis. In economic diplomacy the difficulties of measuring relative power can perhaps be resolved by the use of fairly good proxies for relative economic power. But the limitations of a realist approach still remain in that it pays insufficient attention to the role of international institutions and regimes and domestic factors.

International regimes and institutions attenuate the use of relative economic power. Stronger rule-based trade and investment regimes act as a clear constraint on the use of discretion and thus economic power by states. The network of institutions and regimes has also become denser, despite the shift towards liberal policies. Economic diplomacy must therefore include an assessment of the role of international institutions and regimes.

Domestic theories can be divided into societal and state-centred approaches. The societal models provide rich material for analysis and can be used to determine the factors shaping negotiations and the win-set or scope for agreement. The societal approaches also provide the basis for rationalist models in which government is seen as the agent for a set of national interests, which constitute the principal. Although powerful, rationalist models have the weakness that they tend to assume the state is a unitary actor, negotiating on the basis of fixed national preferences, and that they neglect the role of domestic institutions. It is therefore important to include an assessment of how decisions are reached within national governments and the institutional framework within which interest aggregation takes place. Domestic institutions also determine the degree of agent slack and the ratification process. Constructivist theories can further enrich analysis by focusing on how preferences can be changed through a process of dialogue or persuasion. They thus enable our analysis to assess how preferences change over time and why.

Finally the chapter discusses two approaches that combine elements of these various theories and are of special interest to economic diplomacy. The Putnam metaphor has the advantage that it facilitates an analysis of the dynamic interaction between the domestic and international levels involved in any negotiation. Its main weakness is that it does little to help define the dimensions of the national win-sets. The Odell model has the advantage that it focuses more on negotiation strategies and integrates the role of markets. Its main weakness is perhaps that it is difficult to apply to multilateral negotiations. Both the Putnam and Odell models are therefore valuable, although by no means the only possible models that can be used to analyse economic diplomacy. They both share a weakness in that they tend to neglect the international institutional setting within which economic diplomacy takes place. To a greater or lesser degree international rules, regimes and institutions shape all aspects of economic diplomacy and thus the expectations and options for negotiators.

References

Aberbach, J.D., Putnam, R.D. and Rockman, B.A. (1981), *Bureaucrats and Politicians in Western Democracies*, Harvard University Press, Cambridge, MA.

Bayliss, J. and Smith, S. (1998), *The Globalization of World Politics: an Introduction to International Relations*, Oxford University Press, Oxford.

Bayne, N. (2000), *Hanging in There: The G7 and G8 Summit in Maturity and Renewal*, Ashgate, Aldershot.

Breslin, J.W. and Rubin, J.Z. (eds) (1991), *Negotiation Theory and Practice*, PONs Books, Cambridge, MA.

Destler, I.M. (2005), *American Trade Politics*, 4th edition, Institute of International Economics, Washington.

Eichengreen, B. (1998) 'Dental Hygiene and Nuclear War', *International Organization*, Vol. 52, No. 4, pp. 993–1012.

Evans, P., Jacobsen, H.K. and Putnam, R.D. (eds) (1993), *Double-Edged Diplomacy: International Bargaining and Domestic Politics*, University of California Press, Berkeley, CA.

Fasan, O. (2006), 'Compliance with WTO Law in Developing Countries: A Study of South Africa and Nigeria', PhD dissertation, LSE.

Garrett, G. (1998), *Partisan Politics in the Global Economy*, Cambridge University Press, Cambridge.

Gilpin, R. (1987), *The Political Economy of International Relations*, Princeton University Press, Princeton, NJ.

Goldstein, J. (1988), 'Ideas, Interests and American Trade Policy', *International Organization*, Vol. 42, No. 1, pp. 179–217.

Goldstein, J. and Martin, L. (2000), 'Legalization,Trade Liberalization, and Domestic Politics: A Cautionary Note', *International Organization*, Vol. 54, No. 3, pp. 603–32.

Grieco, J. (1990), *Cooperation Among Nations; Europe, America and Non-Tariff Barriers to Trade*, Cornell University Press, Ithaca, NY.

Ikenberry, G.J., Lake, D.A. and Mastandano, M. (eds) (1988), *The State and American Foreign Economic Diplomacy*, Cornell University Press, Ithaca and London.

Keohane, R.O. and Nye, J.S. (2001), 'Between Centralization and Fragmentation: The Club Model of Multilateral Cooperation and Problems of Democratic Legitimacy', *Kennedy School of Government Working Paper No. 01-004*, available at SSRN: http://ssrn.com/abstract=262175.

Kindleberger, C. (1973), *International Economics*, R.D. Irwin, Homewood IL.

Landau, A. (2000), 'Analyzing International Economic Negotiations: Towards a Synthesis of Approaches', *International Negotiation*, Vol. 5, pp. 1–19.

Milner, H. (1997), *Interests, Institutions and Information: Domestic Politics and International Relations*, Princeton University Press, Princeton, NJ.

Milner, H. (1998) 'Rationalizing Politics: The Emerging Synthesis of International, American and Comparative Politics', *International Organization*, Vol. 52, No. 4, pp. 759–86.

Odell, J.S. (2000), *Negotiating the World Economy*, Cornell University Press, Ithaca and London.

Princen, S. (2005), 'Governing through Multiple Forums: The Global Safety Regulation of Genetically Modified Crops and Foods', in Koenig-Archibugi, M. and Zürn, M. (eds), *New Modes of Governance in the Global System*, Palgrave, Basingstoke.

Putnam, R.D. (1988), 'Diplomacy and Domestic Politics: The Logic of Two-Level Games', *International Organization*, Vol. 42, No. 3, pp. 427–60.

Putnam, R.D. and Bayne, N. (1987), *Hanging Together: Cooperation and Conflict in the Seven-Power Summits*, SAGE, London.

Sebenius, J.K. (1983), 'Negotiation Arithmetic: Adding and Subtracting Issues and Parties', *International Organization*, Vol. 37, pp. 281–316.

Spero, J.E. and Hart, J. (2003), *The Politics of International Economic Relations*, Thompson/Wadsworth, Belmont CA.

Strange, S. (1988), *States and Markets: an Introduction to Political Economy*, Pinter, London.

Tollison, R.D. and Willett, T.D. (1979), 'An Economic Theory of Mutually Advantageous Issue Linkages in International Negotiations', *International Organization*, Vol. 33, No. 4, pp. 425–49.

Ulbert, C. and Risse, T (2005), 'Deliberately Changing the Discourse: What Does Make Arguing Effective?', *Acta Politica*, Vol. 40, No. 3, pp. 351–67.

Woolcock, S. (2000), 'European Trade Policy: Global Pressures and Domestic Constraints', in Wallace, H. and Wallace, W. (eds), *Policy Making in the European Union*, 4th edition, Oxford University Press, Oxford.

Woolcock, S. (ed.) (2006), *Trade and Investment Regulation: the Role of Regional and Bilateral Agreements,* UN University Press, Tokyo.

WTO (2003), Ministerial Statement of World Trade Organization Ministerial Conference, 5th Session, Cancun 10-14 September, Document WT/MIN(03)20 of 23 September 2003.

WTO (2004), Decision adopted by the General Council on 1 August 2004 (the July Package), Document WT/L/579 of 2 August 2004.

Chapter 3

Economic Diplomacy in Practice

Nicholas Bayne

This chapter examines the practice of economic diplomacy, concentrating on what is done by national governments. It starts by analysing the activities of permanent officials or bureaucrats. These are still the people who conduct most international negotiations in economic diplomacy; and while formal decision-making powers may rest with ministers or legislatures, these powers are usually exercised on the basis of preparatory work done by officials. But as the chapter proceeds, it traces the interaction of bureaucrats with other state and non-state actors. All these actors are discussed in greater detail in Chapters 4 and 5.

The chapter begins with the story of the fifth International Tin Agreement (ITA). Though it dates from the 1980s, it foreshadows the new economic diplomacy, illustrating both how different tensions operate within government and what methods are used to resolve them. The main body of the chapter is divided into three parts:

- the first goes through the sequence of *domestic decision-making* in government;
- the second analyses the process of *international negotiation* and relates this to the domestic sequence;
- the third examines *negotiating strategies* that illustrate the interaction between domestic and international levels.

The conclusions relate both decision-making and negotiation to the tensions of economic diplomacy identified in Chapter 1.

The Story of the Fifth International Tin Agreement

The aim of the International Tin Agreement (ITA) was to iron out short-term fluctuations in the world price of tin by the use of a buffer stock. The buffer stock manager sold tin if the price rose too high, bought tin if it fell too low and had a fund for this purpose. The intervention prices were set by the International Tin Council, composed of major producers and consumers of tin. The United Kingdom had always been a member of the Council. But when the ITA came up for renewal for the fifth time in the 1980s, the UK had to follow a policy that was agreed unanimously within the European Community (EC).[1]

The UK then had a separate Departments of Industry, which was responsible for policy on the ITA. The officials concerned took the view that the UK should not join the new Agreement, for economic reasons. They argued that the effect of the Agreement over the years had been to keep the price of tin artificially high. This was bad for British industrial users of tin, who had to pay too much and were forced to seek substitutes. It was even bad for the operators of British tin mines, who saw their market shrinking. Industry officials foresaw that upward pressure on the price would cause the ITA to collapse within three years.

Officials in the Foreign and Commonwealth Office (FCO) strongly disagreed with Industry and argued that the UK should join the new ITA, just as it had joined all previous tin agreements.[2] The FCO was not convinced by Industry's economics. The Agreement had served its purpose well over twenty years, which suggested a fair balance of supply and demand. The FCO relied on political arguments in favour of joining. If the UK decided not to join, then the EC as a whole could not join, as it was not unanimous. With such a large group of consumers absent the Agreement could not survive. This would alienate the other Member States of the EC, most of whom wanted to join; it would alienate developing countries, who attached importance to this and other commodity agreements; in particular, it would alienate Malaysia, the largest tin producer. Britain had already had several rows with Malaysia in the 1980s, after Prime Minister Mahathir Mohammed came to power, and did not want another. FCO officials had firm instructions on that from Peter Carrington, then British Foreign Minister.

The Department of Industry and the FCO reached deadlock. So they looked for allies in other ministries. The Department of Trade supported the FCO, as they were responsible for the UN Conference on Trade and Development (UNCTAD), which encouraged commodity agreements.[3] But the Treasury supported Industry, as they did not want Britain to pay money into an agreement that might collapse. So there was still an equal balance of forces.

As officials could not agree, the problem went to a Committee of Ministers, which brought in yet more departments. The Minister of Agriculture and his officials were against the tin agreement, as they did not like those commodity agreements that covered agricultural products.[4] But the Minister of Defence, like his officials, favoured joining it, as he hoped for defence sales to Malaysia.

---

1 The common EC regime for commodity agreements, called 'Proba 20', was only agreed in 1982. It did not apply when the ITA had last been renewed, though the UK was already in the EC. For European decision-making in trade issues generally, see Chapter 13 below and Woolcock 2005.

2 The author was the official mainly concerned in the FCO.

3 For an account of the operation of commodity agreements at this time and the role of UNCTAD, see Spero and Hart 2003, 185, 241–9.

4 At the time these covered cocoa, coffee, tropical timber and wheat.

So both ministers and bureaucrats were split down the middle and there was still no decision.

In these conditions the problem had to go to the Prime Minister, then Margaret Thatcher, for her to arbitrate. She was known to be inclined against the Agreement, largely because the Americans, under President Ronald Reagan, had decided they would not join. But before she made a decision, she and Carrington went off to an Anglo-German summit, to meet Helmut Schmidt as Chancellor and Hans Dietrich Genscher as Foreign Minister.

The risks were high for the FCO at this summit, as Germany was the only other EC Member State that had doubts about the International Tin Agreement. If Germany should decide not to join, that would undermine the FCO's case, while strengthening Industry's position. Both Genscher and Schmidt were undecided when the summit began. In the event, Carrington persuaded Genscher that the right course was to join; Genscher then persuaded his chancellor Schmidt; and Schmidt persuaded Thatcher. Britain and Germany endorsed an EC position in favour of the new agreement, which was duly adopted and entered into force.

This episode reveals unusually starkly the first two tensions in economic diplomacy: between the Department of Industry's economic case and the FCO's political case; and between the FCO's international arguments and Industry's domestic ones. It illustrates multi-level economic diplomacy, with interaction between the bilateral (Anglo-German), regional (the EC) and plurilateral levels (the ITA). It shows how heads of government get involved, both as domestic arbiters in decision-making and as players on the international scene. Carrington's manoeuvre is also an admirable example of skilful two-level game diplomacy.

The sequel illustrates the third tension in economic diplomacy, hitherto neglected in the story: between government and other forces, including the market. Three years later, market pressures caused the buffer stock manager to overspend his fund in supporting the tin price. The Fifth ITA became insolvent and collapsed, just as forecast, with heavy losses to the subscribing countries.

Decision-Making in Government: the Domestic Sequence

This part of the chapter looks generally at the process of decision-making by governments in economic diplomacy. It analyses the process as a sequence of six stages, as follows:

1) identifying the lead department;
2) external and internal consultation;
3) political authority;
4) democratic legitimisation;
5) international negotiation;
6) ratification of agreement.

This sequential treatment is deliberately simplified, in two respects. First, some of the stages may happen simultaneously, not in succession. Second, the sequence may have to be repeated, in whole or part, as decision-making proceeds, either because of new domestic developments or because of its interaction with international negotiations. Economic diplomacy is rarely a linear process; it is an iterative and cyclical activity, which may go round the same course several times.

Identifying the Lead Department

The first stage in the domestic sequence is to identify the lead department for the subject in question. This is the department whose spokesmen will conduct international negotiations, whose minister will answer in the legislature and whose budget will bear any costs. In political diplomacy the lead department is almost always the foreign ministry. In economic diplomacy in developed countries this seldom happens. Usually the lead goes, by well-established precedent, to the relevant home department: the finance ministry leads on international finance, the agriculture ministry on external agricultural issues, the environment ministry on the global environment. The recent growth in the subject-matter of economic diplomacy does not affect this basic principle. It is usually the result of a domestic policy subject, like employment or education, becoming the subject of greater international pressure. This means that a home department is already available to take the lead.

This general principle requires some important qualifications, however, in relation to the role of foreign ministries and the treatment of international trade. In developed countries, when the foreign ministry gets the lead in economic diplomacy, it is usually for two reasons. One is where economic relations have an unusually high political content, so that economic diplomacy is mainly concerned with reconciling the first tension, between international economics and international politics. This applied in the past to economic relations with Communist countries. The other reason is where the subject covers a very wide range of external interests, with none predominating. Thus, while G8 summits cover trade, finance, development,the environment and other economic issues, the lead department, in the UK and most other member countries, is the foreign ministry. In developing countries, on the other hand, foreign ministries often have much greater authority in economic as well as political diplomacy and the power of home departments (except for finance ministries) is less developed.

International trade negotiations, being on the borderline between external and domestic policy, get varying treatment in different countries. Some favour the domestic aspects, others the international ones. In EU Member States, like Germany, France and Britain, the lead ministry is normally a large home department, which contributes to the formation of the common European negotiating position. In Japan, however, the Foreign Ministry has the lead, not the Ministry for Economics, Trade and Industry (METI). In Canada, Australia and New Zealand, responsibility for foreign affairs and international trade is integrated in a single department. Finally, in the United States and European Union (the two largest players in trade negotiations) responsibility is given to a separate body: the US Trade Representative (USTR), whose office is an agency of the White House; and the EU Trade Commissioner, backed by Directorate General (DG) Trade of the Commission (Destler 2005; Wallace and Wallace 2005; Bomberg and Stubb 2003).

The lead department can be changed, though rarely. This can happen, for example, when governments change and redistribute Cabinet responsibilities. Originally the lead department for the British 'Know-How Fund', created in 1989 to provide technical assistance to Russia and other Central and East European countries, was the FCO. When the new Labour government came to power in 1997, it promoted the department responsible for overseas aid, the Department for International Development (DFID), to full Cabinet status and transferred lead responsibility for the Know-How Fund to this department.

External and Internal Consultation

The lead department then launches two consultation processes: *external*, with forces outside central government; and *internal*, with other government departments. Both processes happen simultaneously and interact on one another. Before consultation can start, however, the lead department must decide its own negotiating objectives and tactics and resolve any internal differences. In European economics ministries, for example, the division responsible for trade negotiations in the WTO will be keen to see trade barriers come down. But the division responsible for the textile industry may want to keep the barriers up, so that there is tension between international and domestic pressures. In Canada or Australia, as noted, foreign affairs and international trade are handled by the same department, which must therefore reconcile its international political and economic objectives.

External consultation　The lead department is likely to consult with a wide variety of forces outside central government. As noted in Chapter 1, greater reliance on non-state actors is a strategy increasingly used by government in economic diplomacy. But sometimes their influence can become so strong that departments – whether deliberately or not – become dependent on them or even 'captured' by them. These non-state actors will be analysed in more detail in Chapter 5. This section contains only a brief review of their interaction with officials.

In economic diplomacy departments usually consult *business interests*, to get the views of those whose livelihood is affected by the activity concerned and to test how their policy ideas would be regarded by the markets. The pressure from business may be in conflicting directions. Small firms may have different interests from large firms. Ministries of agriculture listen to farmers, who want high prices for their produce, but also to the food-processing industry, who want their input prices low.

Departments increasingly consult *non-governmental organisations – NGOs*. In many fields, such as development, debt relief, environment and food safety, NGOs are powerful and articulate. They usually become active because they are not content with the line being taken by government – and they are often opposed to business interests as well. It is a delicate decision for government to judge how far to engage them. They may be very vocal and committed, but only represent a minority view in the country at large.

Departments consult *expert opinion*, including academics. Issues in economic diplomacy are often very complex and technical and departments cannot carry all the necessary expertise in-house. Academic experts can be very influential. For example, the ideas behind the conversion of the GATT into the WTO essentially came from Professor John Jackson, an academic at the University of Michigan.[5]

In many subjects, integrating the position of *public bodies outside central government* is becoming an essential part of the consultation process. In international finance, central banks have always been involved. Now other regulatory authorities, e.g. for securities and insurance or for food safety, are becoming influential. Sometimes the responsible bodies are at sub-national level in federal systems. So state insurance regulators in the US and food safety authorities in the German *Länder* get involved in economic diplomacy.

The lead department will also consider how to involve the *media*. Consulting outside forces may have brought the issues into the public domain, while greater transparency is another favoured strategy in the new economic diplomacy. But this is another tricky decision for government. On the one hand the support of the media will be very important later on, to get popular backing for any international agreement reached. So it is worth preparing the media in advance. But if the government's position becomes publicly known at this early stage, it may be harder to change it later in the course of negotiation. The traditional practice is to brief trusted contacts unattributably: the media gets the information and can publish it, but should not attribute it to the government or present it as a fixed government position. However, while this practice may work for press and radio, it has less attractions for television, which is looking for stories with visual impact.

Internal consultation   As well as consulting outside forces, the lead department seeks to get a view agreed across the whole of government. A complex negotiation, like a multilateral trade round, can involve almost every government department, as Chapter 4 will show. But even in a more precise field, such as climate change, the department responsible for the environment, in the lead, would consult ministries of trade and economics, finance, development and foreign affairs. Each would have their departmental instincts: the economics ministry looking for the opportunities and costs for business; the finance ministry wanting to get value for money; the development ministry concerned for the position of poor countries; and the foreign ministry seeking consistency with wider foreign policy. Each ministry would have their own contacts with outside forces – business, NGOs, academics and others. The energy industries, for example, would be closer to the Economics than the Environment Ministry.

---

5   The proposals in Professor Jackson's paper 'Restructuring the GATT System' (Jackson 1990), especially pp. 93–4, were taken over almost exactly in the design of the WTO.

In a straightforward case, the lead department can get the assent of others by correspondence. Where there are conflicting views, these will be resolved at meetings of officials, called and chaired either by the lead department or by a neutral body. In the UK the Cabinet Office, under the Secretary to the Cabinet, often serves as neutral chair and secretariat in economic diplomacy, especially in European Union matters. Most other governments have comparable bodies.

If the departments concerned reach agreement on the negotiating position, this will typically be a compromise position. No department will obtain all its objectives, but each will have to adapt or abandon some. It is important that, once agreement is reached, departments give up those ambitions which are not covered by the agreed position, so that all parts of government say the same thing. This singleness of purpose contributes greatly to effective economic diplomacy, because it gives strength to a negotiating position. It is an aspect of economic diplomacy where the UK is generally thought to be very efficient. Geoffrey Howe, the British Foreign Secretary from 1983 to 1989, records in his memoirs the envy of his European colleagues: "'Your British people", they would say, "are like the Kremlin. They all always say the same thing'" (Howe 1994, 447).

But singleness of purpose of this kind has its downside. If agreement has been reached only with difficulty on a position which all can defend, it may become very hard to adjust it during negotiation. This is particularly evident in the European Union, where often the strain of producing an agreed position among the 27 Member States exhausts any possible negotiating flexibility.

Political Decision

In the account given so far, permanent officials have driven the process. The next stage raises the process to the political level and involves ministers. This can be broken down into three distinct activities.

As a minimum requirement, officials submit their work to ministers for *endorsement*, to give it political authority. If officials have agreed a position, then usually simple ministerial endorsement can be obtained by the lead minister writing to his colleagues or reporting in Cabinet. Each meeting of the European Union's Council of Ministers, for example, begins with decisions taken without discussion, called 'A Points' (Bomberg and Stubb 2003, 50).

The second activity for ministers involves *settling disputes*. Officials may be unable to agree; or ministers may not agree with their officials' advice. In that case ministers themselves have to meet and most governments have formal or informal machinery for this purpose. In the UK, for example, there is an established system of Cabinet Office ministerial committees; the problem could go to one of them or to a smaller, ad hoc group of ministers. Ministers will have somewhat different criteria for judgement than their officials and will be more responsive to parliamentary and popular pressures.[6] Where disagreement persists, even after ministerial discussion, then the head of government gets involved, to

---

6 For a perceptive analysis of the differences between ministers and officials, still relevant today, see Aberbach, Putnam and Rockman 1981.

resolve matters and act as arbiter. Prime ministers' and presidents' time is precious, however, and departments will always try their utmost to settle matters without involving the head of government.

The third activity consists of ministerial *initiative*. This chapter has so far analysed ongoing economic diplomacy, where ministerial authority is sought only after the treatment of an existing issue by officials. But ministers may decide to launch new policies and intervene themselves much earlier in the sequence. The greater involvement of ministers is another favoured strategy in the new economic diplomacy. In particular, heads of government can use their authority to drive forward issues, not waiting to be invoked as arbiter. Heads of government can increasingly draw on their own staffs – in the White House, the Elysée, the Federal German Chancellery and even No 10 Downing Street under Tony Blair as UK Prime Minister – and are using them in the place of lead departments, rather than entrusting the subject to a Cabinet colleague.

Democratic Legitimisation

In non-democratic governments, a decision by ministers or the head of government settles the matter. But in democracies a further process is required, to give the government's agreed position democratic legitimacy and to satisfy its accountability to its electorate. This normally involves a report to the elected legislature and possibly endorsement of the government's decision by a vote. In countries with parliamentary systems this usually comes quite late in the sequence of economic diplomacy. But elsewhere the elected bodies could be involved much earlier and this especially applies to the US Congress. The report to the legislature will usually be accompanied by formal statements and briefing material intended to be published in the press or other media. At this time the government announces its position formally and takes responsibility for it.

Both to the press and to parliament the government may not want to go beyond a general statement, without too much detail, so as to retain some flexibility in the later negotiation. The reaction of parliament and the press will have a stronger impact on ministers than on officials. So forces outside government, like business and NGOs, will try to influence government decisions through parliament and the media too, in addition to direct contacts with officials.

International Negotiation

Stages 1 to 4 complete the domestic decision-making sequence to prepare for an international negotiation. The actual negotiation can be left on one side at this stage, to be considered later in the chapter. For the moment, the assumption is that the negotiation has run its course and international agreement has been reached.

Ratification of Agreement

Once agreement is reached, a number of stages in the earlier domestic sequence are repeated. The lead department negotiator reports to the other departments concerned and seeks their concurrence. The lead department minister briefs other ministerial colleagues, to re-confirm the earlier political authority. The agreement is reported to parliament and, if necessary, legislation is introduced so that the government can meet the commitments it has taken. The government launches a media campaign to ensure the agreement wins public acceptance.

No government wants to find that the agreement it has struck internationally comes apart at this ratification stage. So governments take precautions in advance to avoid this danger. Sometimes these may be formal precautions, as when the US Administration seeks 'fast-track' authority for trade negotiations from Congress (Destler 2005). This means that Congress can either endorse or reject an agreement, but it cannot amend its provisions. Skilful international negotiators will adjust their tactics in anticipation of any problems with ratification and even seek to turn them to their advantage. Even with these precautions, however, all negotiators are taking a gamble when they return to seek ratification for what they have agreed. These risks will vary from country to country, depending both on the general structure of government and the strength of the particular administration in power. This determines the size of the win-set available to the negotiator, as defined in Putnam's analysis (Putnam 1988).

International Negotiations

This review of the domestic sequence in decision-making has deliberately left on one side what happens in international negotiations. It is now time to examine the international sequence and how it meshes with the domestic one. International negotiations can also be analysed in five distinct stages, which can sometimes be linear but will more often be iterative and cyclical, like their domestic counterpart. The stages are:

a) agenda-setting;
b) mandating;
c) negotiating to agreement;
d) adoption of agreement;
e) implementation.

Agenda-setting

Before any negotiation there will be an agenda-setting phase, which identifies what should be subject to international treatment. This phase can be lengthy: for example it took over four years' preparation and a failed ministerial meeting at Seattle before the WTO was ready to launch the Doha Development Agenda in 2001. During this phase governments have usually not committed themselves to firm positions, as it coincides with the Consultation stage in the domestic sequence. This provides opportunities for outside forces, such as business and NGOs, to get their favoured subjects accepted on the agenda. It is often the occasion for international epistemic communities (described in Chapter 4) to establish an intellectual basis for the discussion, before the hard bargaining sets in. Once the negotiation proper begins, however, these outside forces usually have to withdraw, leaving only governments at the table.

An example of how non-state actors – in this case business and academic experts – seek to influence agenda-setting relates to the Commonwealth Heads of Government Meeting (CHOGM) in Durban, South Africa, in late 1999. The CHOGM was held shortly before the WTO met in Seattle, aiming to launch a new trade round. If the Commonwealth, with over 50 members, could decide a common line for Seattle, that should have quite an impact on the agenda to be agreed there. The Commonwealth Business Council (CBC), representing private business in Commonwealth countries, wanted the heads of government to agree at Durban on specific proposals for the new WTO round. The CBC commissioned a report from their academic advisers, who were Razeen Sally and Stephen Woolcock (co-author of this book) of the International Relations Department of the LSE. The CBC report was well received at Durban and enabled Commonwealth trade ministers to be active at Seattle, though the meeting was a disaster for other reasons.

Mandating

Once the decision has been taken to launch the negotiations and the agenda is defined, the government representatives involved need a mandate to negotiate. This is provided by completing the later stages of the domestic sequence, to secure inter-departmental agreement, political authority and democratic legitimisation.

As domestic decision-making procedures vary widely between countries, so will the mandates given to negotiators. They will especially determine how much negotiating flexibility or 'slack' delegations will have, as explained in Chapter 2. Negotiators from the United States and the European Union will have a tightly defined mandate, reflecting the complexity of their domestic decision-making. This will limit their win-sets, in Putnam's terms, and make them hard negotiators. But negotiators from developing countries are often given much greater freedom of action and may be quite detached from the domestic process. Economic diplomacy is more often handled by foreign ministries and less integrated into domestic policy. Representatives of developing countries may operate independently of their capitals and take decisions on their own initiative.

Negotiating to Agreement

This is the core of the negotiating process. Negotiating strategies will be considered in more detail in the next section of this chapter. But throughout the process the negotiators and their teams, at least those from developed countries, will be checking the likely acceptability of the emerging results at the domestic level. For a delegation with only limited negotiating slack, this will be a constant, iterative process.

For example, European negotiators operating in Washington at the IMF and World Bank, or in New York at the United Nations, will take advantage of the difference in time zones. The domestic team in the lead department will find at the start of the working day, in Berlin, Brussels or London, the negotiators' report and request for guidance sent overnight. They will have the morning to consult other parties, by telephone and e-mail or in informal meetings, and prepare a reply to be sent out before the working day begins in the United States. Such activity will usually be confined to bureaucratic contacts. Consulting ministers or outside forces takes longer.

Adoption of Agreement

The negotiations, if successful, will conclude with an agreement. Before the participating governments will commit themselves to such an agreement and be ready to submit it to ratification, there is usually a more formal procedure than prevails while the negotiations are in progress. There is often a pause between reaching agreement on a text (which may be *initialled* by the official negotiator) and giving formal assent to it (which may involve *signature* by a minister).

Depending on the subject, there will be different thresholds of adoption. Informal understandings on familiar subjects, based on voluntary cooperation, may not need to go beyond official level. But any agreement involving a legal commitment or a new departure in policy will usually require political authorisation by ministers. In some countries, such as the United States, the government may consult the legislature before adopting an agreement, to be sure that the subsequent ratification process will go smoothly.

Implementation

Once an agreement has been negotiated internationally and ratified domestically, then it has to be implemented. All governments taking part in an international agreement have an interest in seeing that other parties respect the agreement as faithfully as they do. The effectiveness of this will depend on the structure of the agreement and the institutions sponsoring it. For example:

• Agreements based on voluntary cooperation often rely on peer pressure to ensure implementation. In compact institutions like the OECD this can be effective, but in more diffuse bodies like the United Nations commitments are easily evaded.
• Some voluntary agreements are self-regulating, especially where funds are involved. Countries following IMF programmes are not legally obliged to observe them, but they will not get the desired finance unless they do.
• Other agreements are based on formal rules and legal obligations. Failures of implementation are subject to dispute settlement procedures. These can apply

bilaterally, in regional agreements (like the EU or NAFTA) or multilaterally, especially in the WTO.

Implementation is thus a major factor in deciding between voluntary cooperation and formal rules.

After this analysis of both the domestic and international sequences, Table 3.1 shows how they fit together.

Table 3.1   How domestic decision-making and international negotiation fit together

Domestic	International
1 Identifying the lead department	
2 External and internal consultation	a Agenda-setting
3 Political authority	
4 Legitimisation	b Mandating
5 Negotiation	c Negotiating to agreement
	d Adoption of agreement
6 Ratification	
	e Implementation

Negotiating Strategies

This section returns to the actual process of international negotiation and examines some of the strategies used, especially those that try to take advantage of the domestic process in other negotiating parties. This analysis of negotiating strategies is picked up again in Chapter 15, in the examination of international economic institutions and what governments want from them. The strategies considered here are the following:

1) bargaining among lead negotiators;
   - value claiming bargains;
   - value creating bargains;
   - package deals;
2) exploiting divided counsels;
3) intervention by outside forces;
4) political intervention – playing the head of government card.

Bargaining among Lead Negotiators

Negotiators from the lead departments (who may have people from other departments at their elbows) come to the international table with a double aim: to maximise the area on which they can agree with the other parties; and to demonstrate the benefits of the agreement reached to their partners in the domestic process. As explained in Chapter 2, negotiation can be divided into two methods: distributive bargaining or value claiming – when party A gains, party B loses; and integrative bargaining or value creating, where everybody gains (see Putnam 1988 and Odell 2000, 31–4).

Value claiming It is instinctive to think of negotiators bargaining so as to gain advantage at the expense of the other parties; a gain for me means a loss for you. Popular opinion – like parliaments and the media – often looks at negotiations in this way. The United States, for reasons explained in Chapter 10, often favours value claiming strategies. But if negotiators only concentrate on their gains, this is not likely to be a fruitful approach to economic diplomacy. An agreement is unlikely to be concluded where one or more parties are clearly the losers. Such an agreement is unlikely to be ratified back home and, even if it were, the losing side would always look for ways to escape or overturn it. The US Administration was unsuccessful in its value claiming approach to a new round of negotiations in the WTO at Seattle in late 1999. It proposed an agenda which brought obvious gain to the United States but did not offer enough to anyone else.

Value creating So skilful negotiators in economic diplomacy look for value creating deals where all parties can regard themselves as having benefitted. The problem here is that value creating deals are difficult to identify. For example, in climate change negotiations, it would appear that everyone would benefit from the reduction of emissions of greenhouse gases worldwide. But developing countries point out that this is in fact an unequal bargain, as reducing emissions inhibits their growth more than it does for mature industrial countries. So while they subscribe to the UN Framework Treaty on Climate Change, they have so far resisted making commitments under the Kyoto Protocol in the absence of compensation from rich countries.

Package deals In practice, many value creating agreements turn out to be packages of a number of value claiming deals. In each individual deal, some countries gain more than others, but the total package adds up in such a way as to provide something for everyone. For example, at the 2002 G8 Kananaskis summit the Americans agreed to replenish the World Bank's Trust Fund for debt relief in return for European commitments to finance the clean-up of nuclear installations in Russia (Bayne 2005, 135, 218–19). One consequence of this is that international economic negotiations quite often proceed by large package deals. For example, both the Uruguay Round in the GATT, concluded in 1994, and the Doha Development Agenda in the WTO, launched in 2001, consisted of a 'single undertaking', so that nothing was agreed until everything was agreed (Croome

1999; Preeg 1995; Laird 2002). This strategy increases the chances of there being something for everyone, as well as the adverse consequences for a government that causes such a deal to collapse.

Exploiting Divided Counsels

It may be that the ingenuity of negotiators in constructing value creating bargains and package deals is not enough to produce agreement. So governments look for ways to take advantage of the domestic processes in other parties. Each government in the negotiations knows that the others have been through a comparable process of consultation and political decision. A skilful negotiator looks for ways to exploit evidence of divided counsels in other governments.

One method is to play on known departmental rivalries. In some cases officials may feel closer to their colleagues from the same ministry abroad, whom they see as allies, than to officials from other ministries at home, whom they regard as rivals. Normally the Japanese government is very cohesive, but there is sometimes an opportunity to use this tactic in trade negotiations. Because the Foreign Ministry has the lead, rather than the Ministry for Economics, Trade and Industry (METI), the METI may therefore feel left out. The European economics ministries have close links with their sister ministry in Japan and may find the METI more responsive than the Foreign Ministry to its arguments to get the Japanese position changed.

Even where there are no built-in rivalries, it is normal that the agreed position of a government is more limited than individual departments would prefer. In principle, departments should abandon their wider objectives and rally behind the agreed position. But many departments in practice cannot or will not abide by this discipline. They let it become known that they could accept or even prefer a different position. The British, as noted, are usually very disciplined internally and so are the French. Other countries are more given to fighting out their inter-departmental battles in public or at the negotiating table – such as the Americans and the Germans. This makes them obvious targets for others to exploit these divided counsels.

The same tactic can also be practised against the collective negotiating position of the European Union when the common purpose of the Member States is fragile. In 1995 Canada had a bitter dispute with Spain about fishing in the North Atlantic. The Spanish expected solid European support for their position, because the EU operates a Common Fisheries Policy. But within the EU, the British and Irish had the same complaints about Spanish over-fishing as the Canadians had. They ensured that the EU and Canada struck a deal which increased the discipline over everyone's fishing practices.

Finally, it is possible for countries to exploit the tension between politics and economics in their negotiating partners. At the beginning of the 2000s Turkey and Argentina were negotiating packages with the IMF to deal with financial crises. When the Bush Administration first took office, the US Treasury declared that it would not agree to further IMF support for such cases. But the American position soon softened towards both countries, for political reasons: Turkey was seen as being in the front line in the fight against terrorism, while the US was reluctant to abandon a Latin American ally.[7]

Intervention by Outside Forces

While governments try to take advantage of domestically divided counsels to move international decisions in their favour, outside actors – business, NGOs and others – may do the same. This is now an integral part of economic diplomacy. While individual business firms or NGOs still intervene in economic diplomacy, collective intervention has become the standard practice, as Chapter 5 illustrates. Non-state actors form coalitions to lobby several governments together, as well as the secretariats of international institutions, often on a systematic basis (O'Brien and others 2000).

The long campaign by development NGOs to secure full debt relief for low-income countries illustrates the different tactics used. Before the Birmingham G8 summit of 1998 Christian Aid, a leading British charity, correctly identified Germany as the main obstacle to agreement. It issued its supporters with postcards addressed to the German finance minister, printed with a text in German urging a more generous approach. Fifteen thousand such postcards flooded into the German finance ministry, while a second wave targeted Federal Chancellor Helmut Kohl and the leader of the opposition, Gerhard Schroeder (Bayne 1998). The Kohl government did not change the German position, but after Schroeder and the German Social Democrats (SPD) came to power later in 1998, one of their earliest acts in office was to reverse the stance on debt relief (Bayne 2005). At the Birmingham summit a large peaceful demonstration encircled the meeting site and such expressions of mass support for debt relief became a feature of later summits. But at the same time the campaigners were lobbying internally, to convince both creditor governments and the IMF and World Bank of the intellectual case for change (Mallaby 2004). This culminated in the run-up to the 2005 Gleneagles summit, when an NGO campaign to 'Make Poverty History' gathered worldwide support. No head of government wished to oppose such a movement and the summit endorsed a plan for 100 per cent debt relief for selected countries worked out by the G7 finance ministers.

While business firms seldom engage in public pressure like NGOs, they are equally adept at collective intervention behind the scenes. For example, the WTO's negotiations on financial services twice came near to collapse, in 1993 and 1995, largely because of differences between the US and the EU negotiators. The US wanted too much, while the EU would settle for anything. Then a group of American and European financial service firms came to realise that they had a joint interest in a good result from the negotiations. So they exercised collective pressure on the European and American negotiators to work together – with the result that the negotiations concluded with an agreement in 1997. In the European Union firms regularly influence domestic decision-making in each Member State

---

7   Even so, the extra IMF support agreed in August 2001 was unable to save Argentina from financial collapse at the end of the year. See Blustein 2005.

through national associations like the Confederation of British Industry in the UK. But they also combine to intervene with the European Commission, through BusinessEurope (the union of European business organisations – formerly UNICE), so as to influence decision-making at the EU level.

Business and NGOs usually work separately and often in opposition. But climate change provides an example of an alliance that may become increasingly common. In order to convince the current US Administration (strongly influenced by the energy industry) to take climate change seriously and impose mandatory limits on greenhouse gas emissions, other governments have made common cause with NGOs, non-energy firms, state authorities and members of Congress, in the hope that this domestic pressure will be more effective than international exchanges.

Political Intervention – Playing the Head of Government Card

The international strategies examined so far have been initiated by government officials or by outside forces. However, even in negotiations conducted by officials, ministers often intervene, though they are not themselves at the table. Internationally heads of government may try to break the deadlock when this persists at lower levels, just as they act as arbiters nationally. Now that heads of government, like Tony Blair and George W. Bush, often talk on the telephone, such intervention is becoming more common. This chapter therefore concludes with a few examples of intervention by Blair as UK Prime Minister.

These interventions range from the simple to the more ambitious. A simple intervention took place in 2000, when Blair successfully intervened with US President Clinton to get British exports of cashmere taken off the list of products subject to American retaliatory trade barriers because of the EU policy on bananas. Blair argued to Clinton that the US was alienating its most likely ally in the European trade debate. He tried a similar approach to Bush in 2002, before the US imposed new tariffs on steel imports, but this time his intervention had no effect.

In the run-up to the Gleneagles summit in 2005, Blair repeatedly intervened directly with the other G8 leaders to get each of them committed to increase levels of development aid, especially doubling aid to Africa by 2010. Many of the European leaders rallied early on to a collective EU commitment to raise aid levels to 0.7 per cent of national income. But as the summit approached, there was still resistance from the United States, Japan and Germany. Shortly before Gleneagles, Blair visited Washington and convinced Bush that he should not look less generous than the Europeans. He won over the Japanese Prime Minister, Junichiro Koizumi, at a bilateral meeting at Gleneagles and persuaded Schroeder on the margins of the summit itself. In all three cases Blair got the leaders to go beyond the position being defended by their officials, so as to achieve his objective.

Blair's most ambitious intervention took place early in 1999, with Schroeder over debt relief. As noted earlier, after Schroeder replaced Kohl in office, he himself announced a reversal of policy on debt relief, taking a much more forthcoming approach.[8] However, the finance ministry was still the lead department for this subject in the German government and they continued to drag their feet. At some point Blair contacted Schroeder to draw his attention to this, knowing that Schroeder was not on very good terms with his finance minister, Oskar Lafontaine. The result was that Schroeder removed the lead responsibility for this subject from the finance ministry and transferred it to his own department, the Federal Chancellery. The Chancellery moved the subject along much faster, and the Cologne summit produced a substantial agreement. This was another example of an advanced 'two-level game' move in economic diplomacy, comparable with Carrington's tactic described at the start of this chapter.

Conclusions

This chapter has analysed the methods adopted by governments today, in decision-making and negotiation, to reconcile the three tensions of economic diplomacy, as set out in Chapter 1. The main focus has been on reconciling the second tension – between domestic and international pressures – but the other two tensions have also been examined.

Domestic Decision-making

The domestic sequence is initially concerned with enabling governments to reach common positions internally. It provides both for the allocation of responsibility, at official and ministerial level, and incorporates a series of techniques for reaching agreed views, right up to the use of the head of government as arbiter. This aspect mainly relates to the *efficiency* of government. But as the domestic sequence proceeds, it increasingly focuses on *accountability,* by involving political authority, democratic legitimisation and ratification.

In the process domestic decision-making also addresses the other two tensions, as follows:

- The task of reconciling the first tension, between international economics and politics, falls particularly on foreign ministries. They are regular players in the consultation process, though seldom in the lead except when external political factors are unusually strong.
- The involvement of ministers and heads of government, as endorsers, arbiters and sources of initiative, also injects political elements into the domestic decision-making process.
- To reconcile the third tension, between government and other forces, outside actors, especially business, NGOs and the media, have to be integrated into the decision-making process, so that wider domestic pressures can be satisfied. They are involved not only in confidential consultations with officials but also

---

8 This was done in an article in the *Financial Times* on 21 January 1999.

in the more public lobbying of ministers and parliament. This is a growing trend in the early 2000s, as Chapter 5 will show.

International Negotiation

Economic diplomacy looks for ways in which domestically agreed positions can be deployed successfully in international contexts. The negotiators seek to maximise the scope of agreement in ways that will satisfy not only their own domestic backers but also domestic interests in their negotiating partners, since without that the agreement will fail to secure the necessary ratification. They therefore look, in the first instance, for solutions which provide something for everyone. If such solutions are not readily attainable, negotiators look for ways in which the domestic processes in their partners can be turned to their advantage.

While much of this activity takes place among the circles of officials concerned with the negotiations, it now goes wider and brings in the other strands of economic diplomacy:

- ministers, and especially heads of government, try to advance agreement by introducing additional political arguments;
- outside forces, like business, NGOs and epistemic communities, also seek to intervene, usually by collective action, in order to change the course of the negotiations;
- the implementation of international agreements is relevant to the question whether voluntary cooperation or formal rules will reconcile domestic and international pressures better.

Many of these issues will be examined and illustrated further in the practitioner chapters later in this book.

References

Aberbach, J., Putnam, R.D. and Rockman, B. (1981), *Bureaucrats and Politicians in Western Democracies,* Harvard University Press, Cambridge, MA.

Bayne, N. (1998), 'Britain, the G8 and the Commonwealth', *The Round Table*, No. 348, pp. 445–57.

Bayne, N. (2005), *Staying Together: The G8 Summit Confronts the Twenty-first Century*, Ashgate, Aldershot.

Blustein, P. (2005), *And the Money Kept Rolling In (and Out): Wall Street, the IMF and the Bankruptcy of Argentina*, Public Affairs, New York.

Bomberg, E. and Stubb, A. (2003), *The European Union: How Does it Work?*, Oxford University Press, Oxford.

Croome, J. (1999), *Reshaping the World Trading System: A History of the Uruguay Round*, 2nd edition, World Trade Organization, Geneva.

Destler, I.M. (2005), *American Trade Politics*, 4th edition, Institute of International Economics, Washington.

Howe, G. (1994), *Conflict of Loyalty*, Macmillan, London.

Jackson, J.J. (1990), *Restructuring the GATT System*, Royal Institute of International Affairs, London.

Laird, S. (2002), 'A Round by Any Other Name' *Development Policy Review*, Vol. 20, No. 1, pp. 41–62.

Mallaby, S. (2004), *The World's Banker*, Yale University Press, New Haven, CN.

O'Brien, R., Goetz, A.M., Scholte, J.A. and Williams, M. (2000), *Contesting Global Governance: Multilateral Economic Institutions and Global Social Movements*, Cambridge University Press, Cambridge.

Odell, J. (2000), *Negotiating the World Economy*, Cornell University Press, Ithaca, NY.

Preeg, E. (1995), *Traders in a Brave New World*, University of Chicago Press, Chicago.

Putnam, R.D. (1988), 'Diplomacy and Domestic Politics: The Logic of Two-Level Games', *International Organization*, Vol. 42, No. 4, pp. 427–60.

Spero, J. and Hart, M. (2003), *The Politics of International Economic Relations*, 6th edition, Thompson/Wadsworth, Belmont CA.

Wallace, H., Wallace, W. and Pollack, M.A. (eds) (2005), *Policy-making in the European Union*, 5th edition, Oxford University Press, Oxford.

Woolcock, S. (2005), 'European Trade Policy', in Wallace, H., Wallace, W. and Pollack, M.A. (eds) (2005), *Policy-making in the European Union*, 5th edition, Oxford University Press, Oxford.

Chapter 4

State Actors in Economic Diplomacy

Kate Macdonald and Stephen Woolcock

One of the central purposes of this book is to explore the various ways in which the conduct of economic diplomacy has changed fundamentally during the 1990s and early 2000s. Through most of the period since World War II economic diplomacy has been dominated by governments – and within them by permanent officials. However, as earlier chapters have shown, the end of the Cold War and the advance of globalisation has seen a major increase in the numbers and variety of both government and non-governmental actors involved in domestic decision-making and international negotiation. This chapter aims to provide an overview and mapping of the organisation of state actors at national, transnational and international levels. It will show how the range of actors involved in economic diplomacy is expanding in response to new patterns of economic interconnection and the increasingly intrusive impacts of economic negotiation and decision-making. The following chapter then does the same for non-state actors.

While the primary aim of the chapter is focused on simply mapping and identifying the cast of actors involved in economic diplomacy, it also highlights some of the differences in the roles and influence of these actors across the various issue areas and instruments in economic diplomacy. It considers the ways in which actors' roles are changing as economic diplomacy is transformed in a globalising world, including the often contested sources of the legitimacy of their roles, and thus the potential impacts of changing configurations on the effectiveness and legitimacy of resultant decision-making processes. The analysis presented here and in Chapter 5 is conceptually located within a scholarly literature that includes international political economy, public administration, comparative politics, negotiation theory, global governance, civil society, social movements, group behaviour and collective action, as well as broader political and sociological literatures. The references provided throughout both chapters are intended to assist readers in navigating this somewhat fragmented and disparate collection of relevant scholarly research.

A broad range of state actors are considered in this chapter. First, the concept of the 'state' as a decision-maker in economic diplomacy is unpacked. The various actors involved in economic diplomacy within both executive and legislative branches of government as well as within subnational levels of government are considered, alongside state-based actors at international and transnational levels. The classes of state actors analysed in this chapter are summarised in Table 4.1.

Table 4.1   State actors in economic diplomacy

Executive branch of government
  Heads of government and ministers
  Bureaucracies
  Independent regulatory agencies
Legislative branch of government
  Parliaments
  Political parties
Provincial, state and local government
The international and transnational level
  International organisations
  Transnational policy networks

'States' are often characterised and analysed as monolithic entities, but in fact they are comprised of a multiplicity of distinct groups. In the context of globalisation and with the increased complexity of contemporary policy-making processes and thus the expansion of government bureaucracy more broadly, the number of groups involved in policy-making processes has expanded dramatically. State actors remain based predominantly at national (including subnational) levels, but state-based actors at the international and transnational levels are also becoming increasingly important. The following discussion moves through each in turn.

State Actors at the National Level

The key actors at the national level in most countries can be categorised as part of either the executive or the legislative branches of government, although the balance and interaction between these two branches, and between different actors within them, vary significantly between different institutional systems. In the US for example, policy-making on issues such as trade is unusually decentralised, with the legislature playing a particularly important role (Cohen, Paul et al. 1996). In such cases, policy-making involves the pursuit of compromise and accommodation on one or both of two levels – among the various executive branch departments and agencies having policy jurisdiction, and between the administration and legislature, with the judicial branch making very infrequent appearances when policies or administrative decisions are challenged in the courts (Milner 1997). Thus, while some influential models of international economic policy making (in particular those based on Putnam's 'two-level game') emphasise the need for the executive branch to have agreements ratified by the legislature, it is also important to focus attention on how the executive comes to define the national interest via inter-departmental or inter-agency debates that are often very complex. Discussion of such roles begins by considering the different actors involved in the executive branch of government, and then considers those involved in the legislature.

Executive Branch of Government

The structure of the executive branch of government varies significantly between different political and institutional systems. Of particular significance are differences between presidential executive systems such as that of the US, where both political power and symbolic authority are centred in one individual – the president – and parliamentary systems characterised by a non-executive head of state separated from an executive head of government (Greenwood and Wilson 1990; Mahler 1992). Within all systems, however, we can identify three key executive actors as being of particular importance: politicians (heads of government and ministers), bureaucrats, and independent (or quasi-independent) administrative and regulatory agencies. Each of these is analysed below, together with a discussion of key trends in the changing dynamics of interaction between politicians and bureaucrats and between different government ministries and agencies.

Politicians and Bureaucrats

While the role of *politicians* in policy-making processes varies with different political systems, ministers within a given department typically have the primary political authority and ultimate responsibility for decisions. Often they are concerned not only with the technical merits of a given policy in relation to some conception of the 'national' or 'public' interest, but also with the implications of their decisions for the prospects of themselves or their party retaining power. The role of the *bureaucracy* is theoretically to administer the policy of the executive and to offer specialised advice to the executive rather than to make policy of its own, though often they do the latter also. Max Weber is seen as the father of work in this field, but bureaucracies have been studied from various perspectives: within organisational theory; behavioural theory; and within extensive literatures on public administration.

Except where senior posts are held by political appointees, it is civil servants who have the responsibility of implementing decisions taken by politicians who may well move on to other posts or lose elections. Civil servants will therefore tend to be more concerned than politicians with the practicality of implementing decisions, and may also provide a long term institutional memory, retaining knowledge of previous cases and precedents which bear on any policy debate. This differs, however, between political systems. For example, while many European officials may remain in place for a period that extends beyond the life of one government, in the United States senior officials are political appointees whose term in post coincides with that of the administration (Greenwood and Wilson 1990).

Nevertheless, within contemporary forms of economic diplomacy the *relationship between ministers and departments* is changing, with ministers often taking a more direct and central role in negotiations, particularly around high profile events such as WTO negotiations and summits. Such changes reflect the increasing politicisation of many of these decisions, associated with their increased domestic political impact upon a wider range of constituencies; governments increasingly involve ministers to address international economic issues that have important domestic implications. While the focus here is on departments and ministers, government departments can include both ministerial departments and non-ministerial departments. The latter includes bodies such as customs and excise or departments of inland revenue – formally headed by boards, although often answered for by ministers.

Inter-Departmental Relations

The relationship between different departments and agencies within the executive branch of government is also important to consider. A wide range of different kinds of actors are involved in economic diplomacy, and the degree of decentralisation within the executive branch varies between countries and between policy areas. As explained in Chapter 3, no single executive branch actor can monopolise any significant trade policy decision, so that the organisational path to policy decision-making inevitably requires coordination among many executive branch departments and agencies that have jurisdiction in various foreign trade policy sectors, except in rare instances where presidents intervene on their own to implement trade policy unilaterally. Up to two dozen different executive branch entities may participate in inter-agency committees and working groups, as the executive branch of any government seeks to find a consensus among a wide number of different government departments, each with their own organisational interests and priorities (Cohen et al. 1996; Cohen 1994).

The Uruguay Round of trade negotiations (1986–1994) provides an example of the range of internal government co-ordination required in trade negotiations. These were led by the USTR in the United States and DG Trade of the European Commission (in consultation with the EU Member States in the case of the European Union), but many other departments were involved:

- *Departments of Agriculture* were closely associated with the negotiations, because of the centrality of negotiations on reductions in agricultural support. Ministries of agriculture also regulated food safety standards in many countries, so they were likewise involved in the negotiations of an Agreement on Sanitary and Phyto-Sanitary (SPS) measures.
- *Departments of Industry, Enterprise or the Economy* were involved in the negotiations because of their interest in sponsoring a wide range of industrial sectors. As the negotiations touched not only on tariff levels but also on non-tariff measures, such as quotas for textiles and clothing or tighter WTO control over the use of national subsidies, these departments played a central role.
- *Ministries of science or technology* were concerned with the control of national subsidy programmes as well as the negotiations on Trade Related Intellectual Property Rights (TRIPS).
- *Finance Ministries* were involved in the negotiations because tariff reductions resulted in reduced government revenue and because the negotiations on

services covered financial services, which had been the jealous preserve of finance ministries or treasuries for many years.

• The services negotiations also involved *ministries responsible for transport, telecommunications, health and other public services,* which were all subject to negotiations and some liberalisation commitments.

• *Ministries of the Interior or Home Offices* were concerned with the services negotiations because they covered the free movement of people and thus touched on immigration and migration issues.

Towards the end of the Uruguay Round, the environment began to figure as a major potential issue. Labour standards were also proposed as a topic that should be added to the WTO agenda, at the time of the completion of the Uruguay Round. This meant that *ministries responsible for environmental standards and regulation* were involved in the negotiations, as were *employment or labour affairs departments.* These WTO negotiations represent an instance of economic diplomacy with unusually broad participation. Many cases of economic diplomacy are much more specific and focused, with the number of agencies involved being correspondingly lower. In general, however, the advance of 'deep integration' within the global economy continues to see this number rise.

Independent Regulatory Agencies

Another key group of actors within the executive branch involves independent regulators and administrative agencies. Regulatory agencies – encompassing a broad array of independent and semi-autonomous bodies – have been described as the fourth branch of government (after the executive, legislature and judiciary). They comprise a miscellaneous group, exhibiting some of the features normally associated with departments, but generally operating independently of ministers unless major political questions are involved. Many such bodies are statutory, formed under an act itself, such as the Health and Safety Commission in Britain. Other founding instruments may be a royal charter, treasury minute or the articles of a non-profit company (Greenwood and Wilson 1990). While such bodies commonly have restricted authority, a limited arsenal of political resources and a lack of independent finance, their strong organisational and information resources (particularly when their functions involve specialised professional expertise) often enable them to serve as important actors in the policy-making process.

The use of such agencies is long established practice in the United States, where limitations on government intervention have led 'independent' regulatory agencies frequently to be used to correct perceived market failures (Woolcock 1998). In Europe and elsewhere governments in the past have been more willing to intervene directly to correct market failures. But due to trends towards privatisation and growing support for independent regulation, many countries are making greater use of such agencies. Examples of these include: central banks; financial market regulators; competition and anti-trust authorities; and agencies regulating food and drug safety, access to telecommunications markets and sometimes even trade measures, such as the ITC in the United States (Majone 1997; Gilardi 2001; Thatcher 2002).

The importance of such regulatory bodies in economic diplomacy can be illustrated in many sectors. For example, in 2000 there was an important debate concerning access conditions for public telephone networks for mobile digital telephony and the standards to be set for the next generation of mobile technology. In most countries it was regulatory agencies, such as the Federal Communications Commission (FCC) in the US, OFTEL in the UK or the Directorates General (DGs) for Information Society and Competition in the European Commission, that determined the terms and conditions for competition between the existing (monopoly) common carriers and the new mobile suppliers. A comparable debate took place over the introduction of digital television (Hart 2004). Similar roles are played by regulators in financial markets and in risk assessment that can determine access to a range of goods and services markets. Such bodies are therefore likely to play a continued and important role in economic diplomacy as governments seek to delegate detailed technical regulation to specialist bodies.

Legislative Branch of Government

In the context of international economic decision-making relevant to economic diplomacy, much analysis of the legislative branch of government has focused on its role in ratifying international agreements negotiated by the executive (Putnam 1988; Milner 1997). Within the wider context of the national decision-making process, legislatures of course perform a number of other important functions, including criticism and control of the other branches of government (most notably the executive), as well as promoting public deliberation around major policy questions, and performing a central lawmaking function.

However, often legislatures are not directly involved in the negotiation processes of economic diplomacy, except to the extent that a credible power of veto by the legislature when it comes to ratifying agreements obliges negotiators in the executive to ensure that the legislature is fully informed. The general trend in most countries has been towards rising executive power at the expense of the legislature, as legislative bodies struggle to keep up with the expanding size and resources of executive bureaucracies, particularly as the complexity and technical demands of the policy-making process continue to increase. National legislatures tend to have even less control over monetary policy than over trade or other policies, especially following the shift towards greater acceptance of independent central banks. Despite these constraints on direct involvement of the legislative branch of government in the detailed conduct of economic diplomacy, it still wields important influence over the ultimate outcomes. As with the executive branch of government, there are multiple actors in the legislature: discussion here focuses particularly on parliaments and political parties. These are also important for the executive, but their impact is often more direct in legislatures.

Parliaments

At the core of the legislative branch of government are national (and in some cases subnational) parliaments. While labels differ, parliaments or legislative bodies are generally characterised by the formal equality between their members, and the fact that their members' authority derives from their claim to represent the rest of the community (Mahler 1992). The specific structure of parliaments differs between countries. The electoral system in particular, because of its influence over the way in which legislators are selected, importantly affects the ways in which pressure groups and interest-based organisations contribute to the legislative decision-making process. Other differences include the size of the legislature, whether there is one house or two, and how power relations between houses operate.

The role of parliaments in the conduct of economic diplomacy also varies significantly between contexts, depending on the constitutional powers assigned to the legislative branch of government. For example, the US Congress has constitutional powers in the field of commercial policy while the powers of the European Parliament are heavily circumscribed. Accordingly, the US Congress plays a key role in the agenda-setting, negotiation and ratification phases of any negotiation, for which the US Administration requires authority from the Congress. In Europe, however, national and European parliaments only ratify an agreement once it has already been adopted by the Member State governments in the Council. The European agenda for any trade negotiation is therefore largely set by the Member State governments in the Council of Ministers, acting on a proposal from the European Commission, with national and European parliaments having only an indirect impact. Because their veto power is not credible, parliaments have tended not to be taken very seriously by European trade negotiators. (Chapter 13 provides more details on the EU.)

In some systems, *legislative committees* are important actors, enabling more serious and complex discussion on highly specialised matters to occur. In the legislative branch in the US, a broad range of standing committees participate in the formation of various facets of trade policy (Cohen, Paul et al. 1996). However, the influence of such committees, as with the rest of the legislative branch of government, is often constrained, particularly by their frequent dependence upon executive agencies to supply them with the information that is essential in technical and complex decision-making processes. The situation varies significantly between countries, however. US Senate committees, for example, have far more in the way of committee staff and resources than do committees of other national legislatures (Mahler 1992).

Political Parties

The structure of political parties within a given political system also affects decision-making dynamics within the legislative branch of government. Within the political system as a whole, political parties assist in the representation function and serve as a transmission channel linking public opinions from various groups within society to government officials. Decision-making processes within government are often influenced by party policy or doctrine and by the desire for re-election at a party level. Within the legislature, political parties provide candidates for formal legislative positions such as the speaker, deputy speakers and committee chairs, and influence individual legislative behaviour. The importance of this latter function varies depending on the strength of party discipline within a given context, as well as on the significance and strength of any coalitions involved in the formation of government. In the British House of Commons for example, party discipline is very strong, whereas in the US legislature it is considerably weaker. Systems with strong party discipline within a governing party will find it easier to ratify an agreement than those in which there is weak party discipline, or coalition government. The position of the party on any international agreement is also less influential in cases of weak party discipline or weak and factionalised coalition government.

As politicians attempt to balance the medium or long term benefits of increased economic growth arising from greater international cooperation against the short term political and economic costs of any agreement, their political calculations are often influenced by imbalances in electoral representation. The latter arise from systems of voting and electoral representation inherent in the design of parliamentary systems, as well as from features of the party system operating within a given legislature. Commonly, rural or agricultural constituencies are disproportionately represented in terms of the number of electors, because of relatively sparser rural populations and the slow pace of electoral reform to adjust boundaries. The organisation of major political parties around rural constituencies can compound the effects of such institutional factors, particularly in the case of coalition governments.

This disproportionate political influence wielded by rural constituencies in many countries helps to explain why the agricultural sector has benefited from greater support and protection in many European countries, Japan and elsewhere, and thus why agricultural reform has been frustrated for so many years. For example, in Germany the coalition of the Christian Democratic Union (CDU) and the Christian Social Union (CSU) under Helmut Kohl of the late 1980s and early 1990s depended on rural votes in Bavaria, where the CSU is based. Concessions in agricultural trade negotiations, which would have resulted in fewer subsidies for the small and relatively inefficient Bavarian farmers, could have led to lost votes for the CSU, which would have undermined the coalition government. This was one of the reasons Germany resisted reform of the Common Agricultural Policy (CAP) and any concessions in the agricultural negotiations in the Uruguay Round. It was only when reform of the subsidy programme provided compensation or side payments to the smaller farmers in Bavaria that the German Federal Government was able to support concessions. Similar dynamics have been prevalent in France, where the government has frequently been unwilling to make concessions on agriculture because of the cost in terms of votes. In Japan such dynamics have also been highly influential, with the Liberal Democratic Party's (LDP) strongholds in rural constituencies ensuring that the Japanese government has persistently opposed concessions on rice imports.

Provincial, State and Local Government

As the scope of economic diplomacy expands to encompass issues that fall within the domain of subnational government, actors at this level are increasingly involved in the conduct of this diplomacy. Such issues include investment, public procurement, and the regulation of areas such as insurance, financial services and health and safety. Sometimes the role of subnational government actors in such areas is marginal; in other cases it is substantial. For example, 70 per cent of public procurement – which can account for anything up to 10 per cent of GDP in developed economies – is accounted for by subnational or subfederal level government. Some financial and other services are also regulated at subnational or subfederal levels. As 'deep integration' continues to encompass an expanding range of issues relating to subnationally governed services and investment, the role of government actors at this level is likely to increase in future. Our consideration of government actors must therefore include both state and local governments.

Provincial and State Governments

Within federal systems such as the United States, Australia, Canada and Germany state and provincial governments often aspire to pursue economic diplomacy at their own level.[1] The impact of federal systems upon the conduct of inter-governmental relations in specific decision-making contexts varies between countries according to the size of the federation, the homogeneity of the units and the constitutional and legislative frameworks within which the levels of government operate together; also, elements of the wider political system such as political parties, interest groups, political culture and administrative practices can be influential.

Local Governments

In many fields of policy-making, local government acts both as a provider of local services, and as a means of legitimising decision-making processes by facilitating greater citizen participation and responsiveness of policy makers to local priorities (Greenwood and Wilson 1990; Chandler 1993). The authority and independence of local government, however, is often much weaker than that of state governments. Within federal systems neither national nor regional governments are constitutionally subordinate to the other. In contrast, the powers of local authorities are typically grounded in discretionary Acts of Parliament, and much of their finance also stems ultimately from Parliament. However, despite the legal and financial subordination of local to higher government levels, local government involvement via deliberative processes and networked modes of intergovernmental coordination can sometimes be of considerable practical

---

1   There is much work in public administration and comparative government literatures looking at the roles of federal systems, and the role and influence of state governments in different systems (Watts 1970).

significance, particularly where they gain authority in deliberative processes by virtue of their claim to represent local constituencies on particular issues (Greenwood and Wilson 1990).

State and local governments participate actively in international economic policy-making across a range of issue areas. In some instances this economic diplomacy can be ambitious, such as when the US state of Massachusetts sought to impose sanctions against Myanmar (Burma) on human rights grounds. More commonly, the involvement of state and regional governments is focused either on issues relating to government procurement or services provision, or on a range of infrastructure and investment issues relevant to local and state government policies that aim to strengthen state and regional competitiveness within global markets.

The development of economic 'clusters' (that is, geographic concentrations of interconnected companies, commonly based around shared infrastructure and human capital resources) is of particular importance. Local and state governments are actively promoting policies to support local economies and attract foreign investment for this purpose, as such clusters increasingly shape the geographies of national, regional, state, and even metropolitan economies (Castells 1994; Goodwin and Painter 1996; Jones 1998; Porter 2000; Sassen 2001). Because clusters can substantially increase economic activity in a region, state and local authorities compete directly with each other to attract inward investment to their local areas. These new dynamics of geographical competition, and the increased importance of subnational government they imply, can therefore lead to the emergence of new roles for subnational government actors in economic diplomacy. However, the capacity of local governments to exercise decisive influence over outcomes remains constrained by limits to both their formal powers and their opportunities for informal influence, in the context of national policy-making processes in which more centralised levels of government generally dominate.

The International and Transnational Level

International Organisations

Involvement by state actors in the conduct of economic diplomacy at the international level occurs most visibly via recognised international organisations.[2] There are more than 300 international organisations, ranging from large organisations like the IMF, World Bank and ILO, through medium-sized organisations like the WTO to smaller specialist bodies such as the International Standards Organisation (ISO). Other relevant international organisations include the range of new UN organisations created through the Rio process, the OECD, the Commonwealth and the G8, all of which are active in differing aspects of

---

2   Some of these international organisations – namely the EU, the WTO, the IMF and the World Bank – have entire chapters dedicated to them later in the book; they are therefore discussed only briefly here.

contemporary economic diplomacy – see Chapter 15. A number of regional organisations are involved in managing and regulating international trade and other forms of economic integration. Examples include regional development banks, loose economic groupings such as Asia-Pacific Economic Cooperation (APEC), and more ambitious projects of regional integration such as the EU. There are also a rapidly growing number of bilateral institutional frameworks being established as part of free trade and other bilateral arrangements. While the legitimacy of many international organisations – particularly those associated most strongly with the promotion of neo-liberal policy agendas on a global scale, such as the WTO, IMF and World Bank – has been subject to widespread critique in recent years, governments make increasing use of such organisations, which can become actors in economic diplomacy in their own right.

The autonomy of such organisations in relation to their constituent member states is, however, a matter of ongoing scholarly debate, and it varies widely between different cases. For example, the staff of the IMF and World Bank clearly can have an impact on policy development, even if final decision-making power rests with national governments. However, in the case of the WTO, the secretariat is much more constrained in what it can do directly, with all policy proposals coming from WTO member countries rather than the secretariat; nevertheless, the secretariat continues to be active in brokering compromises between conflicting state positions. If the negotiations are taking place within an international organisation, such as the WTO or UNEP, civil servants employed by these organisations have an interest in finding compromises, and such actors can therefore shape the dynamics of economic diplomacy. These international civil servants can also contribute to shaping policy by clarifying the potential scope and impact of any agreement and by coordinating the flow of information, thus smoothing the ground for successful negotiations between individual states.

State Actors in Transnational Policy Networks

State involvement in transnational policy networks encompasses both networks that are exclusively inter-governmental in form, and those that bring in wider groups of actors. Policy-makers commonly turn to 'experts' of various kinds when it comes to interpreting technical issues, such as when negotiations concern international standards or technical aspects of rules of origin. By collecting information that is of direct relevance to policy-making and communicating with each other across national borders, such experts can shape both national policy preferences and common outcomes at the international level.

In some cases these policy networks are reasonably limited in scope, involving direct inter-agency coordination between parallel government agencies in two or more countries. The role of state actors within intergovernmental networks of this kind has been analysed in particular by Anne-Marie Slaughter, who examines the increasing role in international policy-making processes of networks of homologous government actors such as financial regulators, judges or even legislators (Slaughter 2000, 2005). In other cases such networks are broader and more diffuse, and tend to be analysed more commonly within frameworks that refer to 'elite policy networks' or 'epistemic communities'. Haas (1992) defines an epistemic community as a 'network of experts with recognised expertise and competence and an authoritative claim to policy-relevant knowledge in the issue concerned'. He also argues that for their policy coordination function to operate effectively, such 'communities' must share a common set of values and objectives, even though their means of achieving these objectives may vary.

While states and their agencies participate directly in both these kinds of networks, officials of international agencies and organisations are also often important participants. For example, the OECD has frequently participated in such 'epistemic communities' or policy networks. It helped to build a better understanding of the true costs of agricultural subsidies within a range of national agricultural programmes, paving the way for agreement on agricultural trade policy issues during the Uruguay Round. It also contributed to the development of the now widely accepted paradigm that characterises services as part of the international trade agenda (Drake and Nicolaidis 1992).

In other cases, private sector or academic experts are used by governments, as in technical committees of the international bodies setting standards for food safety or digital mobile telephony. Global warming provides one important example of how the facilitation of improved knowledge through state involvement in more broadly based networks has had a major impact on policy outcomes. For many years a range of governments resisted international cooperation to reduce greenhouse gases because there was no consensus on the fact of global warming. This led to the creation of the Inter-governmental Panel on Climate Change (IPCC), which is an international group of scientists brought together by the UN Environment Programme (UNEP) and the World Meteorological Organisation (WMO) to assess the evidence for global warming and make recommendations to governments. The evidence produced by successive IPCC reports has played an important role in obliging more sceptical governments to accept environmental concerns as a serious issue on the international political agenda.

Conclusions

This chapter has shown how developments in economic diplomacy are having an impact on the role and number of state actors involved. Within national governments, a much greater number of departments are now becoming involved in international negotiations, compared with the situation before the advance of globalisation. This has created new kinds of tensions between different departmental interests, which economic diplomacy must reconcile. Relationships between executives and legislatures, and between bureaucracies, ministers and heads of government, are also changing in many cases. There is also the subnational level government to be taken into account as this is becoming more active in economic diplomacy, both through its influence on policies that shape national markets and in its efforts to ensure that the state, province or region benefits from globalisation. At the international level, inter-governmental and transnational forms of networked coordination are taking on important new roles, alongside international organisations. Finally, the rise of non-state actors and their interaction with government has had wider implications for how state actors operate. These will be considered at the end of the next chapter.

References

Castells, M. (1994). 'European Cities, the Informational Society and the Global Economy', *New Left Review*, Vol. I/204, pp. 18–32.

Chandler, J.A. (ed.) (1993), *Local Government in Liberal Democracies: An Introductory Survey*, Routledge, New York.

Cohen, S. (1994), *The Making of United States International Economic Policy: Principles, Problems, and Proposals for Reform*, Praeger, Westport, VA.

Cohen, S., Paul, J. et al. (1996), *Fundamentals of US Foreign Trade Policy: Economics, Politics, Laws and Issues*, Westview Press, Boulder, CO.

Drake, W.J. and Nicolaidis, K. (1992), 'Ideas, Interests, and Institutionalization: "Trade in Services" and the Uruguay Round', *International Organisation*, Vol. 46, No. 1, pp. 37–100.

Gilardi, F. (2001), *Principal-Agent Models Go to Europe: Independent Regulatory Agencies as Ultimate Step of Delegation*, paper presented at the ECPR General Conference, Canterbury, UK, accessible at: http://www.leidenuniv.nl/fsw/ecpr/pubchoice/gilardi. pdf.

Gilardi, F. (2002), 'Policy Credibility and Delegation to Independent Regulatory Agencies: a Comparative Empirical Analysis', *Journal of European Public Policy*, Vol. 9, No. 6, pp. 873–93.

Goodwin, M. and Painter, J. (1996), 'Local Governance, the Crises of Fordism and the Changing Geographies of Regulation', *Transactions, Institute of British Geographers*, Vol. 21, pp. 635–48.

Greenwood, J. and Wilson, D. (1990), *Public Administration in Britain Today*, Unwin Hyman, London.

Haas, P. (1992), 'Epistemic Communities and International Policy Coordination: Introduction', *International Organization*, Vol. 46, No. 1, pp. 1–35.

Hart, J. (2004), *Technology, Television and Competition: the Politics of Digital TV*, Cambridge University Press, Cambridge.

Jones, M. (1998), 'Restructuring the Local State: Economic Governance or Social Regulation?', *Political Geography*, pp. 959–88.

Mahler, G. (1992), *Comparative Politics: An Institutional and Cross-National Approach*, Prentice Hall, New Jersey.

Majone, G. (1997), *The Agency Model: The Growth of Regulation and Regulatory Institutions in the European Union*, http://aei.pitt.edu/786/01/scop97_3_2.pdf.

Milner, H. (1988), *Resisting Protectionism: Global Industries and the Politics of International Trade*, Princeton University Press, Princeton, NJ.

Porter, M.E. (2000), 'Location, Competition, and Economic Development: Local Clusters in a Global Economy', *Economic Development Quarterly*, Vol. 14, No. 1, pp. 15–34.

Putnam, R.D. (1988). 'Diplomacy and Domestic Politics: The Logic of Two-Level Games.' *International Organisation*, Vol. 42, No. 3, pp. 427–60.

Sassen, S. (2001), *The Global City: New York, London, Tokyo*, Princeton University Press, Princeton, NJ.

Slaughter, A.-M. (2000), 'Governing the Global Economy through Government Networks', in Byers, M. (ed.), *The Role of Law in International Politics : Essays in International Relations and International Law*, Oxford University Press, Oxford.

Slaughter, A.-M. (2005), 'Disaggregated Sovereignty: Towards the Public Accountability of Global Government Networks', in Held, D. and Koenig-Archibugi, M. (eds), *Global Governance and Public Accountability*, Blackwell, Oxford.

Thatcher, M. (2002), 'Delegation to Independent Regulatory Agencies: Pressures, Functions and Contextual Mediation', *West European Politics*, Vol. 25, No. 1, pp. 125–47.

Watts, R. (1970), *Administration in Federal Systems*, Hutchinson Educational Ltd, London.

Woolcock, S. (1998), 'European and American Approaches to Regulation: Continuing Divergence?', in Van Scherpenberg, J. and Thiel, E. (eds), *Towards Rival Regionalism? US and EU Economic Integration and the Risk of Transatlantic Regulatory Rift*, Stiftung Wissenschaft und Politik, Eberhausen.

Chapter 5

Non-State Actors in Economic Diplomacy

Kate MacDonald and Stephen Woolcock

Both the centrality and the legitimacy of the state's role in policy-making has tended to be taken for granted within much domestic and international political scholarship and practice – at least in the context of liberal democratic institutional arrangements. It is generally expected that state actors will have a range of central roles in the conduct of economic diplomacy, including representation of particular interest groups or constituencies, technical administration and representation of national interests on the international stage. Both the efficacy and legitimacy of these roles are being challenged due to effects of globalisation such as increased pressures from global capital, increasingly 'deep integration' of national economies and the changing character and rising influence of the non-state actors that comprise the subject of this chapter.

Non-state actors include pressure groups of conventional kinds, including business, labour and agricultural interests, organised around enduring national constituencies and lobbying government to promote their own group interests in policy-making processes. Such actors are analysed most extensively within the broader literatures on civil society, corporatism and collective action (Olson 1965; Truman 1981; Ball and Millard 1986; Mahler 1992). In addition, an increasing number of networked social movements are organising around new issues – often with transnational territorial reach. These groups, along with a wide array of professional bodies and other non-state actors, play increasingly important roles within both networked and directly delegated processes of international economic decision-making.

While the term 'pressure group' seems to imply sanctions, conflict and competing exercise of power – as assumed by many interest-based analyses of lobby groups and rent-seeking – such groups also commonly seek to realise their aims via persuasive strategies. Working through both the media and more grassroots forms of public engagement, as well as via direct participation in deliberative processes with policy-makers, such actors commonly seek to influence policy outcomes by 'framing' issues in ways that are consistent with their own values and interests, and thus persuading decision-makers and the public more broadly that the promotion of their particularistic positions is consistent with defence of a broader public interest. Thus while rationalist and institutionalist traditions have dominated many older, interest-based analyses of non-state actors, constructivist theorists have been increasingly influential within much of the more recent literature examining actors of these kinds.

Strategies of both pressure and persuasion are deployed by such actors at national, international and transnational levels. At the national level, modes of non-state engagement with state decision-making processes have changed significantly in recent years, partly in response to the decline in corporatist modes of government in some countries, and partly in response to a rise in networked or societal modes of regulation and governance domestically (Majone 1994; Moran 2003).

For our purposes, however, the most significant changes have been those affecting the modes of engagement of non-state actors with decision-makers at the international level. Traditional strategies still persist, in which these actors lobby state actors nationally in the hope that their preferred positions will be incorporated within the definition of the 'national interest' and taken forward into international fora. But increasingly, such actors mobilise beyond national borders to leverage direct pressure on decision-makers at the international level. This chapter examines the strategies of the groups listed in Table 5.1.

Table 5.1   Non-state actors in economic diplomacy

Agricultural lobbies
Business interest groups
Trade unions
Consumer organisations
Transnational civil society: social movements and advocacy networks
Non-state actors in policy and regulatory networks

Non-state actors sometimes participate directly within international organisations. These range from environmental NGOs that are actively involved in the work of UNEP and the UN Commission on Sustainable Development (CSD) and have observer status in discussions about implementing the Montreal Protocol on the reduction of the production of ozone-depleting substances, through to Consumers International, that has representation on (or at least access to the work of) UN bodies such as the Codex Alimentarius Committee of the Food and Agriculture Organisation, which develops food safety standards. In other cases, non-state actors participate via more weakly institutionalised modalities, such as those available for civil society 'participation' in decision-making processes of the IMF and World Bank.

In cases where NGO participation continues to be resisted by state-based decision-makers at the international level – despite often sustained campaigns by non-state actors that are demanding a stronger voice in decision-making processes – they often organise to make their voices heard by mobilising around defined meetings or events such as at the World Economic Forum and WTO Ministerials, or organise alternative, parallel events such as the World Social Forum (O'Brien and Goetz 2000). The official events and summits are symbolically charged and attract high profile media attention. They therefore often provide ideal opportunities for such groups to exercise strategies of 'persuasion' favoured by many, since the degree to which they succeed in 'framing' issues via their advocacy strategies is highly dependent on the amplification of their messages by global media.

In such cases, these non-state actors frequently justify their demands for an increasing role within a globalising political economy on the basis of claims that the legitimacy of existing processes of state-based decision-making can no longer be taken for granted. They argue that greater civil society participation in such decision-making processes would increase transparency, accountability and legitimacy, by enabling more effective representation of diverse views, better scrutiny of decision-making processes, and in some cases better informed and more effective policy outcomes.

The Evolution of Non-State Actors from the National to Transnational Domain

In light of the greater visibility and direct participation of non-state groups in international processes of economic policy making, much analysis and debate has focused upon the question of the extent to which these groups continue to operate as nationally based actors, or the extent to which their modes of organisation are increasingly globalised. The analysis presented in the following sections presents a somewhat more complex story, in which organisational groupings are gradually and unevenly shifting from national towards both international and transnational modes of organisation, while the territorial grounding of such actors – even those whose attempts to influence policy-making processes involve predominantly transnational strategies – remains of great importance. The following discussion of each separate category of non-state actor distinguishes the differing ways in which transnational modes of non-state mobilisation coexist and interact with enduring forms of national non-state organisation in each case.

Agricultural Lobbies

Agriculture is well established as a case of special importance in the international political economy with respect to the influence of organised interest groups. The dominance of arguments based on 'agricultural exceptionalism' in the years following World War II played an important role in justifying special treatment for this sector in the form of extensive governmental assistance and protection (Wilson 1981; Halpin 2005). Such arguments tended to characterise the agricultural sector as hazardous (due to unstable weather and market conditions) and of particular importance to promoting crucial national policy goals (including autonomous food security and rural and regional development), thus justifying special treatment for this sector. In the US and Europe, both single commodity associations and more broadly based groupings such as the National Farmers Union and American Agriculture Movement play central roles (Cigler 1991). While similar kinds of groups commonly operate in developing countries, a broader range of agricultural actors can also play important roles, including groups such as lobbies of the landless, cooperatives, peasant movements, and in some cases influential landowning individuals or families (Ball and Millard 1986; Misquitta 1991).

Organised interest groups within agriculture are commonly associated with protectionism, and indeed this is the primary objective of many. However, agricultural groups such as wheat growers in countries like the United States or Australia also commonly form well organised elements of pro-liberalisation lobbies. The range of issues on which agricultural lobbies have organised tend to differ between developing and industrialised countries. Protectionism and liberalisation are also the main axes along which agricultural groups have organised in developing countries, such as protests against regional free trade agreements by Latin American peasant movements. However, the core interests of such groups have also been identified with wider aspects of the economic diplomacy agenda, as illustrated for example by the role of agricultural movements in countries such as India in resisting the application of patent provisions within TRIPS to certain varieties of seeds (Borowiak 2004).

Despite their substantial influence over the politics of international trade, agricultural interest groups have tended to display much weaker organisation at the international level than have many other interest groups. For example, the International Federation of Agricultural Producers and the Committee of Agricultural Organisations in the EU for the most part are aggregations dominated by national groups that function mainly to provide some superficial coordination, as required to form a united front at international forums. The established pattern of *national* embeddedness, whereby agricultural interest groups have historically occupied a special role within their national political systems, can help explain why *international* federations of national organisations at global or regional levels have remained relatively weak (Halpin 2005).

The restructuring of domestic agricultural industries, together with challenges to conventional partnerships between governments and national interest groups that are arising in the context of contemporary changes within the global political economy, often increase the willingness of governments to leave production prices and questions of farm survival to be determined by market forces. These trends have led to a decline in the influence of farm interest groups over national policy-making processes in many cases. Most analysts concur that increasingly, the regulation of agricultural and food production is being shaped at multiple levels by a mix of global, supranational, national and subnational regulations and institutions (Halpin 2005). Thus, while the influence of such groups on agricultural governance remains significant, it appears likely that agricultural pressure groups will need to increasingly organise on a transnational level if they are to be successful in the future.

Business Interest Groups

At both national and international levels, private business actors can mobilise via various organisational structures: confederations of industry, which seek to represent wide sections of business; industry or sector trade associations; and individual firms lobbying governments directly. Companies will tend to use all three levels of lobbying, depending on which is most appropriate and effective.

Confederations These will often be used to represent a general business interest, like opposition to social or labour clauses in free trade agreements. Although such confederations often coordinate their activities internationally, they tend to represent national positions. The Japanese Keidanren is an important example of such a national confederation: the corporatist tradition of much of Japanese business has enabled the Keidanren to provide a coherent focus for Japanese industry. European confederations of industry have also been important, with the German Bundesverbund der Deutsche Industrie (BDI) and Bundesverbund der Deutschen Arbeitgeber (BDA), Confindustria in Italy and the British Confederation of British Industry (CBI) being perhaps the most influential. At a European level, BusinessEurope (the former Union of European Industry and Employers' Confederations – UNICE) includes all national confederations of the EU Member States, as well as other European confederations such as the Swiss. Such associations also exist in the US – for example the National Association of Manufacturers (which represents the larger industrial companies), the Chamber of Commerce (which represents the smaller companies) and long established organisations such as the US Council for International Business. However, the weaker corporatist tradition in the US has meant that formal federations are relatively less influential than in Europe or Japan. In contrast, much of the lobbying power in Washington comes from more ad hoc coalitions of companies, which tend to have a more focused agenda and can also be more flexible than the standing confederations.

Sector associations These tend to be involved in seeking protection from import competition or promoting market liberalisation abroad. Each country has a large number of sector trade associations that have varying degrees of influence, from the heavy hitters such as in the steel and agriculture sectors, through to cuddly toys. Such sectoral associations participate actively in processes of international economic policy-making, some lobbying for protection and some for liberalisation. The systems that represent business interests in this policy-making process differ by country. The US system of autonomous groups and corporate offices contrasts with the more orderly networks of business associations that serve to define and communicate business viewpoints in other countries. Different again are the situations in Germany and Japan, where legal systems are more supportive of business associations, government may provide direct financial support to business groups, and business organisations are expected to adopt positions that promote societal and industry interests rather than just the interests of individual companies (Milner 1988).

Individual firms These tend to lobby independently on issues of concern when they cannot get broader support, or when the issue is company specific, such as subsidies for civil aircraft production. Such strategies are particularly viable in the case of multinational companies (MNCs) with a global reach, many of whom can clearly be seen also as transnational actors in their own right, with the capacity to pursue their interests without reference to any formal organisations. Some individual companies use advertising campaigns or social responsibility policies as means of influencing the climate of public and consumer opinion and government regulation, while many major American companies have established public affairs departments and sometimes a permanent lobbying presence in Washington to monitor governmental events and express corporate positions on policy issues (Lehne 1993).

The international level   Internationally, business is organised in different forms. Organisations such as the International Chamber of Commerce (ICC) can be categorised as global membership organisations. Established in 1919 the ICC brings together individual companies, sector level trade associations as well as national confederations. The ICC represents some 800 national chambers of commerce in over 130 countries. The main functions of the ICC are to promote open markets through scrutinising and lobbying national governments and international organisations, and the development and promotion of voluntary codes of conduct or rules for businesses. With regard to the former, the ICC draws on a large number of specialist working groups and experts (over 500 experts) and has access to discussions in the UN and other international organisations.[1]

Business participation also takes place at plurilateral and regional levels. For example, the Business and Industry Advisory Committee (BIAC) has for many years provided business views and input into the deliberations of the OECD. BIAC consists of the leading confederations of business or industry in the OECD countries. In some cases these are bodies specialising in international business or commercial issues, such as the US Council for International Business in the US; in other cases they are national confederations. The impact of the various BIAC committees has varied, depending on the issues under discussion and the quality of participants. On issues such as the development of OECD work on investment policy, the BIAC has played an important role.

Business also takes part in the policy-making process via international business dialogues, such as the Transatlantic Business Dialogue (TABD) and its followers in other bilateral relationships. The Transatlantic Business Dialogue (TABD) was established in 1995, first as a group of chief executives on each side of the Atlantic discussing the agenda for transatlantic commercial relations. Subsequently expert groups were added to seek common approaches or positions on some fairly detailed but important aspects of transatlantic commercial relations. In recent years there has been a general growth in the application of this approach to bilateral commercial relations between countries or regions, so that there are business dialogues associated with many bilateral agreements.

Coalitions of businesses   Business can also organise itself on a transnational basis via coalitions that come together to pursue specific aims. In some cases these

---

1   Further details are on the ICC website, http://www.iccwbo.com.

coalitions may be broad and in other cases regional or sector specific. Perhaps the most well known coalition of companies is the World Economic Forum (WEF), which was formed in 1971 with a meeting of European companies in Davos, and has since then expanded into a global organisation with over 1000 companies supporting it. It has the aim of creating 'partnerships between member companies and political, intellectual and other leaders to discuss and advance key issues on the global agenda'. At the regional level coalitions such as the European Round Table of Industrialists have been created to try to provide a more dynamic representation of industry by directly involving chief executives of companies rather than officials of associations.

Businesses also form sector coalitions at an international level in order to further their interests. For example, there is a network of coalitions of service industries that has evolved since the 1980s to provide effective business input into negotiations on trade in services – both multilaterally in the WTO and in bilateral negotiations. Similarly, the pharmaceutical sector has been active in international coalitions to promote both common approaches to such issues as clinical testing, and common positions in the TRIPS negotiations within the GATT/WTO (Sell 2003).

Businesses – acting either individually or collectively – can exercise substantial influence over the policy-making process in a number of ways. In some cases businesses are able to use their market power to threaten, induce or coerce governments (Korten 1995). For example, a business organisation may approach its national government with the argument that, if the regulatory or tax burden on its business is not eased, investment, jobs and economic prosperity will move elsewhere. Businesses can also use 'softer' forms of power, via the often extensive reliance of trade officials on private sector groups for important data and technical analysis concerning sectoral and foreign trade issues. This enables data provided by private advocates to feed directly and often influentially into the government's trade policy making process (Cohen, Paul et al. 1996).

Sometimes the influence of business groups depends on the structure of consultation with government. In some countries this is via a corporatist structure. In the US, however, the private sector influences policy-making directly via a permanent three-tiered network of private advisory committees statutorily created by Congress. The advisory committees are charged with counselling the administration's trade negotiator on the details of the private sector's attitudes on general trade policy, specific negotiating objectives and bargaining positions. US trade law formally stipulates that before the executive branch can submit trade legislation to Congress for approval under the fast track process, the advisory committees must first produce written evaluations that assess whether the proposed agreement is compatible with US commercial interests (Cohen, Paul et al. 1996).

While these different sources of business influence over policy-making processes can sometimes be in conflict, all contribute to forging an active and growing role for business actors in the conduct of economic diplomacy.

Trade Unions

At the *national level,* union organisations of traditional kinds – organised both sectorally and within national umbrella organisations – continue to exert an important influence on state policy-makers involved in economic diplomacy, via traditional pressure group tactics, via their institutionalised involvement within corporatist structures, and in many countries via political parties. Some national union organisations are clearly more cohesive and stronger than others, although union membership has declined in most countries since the 1970s due to falling industrial membership, the reorganisation of work within a global economy, low levels of unionisation within growing service sectors and a general decline in the popularity of corporatist modes of government in many countries (Johnson 1991; Munck and Waterman 1999).

At the *international level,* organised labour coordinates its position within the the International Trade Union Confederation (ITUC), the successor to the International Confederation of Free Trade Unions (ICFTU), which is based in Brussels but represents unions from around the world. Organised labour is represented in the ILO and in the Trade Union Advisory Committee (TUAC) of the OECD, but the latter has had relatively little influence. Compared to business, the labour movement has many fewer resources at its disposal, and fewer links with international institutions.

Under conditions of globalisation, labour is also increasingly organising itself on a *transnational level,* often using less hierarchical and more networked structures, and engaging more intensively with other kinds of social actors. While the organisational mode of labour has traditionally been formalised within a broadly hierarchical structure, 'social movement unionism' might be seen as referring not only to alliances between unions and wider social groups, but also to a broader engagement with non-unionised workers, social movements and broader social issues, and with an openness to new networked forms of organisation, within and between organisations (Munck and Waterman 1999). On many issues there are conflicts between unions and workers in the North and the South (such as around the issue of the social clause in the WTO) but on other issues labour organisations from the global North and South work together within common coalitions.

Organised unions of all these kinds engage with and influence processes of economic diplomacy at various levels. As well as influencing national policy-makers, they seek to shape outcomes at regional as well as plurilateral and global levels, such as by organising in support of the Social Chapter of the European Treaties and the North American Agreement on Labour Cooperation, a side agreement to the North American Free Trade Agreement (NAFTA). Early in 1996, leaders of the world's largest trade unions pledged, while lobbying the World Economic Forum in Davos, to fight attempts to drive down workers' living standards. The ICFTU worked as part of broader social alliances by attending the Beijing Women's Conference and the 1995 UN World Summit for Social Development, where the ICFTU played a prominent role in drafting the 'Ten Commitments', including basic labour rights, which governments would supposedly honour (Munck and Waterman 1999). In recent decades, the international labour movement has also explored more innovative forms of actions, such as increased cooperation between Canadian, US and Mexican workers in response to NAFTA, the increasing use by labour groups of transnational forms of pressure that involve direct engagements with companies, and the use of consumer based tactics such as those deployed within the prominent 'anti-sweatshop campaigns' of the late 1990s. At other times, transnational networks of labour activists have attempted to influence policy-making via more conventional, state-based decision-making sites; for example, attempts to utilise the Generalised System of Preferences system as means of pressuring countries violating agreed international labour standards (Compa and Vogt 2001).

Consumer Organisations

Consumer organisations constitute another important category of interest group that has frequently influenced processes of economic diplomacy. Almost all countries have some form of consumer representation, although their strength varies.[2] Some consumer organisations are quite close to the state, but most are independent, non-governmental bodies, typically organised within relatively formal and hierarchically ordered institutional structures. At an international level, Consumers International has represented national organisations since 1960 and is governed by a Council elected by the national organisations. In general, European consumer organisations, like European business and industry associations, are more institutionalised and centralised, and national consumer groups there tend to support the Bureau of European Union Consumers in developing a common position. Consumer organisations in the US tend to be less centralised and more likely to compete to shape policy. In Europe, consumer organisations are also more likely to be formally integrated into the policy process.

Consumer groups have been drawn more and more into the debate on globalisation, as a result of their involvement in issues such as food safety. Consumer organisations had initially sought to promote 'sustainable consumption', for example through the use of labelling schemes that empower consumers and enable them to choose products based on knowledge of their impact on the environment, or whether child labour has been used in their production. But trade disputes over beef hormones and the use of genetically modified crops in food have heightened awareness of how international trade, and in particular the rules governing international trade, impinge upon consumer choice. Consumer confidence in established, science-based food safety regulation was also shattered by the fiasco of BSE (mad cow disease) and by other cases in which 'sound science' appeared to get it wrong. Consumer groups and environmental NGOs therefore

---

2   See the Consumers International website http://www.consumersinternational.org for details of these organisations.

shared a common critique of the established practices and value systems that governed environmental and food safety regulation.

Transnational Civil Society: Social Movements and Advocacy Networks

With the advent of globalisation and the increasingly transnational organisation of production, investment and policy-making processes, organisations that form part of 'civil society' are increasingly networking and organising across similarly transnational scales. A number of these groups have not only *organised* in new ways, but have also defined their activities around new sets of social interests and concerns. Such groups have been variously labelled and analysed as 'global civil society', 'global social movements' and 'transnational advocacy networks'. These are characterised by many analysts as representing a qualitatively different form of transformative politics; such analysts stress the autonomy of these movements from party politics and in many cases their organisation around values or goals that do not map onto their own group's self-interest (Keck and Sikkink 1998; Scholte and O'Brien 1999; Scholte 2000; Tarrow 2005).

The motivations of such transnational social actors are commonly represented as forming part of a 'backlash' against the globalisation of markets (Klein 2000; Broad 2002; Green and Griffith 2002). While many of these groups share a common hostility towards the prevailing liberal paradigm that has shaped economic diplomacy throughout the 1980s and 1990s, they are extremely heterogeneous in their composition, values and demands. Nevertheless, in general the issues in which they have been most active and influential have tended to be those relating to new issues of concern raised by the global economy, including world poverty and debt, together with more traditional social justice concerns such as workers rights, corporate regulation and the environment. Two examples – of development NGOs and environmental NGOs – are briefly considered here.

Development NGOs

The interests of development NGOs are to some extent consistent with those of labour in the sense that both point to the inequalities created by globalising markets and the continuing poverty in many developing countries. However, the increasing involvement of such actors in economic diplomacy also reflects a broadening of the economic diplomacy agenda to encompass issues related to global poverty and development. Such issues were previously regarded by many – including many development NGOs themselves – as concerns most appropriately dealt with at the national or local level, rather than within processes of international economic decision-making. However during the 1990s, a number of leading development NGOs, such as Actionaid, Christian Aid, Oxfam and Save The Children, came to the view that a project-based approach to development aid was insufficient by itself given its failure to confront the underlying causes of persistent poverty, which many considered to be grounded in the prevailing system of international rules governing both production and trade. Increasingly, they therefore adopted strategies that placed greater emphasis upon advocating the interests of developing countries in international organisations such as the IMF and WTO, within which many such rules were formulated and in some cases enforced. In this context, such development NGOs began to challenge the conventional wisdom of the liberal 'Washington Consensus' that market liberalisation was the best strategy for development. This provided a common cause between labour and development NGOs, although they differed on issues such as the use of trade sanctions to ensure that international labour standards were enforced.

Environmental NGOs

This group of NGOs is just as powerful – possibly more so – than organised labour and the development NGOs. They draw on broad and growing support for 'sustainable development' among political parties and more general public opinion, especially in the developed economies. The mobilisation of such actors in the field of the environment was driven by the need to protect global commons, such as the ozone layer, biodiversity and endangered species. In some cases, environment NGOs mounted a direct challenge to the orthodox norms of liberal economics, which were seen as failing to address adequately the environmental externalities resulting from existing forms of development. In other cases, environmental groups have facilitated research into the effects of new products and technologies on the environment, demonstrating that existing scientific knowledge on the environmental impact of industrialisation was far from certain and embodied a set of values which were, in the view of such groups, skewed towards growth per se rather than sustainable growth. Such examples highlight the influence gained via global civil society's challenging of the value systems on which market regulation has often come to be based, and their strategic deployment of information to promote designated values and interests within international policy-making processes.

Non-State Actors in Policy and Regulatory Frameworks

In the activities described so far in this chapter, the non-state actors concerned are acting on their own behalf. But they can also fill quite a different function, in which they assume – in whole or part – direct responsibility for policy-making or regulation.

Chapter 4 explained how independent state regulatory agencies are increasingly active in economic diplomacy. In some cases, however, the negotiation of rules and regimes is not done by public agencies, but rather is delegated almost entirely to private sector groups. Sometimes, it is *individual companies* that are directly involved in such standard-setting processes. For example, standards for mutual recognition of drug testing in the pharmaceuticals sector were negotiated between American, European and Japanese pharmaceutical companies within the framework of an international agreement of the early

1980s. In other cases the key actors in such processes are *business sectoral associations*. For example, toy manufacturers have an important role to play with regard to the adoption and implementation of safety standards for toys. In the case of food safety standards, companies and associations often work alongside scientific experts, governments and consumer groups, such as in the Codex Alimentarius Commission. *Professional associations* are also important actors in relation to many delegated policy-making functions. Such groups are particularly important in the case of accounting and financial standards. The International Federation of Stock Exchanges, the International Council of Securities Associations and the International Accounting Standards Committee provide examples of international economic forums in which non-state actors of these kinds are delegated direct responsibilities for decision-making. Similarly, mutual recognition agreements, such as between the European Union and the United States, involve negotiations between professional bodies concerning the mutual recognition of professional qualifications.

In addition, the transnational policy networks and epistemic communities already examined in Chapter 4 often include non-state actors as indispensable participants, whether alongside state actors or entirely on their own. *Individual 'experts'* – whether from industry or academia – commonly participate in such networks in their individual capacity. *Professional associations, universities* and *think tanks* of various kinds all make significant contributions in transnational policy networks, as can many *non-governmental organisations*. These non-state actors participate in the generation of new discourses, in the dissemination of ideas and arguments favouring particular positions, and in many cases also in the generation of new information.

The participation of non-state actors in policy networks is rarely controversial. But the delegation of direct policy or regulatory responsibility to them raises important questions of efficiency and accountability in relation to the state/non-state dividing line. Roles for non-state actors are commonly justified on the basis of arguments concerning their superior technical expertise in relation to complex and rapidly changing policy questions. However, many regard such transfers of policy making authority to unaccountable private actors as extremely problematic from the perspective of transparency and democratic accountability criteria (Haufler 2001; Cutler 2003). The legitimacy of such private policy making arrangements in the conduct of economic diplomacy thus continues to be debated.

Conclusions

This chapter, following on from the previous chapter on state actors, has highlighted a number of lessons regarding the identity, roles and influence of different categories of actors within contemporary processes of economic diplomacy.

The more intrusive nature of economic negotiations between countries in recent years has meant that more and more interest groups are affected by and interested in the decision-making process. In particular, a range of societal actors have become better equipped to organise and mobilise transnationally, thus enabling them to exert direct pressure on decision-making beyond their own state borders.

Analysis in this and the preceding chapter has also highlighted how these shifting configurations and roles of actors are the result of fundamental changes within the international political economy. As geographies of economic and social interconnection are transformed, and processes of deep integration advance, tidy distinctions between *national* and *international* economic policy can no longer be sustained. This obliges economic diplomacy to go much deeper into domestic policy-making, and requires social actors to identify shared interests and mobilise more effectively across transnational spaces.

There are a number of questions regarding the implications of such changes for the effectiveness, accountability and overarching legitimacy of policy-making processes. In relation to *effectiveness*, does the expansion in the number of actors lead to the introduction into decision-making processes of better information, thus enabling better informed decisions, and better capacity to find mutually beneficial negotiated outcomes? Or does the increasingly tangled web of actors create barriers to effective deliberation, in the form of increased conflict and 'transaction costs' within the negotiation process? In relation to *legitimacy*, the increased scope of economic diplomacy is creating real pressures for greater democratic accountability, as more and more interest groups see their domestic policy preferences influenced and in some cases undermined by international negotiations and agreements. This raises increasingly pressing questions regarding the implications of these changes for democratic criteria such as transparency and accountability. These are broader questions that run through the whole discussion of economic diplomacy. The discussion of non-state actors, along with that of state actors in the previous chapter, serves as a contribution to our general understanding of these issues.

Readers inclined towards a more structural view of political economy may feel that much of this analysis of actors, while perhaps descriptively interesting, is ultimately of little relevance to the determination of 'winners' and 'losers' in processes of economic diplomacy, since international capital, or state-based elites, or the imperatives of the 'international system', will structurally determine most of the important outcomes irrespective of what given actors do or say. However, the analytic approach taken in this book, placing the key actors in economic diplomacy centre stage, invites the view that an analysis of actors, their goals, their strategies and their relative sources of power and influence, can contribute to a better understanding of the forces driving outcomes within economic diplomacy, even although events driven by the competing wills of participating actors may also be shaped and constrained in important ways by structural factors.

While these questions remain to be explored and debated further, what emerges clearly from this chapter is that the increased involvement of non-state actors in economic diplomacy has created new empirical and normative challenges along all three of the tensions of economic diplomacy highlighted in Chapter 1 of this book: economic-political, international-domestic and state-non-state. Such challenges go to the heart of questions about how to implement effective and legitimate decision-making structures and processes that will enable both state and non-state participants within a new economic diplomacy to steer and manage the complexities and dynamics of contemporary economic globalisation.

References

Ball, A. and Millard, F. (1986), *Pressure Politics in Industrial Societies: A Comparative Introduction*, Macmillan Education, Houndmills.

Borowiak, C. (2004), 'Farmers' Rights: Intellectual Property Regimes and the Struggle over Seeds', *Politics and Society*, Vol. 32, No. 4, pp. 511–43.

Broad, R. (2002), *Global Backlash: Citizen Initiatives for a Just World Economy*, Rowman and Littlefield Publishers, Lanham, MD.

Cigler, A. (1991), 'Organisational Maintenance and Political Activity on the Cheap: the American Agriculture Movement', in Cigler, A. and Loomis, B. (eds), *Interest Group Politics*, Congressional Quarterly Press, Washington, DC.

Cohen, S., Paul, J. et al. (1996), *Fundamentals of US Foreign Trade Policy: Economics, Politics, Laws and Issues*, Westview Press, Boulder, CO.

Compa, L. and Vogt, J. (2001), 'Labor Rights in the Generalized System of Preferences: A 20-Year Review', *Comparative Labor Law and Policy Journal*, Vol. 22, No. 2/3, pp. 199–238.

Cutler, C. (2003), *Private Power and Global Authority: Transnational Merchant Law in the Global Political Economy*, Cambridge University Press, Cambridge.

Green, D. and Griffith, M. (2002), 'Globalisation and its Discontents, *International Affairs*, Vol. 78, No. 1, pp. 49–68.

Halpin, D. (ed.) (2005), *Surviving Global Change? Agricultural Interest Groups in Comparative Perspective*, Ashgate, Aldershot.

Haufler, V. (2001), *A Public Role for the Private Sector: Industry Self-Regulation in a Global Economy*, Carnegie Endowment for International Peace, Washington, DC.

Johnson, P. (1991), 'Organised Labor in an Era of Blue Collar Decline', in Cigler, A. and Loomis, B. (eds), *Interest Group Politics*, Congressional Quarterly Press, Washington, DC.

Keck, M.E. and Sikkink, K. (1998), *Activists Beyond Borders : Advocacy Networks in International Politics*, Cornell University Press, Ithaca, NY.

Klein, N. (2000), *No Logo*, Vintage Canada, Toronto.

Korten, D. (1995), *When Corporations Rule the World*, Kumarian Press and Berrett-Koehler Publishers, San Francisco.

Lehne, R. (1993), *Industry and Politics: United States in Comparative Perspective*, Prentice Hall, New Jersey.

Mahler, G. (1992), *Comparative Politics: An Institutional and Cross-National Approach*, Prentice Hall, New Jersey.

Majone, G. (1994), 'The Rise of the Regulatory State in Europe', *West European Politics*, Vol. 17, No. 3, pp. 77–101.

Milner, H. (1997), *Interests, Institutions and Information: Domestic Politics and International Relations*, Princeton University Press, Princeton, NJ.

Misquitta, L. (1991), *Pressure Groups and Democracy in India*, New Delhi, Sterling Publishers Private Limited.

Moran, M. (2003), *The British Regulatory State: High Modernism and Hyper-Innovation*, Oxford University Press, Oxford.

Munck, R. and Waterman, P. (1999), *Labour Worldwide in the Era of Globalization*, Macmillan Press, Houndmills.

O'Brien, R. and. Goetz, A. M (2000), *Contesting Global Governance: Multilateral Economic Institutions and Global Social Movements*, Cambridge University Press, Cambridge.

Olson, M. (1965), *The Logic of Collective Action*, Harvard University Press, Cambridge, MA.

Scholte, J.A. (2000), 'Global Civil Society', in Woods, N. (ed.), *The Political Economy of Globalisation*, Macmillan Press, London,.

Scholte, J.A. and O'Brien, R. (1999), 'The WTO and Civil Society', *Journal of World Trade*, Vol. 33, No. 1, pp. 107–24.

Sell, S. (2003), *Private Power, Public Law: The Globalization of Intellectual Property Rights*, Cambridge University Press, Cambridge.

Tarrow, S. (2005), *The New Transnational Activism*, Cambridge University Press, Cambridge.

Truman, D. (1981), *The Governmental Process: Political Interests and Public Opinion*, Greenwood Press.

Waterman, P. (1999), 'The New Social Unionism: A New Union Model for a New World Order', in Munck, R. and Waterman, P. (eds), *Labour Worldwide in the Era of Globalization*, Macmillan Press, Houndmills.

Wilson, G. (1981), *Interest Groups in the United States*, Clarendon Press, Oxford.

Useful Websites

Consumers International: http://www.consumersinternational.org.
International Chamber of Commerce: http://www.iccwbo.org.

Chapter 6

Making Government Policy: A Case Study of the G8

Martin Donnelly

State policy-making, domestic or foreign, is a complex process. Modern policy formulation seeks to be strategic in nature and focused on outcomes. It takes account of the interests of a wide range of stakeholders, including external stakeholders. It aims to be flexible and innovative, bringing together the contributions of both external and internal stakeholders to deliver new, creative solutions to policy challenges.

The G8 process is a good example of how multilateral foreign policy is developed in the real world. This chapter provides a case study of how the G8 functioned between the end of the US Presidency in 2004, through the UK and Russian Presidencies in 2005 and 2006, and into the German Presidency of 2007. It explains how the United Kingdom used the G8 process to achieve far-reaching, cooperative outcomes from the 2005 Gleneagles Summit, which were further pursued at later summits. The case study demonstrates how the core principles of modern policy-making can be applied through changing circumstances, with changing policy leads, and with variable amounts of success. In addition, this chapter gives brief background to the G8 as an institution and analyses the G8 process and the impact of the G8's policy commitments.[1]

Introduction to the G8

The G8 is unique on the international stage in that, although it is regularly mentioned as one of the world's most influential supranational bodies along with the UN and EU, it is informal, flexible and small. It has remained true to its roots as a club of leaders: it has no permanent base, no premises to call its own, no formal secretariat and no budget. Its origins lie in the 1973 oil crisis and subsequent global recession. The French built on the 'Library Group' (a gathering of senior officials from the United States, Europe, and Japan to discuss economic issues) by inviting the heads of six major industrialised economies to a meeting in Rambouillet and proposing regular meetings. Canada participated from 1976, the European Union (represented by the European Commission and Presidency)

---

1   A comparable analysis of the G8 summits from 1998 to 2000 is in Budd 2003.

from 1977 and Russia, with full membership, from 1998, when G7 became G8 (Putnam and Bayne 1987; Bayne 2005).

So with only eight members, plus the European Commission, meetings are small and decision-making, when consensus is achieved, can be rapid. But at the same time the lack of secretariat, other than the logistical support of the rotating presidency, means there is very little G8 institutional memory, to record the outcomes of meetings, and force the G8 to follow an inherited agenda. Much rests on the observance of unwritten convention, personalities and an effective chair. Although the grouping brings together eight of the world's leading powers, accounting for over two-thirds of world GDP (World Bank 2006), there is no formal budget, meaning that there are few direct or independent G8 levers. The very clear concentration of global wealth in the G8 means that media and public expectations of summits are extremely high – and can often go unmet.

The uniqueness of the G8 as a grouping is reflected in the way it works. Unlike the UN or EU with their permanent headquarters and regular meetings at a variety of levels, the G8 has retained its light footprint. Although there was a period in the late 1980s and early 1990s when the growing involvement of other ministers weighed heavily on the summit, since 1998 the summits have returned to the original concept of a leaders' 'fireside chat'. So, although in any given presidency there is a wide range of supplementary meetings of ministers and experts in specific policy areas, the focus of world attention remains the annual G8 summit of heads of governments.

Summit Preparation

Although the summits themselves have a comparatively light bureaucracy compared to many international meetings, behind them lies an intense, year-long process of preparation. This is characterised by the same traditions of small groupings, informal exchanges and quick decision-making that characterise the G8 summits themselves.

G8 Summits are prepared by the 'sherpa' group of senior civil servants appointed by their heads of government. Sherpas are the personal appointees of their leader. In the UK the post goes traditionally to the Principal Private Secretary to the Prime Minister (although in the UK's Presidency year in 2005 Tony Blair chose Sir Michael Jay, Permanent Under-Secretary at the Foreign and Commonwealth Office, to be his sherpa). Sherpas meet on an almost monthly basis in the run-up to a summit, and there is constant day to day contact between their staff.[2]

Similar to leaders' participation at the summits themselves, sherpas meet alone in a room, with the assistant to the presidency sherpa the only non-sherpa in the room, to allow for frank and informal discussion. The sherpas' role is clear: as officials close to their leaders they are uniquely placed to articulate his

2   There is a parallel network of G8 Africa Personal Representatives (APRs), dating from 2001.

or her political wishes, and to translate them into deliverables suitable for the G8 summits. But sherpas do not make policy in isolation. They rely on their domestic policy-making mechanisms to feed in ideas, operating on the traditional foundations of the policy-making process: understanding the problem; developing solutions; implementing or testing those solutions; and evaluating the results.

Whereas sherpas give an overall political direction to development of G8 policy, this is turned into communiqué language and firm outcomes by the G8 subsidiary groups. The foreign affairs sous-sherpas (FASS), generally foreign ministry directors general of economic affairs, focus on preparing the key texts on most economic policy issues to be agreed at the summit, such as trade, development or the environment. The finance sous-sherpas (FSS), finance ministry directors, concentrate on summit texts with a macroeconomic or financial focus, usually for finance ministers to agree at their separate meeting before the summit. The foreign ministry political directors' (PD) group deals with more traditional foreign policy issues. Although they meet several times per year, their job is less focused on the summit alone, given that they also prepare for G8 foreign ministers' meetings, usually held twice a year before the summit and during the UN General Assembly's ministerial week.

Beyond the sherpa, FASS, FSS and PD track, other officials meet under the G8 banner to discuss a wide range of issues including non-proliferation (G8 non-proliferation directors); nuclear safety and security (G8 nuclear safety and security group); counter-terrorism and organised crime (G8 Roma-Lyon group); and others. Statements from these groups are fed up through sherpas to be adopted by leaders at the summit.

The 2005 Gleneagles Summit: Framing the Terms of the Policy Debate

Policy decisions in the G8 reflect the nature of the grouping and the G8 summits themselves. Just as the summits are private, informal meetings of leaders, to which invitations are issued in the name of the host him- or herself, so the policy focus of each summit is the decision of the host.

Planning for the next year's G8 presidency usually starts immediately after the present year's G8 summit: it is traditional for the incoming presidency to give an indication of the next year's G8 themes in their post-summit press conference. The UK Prime Minister, Tony Blair, acted in accordance with this tradition following the Sea Island Summit in June 2004, chaired by the US. Immediately on his return from Sea Island, in his 14 June statement to the British Parliament about the summit, he identified Africa and climate change as the two priorities for the UK Presidency of the G8 in 2005.

These issues reflected the scope of the G8's work. Although the summit process was originally developed to discuss macroeconomic and financial issues, as time has gone by the G8 has exemplified the flexibility inherent in the policy-making process. As the original genesis of the summits – the oil shocks and economic crises of the 1970s – has receded, so the G8 has adapted to address new emerging challenges – the challenges posed by globalisation, aid and development, and a more interdependent world.

Since the late 1990s the G8 has focused its work on Africa. At the Kananaskis Summit in 2002 the G8 renewed its partnership with Africa. Prime Minister Blair's choice of Africa as a key UK priority built on this earlier commitment. Similarly, although the issue of climate change per se had not been a major theme of previous G8 discussions, the G8 had discussed renewable energy at the Okinawa Summit in 2000 and a task force reported back to the G8 at the Genoa Summit in 2001. Prime Minister Blair's selection of both Africa and climate change, therefore, while being his personal choice, built on shared foundations. He told the World Economic Forum in Davos in January 2005 that he had chosen the two issues because there were 'differences that need to be reconciled; and if they could be reconciled or at least moved forward, it would make a huge difference to the prospects of international unity, as well as to people's lives and our future survival' (Blair 2005).

The Prime Minister's speech at Davos at the start of the UK's G8 Presidency set the tone for the rest of the year. On Africa, he outlined the challenge: how to solve the problem of African poverty and conflict on the basis of a renewed partnership between African governments and those of the developed world; and how to shift away from the donor/recipient relationship of old, to a relationship where there was an uplift in aid and debt relief, support for African peacekeeping efforts, and an opening of developed country markets, all based on the obligation of good governance from the African side.

On climate change, the problem went somewhat wider, given the lack of full international consensus on the nature of the problem. So Prime Minister Blair's challenge was in some ways simpler than that posed by Africa: he wanted the G8 to set a direction of travel, sending a strong signal that the G8 was committed to tackling climate change; to develop a package of practical measures to cut emissions, focused on technology; and to develop a partnership with the rapidly developing economies not originally bound by the Kyoto Protocol to tackle the issue.

The Preparation Process for Gleneagles

With the problem defined, the traditional policy-making machinery swung into motion. As well as using governmental sources to develop policy options for the Gleneagles G8 Summit, the UK G8 Presidency was unusual in the extent to which it relied on external advice from stakeholders to develop outcomes for the summit.

The use of external stakeholders was particularly well developed on the Africa aspects of the agenda. Even before the UK's Presidency of the G8 started, Prime Minister Blair launched the Commission for Africa (CfA) in 2004. The CfA, under his leadership and working with the benefit of a secretariat based in London, brought together a range of expertise to analyse the problems faced by

Africa, and to develop a series of recommendations to remove the obstacles to development (Commission for Africa 2005).

Beyond the CfA the UK Presidency developed an extensive programme of outreach to NGOs and civil society stakeholders with an interest in the African agenda. 2005 was the twentieth anniversary of Live Aid concerts to raise funds for Africa. It marked a key milestone of progress towards the UN Millenium Development Goals (see http://www.un.org/millenniumgoals/). As such there was a great deal of public interest in the Africa agenda. As part of the response to this interest, the UK embarked on an ambitious programme of outreach to external stakeholders.

For the UK's engagement strategy in 2005 Prime Minister Blair met with representatives of NGOs, business and trades unions. His sherpa, Michael Jay, held a series of what became monthly meetings with NGOs in the run up to the summit.[3] The engagement policy did not stop at UK NGOs: during the course of visits to other G8 capitals the UK Sherpa and FASS met with NGOs from other G8 partner countries. Michael Jay also hosted a meeting with NGOs in the margins of the March sherpa meeting; five sherpas attended in person and (for the first time) each G8 country was represented.

Meetings with civil society were bolstered by a meeting of development ministers in May 2005. As with the NGO meetings, this was separate from the formal G8 summit preparation process, but produced outcomes which fed into the policy background in the run-up to the summit. Ultimately this wide-ranging and comprehensive programme of engagement helped achieve better results, secure wider buy-in to the policy outcomes agreed, and communicate the results of all strands of the G8's work to a wider audience.

Outreach to civil society was not limited to the Africa agenda. On climate change the UK Presidency also set out to work with leading experts on climate change and energy policy so as to deliver evidence based outcomes at the Gleneagles Summit itself. The Hadley Center, a leading climate research institution, organised a meeting of experts to discuss emerging evidence on the science of climate change. This event was complemented by a public statement by the G8 National Academies of Science underlining their common understanding of the role that emissions of carbon dioxide caused by human activity were playing in climate change. The statement also pointed the way to what needed to be done to tackle the effects of climate change and called for the G8 to show political leadership in developing a response.

Engagement with outside stakeholders was not restricted to civil society. At Davos in January 2005 the Prime Minister asked representatives of 25 leading transnational companies to consider the issue of climate change. They reported back on 9 June, requesting G8 leaders to send a strong signal to markets on their commitment to manage climate change through an agreed international

---

3   Action Aid, the Catholic Agency for Overseas Development (CAFOD), Christian Aid, Comic Relief, Debt AIDS Trade Africa (DATA), the Global Campaign Against Poverty (GCAP), Global Watch, the Jubilee Debt Campaign and Stop AIDS were some of the NGOs who attended the meetings.

framework. As with the Africa process, an environment ministers' meeting was
held in April, which fed policy ideas into the G8 summit process.

Just as engagement with external non-governmental stakeholders was
considered key to the development of successful outcomes from the Gleneagles
Summit, the UK Presidency was concerned to ensure that non-G8 governments
were engaged in the summit process and at the summit itself, as a means of
delivering a truly global response to the global challenges the G8 was considering.
In this too, the UK was continuing a long G8 tradition of engagement with non-
G8 members. Before it became a member of the G8 at the Birmingham Summit
in 1998, Russia had played an increasing role in the G7 Summits from 1991
onwards. A range of African leaders had attended all G8 Summits since 2002.
Leaders of the major emerging economies were first invited to the G8 Summit at
Evian, under the French Presidency, in 2003, while Middle Eastern leaders were
invited to the US Sea Island Summit in 2004 (Bayne 2005, 206–7).

Given the global nature of the climate change challenge, the UK invited China,
India, Brazil, Mexico and South Africa to attend the Gleneagles Summit and to
take part in the discussions on climate change. Similarly, the leaders of Algeria,
Ethiopia, Ghana, Nigeria, Senegal, South Africa and Tanzania were invited
to take part in the discussions on Africa at the summit. The UK took care to
involve these outreach partners closely in preparations for the summit: the UK
Foreign Affairs Sous-Sherpa and Sherpa both met their outreach counterparts, as
preparations for the summit advanced, and UK ministers and the Prime Minister
engaged with all partners before the summit to ensure that their concerns were
being heard. Close involvement with some of the key players on climate change,
and with those dealing on a daily basis with the challenges faced by Africa,
helped the development of substantive deliverables at the summit itself, which
were supported by a far wider constituency than the G8 alone.

Meeting the challenge of delivering these ambitious outcomes required
a joined-up approach across all government departments. The Foreign
and Commonwealth Office took the lead in co-ordinating UK government
preparations, supporting the sherpa and FASS during negotiations in the run
up to the summit. However, success was dependent on support from a range of
other departments who lead in Whitehall on topics on the G8 agenda, including
HM Treasury, the Department for International Development (DFID), the
Department for Environment, Food and Rural Affairs (DEFRA) and the
former Department for Trade and Industry (DTI). Effective communication
between the Prime Minister's staff at No 10 Downing Street and all departments
involved ensured that a coherent government line was consistently delivered,
thus increasing the UK's ability to persuade countries and groups that had the
power to influence outcomes.

Delivering Results at Gleneagles

Having defined the problem, and identified stakeholders, the traditional search
for policy solutions began. Much of the negotiations on summit deliverables

took place in the narrow sherpa, FASS and FSS groups, although other bilateral channels were also used. The challenge the UK set itself was to ensure the G8 took specific action, backing up the rhetoric of previous summits, to commit to firm allocations of resources, which would make a real difference to the situation in Africa, and to change the terms of the debate on climate change. .

On Africa, the UK secured significant progress. Building on the Commission for Africa's report, and taking into account the comments of civil society stakeholders and African leaders, the G8 agreed a comprehensive package of measures at the Gleneagles Summit. The solutions the G8 reached built on the good practice of previous summits while taking a new approach to the challenges of Africa, rooted firmly in a partnership with African countries themselves.[4]

Among the key achievements of the G8 summit were the agreements reached on increases in aid and debt relief, pre-requisites for the delivery of real improvements across a range of areas and the focus of the hardest negotiations in the different summit preparatory meetings. Following the EU's commitment to increase development spending in May 2005, the announcement of increases in US aid in June, and Japanese, Canadian and Russian commitments at the Summit itself, the G8 leaders were able to announce that they would double aid to Africa by 2010, as part of a commitment to increase overall spending on development aid by $50 billion also by 2010. At the summit leaders also confirmed the 11 June decision by finance ministers to cancel 100 per cent of the debts owed by Heavily Indebted Poor Countries to the IMF, World Bank and African Development Fund.

With the back-up of this extra funding, the G8 and African countries were able to commit to significant actions, designed to secure a step change in delivering progress towards the Millennium Development Goals on the continent. The G8 committed firmly to supporting commitments from African leaders to the principles of good governance and anti-corruption, by encouraging the development of African-led solutions. The G8 promised to help Africa tackle the conflicts which hold back the development of the continent, including by supporting the African Union and African nations' capacity to deal with conflict and maintain the peace in Africa. The G8 also promised to support African institutions such as the African Union and the New Partnership for Africa's Development (NEPAD) in their efforts to improve governance in Africa.

The G8 also committed significant support to developing the human potential of Africa, backing the 'Education for All' Fast-Track Initiative, originally launched at the 2002 Kananaskis G8 Summit (see http://www1.worldbank.org/education/efafti). It continued its efforts to tackle HIV/AIDS, tuberculosis, malaria and polio, among other diseases. In particular, the G8 committed to developing a package on HIV prevention, treatment and care with the aim of providing as close as possible to universal access to treatment for all those who needed it by 2010.

---

4 The Gleneagles documents on Africa and other subjects are accessible at the UK G8 Presidency website, http://www.g8.gov.uk, and the website of the University of Toronto G8 Research Group, http://www.g8.utoronto.ca, which has a complete archive of G7 and G8 documents.

Recognising the prime role that private enterprise will play in bringing Africa out of poverty, the G8 committed to improving the capacity of Africa to promote growth. A key part of this was a promise to help developing countries build the physical, human and institutional capacity to trade. As well as support for infrastructure development, the G8 recognised that it had its part to play in improving the trading regime for African countries. The G8 therefore recommitted to working hard to delivering the WTO's Doha Development Agenda as part of its commitment to strengthening the multilateral trading system. The engagement of African countries in the summit preparation process ensured their firm commitment to the wide range of outcomes agreed.

Outcomes on climate change were no less significant. For the first time all the G8 agreed in a public statement that 'climate change was a serious and long-term challenge that has the potential to affect every part of the globe'. The G8 committed to taking firm action to tackle the threat, and adopted a comprehensive Action Plan on Climate Change, Clean Energy and Sustainable Development. The Plan sets out clear priorities for the G8 in transforming the way the G8 countries use energy, including through comprehensive energy efficiency measures in buildings, appliances and transport. It also includes commitments on the greater use of clean and renewable energy and the promotion of investments in clean technologies in the developing world. As part of the Action Plan the G8 tasked the International Energy Agency (IEA) with carrying out a range of work on energy efficiency (see Chapter 16 below). It also asked the World Bank to take the lead in establishing a new framework for clean energy and development, including investment and financing.

As well as this series of specific measures, the G8 also agreed to launch, together with the top 20 emitters of carbon, the Gleneagles Dialogue on Climate Change, Clean Energy and Sustainable Development as a means of addressing the challenge of climate change outside the traditional UN structures; as a means of monitoring implementation of the actions included in the Gleneagles Action Plan; and as a means of sharing best practice between participating governments.

Again, the involvement of the key emerging economies in the summit preparation process helped to achieve strong summit commitments on climate change and make the ensuing Gleneagles Dialogue meeting a success. The first meeting of the Gleneagles Dialogue on Climate Change, Clean Energy and Sustainable Development was held in the UK in November 2005. The meeting fulfilled its primary purpose of providing an informal political space to discuss cooperation to combat the challenge of climate change, without the negotiating pressures of the UN process. Dialogue partners agreed to work together on the deployment of clean technologies; incentives for large scale private investment in low carbon technologies; a new model for cooperation between developed and developing countries; and reinforcing action on adapting to the impacts of climate change.

The second meeting of the Dialogue, held in Mexico in October 2006, developed cooperation still further. Dialogue partners agreed that climate change was happening now, and affecting everyday lives; that the economics showed that early action was necessary; that, while the private sector understood that carbon emissions had a price, policy makers needed to give the private sector the long-term perspective; and that the implementation of energy efficiency measures could make a significant reduction in emissions immediately at low cost, using available technology. Germany will host the next meeting of the Gleneagles Dialogue in September 2007, maintaining the G8's cooperation with non-G8 partners on issues of global significance.

Implementation of Commitments through St Petersburg and Beyond

Following the achievement of the summit, and agreement on these ambitious outcomes, the challenge for the UK, and the G8 as a whole, remained to ensure speedy implementation of the Gleneagles commitments, in line with the core principles of good policy-making – that it is based on outcomes – and these outcomes are constantly evaluated and tested.

The Russian Federation took over the presidency of the G8 in January 2006 (http://www.g8russia.ru). President Vladimir Putin had announced at his press conference at the end of the Gleneagles Summit that the Russian G8 agenda would focus on energy security, infectious diseases and education. Putin's choice of priorities was in keeping with the G8 tradition of balancing continuity with the opportunity to discuss and explore new areas for cooperation. It soon became clear that the energy security strand would touch upon the areas of energy efficiency and climate change, while both infectious diseases and education had a development angle.

The St Petersburg Summit made important progress in taking forward Gleneagles commitments through discussions on infectious diseases and education. The Africa progress report adopted by leaders at the summit set out progress made on delivering the wide range of G8 Africa commitments and included detail on next steps, including the importance of the G8 honouring its commitments on aid, further debt cancellation and action on peacekeeping and anti-corruption work.[5]

In the energy security text signed at the summit, leaders committed to the principles of open, efficient and competitive markets as a way to ensure security of energy supply. The text reiterated the conclusion reached at Gleneagles, that dangerous climate change needs an urgent, global response. The communiqué also promoted the wider use of renewable and alternative energy sources and supported a number of practical energy efficiency measures.

The media spotlight on the weekend of the St Petersburg Summit refocused attention on climate change and Africa and helped to consolidate the position of these two topics at the top of the international agenda. Russia also worked hard to engage with stakeholders. At a 'Civil 8' meeting in Moscow held shortly before the summit, President Putin met with over 650 civil society representatives from around the world. Similarly, just as the UK Presidency invited the leaders

---

5   The St Petersburg documents are accessible at the Russian G8 Presidency website, http://www.g8russia.ru, as well as on http://www.g8.utoronto.ca.

of China, India, Brazil, Mexico and South Africa to Gleneagles, so Russia invited them to St Petersburg, together with the heads of various international and regional organisations. Again, the involvement of these outreach partners at the summit helped bind a wider constituency into the conclusions of the G8 grouping, and reinforced the G8's ability to speak with authority on issues of truly global concern.

For the UK, progress towards implementation of previous G8 commitments is monitored not just through the annual summit but also through domestic reviews. In the case of Africa commitments, the Department for International Development (DFID) publishes a regular evaluation of milestones reached. Following Gleneagles, the UK government devised a 'Gleneagles Implementation Plan for Africa'. The plan has a series of UK-identified international milestones mapping out progress towards full implementation of the Gleneagles commitments. The plan detailed outcomes the UK expected to achieve by the end of 2006 in order to be on track to deliver Africa commitments made at Gleneagles. To maintain momentum on delivery of these commitments, the UK also identified a further set of milestones beyond the Russian G8 presidency, leading up to outcomes it would like the international community to deliver by the time of the Heiligendamm Summit in June 2007, chaired by Germany. The plan is updated monthly and placed in the libraries of both Houses of the British Parliament and on the website of the Department for International Development (see http://www.dfid.gov.uk).

Conclusion

The German G8 Presidency has focused on the global economy and Africa, under the overarching theme of 'growth and responsibility' (http://www.g-8. de). Climate change and energy efficiency are key components of the focus on the global economy, building on the Stern Review on the Economics of Climate Change issued in October 2006 (Stern 2006). The message of the Stern Review was that it is essential to tackle the threat of climate change now if we are to secure global security and prosperity.

At the Heiligendamm Summit, the G8 leaders made unprecedented progress. They agreed the need for a global emission reduction goal and committed to discuss a post-2012 international climate change framework in conjunction with the Plus-5, under the United Nations Framework Convention on Climate Change (UNFCCC). Additionally the US pledged to host a meeting of major energy consuming and greenhouse gas emitting countries to support the UNFCCC process.

The German focus on Africa has resulted in the G8 reaffirming its Gleneagles aid commitments of an extra $50bn per year globally by 2010, an extra $25bn for Africa, and a pledge to deliver universal access to HIV/AIDS prevention, treatment and care services by 2010. Additional commitments include meeting the estimated shortfall of the Education For All Fast Track Initiative by $500m (for 2007), support for strengthening health systems, better coordination of international assistance, and support for sustainable financing of African peacekeeping.

Each G8 Presidency takes forward its own agenda, relying on the goodwill of others to help produce an agreed outcome. This chapter has outlined how the informal nature of the G8 has nonetheless provided continuity of work on the two central themes of the 2005 UK Presidency, reflecting the underlying political consensus created at Gleneagles, and the continued importance of African development and climate security to global welfare. A focus on issues of genuine global importance and agreement on substantive outcomes provides the best guarantee of the continued relevance of the G8 and its outreach process in the years ahead.

References

Bayne, N. (2005), *Hanging Together: The G8 Summit Confronts the Twenty-first Century*, Ashgate, Aldershot.

Blair, T. (2005), Special Address by Tony Blair at the World Economic Forum in Davos, 27 January 2005, accessible at http://www.g8.gov.uk.

Budd, C. (2003), 'G8 Summits and Their Preparation', in Bayne, N. and Woolcock, S. (eds), *The New Economic Diplomacy: Decision-Making and Negotiation in International Economic Relations*, 1st edition, Ashgate, Aldershot, pp. 139–146.

Commission for Africa (2005), *Our Common Interest: An Argument*, Penguin Books, London.

Putnam, R.D. and Bayne, N. (1987), *Hanging Together: Cooperation and Conflict in the Seven-Power Summits*, SAGE, London.

Stern, N. (2006), *Stern Review on the Economics of Climate Change*, Cambridge University Press, Cambridge.

World Bank (2006), *World Development Report 2006*, World Bank, Washington.

Useful Websites

German G8 Presidency (2007): http://www.g-8.de.

G8 Research Group, University of Toronto: http://www.g8.utoronto.ca.

Russian G8 Presidency (2006): http://www.g8russia.ru.

UK Department for International Development: http://www.dfid.gov.uk.

UK G8 Presidency (2005): http://www.g8.gov.uk.

United Nations Millennium Goals: http://www.un.org/millenniumgoals/.

World Bank 'Education for All' Programme: http://www1.worldbank.org/education/efafti/.

Chapter 7

Business in Economic Diplomacy

Reinhard Quick

The chemical industry is essential to a broad range of manufacturing and agricultural industries, with virtually every product – from automobiles to zippers – using chemical inputs. Worldwide, the output of the industry is valued at $ 1.9 trillion annually. Of that output forty per cent – $ 792 billion – is traded globally accounting for more than 10 per cent of world merchandise exports in 2003. The chemical industry also employs 7 million people worldwide.[1]

This chapter describes the role of business advocacy in international environment and trade negotiations using the chemical industry as an example. The above citation not only demonstrates the importance of the chemical industry as the producer of inputs for other manufacturers but it also shows its strong participation in international trade.[2] The chemical industry is one of the most regulated industries, locally, regionally and supra- or internationally. At the international level many organisations deal with chemicals, be it trade in chemicals, chemical safety or the sound management of chemicals.

In the area of trade the World Trade Organization (WTO) is the central international institution on which the chemical industry concentrates its advocacy activities. In the area of environment a focal point such as the WTO for trade does not exist. The United Nations Environment Programme (UNEP) is an important body with respect to the environmental issues of the chemical industry. Under the auspices of UNEP several international environmental agreements have been negotiated which are of importance to the chemical industry, such as the Basle Convention (dealing with hazardous waste), the Montreal Protocol (banning CFCs), the Rotterdam Convention (dealing with trade in hazardous chemicals) and the Stockholm Convention (prohibiting persistent organic pollutants or POPs).

Other international bodies also deal with chemicals and the environment. In order to coordinate the different activities of these organisations the Inter-Organization Programme for the Sound Management of Chemicals (IOMC)

---

1   Citation from Document WTO/TN/MA/W/58 of 4 July 2005, Communication on Tariff Liberalization in the Chemicals Sector made by Canada, Japan, Norway, Separate Customs Territory of Taiwan, Penghu, Kinmen and Matsu, Singapore, Switzerland, and the United States (WTO 2005).

2   CEFIC *Facts and Figures*, accessible at http://www.cefic.org/factsandfigures/, provides further information about the chemical industry.

has been established. Seven organisations belong to IOMC: the Food and Agriculture Organization (FAO), the International Labour Organization (ILO), the OECD, UNEP, the United Nations Industrial Development Organization (UNIDO), the United Nations Institute for Training and Research (UNITAR) and the World Health Organization (WHO). IOMC together with UNEP and the Intergovernmental Forum on Chemical Safety (IFCS) convened the 2006 International Conference on Chemical Safety which took place in Dubai, United Arab Emirates. The Conference endorsed the Strategic Approach to International Chemicals Management (SAICM).

Besides IOMC, the United Nations Commission on Sustainable Development (UNCSD), the United Nations Conference on Environment and Development (UNCED) as well as the World Summit for Sustainable Development (WSSD) also address issues related to chemicals.

This chapter describes the chemical industry's advocacy structure using advocacy activities in relation to UNEP and the WTO as an example. First, the chapter concentrates on the advocacy structure and on civil society participation in international decision-making. Thereafter the chapter will discuss advocacy activities on the basis of specific examples.

The Structure of the Chemical Industry's Advocacy

The cradle of the chemical industry lies in Europe. Until 2005 the European chemical industry (in the then 25 EU Member States) was the biggest in the world. Given the strong economic growth of Asia, the Asian chemical industry has taken the lead in 2005. The United States, Japan, China and Germany are the leading chemical producer countries of the world. Almost half of the world's 30 biggest chemical companies have their headquarters in Europe (CEFIC *Facts and Figures*).

Any successful advocacy structure is bound to follow the (legislative) decision-making process. The chemical industry's advocacy structure follows this rule. Since 'all politics is local', the basis for the industry's advocacy in the international arena are national industry federations, such as the American Chemistry Council (ACC) of the United States, the German Verband der Chemischen Industrie, e.V. (VCI), the French Union des Industries Chimiques (UIC), the UK Chemical Industries' Association (CIA), the Italian Federchimica or the Japan Chemical Industry Association (JCIA).[3] Chemical companies producing in these countries are members of the respective national associations on a voluntary basis. The national associations convey their views on international issues to their respective governments. Given the supranational decision-making structure of the European Union, there is also a European Chemical Industry Council, CEFIC. The members of CEFIC are national chemical industry federations and companies, the latter being divided into two groups: corporate and business members.

---

3   The websites of these federations and of other organisations mentioned below are listed at the end of this chapter.

At world-wide level the industry is represented by the International Council of Chemical Associations (ICCA). The ICCA is the voice of the chemical industry vis-à-vis the above mentioned international organisations, dealing with policy issues of international significance such as trade policy, policies related to health, safety and the environment, climate change, the safety of international transport, intellectual property and efforts to eliminate chemical weapons or the diversion of chemicals for the production of illegal drugs. ICCA consists of national chemical industry associations: three North American (the associations of Canada, US and Mexico); four South American (the associations of Brazil, Argentina, Uruguay and Chile as well as the association representing Mercosur as such); one European (22 national associations plus six associate members); two Australasian (Australia and New Zealand); one African (South Africa); and one Asian (Japan). Several Asian nations are associate members and await full membership status. ICCA has no permanent secretariat; the secretarial functions are provided on a rolling basis by ACC or CEFIC.

The advocacy process is developed bottom-up. The issues are discussed at national level from which joint European or international positions emerge. ICCA, for example, has a Technical Affairs Group which develops the ICCA input on all international environmental matters, such as chemical safety and the sound management of chemicals, as well as a Trade Policy Group which develops the ICCA input into the WTO. ICCA positions are adopted by the ICCA governing bodies.

Timing is of crucial importance. The industry has to be active during the negotiations of an international agreement and has to develop its positions before decisions are taken. Once the negotiations have been completed another national advocacy initiative takes place, namely the advocacy concerning the national or supranational ratification process. National advocacy is crucial for any international process.[4]

Parallel to the chemical industry's advocacy structure the industry also utilises horizontal industry/business organisations for its advocacy purposes. The chemical industry provides input on international issues to horizontal industry/business organisations, which in turn provide their input to national governments or, via their European or international bodies, to international organisations. This advocacy process also starts at a national level and broadens the advocacy scope. In particular in the trade policy area chemical industry positions often form the basis for overall industry positions. Once adopted these positions are then presented by the overall industry federation to the national government, for example, the Bundesverband der Deutschen Industrie, e.V (BDI) to the German government, or via BusinessEurope (formerly UNICE) to the European Commission. At the international level the International Chamber of Commerce (ICC), the Business and Industry Advisory Committee of the OECD (BIAC) or the World Business

---

4   In the European context, the importance of the national advocacy process is sometimes ignored by some 'global' companies, since they look at Europe as a homogeneous entity taking purely European decisions and not as a heterogeneous entity taking European decisions with a strong national component.

Council for Sustainable Development (WBCSD) represent international business views vis-à-vis international organisations. National chemical associations and companies are also active in these groups.

Civil Society Participation in International Decision Making

The Exemplary Case of UNEP

> An effective engagement of civil society at governance and programmatic levels is critical to strengthen the environmental pillar of sustainable development, and foster action to concretely implement Agenda 21.[5]

The Stockholm Declaration of the 1972 Stockholm Conference on the Human Environment recognises in paragraph 7 the important role of citizens, communities, enterprises and institutions at every level in achieving its environmental goal (Stockholm Declaration 1972). Also Section III of Agenda 21, adopted by UNCED in 1992, refers to the important role of civil society in achieving sustainable development (UNCED 1992).

Since its creation in 1972 UNEP has established a special relationship with civil society. It acknowledges the role of civil society in addressing environmental concerns and provides civil society with the possibility to shape the intergovernmental decision-making process during which operational policies and work programmes are established. To this end UNEP has adopted an accreditation system which grants civil society organisations a consultative status.[6]

Accredited organisations, which include ICC, ICCA and WBCSD, have the possibility:

- to receive unedited working documents of the UNEP Governing Council/ Global Ministerial Environmental Forum at the same time as the UNEP Committee of the Permanent Representatives;
- to submit to the UNEP Secretariat written contributions to these unedited working documents of the Governing Council/Global Ministerial Environment Forum, for distribution to the governments.

During the sessions of the UNEP Governing Council/Global Ministerial Environment Forum accredited organisations have the opportunity:

---

5   Citation from UNEP website: http://www.unep.org/civil_society/About/index. asp/.

6   See http://www.unep.org/civil_society/About/accreditation.asp, for UNEP procedures on Accreditation and Consultative Status at the Governing Council. The list of accredited organisations with observer status to the UNEP Governing Council/Global Ministerial Environment Forum (GC/GMEF) can be found at: http://www.unep.org/ civil_society/PDF_docs/accreditation_NGOs.pdf.

- to attend the plenary, the Committee of the Whole and the Ministerial Consultations discussions as observers;
- to circulate written statements to governments through the UNEP Secretariat;
- to make oral statements during the discussions of the Governing Council/Global Ministerial Environment Forum at the invitation of the Chairperson.

In conjunction with the meetings of the Governing Council and the Global Ministerial Environment Forum, UNEP organises the Global Civil Society Forum on a yearly basis. The Forum discusses policy issues related to water, chemicals management, gender and the environment, globalisation, etc.

Based on the classification adopted by UNCED, UNEP classifies civil society organisations into nine major groups, of which 'business and industry' is one. The UNEP division of technology, industry and economics (UNEP DTIE) is the focal point for business and industry associations working on UNEP issues. A subsection of this division is responsible for chemicals. The chemicals subdivision of UNEP primarily works on issues related to chemical safety, such as the sound management of hazardous chemicals, safe production, use and disposal of chemicals.[7]

Given the multitude of issues dealt with by UNEP concerning the chemical industry ICCA has been an accredited organisation since 1998.[8] The example of SAICM (discussed later in the chapter) demonstrates that ICCA avails itself of the possibilities and opportunities granted to it as an accredited organisation. Business considers UNEP's relationship with civil society as an exemplary model that could and should be copied by other international organisations. The strategy paper on 'Enhancing Civil Society Engagement in the Work of the United Nations Environment Programme' distinguishes between the private sector and other civil society organisation (traditional NGOs) and concludes that UNEP should strengthen the role of 'traditional' NGOs and not that of the private sector (UNEP 2002, 4–5). It nevertheless recognises the role of business in promoting UNEP's goals and suggests strengthening the current approaches to the private sector through UNEP DTIE as well as strengthening mediation between the private sector and other civil society organisations.

The WTO's Love-Hate Relationship with Civil Society

The Agreement establishing the World Trade Organization contains in Article V, paragraph 2 a specific reference to NGOs which says that: 'The General Council

---

7   See http://www.unep.org/resources/business/Focus_Areas/ for the UNEP Division of Technology, Industry and Economics. For an overview of the activities of the chemicals division see http://www.chemunep.ch/irptc/.

8   See the UNEP Civil Society Directory at http://www.unep.org/dpdl/civil_society/directory/process2asp?90 and UNEP Major Groups Directory at: http://www.unep.org/civil_society/Registration/index2asp?idno=375.

may make appropriate arrangements for consultation and cooperation with non-governmental organisations concerned with matters related to those of the WTO'. Article V, paragraph 2 has been implemented by the Guidelines for Arrangement on Relations with Non-Governmental Organizations adopted by the WTO's General Council (WTO 1996). With these guidelines the WTO recognises the role that civil society organisations can play to increase the awareness of the public in respect of WTO activities and sets out some fundamental principles concerning improved transparency and communications with NGOs.

The interaction between the WTO and NGOs should lead to:

- a prompt de-restriction of WTO documents;
- the organisation of symposia for NGOs on specific WTO issues;
- the participation of chairpersons of WTO Council and Committees in discussions and meetings with NGOs in their personal capacity;
- informal arrangements to receive the information NGOs may wish to make available for consultation by interested delegations;
- the continuation of the past practice of the WTO Secretariat in responding to requests for general information and briefings about the WTO.

The Guidelines also identify the limits of civil society participation in WTO matters. The concluding paragraph says:

> Members have pointed to the special character of the WTO which is both a legally binding intergovernmental treaty of rights and obligations among its Members and a forum for negotiations. As a result of extensive discussions, there is currently a broadly held view that it would not be possible for NGOs to be directly involved in the work of the WTO or its meetings. Closer consultation and cooperation with NGOs can also be met constructively through appropriate processes at the national level where lies primary responsibility for taking into account the different elements of public interest which are brought to bear on trade-policy making. (WTO 1996)

The WTO does not provide for a general accreditation system for civil society organisations, nor does it give civil society the possibility to attend WTO meetings. In particular the meetings of the General Council or the meetings of the different WTO Committees established to administer the various WTO Agreements cannot be accessed by NGOs. Accreditation is only possible for WTO Ministerial Conferences, yet NGOs are only allowed to attend the plenary session. This restriction is a clear result of the limits of civil society participation in WTO matters. During the conferences the WTO Secretariat and the host country set up an NGO Centre where debriefing sessions and other NGO meetings take place. Also WTO members debrief their national civil society representatives about the developments of the conference.

Given the clear and limited role for civil society during WTO Ministerial Conferences the practice has evolved according to which NGOs organise their own meetings with WTO members either openly or privately. For example, during the

Hong Kong Ministerial Conference a whole range of NGO public meetings took place in parallel to the negotiations.[9] Some WTO members also invite members of civil society organisations to become part of their official WTO delegation. These members have access to the more restricted parts of the conference and as a consequence much better access to developments and documents than 'ordinarily' accredited NGOs.

Another implementation step of the above mentioned Guidelines is the monthly list of NGO position papers received by the WTO Secretariat.[10] This list contains position papers on WTO issues adopted by the private sector, such as ICCA, CEFIC, BusinessEurope and BDI, as well as papers of other NGOs, such as Oxfam, Greenpeace or the World-Wide Fund for Nature (WWF).

The WTO Secretariat also organises public symposia on WTO issues which give civil society ample opportunities to present their views on WTO-related matters.[11] It is interesting to note that the various parts of civil society do not use these symposia to exchange their often conflicting views on WTO among themselves; rather they tend to attend those sessions of the symposium where they can meet their peers.

Since the disastrous Seattle WTO Ministerial Conference the question how to improve civil society's access to the WTO has been a top issue on the WTO's agenda. The membership is however deeply divided on this issue. Some countries, such as the United States, are of the view that the WTO should open its doors to civil society and provide for a broad participation comparable to the United Nations' system. Others, such as the European Union, are not as radical as the US but would nevertheless open the WTO doors more widely to civil society. Others again, among them most developing countries, reject the participation of civil society in WTO meetings.[12]

The deep division of the WTO membership on this issue became evident also in the WTO's Asbestos Case, where the Appellate Body adopted an Additional Procedure on how to deal with *amicus curiae* briefs, which it expected to receive in great numbers.[13] In the end the Appellate Body received eleven applications for leave to file a written brief (one of which was from CEFIC), yet denied all requests to file such a brief for failure to comply sufficiently with the requirements set out in the Additional Procedure (Van den Bosche 2005, 196ff.). The WTO membership was not very pleased with this initiative by the Appellate Body and adopted the following observation after a reportedly tumultuous debate:

---

9   The list of the Public Meetings can be found at: http://www.wto.org/english/thewto_e/min05_e/ngo_meetings_e.pdf.

10   See http://www.wto.org/english/forums_e/pospap_e.htm for the list of position papers received by the WTO Secretariat.

11   See http://www.wto.org/english/forums_e/public_forum_e/programme_e.htm for the programme of the Public Forum held in September 2006.

12   For a more detailed discussion of this issue, see Van den Bosche 2005, pp.154ff.

13   *Amicus curiae* stands for friend of the court. In the WTO context *amicus curiae* briefs are submissions by non-WTO members, in particular NGOs, individuals and others, in a specific dispute settlement case.

There was broad agreement that the rights and obligations under the DSU [Dispute Settlement Understanding] belonged to WTO Members. It had been repeatedly stated that the WTO was a member-driven organization. Therefore most delegations had concluded that since there was no specific provision regarding amicus briefs such briefs should not be accepted. Some delegations were of the view that amicus briefs could be used in some cases and there was at least one delegation who believed that there was both a legal and a substantive reason to use amicus briefs. There was no agreement on this point. (WTO 2001)

The Chemical Industry's Advocacy Activities in Environment and Trade Negotiations

In the following section two examples of chemical industry advocacy activities will be discussed: the Strategic Approach to International Chemicals Management (SAICM) and the industrial tariff negotiations of the WTO's Doha Development Agenda (DDA). The first example refers to negotiations that have been concluded successfully, the second to negotiations that still await conclusion.

Strategic Approach to International Chemicals Management (SAICM)

The Strategic Approach to International Chemicals Management was adopted in early 2006 by the International Conference on Chemicals Management (ICCM) which took place in Dubai, United Arab Emirates. SAICM comprises three core texts: the Dubai Declaration, the Overarching Policy Strategy and a Global Plan of Action. It is a policy framework for international action on chemical hazards.[14]

The origins of international chemicals management can be traced back to the so-called UN Earth Summit, the United Nations Conference on Environment and Development (UNCED) of 1992, which adopted, *inter alia*, the Rio Declaration and Agenda 21 (UNCED 1992). Agenda 21 is a comprehensive plan of action for governments and stakeholders covering all areas in which human activities can have an impact on the environment. Chapter 19 of Agenda 21 entitled Environmentally Sound Management of Toxic Chemicals establishes key areas for the sound management of chemicals, such as risk reduction, knowledge and information, governance, capacity building and technical cooperation as well as illegal traffic.

As a consequence of Agenda 21 the Intergovernmental Forum on Chemical Safety (IFCS) and the Inter-Organization Programme for the Sound Management of Chemicals (IOMC) were established. Chapter 19 of Agenda 21 was reaffirmed by the World Summit on Sustainable Development (WSSD) held in 2002 in Johannesburg, South Africa. In particular, paragraph 23 of the Johannesburg Implementation Plan aims to achieve, by 2020, 'that chemicals are used and produced in ways that lead to the minimization of significant adverse effects on human health and the environment' (WSSD 2002).

---

14 See the UNEP SAICM home page at: http://www.chem.unep.ch/saicm/iccm_sec. htm.

The developments which led to the adoption of SAICM began in February 2002 when the Governing Council of UNEP adopted a decision which expressly states the need to further develop a strategic approach to international chemicals management.[15] SAICM has been developed by a multi-stakeholder Preparatory Committee, co-convened by UNEP, the IFCS and the IOMC.

The Dubai Declaration of 2006 is a political commitment by all stakeholders to achieve sustainable development through a sound management of chemicals. It refers to the responsibilities of governments, the private sector and other non-governmental organisations. It reiterates *inter alia* the need to take concerted action at international level and recognises the efforts made by the private sector and other non-governmental organisations to promote chemical safety. It underlines the lack of capacity of developing countries to handle chemicals safely and repeats the need for concerted action to arrive at fundamental changes in the way societies handle chemicals. In adopting the Declaration the signatories also accepted the Overarching Policy Strategy and recommended the use and further development of the Global Plan of Action.

The Overarching Policy Strategy (OPS) contains the core elements of chemicals management and is aimed at achieving the WSSD 2020 objectives. Its scope includes: (a) environmental, economic, health and labour aspects of chemical safety, and (b) agricultural and industrial chemicals, with a view to promoting sustainable development and covering chemicals at all stages of their life-cycle, including in products. Its statement of needs refers to progress already made and to the still unsatisfactory situations with respect to chemical safety that need improvement at all levels. It explicitly refers to the following key issues for chemical safety and the sound management of chemicals: risk reduction, knowledge and information, governance, capacity building and technical cooperation as well as illegal traffic. Measures to implement these key issues should be based on scientific evidence and methods, socio-economic aspects and precaution. The OPS is not legally binding. The private sector is encouraged to contribute to the aims of the OPS by voluntary initiatives.

The Global Action Plan is considered to be the working tool for the implementation of the OPS. It contains the same key issues as the OPS and extensive tables on:

- measures to support risk reduction;
- strengthening knowledge and information;
- governance: strengthening of institutions, law and policy;
- enhancing capacity building;
- addressing illegal international traffic;
- improved general practices.

ICCA has been actively involved in the preparation of SAICM and has participated in the meetings of the Preparatory Committee which took place in

---

15 The decision can be found at: http://www.chem.unep.ch/saicm/SAICM/draftelements/ssvii3.pdf.

2003, 2004 and 2005.[16] It also took part in the Dubai Conference where it informed the participants about its voluntary initiatives to improve chemical safety and the sound management of chemicals. ICCA has adopted a position paper on SAICM and has supported the adoption of the Strategy with its three principal core texts.[17] More importantly, in the course of the SAICM negotiations ICCA has adapted its Responsible Care© Programme and has presented at Dubai both its Responsible Care© Global Charter and its Global Product Strategy.[18] Both initiatives are considered by the chemical industry as a direct contribution to the implementation of SAICM. They implement the crucial elements contained in the OPS, such as:

- risk reduction measures through improvement and further development of product stewardship in the whole value chain;
- closer cooperation with governments and other stakeholders in a partnership approach;
- improved knowledge and information on chemicals;
- public access to information taking confidentiality issues into account;
- capacity building.

One of the concrete aims of the Global Product Strategy is the elaboration of risk assessments and the implementation of risk management measures based on these risk assessments for all chemical substances by 2018. This will be quite a challenge for all chemical companies located outside the European Union. Instead companies inside the EU and those exporting chemical substances to the EU will have to comply with the recently adopted REACH Regulation which obliges companies to provide both risk assessments and risk management measures when registering their chemical substances with the European Union's Chemicals Agency (European Union 2006).

With respect to capacity building the ICCA has made proposals outlining five concrete projects which are being discussed at the moment with UNEP.

The transparent, participatory and deliberative process which led to the conclusion of SAICM seems to have worked well, since governments and other stakeholders praise the results and consider that they have been part of a process to which they could make a contribution.[19] The real challenge of SAICM however

---

16　The minutes of the Preparatory Meetings are at: http://www.chem.unep.ch/saicm/saicm_development.htm.

17　ICCA *Position Paper on SAICM* of 9 June 2005 (ICCA 2005a), at: http://www.icca-chem.org/section06.html. 'International Council of Chemical Associations Welcomes Approval of SAICM', ICCA Press Release, 9 February 2006, at: http://www.icca-at-dubai.org.

18　For detailed descriptions of these programmes and documents, see: http://www.responsiblecare.org/; http://rclg.alert.com.mt/flashpresenation.html; and http://www.icca-chem.org/section02d.html.

19　See UNEP Press Release at: http://www.chem.unep.ch/saicm/iccm_sec.htm; EU Press Release IP 06/129; and ICCA Press Release, note 17 above.

lies in translating the different elements of the core texts, in particular the OPS, into national processes and international agreements in order to achieve the WSSD 2020 objectives, especially the elaboration of risk assessments and the implementation of risk management measures based on these assessments for all chemical substances

Chemical Tariff Elimination: the WTO's Industrial Tariff Negotiations in the DDA

In order to understand the chemical industry's position on the Non-Agricultural Market Access (NAMA) negotiations in the DDA – namely to eliminate chemical tariffs altogether – one must look at the results of the tariff negotiations of the Uruguay Round. During the Round the ICCA called upon governments to agree on a harmonisation of chemical tariffs at a low level (ICCA 1991). The ICCA proposal found its way into the final results of negotiations as a so-called sectoral agreement (Schanz 1995, 107–10).

The Chemical Tariff Harmonization Agreement (CTHA) of the Uruguay Round provides for the reduction of chemical tariffs to zero, 5.5 per cent or 6.5 per cent for the HS Chapters 28 to 39 and includes inorganic and organic chemicals, fertilisers and plant protection products, soaps and cosmetics, and plastics. Chemical tariffs below the harmonised level remain unchanged. The agreement does not allow for any exceptions. Instead it provides for three time periods during which CTHA members have to reduce chemical tariffs to the harmonised level: five years for all tariffs which were equal to or below 10 per cent, ten years for all tariffs which were above 10 per cent and below 25 per cent, and 15 years for all tariffs above 25 per cent. The agreement came into force on 1 January 1995 and is now being applied by 50 WTO members.[20] For pharmaceuticals CTHA was complemented with a Tariff Elimination Agreement which came into force on 1 January 1997 and is being applied by 32 WTO members.[21] This covers HS Chapter 30 and specific parts of HS Chapter 29, as well as active pharmaceutical ingredients and sole use intermediates. These last two categories have to be listed individually, annexed to the tariff schedules and updated every three years.

Given the success of CTHA and the continued globalisation of the chemical industry, ICCA set itself the goal in 1999 to eliminate chemical tariffs by 2010.[22] The chemical industry never believed in a WTO without trade rounds and therefore supported a comprehensive new round of trade negotiations as early

---

20 Armenia, Australia (de facto), Bulgaria, Canada, Chile (de facto), China, Ecuador, European Union (25 members), Hong Kong China, Iceland, Japan, Jordan, Kirgizstan, Korea, Mongolia, New Zealand (de facto), Norway, Oman, Panama, Qatar, Singapore, Switzerland, Taiwan, Turkey (de facto), United Arab Emirates and United States.

21 Australia, Canada, European Union (25), Iceland, Japan, Norway, Switzerland and United States.

22 See http://www.cefic.be/Templates/shwPublications.asp?NID=2&T=3&S=9&P=4 for *CEFIC Comments on a New Multilateral Trade Round*, 15 March 1999 (CEFIC 1999).

as 1999. The industry's spirit of continuous trade liberalisation stood quite in contrast to the difficult birth of the new trade round eventually agreed upon in 2001 (WTO 2001a).

The Doha mandate speaks of reduction or, as appropriate, elimination of tariffs but does not explicitly refer to sectoral tariff elimination (WTO 2001a, paragraph 16). The first such reference can be found in Annex B of the July 2004 package which states that sectoral tariff elimination is a key element to achieving the objectives of the NAMA negotiations (WTO 2004, paragraph 7). The Hong Kong Ministerial Declaration goes one step further and asks the negotiating group to identify these sectors, specifying that participation in such sectoral initiatives should be non-mandatory (WTO 2005, paragraph 19).

In its position on NAMA the chemical industry goes beyond the position of European industry generally. The latter asks for an ambitious non-linear formula with the highest tariff at a maximum of 15 per cent (bound).[23] The chemical industry wants a comprehensive chemical tariff elimination agreement.[24] Given the harmonisation of chemical tariffs agreed upon in the Uruguay Round, real market access for chemical products should consist in the elimination of chemical tariffs and not in a further reduction of already low tariffs.

Since the conclusion of the Uruguay Round chemical trade has nearly doubled (CEFIC *Facts and Figures*). CTHA has certainly contributed to this increase. This growth also demonstrates the need to further liberalise trade in chemicals as most of them are inputs for the production of other goods. If countries want to have a competitive manufacturing sector they should not burden it with extra costs, that is, the tariffs on the imported chemicals, but rather strive to eliminate them.

Today the average bound chemical tariffs are relatively low in industrial countries but quite high in emerging countries. Furthermore there is a discrepancy between applied and bound rates of chemicals. Many developing countries apply lower chemical rates than the rate they have bound in the WTO.

The discrepancy between bound and applied tariff rates in emerging countries is at the centre of the debate in the NAMA negotiations. Since the negotiators have decided that the tariff cuts will be calculated on the basis of the bound rates one can easily imagine that some countries will only agree on 'paper' cuts but not on cuts in the applied rates. This leads to a dilemma: the already low average tariffs in the industrialised world will be reduced even further, while the high average industrial tariffs in emerging countries will not be reduced to a level which can be overcome by competitive industries. The goal of getting real market access in emerging countries will not be achieved. Once the DDA result is implemented, the industrialised world will have no bargaining chip left to obtain further tariff cuts in emerging countries. Therefore the industrialised world, fully supported by

---

23 See http://www.busnesseurope.eu/content/default.asp?PageId=435, BusinessEurope *Position on Non-Agricultural Market Access Negotiations* (BusinessEurope 2002).

24 See http://www.icca-chem.org/section06e.html for ICCA *Market Access for the Doha Development Agenda*, May 2005 (ICCA 2005).

business, expects the emerging countries to make substantial tariff concessions now.

This position of the industrialised world has been heavily criticised by the emerging countries, and in particular by India and Brazil, which claim that their tariff cuts should not be as significant as the cuts of the industrial countries. As a justification for their claim they refer to the Doha mandate, which says: 'The negotiations shall take fully into account the special needs and interests of developing and least developed country participants, including through less than full reciprocity in reduction commitments ...' (WTO 2001a, paragraph 16).

It is interesting to note that the coalition of emerging, developing and least developed countries has so far been very successful in blocking the NAMA requests made by the industrial countries. The WTO membership seems to have enormous difficulties agreeing on a liberalisation package which produces real cuts in applied industrial tariffs and at the same time is in line with the development aspect of the negotiations.[25] In essence the question is whether the emerging countries should benefit from the development exceptions or not. Since the DDA should result in increased South-South trade and should enable all WTO members, but in particular developing countries, to benefit from such trade, industrial and emerging countries have to open their markets.[26] Hence emerging countries cannot insist on the flexibilities provided for by the NAMA package.

The Hong Kong Declaration has not solved but rather postponed this conflict. The modalities have not been properly addressed. As a result, the negotiators are expected to find the magic tariff cutting formula and the coefficients on the one side, whilst agreeing on flexibilities and exceptions on the other. The Declaration simply repeats these elements without indicating a way forward; it further complicates the negotiations by requiring that market access for agriculture and NAMA should have a comparatively high level of ambition (WTO 2005a, paragraph 24).

The sectoral tariff negotiations are part of this complicated picture. The way forward is not clear and some emerging countries in particular India and Brazil oppose them. For the chemical industry the problematic issues of the sectoral negotiations are:

* country coverage;
* exceptions;
* special and differential treatment.

As to country coverage the industry suggests that all WTO members with a viable chemical industry participate, 'viable' meaning a domestic chemical production of $3 billion per year. This is a new benchmark in the WTO, which in the past looked at shares of world trade and not at domestic production. However chemical

---

25 For an overview of all submissions made until 4 April 2006, see WTO 2006b.

26 An interesting study on how the high and often unbound industrial tariffs in countries such as India, Brazil, Egypt, Malaysia, South Africa and Turkey constitute an obstacle for trade between those countries is in NFTC Report 2005.

production is a more accurate indicator, since it applies to countries which have a considerable domestic production but do not trade. A future agreement should also contain a provision specifying that countries which have reached this threshold should join in. According to the latest industry figures about 30 countries (EU = 1) would be covered by the threshold and should, therefore, be part of the sectoral tariff elimination agreement.

As to exceptions, the ICCA follows the CTHA format and suggests product coverage (chs HS 28–39) without exceptions. Flexibility will be introduced by distinguishing between CTHA and non-CTHA members and through phasing, that is, the elimination of tariffs in three steps: CTHA countries should eliminate their chemical tariffs within five years, countries not participating in CTHA should reduce their tariffs within ten years for tariffs which are lower than 25 per cent and within 15 years for those which are higher than 25 per cent. The reductions should be accomplished annually. Special and differential treatment will be acknowledged by the $3 billion threshold and the longer phasing period for non-CTHA members. CTHA members will have to reduce their tariffs faster than non-CTHA members and will therefore offer developing countries more market access. Furthermore, only the most important chemical producing nations would have to sign the agreement, thus leaving approximately 90 WTO members free to decide whether to join or not. ICCA supports the idea of a 'round for free' for the least developed countries.

The sectoral negotiations have not yet progressed very far. In July 2005 several countries suggested the elimination of chemical tariffs.[27] They elaborated on their suggestions in 2006.[28] Given the suspension of the negotiations decided in July 2006 it is subject to speculation whether the WTO will be able to conclude the NAMA negotiations and indeed the whole DDA round successfully. Too many deadlines have been missed so far and the political will to liberalise trade further is still lacking. Also, even if the DDA is concluded, it is not guaranteed that the results will include a chemical sector tariff elimination agreement at all, let alone its contents.

Conclusions

International agreements are negotiated and adopted by governments, not other stakeholders. In some cases these negotiations are authorised by the legislature

---

27 See WTO 2005, note 1 above; also WTO 2003, Japan's Submission on 'Zero-for-Zero' and 'Harmonisation', and WTO 2006, Communication by Singapore on an Update on the Negotiations on the Sectoral Tariff Component.

28 See for example WTO 2006a, Progress Report: Sectoral Discussions on Tariff Elimination in the Chemical Sector, Communication from the United States. This report gives an overview of the discussions held so far and of the issues of a sectoral chemical tariff elimination agreement. Also WTO 2006c, Communication on Tariff Liberalization in the Chemical Sector by Canada, Norway, Singapore, Switzerland, the Separate Customs Territory of Taiwan, Penghu, Kinmen and Matsu, and the United States.

with a negotiating mandate, in others governments have constitutional authority to negotiate. Once negotiated many international agreements have to undergo a national ratification process by which the legislature accepts the results of the negotiations and implements them, if necessary. The international agreement itself specifies when it will enter into force, often after a given number of ratifications.

A successful advocacy process accepts the roles governments and other stakeholders have in this process. The private sector and other non-governmental organisations prepare their input in order to convince governments to accept their views. They do so using substantive arguments related to the issues of the negotiations. They support their arguments with political 'weight', which governments do take into account when formulating their positions: the business community uses its economic weight, trade unions use the political power of the work force and other NGOs use their capability to shape public opinion. Yet without substance the political weight is rarely decisive even if the media would like to make us believe otherwise. Opinion-forming concerning an international issue is an iterative process which starts bottom-up and relies predominantly on substantive arguments about the issue at stake.

The two examples have shown different levels of transparency and participation of civil society in international negotiations: the open and deliberative UNEP process and the more limited WTO process which is less transparent and less participatory. Civil society has adapted its advocacy activities to the respective processes and has found a modus vivendi with both. After all, civil society aims at influencing the national governments participating in these negotiations. In an open and participatory process the views of the stakeholders are made public and are subject to public scrutiny. In a less open and less participatory process these views are made known to the government, yet they are not necessarily publicly known or discussed, let alone scrutinised. Both processes however lead to the formulation of a position which the national government has to defend publicly and for which it is held responsible and accountable.

References

BusinessEurope (2006), BusinessEurope *Position on Non-Agricultural Market Access Negotiations* at http://www.businesseurope.eu/content/default.asp?PageId=435.
CEFIC *Facts and Figures*, accessible at http://www.cefic.org/factsandfigures.
CEFIC (1999), *CEFIC Comments on a New Multilateral Trade Round*, 15 March 1999, at: http://www.cefic.be/Templates/shwPublications.asp?NID=2&T=3&S=9&P=4.
European Union (2006), REACH Regulation, EU Official Journal, L 396 of 30 December 2006.
ICCA (1991), *ICCA Position on the Joint Framework Agreement for Tariff Harmonization in the Uruguay Round*, 28 October 1991, see http://www.icca-chem.org/section06e.html.
ICCA (2005), ICCA *Market Access for the Doha Development Agenda*, May 2005, at http://www.icca-chem.org/section06e.html.

ICCA (2005a), ICCA *Position Paper on SAICM* of 9 June 2005, accessible at http://www. icca-chem.org/section06.html.

NFTC Report (2005), *Making the Case for Ambitious Tariff Cuts in the WTO's Non-agricultural Market Access Negotiations*, National Foreign Trade Council WTO Tariff Analysis Project, May 2005, see http://www.nftc.com.

Schanz, K-U. (1995), 'Der Marktzugang im WTO-Welthandelssystem: Zollsenkungen auf Industrieprodukten und Neuerungen bei den Ausgleichsmassnahmen für Dumping und Subventionen', in Cottier, T. (ed.), *GATT-Uruguay Round*, Verlag Stämpfli & Cie, Berne.

Stockholm Declaration (1972) of the Stockholm Conference on the Human Environment, accessible at http://www.unep.org/Law/PDF/Stockholm_Declaration.pdf.

UNCED (1992), Agenda 21 adopted at UN Conference on Environment and Development, accessible at http://www.un.org/esa/sustdev/documents/agenda21/english/agenda21toc. htm.

UNEP (2002), Enhancing Civil Society Engagement in the Work of the United Nations Environment Programme, Document UNEP/GD.22/INF/13 of 21 November 2002.

Van den Bosche, P. (2005), *The Law and Policy of the World Trade Organization*, Cambridge University Press, Cambridge.

WSSD (2002), Report of the World Summit on Sustainable Development, UN Document A/CONF/199/20*, accessible at http://www.un.org/doc/UNDOC/GEN/N02/636/93/ PDF/N0263693.pdf?OpenElement.

WTO (1996), Guidelines for Arrangement on Relations with Non-Governmental Organizations, Document WTO/L/62 of 23 July 1996.

WTO (2001), Minutes of the General Council Meeting of 22 November 2000, Document WTO/WT/GC/M/60 of 23 January 2001.

WTO (2001a), Doha Ministerial Declaration, Document WTO/WT/MIN(01)/DEC1 of 20 November 2001.

WTO (2003), Japan's Submission on 'Zero-for-Zero' and 'Harmonisation', Document WTO/TN/MA/W/15/Add.2 of 4 March 2003.

WTO (2004), Document WTO/WT/L/579 of 2 August 2004.

WTO (2005), Communication on Tariff Liberalization in the Chemicals Sector made by Canada, Japan, Norway, Separate Customs Territory of Taiwan, Penghu, Kinmen and Matsu, Singapore, Switzerland, and the United States, Document WTO/TN/ MA/W/58 of 4 July 2005.

WTO (2005a), Hong Kong Ministerial Declaration, Document WTO/WT/MIN(05)/DEC, of 22 December 2005.

WTO (2006), Communication by Singapore on an Update on the Negotiations on the Sectoral Tariff Component, Document WTO/TN/MA/W/8/Add.1 of 1 February 2006.

WTO (2006a), Progress Report: Sectoral Discussions on Tariff Elimination in the Chemical Sector, Communication from the United States, Document WTO/TN/MA/W/18/Add. 13 of 4 April 2006.

WTO (2006b), List of Documents, Note by the Secretariat, WTO/TN/MA/S/16/Rev.4 of 5 April 2006.

WTO (2006c), Communication on Tariff Liberalization in the Chemical Sector by Canada, Norway, Singapore, Switzerland, the Separate Customs Territory of Taiwan, Penghu, Kinmen and Matsu, and the United States, Document WTO/MA/W/72 of 15 May 2006.

Useful Websites

American Chemistry Council: http://www.americanchemistry.com.
Bundesverband der Deutschen Industrie, e.V: http://www.bdi-online.de.
Business and Industry Advisory Council (OECD): http://www.biac.org.
BusinessEurope (formerly UNICE): http://www.businesseurope.eu.
Chemical Industries Association (UK): http://www.cia.org.uk.
European Chemical Industry Council: http://www.cefic.org.
Federchimica (Italy): http://www2.federchimica.it.
Intergovernmental Forum on Chemical Safety: http://www.who.int/ifcs/en/.
International Chamber of Commerce: http://www.iccwbo.org.
International Council of Chemical Associations: http://www.icca-chem.org.
Inter-Organization Programme for the Sound Management of Chemicals: http://www.who.int/iomc/en/.
Japan Chemical Industry Association: http://www.nikkakyo.org.
Union des Industries Chimiques (France): http://www.uic.fr.
United Nations Environment Programme: http://www.unep.org.
Verband der Chemischen Industrie, e. V. (Germany): http://www.vci.de.
World Business Council for Sustainable Development: http://www.wbcsd.org.
World Summit on Sustainable Development: http://www.un.org/events/wssd/.
World Trade Organization: http://www.wto.org.

Chapter 8

Is Economic Policy Democratic? And Should It Be? Questions for NGOs

Phil Evans

One of the great clarion cries of the non-governmental world since the signing of the multilateral trade agreements of the Uruguay Round, at Marrakesh in 1994, has been that the WTO is not democratic. Allied to this is the argument that greater involvement of the NGO community in trade policy-making will enhance the democratic accountability of the WTO and will rebalance the agenda of the organisation away from a perceived bias towards corporate interests.

This statement of the situation as seen from many parts of the NGO world has become both an accepted fact among most NGOs and part of the new orthodoxy of the global trade community. Indeed, the involvement of NGOs in the trade policy system in most developed countries has increased quite markedly in the last few years. However, the manner of this involvement has tended to leave government officials and NGOs frustrated and disillusioned.

In more recent years, in some countries, the area of competition policy has emerged blinking into the civil society light in a style not dissimilar to the post-Seattle trade policy world. Of course competition policy, as a trade issue, has been the subject of much (often grossly ill-informed) debate in post-Singapore WTO Ministerials. However, competition policy is largely a domestic, or at best regional, policy arena, with some important international overflows. Like trade policy, it is an area of regulation that has been largely immune from public interest and scrutiny; and like trade policy it has only recently had to contend with the need to deal with civil society groups with agendas beyond the strictly regulatory. The frustration and disillusionment seen in trade policy have yet to be replicated fully in competition policy, although it can be argued this is largely because the contact has been so recent.

In discussing the nature of the relationship between democracy and economic policy it is useful to compare trade policy, a largely international policy arena with domestic overlaps, with competition policy, a largely national policy arena with international overlaps. To chart these relationships one has to first ask a number of basic questions. One has to identify the sort of politics that economic politics is; one has to find out whether economic politics is national, regional or global politics; and one has to see how the answers to these questions have changed over time.

What Sort of Politics is Economic Politics?

The notion of democratic accountability is very much like the fable of the six blind men and the elephant – everyone feels a small part of the beast and thinks it to be a different creature; one feels the trunk and thinks it to be a snake; one the leg and thinks it to be a tree. Democratic accountability is similar in that some will see it only in the representation of people through the ballot box; some will grasp it and see it only when their interest group manages to persuade a government of a particular policy; yet more will see it when a government minister bows to 'popular pressure'.

Of course for the purists democracy is 'a system of government by the whole population, usually through elected representatives'.[1] This is hardly an earthshaking definition. However, it is probably the most widely accepted definition and one that places the locus of democracy and accountability in the elected representatives of the populace voting under universal suffrage. However, such a basic, and rather rose-tinted-spectacle view of democratic accountability fails to take into account that rather important element of the process: politics.

Democracy and Politics

The manner in which politics evolves from the democratic will of a people is far from straightforward. What is clear from the study of the real world operation of politics is that it does not play by some form of model set of rules. Real world politics is a far cry from the 'Mr Smith Goes to Washington' view of the world. Again, this is not a particularly new view of politics. However, it is important to identify exactly what we are dealing with in economic policy if we are to trace its links to democratic accountability. It is also important because of the vision of democratic accountability that is espoused (consciously or unconsciously) by commentators in this debate.

What has clearly emerged in the last 30 years of the study of regulation and politics is that it is a terribly messy affair. Interestingly, and appropriately for this issue, most of the best work on the complications of modern politics has occurred in the United States. Two of the most interesting issues in this modern literature of regulation and politics are the role of the interest group and the different 'types' of politics that are found in modern democratic discourse. In relation to trade policy a dual approach is needed. One has to first heed the literature on interest groups and then apply it to the type of politics that is found in the realm of trade policy.

The accumulated scholarship on the relationship of interest groups and politics is best summed up in the US Annual Report of the Council of Economic Advisers of 1994:

---

1 Oxford English Dictionary, online edition.

> As recognised by both the framers of the Constitution and modern scholars of public choice, all political systems provide interest groups with an incentive for 'rent-seeking' that is, manipulation of collective action for private benefit ... [Rent seeking] can lead government agencies to make decisions that benefit a particular interest group even though they are costly to society as a whole. (Zajac 1995)

This model of the interest group as a rent seeking body is common in the literature and indeed is common in most political systems. In trade policy the great Jagdish Bhagwati has taken this approach further and coined the term 'directly unproductive profit-seeking' activity in relation to the seeking of trade protection by industry (Bhagwati and Srinvasan 1982).

In competition policy the notion of rent seeking activity is intrinsic to the operation of the system. Just as trade policy has tended to exclude agriculture (for example) from its purview, so competition policy has seen certain sectors, over time, excluded from its remit. Such exclusions have tended to take the form of specific exemptions from laws for a sector. Thus in the US the collective selling of sports rights, and indeed other aspects of sports markets, are explicitly excluded from competition law. In Europe exclusions range from the outright (agricultural cooperatives in certain forms) through the broad (until recently liner conferences) to the more narrow (specific rules for the distribution of new cars). These exclusions have come about because of the capture of the political or legislative process by vested interests.

It has to be pointed out that the rent seeking interest group is broadly defined. When one hears of civil society and interest groups today one tends to only hear of them in a 'public interest' sense. It has to be noted that there are enormous difficulties with the term 'public interest': who defines it, who classifies the means of promoting the 'public good' and how is such a definition influenced? What is clear from the literature on regulation is that the definition of interest group is sufficiently broad to include the business community. Indeed, one can argue that the definition requires the inclusion of the business community; for without the business world the creation of trade policy is a little like Hamlet without the Prince.

Indeed the term 'public interest' has very different meanings if one considers it in a competition policy environment rather than a trade policy one. During much of the post war development of European competition policy the regime was charged with protecting the public interest. Unfortunately, the public interest largely became a cover for protectionism. It became a handy shroud to cover the need to restrict competition for the benefit of a merging firm or a practice clearly against the consumer interest, but that could be excused as having 'wider' ramifications. The most specious of these perhaps came in the many investigations into the distribution of perfumes. Perfume firms argued that they needed control over their distribution arms to maintain the correct 'ambience' for their products. Such an ambience, of course, could not be maintained in supermarkets or other stores likely to discount the products. Here, the public interest in maintaining a business model based on exclusivity was clearly at odds with a consumers' economic interest or right to choice.

Perhaps the most insightful (and useful) application of the interest group model of politics is found in the work of James Q. Wilson (Wilson 1980). Wilson's model of political activity fits neatly into a four part box reproduced in Figure 8.1 below.

	COSTS	
	Concentrated	**Diffuse**
BENEFITS		
Concentrated	Interest group politics	Client politics
	Controversy/	*Government action*
	uncertain government action	
Diffuse	Entrepreneurial politics	Majoritarian politics
	Government action	*Uncertain government action*

Figure 8.1   Models of politics

The enormous benefit of the Wilsonian approach is that politics is divided along two axes: the benefits and costs. It is clear that in political activity one always seeks to derive a benefit (be it a specific one or societal one) and for this to occur another group must suffer some form of loss. The beauty of the Wilson model is that one can divide up the types of political activity that one sees in day to day life.

Concentrated Benefits and Concentrated Costs

When one sees set piece battles between interest groups over a policy, one can observe this model clearly in play. The battle becomes controversial as the benefits and costs are both concentrated on specific groups of interest. Such a type of politics leads to heated debates and genuine battles for the ear of the government. Here government action is not certain and will hinge on the success of one party over another. Such battles can occur in areas such as laws governing agriculture, where farmers and retailers fight it out over regulatory issues. More recently such fights have occurred in the United States between producers of steel and their consumers (like car makers). These sorts of battles are classic examples of 'interest group' politics.

In competition policy the model is slightly more complex as parties often battle before an independent regulatory body. Indeed every merger case involving an oligopolistic industry is likely to trigger third parties in the industry to express an 'interest' in not seeing the merger happen. Mergers are thus likely to follow an interest group model, with large sums of money being spent on lawyers and economists to argue the case for and against a particular merger. While trade policy sees a politician balance the domestic interest group battle opposite another politician doing the same, in competition policy the judge of the interest group battle is either literally a judge, in the US for example, or has a fairly tight set of administrative and legal rules by which he or she can judge the case.

Concentrated Benefits and Diffuse Costs

This sort of political activity centres around a small group that derives enormous benefit from a policy, but can pass on the cost to a very large number of other citizens in small increments. This model of politics tends to lead to 'client politics' where the governmental actor is 'captured' by the interest group that seizes the benefit of regulation. All agricultural policies in the developed world are clear examples of client politics – the very, very few (farmers) capture huge gains at the expense of the great majority (the consumer).

In competition policy the problem of regulatory 'capture' tends to be most acute in regulated industries. These industries, primarily in the utility and telecommunications sectors, tend to have been in state control until relatively recently. In recent memory it is also true that at a European level a number of powerful industries, such as liner shipping and automotive retailing, for example, managed to have their anti-competitive activities sanctioned by the competition regulator.

Diffuse Benefits and Diffuse Costs

This model of politics is closer to the Frank Capra view of life than any of the others. Here, operating under 'majoritarian politics' the benefits and costs are so evenly spread and small that society and politicians can debate the greater good of society and engage in discussion across political lines. The sorts of issues amenable to such activities tend to be almost entirely social and moral in nature. Of course, in a zero sum game world of political activity (where only so many parliamentary hours exist), such policy debates can be squeezed out by client and interest group political issues.

Concentrated Costs and Diffuse Benefits

The 'entrepreneurial' model of politics is perhaps the most interesting one for interest groups to run. Here a cost is borne by a very small segment of the society and the benefits that accrue from this policy are small and evenly spread. The manner in which such a campaign is run is a challenge to any interest group. The clearest examples of such policies are those in the environmental field. The Climate Change Levy introduced in Britain, for example, imposes a large cost on a very small number of players (heavy industrial firms) and produces a small benefit to almost everyone (cleaner air). Wilson argues that the only effective means of running and winning such a battle is for the interest group proposing the policy to appeal to broad societal mores and ethical principles.

So Where Does Economic Policy Fit In?

The Importance of History

One of the core problems of the current debate about trade policy and democracy is its ahistorical nature. Most participants in the debate are both new to trade policy and profoundly ignorant of where trade policy has come from. I would argue that to fully understand the relationship of trade policy to politics one has to take a broad historical view. As so often, the current debate about trade policy starts with the passing of the 1930 Tariff Act, better known as the Smoot-Hawley Act. Smoot-Hawley is important for two main reasons. Firstly, it became associated with the deepening of the US depression (already underway by 1930, but exacerbated by the collapse in trade following the Tariff Act) and thence with World War II. Secondly, it was the last general tariff-raising act of its kind. The raising of tariff levels collectively to 60 per cent of the value of imports triggered retaliatory action on the part of US trading partners and a collapse in world trade.

The link between the Smoot-Hawley Act and the onset of World War II is a controversial one. However, this is not actually very important for the purposes of this argument. What is important is that the legislators of the day, and their descendants to this day, saw a link between radically increased protectionism, economic conflict and military conflict. For those legislators emerging from World War II the desire to avoid any repeat of Smoot-Hawley was a significant one.

In many ways Smoot-Hawley was a high watermark for a certain style of US trade policy. Indeed, Smoot-Hawley was the last in a series of very specific tariff raising laws that had set the tone of trade law and policy for a little over a century. The level of specific tariffs had been one of the key battleground political issues in that preceding century and reflected the Congressional centrality in the making of trade policy. However, while the tale of the century to 1930 had been one of Congressional centrality and high tariffs, the tale begun just four years later led in completely the opposite direction.

By 1934 the United States had begun negotiating reciprocal trade agreements with other countries aimed at reducing tariffs and stimulating trade. The Reciprocal Trade Agreements Act of 1934 is likewise important for two key reasons. Firstly, it indicated a desire of the US to undo the damage of the Smoot-Hawley Act of 1930 and secondly, it was the first statement by Congress that it wished to withdraw from specific trade policy formation.

The 1934 Act authorised the executive to reduce tariffs on items of interest to trading partners by up to 50 per cent without recourse to Congress. This authority was repeatedly reaffirmed right up to the 1970s. The US Congress had effectively withdrawn itself from the setting of tariffs. It has to be remembered that constitutionally Congress has the sole authority over trade policy; what the 1934 Act clearly indicated was that Congress could not trust itself to do the job. The self-awareness in Congress, that they could not trust themselves to do the job properly, lasted for little over 50 years. During that time the US trade policy community established a network of institutions and mechanisms designed to place a buffer between the politicians and the making and implementing of trade policy.

This process reached its apogee in the first granting of 'fast-track' trade authorisation in 1974. Under fast-track, when the Administration submitted a trade agreement for ratification, Congress could accept it or reject it, but could not amend it. The granting of fast-track grew from the general tariff authorisation of the 1934 Act and extended it to new negotiating areas to reflect the increased importance of non-tariff barriers. Fast-track allowed the President and his executive to negotiate trade agreements within parameters without fear that Congress would pick apart each element of the deal and add pet projects or scupper particular bits. What has happened of late is that the idea of fast-track has come under attack for not reflecting the 'will of the people' and, following the furore over NAFTA, has become a hot political issue.

The idea that there is a politics of competition policy is less well accepted. Indeed there are only a few political scientists who study competition policy in any serious manner. However, if one charts the origins of competition law and policy one sees a profoundly political system of regulation. While competition policy has been around for some considerable time its modern incarnation is usually traced to the US Sherman Act of 1890. This first modern encapsulation was very much a creature of its time and even the term antitrust refers to the efforts of Congress to control the large 'trusts' or monopolistic firms that were controlling much of the commerce of the period. Indeed the passing of the Sherman Act can, at least in part, be seen as a response to a rural revolt against what was perceived as the perfidy of urban industrial conglomerates. This rural revolt was taken on in Canada and Australia, two of the next countries to adopt the modern incarnation of competition law. It is notable that in the European region competition law came late, and indeed in many countries has only really arrived in the last decade.

Economic Politics Today

The current state of US trade politics has come about for a number of reasons. Firstly, the early 1990s saw a removal of a large number of 'old-style' free traders from US politics. These politicians were steeped in the post-war consensus that equated protectionism with conflict. This group of politicians had constructed the edifice of US trade policy that buffered the policy from undue political influence, for the good of the world. Secondly, these politicians were increasingly likely to be replaced by a more populist model of politician, in many ways harking back to the turn of the century populism of such figures as William Jennings Bryan. This cohort did not share the same world-view as their predecessors; the consensus for freer trade was starting to break down.

This breakdown of the consensus that viewed freer trade as a public good came about at the same time as trade policy itself started to focus on matters of domestic regulation. What is also important about this shift is that the political consensus in favour of trade allowed politicians to champion freer trade and extol its virtues in a public interest manner. With the withdrawal of the political elite from support of freer trade it was left largely to corporate bodies to argue in favour of the benefits of trade. One of the key problems with this is that they tend to do so only when it favours their particular interest. Some argue against freer trade when it suits them (textiles and steel spring to mind) and their involvement signals to opposing forces that they were right all along to think of trade policy as a creature of industry.

The importance of the United States as a driver in world trade cannot be overemphasised. There is no way on earth that the GATT could have been conceived and nurtured without the support of the US. The strategic interests of the United States allowed the GATT to grow and prosper, at some cost to the US in traditional tariff terms. The evolution of US trade policy also occurred directly alongside the evolution of the GATT. So what, one may ask, of other democratic regimes? In the US democratic politics and trade politics were buffered from each other for the good of the world. Democratic politicians recognised that they would damage the greater good if they sought to influence trade policy too directly. In Europe, a similar situation occurred. The great compact of the European Community, and later the European Union, established a complex web of internal negotiations and debates around the Article 113 (now 133) Committee. This web of negotiations acted as a typically European buffer between politicians and trade policy. The regular committee of officials kept the wheels of trade policy oiled and spinning and sought to resolve the core problems of EU trade policy in a totally non-transparent and opaque manner. However, this, again, was done for the best of reasons.

Unlike in the United States, European trade policy has been as much a creature of professional administrators as it has been of politicians. Many of the major trade policy questions were 'settled' a century before the US reached its freer trade consensus. The political consensus on trade thus became embedded in the culture of the administrative system. In the UK, the general tendency towards freer trade is built into the collective culture of the civil service. In France, the desire to protect the farm community (and, it has to be said, almost any industry!) is deeply embedded in the French view of the State and the role of 'la belle France'. The longevity and stability of the trade policy community left the European administration of trade policy to evolve as a meeting of officialdom, rather than as a matter of major political controversy. Bodies like the Article 113 Committee became the embodiment of the awkward consensus of administrators and the implicit statement that politicians did not, and should not, be too heavily involved in trade policy for fear that they would unravel all of the good work of the previous century or so.

In this area competition policy faces a similar set of problems. The desire of certain states to protect specific industries – be they microelectronics or yoghurt – is perhaps at its most difficult in antitrust. Whereas trade policy has specific mechanisms that allow industries to be hived off from liberalisation or traded off for larger gains, it is in competition law and policy that these exemptions face most domestic difficulty. Thus, for example, if a country wishes to support or protect an industry against international competition it can erect some barriers at the border to facilitate this, but will find it much more difficult to erect barriers internally. In Europe, this problem is more acute with restrictions on the use of what is termed 'state aid', where countries grant subsidies or other benefits to firms for investing in certain locations. The fact that such policies are part of competition policy is unique to Europe. In other jurisdictions there are no such controls on whether a local state or city wishes to pay incentives to firms for investing in certain locations.

This is not to say that modern competition law is uniform. In the US there is considerable controversy about how to treat what are termed 'unilateral effects'. These effects are created by individual firms that are, in European terms, in a dominant position. The sort of activities looked at tend to be those that exclude competitors from normal market activities through the erection of barriers to entry or forcing rivals out of business. There has been quite a strong movement in the US to downplay the impact of such activity. The movement has its origins in the 1970s revolt against the state in US economics, and the rise of what is loosely called the Chicago School. The movement argued that the state was often a poor umpire of market activities and needed to be reined in. In contrast corporate activity was viewed as being largely benign and there was increasing pressure to halt government interventions in the marketplace. This form of laissez-faire or perhaps more accurately laissez-passer reached its political peak in the first Reagan administration. The beachhead created in that administration for a more pro-market regulatory regime had a profound effect on antitrust policy and enforcement in the US as it allowed the gradual replacement of more interventionist judges and officials with those more willing to allow firms to engage in what they viewed as 'normal' conduct. Of course such a move did not remove entirely the desire of officials to engage in antitrust enforcement. One could argue that it diverted some of that desire to the state level, where local officials have become more involved in antitrust work, or into the private bar where class action antitrust lawyers have become more aggressive in pursuing damages claims.

In Europe the evolution of modern competition law has been more complicated given the divergent legal traditions in play. What is termed the ordo-liberal tradition in Germany held sway in Brussels during much of the early years of the European Commission. This tradition was much more focused on the law and its interpretation rather than on the economic effect of rules. The US influence on a more economics focused competition law started to have an impact on Europe during the late 1990s and early 2000s. This more 'Anglo-Saxon' view of competition law emerged as economics took a greater hold on the competition enforcement community.

What is quite telling in the European discussions is the fact that the economics debates that were heavily framed by the political shifts that occurred across the western world in the late 1970s onwards, have appeared in Europe in a largely technocratic form. What, at times, were quite ideologically couched debates on single firm conduct in the US, became largely technical discussions in Europe on how to measure exclusionary behaviour or consumer welfare. Indeed that latter term has come to represent to some elements of the US debate a charged term of the Chicago School, while in Europe it has come to signal a strand in the effort to move away from the ordo-liberal legal tradition.

The Evolution of Economic Policy

The idea that trade policy in the United States and Europe was explicitly (in the US) and implicitly (in Europe) removed from politicians for the general good places the current debate in context. Freer trade was seen as the public good that the trading system was there to advance. The administrations of the United States and Europe needed to protect this public good against the viler intentions of the interest groups that would seek to capture the rents from dismantling that public good.

The view of the trading system as the public good in need of protecting fits rather neatly into the Wilsonian box. The century of trade policy prior to Smoot-Hawley in the US was a century of client politics. US politicians recognised that, unchecked, the trading system's benefits would be captured by small interest groups (specific industries like tobacco, textiles, steel and so on) to the disbenefit of the US public and other less well organised industries. Trade policy as client politics was clearly seen as a thing to be avoided. However, the creation of the policy buffer also required the installation of some pressure valves. These pressure valves allowed those seeking protection (and there are always industries seeking protection!) to be channelled through policies like anti-dumping and anti-subsidy laws and later on through trade adjustment assistance for communities. What started to happen during the 1960s and beyond was the emergence of countervailing forces that contested the use of pressure valves. These forces were mainly those of the consuming industries. For example, the seeking of protection by the steel industry (a regular occurrence) started to be met with opposition from industries that imported steel. Trade policy thus evolved from being primarily a client politics system, filtered through buffers and pressure valves, into an interest group system that made outcomes less clear. It has to be noted that in some areas, such as agricultural trade, policy has barely moved from its client politics status!

One of the other key developments in trade policy occurred from the 1970s onwards. The Kennedy and Tokyo Rounds of trade negotiations started to deal with non-tariff issues. One of the results of this was to require broader trade negotiating authorisation from Congress (fast-track). But a longer-term implication involved the type of politics that trade politics would now become. Non-tariff barriers (NTBs) involve a huge range of issues from the simple to spot protectionist wheeze (France directing unwelcome imports to the single customs post at Poitiers) to more troublesome regulatory issues such as labelling of foodstuffs. The ticking off of the simple NTBs during the 1980s and 1990s cut away the obvious problem areas. However, it also started to involve trade policy more directly with national regulatory systems. The response of the trade community was, quite naturally, to apply the clinical methodology of the previous decades to the issues in hand. However, the clinical technocratic world view fitted very poorly with the more complex manner in which domestic policy was formed.

The technocratic approach is fine if you are dealing with client politics regulation – where an industry has gained benefit at the expense of consumers and where this can be dismantled in return for the dismantling of a reciprocal rule abroad. However, as trade negotiations at a global level clung to the diplomatically based reciprocal mercantilism of the past, its agenda was being plunged into the murky world of entrepreneurial and majoritarian politics. While the system could handle interest group politics reasonably well through its vestigial mercantilism, it found itself completely nonplussed by a model of regulation based on majoritarian or entrepreneurial politics. If you look at some of the key problems raised by NGOs in relation to the WTO and its remit and the role of trade policy, one finds a huge number of issues that are majoritarian in nature (where costs and benefits are diffuse) or entrepreneurial (where costs are concentrated and benefits diffuse). The cornerstone issues of the environment, health, welfare and consumer protection are all areas where interest groups have either fought and won battles to impose costs on business to the general good (such as climate change levies and product safety laws), or where complex societal debates have been resolved in compromise positions (many of the developed world health systems in operation).

In competition policy terms the evolution has followed a similar path – up to a point. Competition law in many jurisdictions had flexibility built into it through the use of the 'public interest' or similar test. This test meant that decisions had to be aimed at protecting the public interest. The looseness of this term allowed a good deal of latitude for enforcers and some rather peculiar decisions were made as a result. The public interest test gave enforcers a degree of latitude in some ways similar to that enjoyed by trade negotiators in the days of the more diplomatically based system. When faced with a 'problem' they could use the public interest to resolve that problem by making a decision that normally they would not do. This allowed the system to deal with political pressure or societal concerns in a way that a more juridical system could not.

Since the late 1990s most competition systems have moved, like the WTO after the Uruguay Round, to a more juridical system. Gone is the public interest, to be replaced by a consumer welfare test; departing is dominance, to be replaced by exclusionary conduct; gone is creating or strengthening dominance through merger, to be replaced by significant lessening of competition. What has not gone, however, is that which triggered the need for the wider public interest test.

The WTO moved from a diplomatically-driven, mercantilist bid-offer system to a juridical, mercantilist market access regime. Competition policy moved from a flexible regulatory compliance based regime to a more judicial enforcement based regime. In both cases the regimes removed some flexibility in favour of certainty. Both regimes did this without fully comprehending the impact of this change on the incentive regime such a shift entailed.

Where Do We Go From Here?

If one looks at the relationship between trade policy and mechanisms for democratic accountability from a historical perspective one is struck by the fact that the link was strongest when protectionism was at its most damaging. This has to be borne in mind when calls for greater 'democratic' control of trade policy are voiced. Trade policy is a considerably more complex beast than it was prior to the formation of the GATT. Indeed, there is no longer one simple model of politics that trade policy fits within. In some areas, most notably agriculture, steel and textiles, the old-fashioned client politics is still strong. In other areas the rise of the countervailing force has created a much greater area of political contestability. In others still the more complex realms of entrepreneurial and majoritarian politics butt up against a system of trade negotiation still structured around dealing with client politics at least and interest group politics at most.

One of the great ironies of this new engagement of the trading community with issues of complex domestic regulation is that, at the very time when an appeal to the public good is required to advance an agenda of freer trade, the political consensus in support of that public good has evaporated or is in retreat. The legitimacy of the trading system is under greater scrutiny than at any other time in its history. Prior to the injection of the trading system into the area of domestic regulation, the legitimacy of the GATT sprang from the diplomatic nature of negotiations. The signing of treaties on behalf of a citizenry based on a reciprocal exchange of trade concessions suited a tariff-based model very well. However, with the signing of the Uruguay Round this diplomatic process, with significant leeway built in for states, was replaced with a highly juridical process based on binding interpretation of often vague laws.

The system of regulation at the WTO thus became much more akin to a nation state; citizens (members) signed up to all laws in return for protection against transgressors and acceptance that punishment could be meted out if they themselves transgressed. However, unlike a nation state the WTO did not develop a governing administration that reflected the job in hand, nor did it establish (nor could it) legislative arms that were able to reflect the will of its citizens. The WTO was left lopsided, with a binding constitution negotiated primarily by a very small number of members, a theoretically strong judicial arm, but no legislative or administrative heart. The unwillingness of members to change the WTO into anything other than the GATT writ large has left the legitimacy of the GATT stretched to breaking point and beyond in trying to accommodate the broadened agenda and judicial structure of new treaties.

As argued above the more juridical shift in trade policy was mirrored in competition law and policy. The removal of the public interest and its replacement with a focus on a more economically literate consumer welfare test was viewed at the time as a tidying up of the area. What was not foreseen was the fact that the gradual removal of competition policy from the political realm did not mean the removal of politics from competition policy. The gradual realisation of the shift in trade policy occurred within around three or so years after the signing of the Uruguay Round. While most significant legal reforms in competition policy can be traced to the turn of the millennium, the reinvolvement of politics has taken a little longer. The reinjection of politics has occurred alongside a slew of cases involving large firms with a transnational dimension. This has particularly been the case involving inquiries into the supermarket retailing sectors. The inquiries in these areas have seen activists from the trade arena enter the competition arena to try to curtail the activities of large retail firms. We have also seen alliances formed between different parties to engage directly with the competition enforcement process.

What is troubling for the competition community is the fact that they have never really had to deal with a concerted effort from civil society before and are ill-suited to engage with them. The regulatory community has, until recently, been a relatively small and closed world. A good deal of this closure was caused by the technical nature of the discussion and the skillset needed to engage in this debate. What is interesting in the recent incursion of civil society into the competition field is not that the community has widened, more that different camps have been formed. While civil society engaged fairly early on with the concepts of trade policy with relative ease, it has not really attempted to do so with competition policy. Instead it has chosen to cast the narrowing of the overview of competition policy as part of the problem – thus the focus on consumer welfare is seen as too narrow. In essence the new forces of civil society engagement have tended to favour a return to a looser, more flexible public interest test that would allow their wider concerns over the environmental or social welfare to be superimposed on a competition law investigation.

The position we are left with in both trade and competition policy is little more than a mess. The trade and competition communities have avoided, or moved away from, democratic control for good reasons. In both cases the position was based on democratically elected politicians accepting that the real world of politics meant that they would succumb to the basest of instincts and damage the greater good for their citizens by interfering in trade or competition issues. This worked well for as long as the realms of trade and competition policy were those of the tariff level, the blatantly protectionist rule or regulation or the simple merger or abuse of dominance. As long as economic policy focused on this it was safe from an unravelling of legitimacy. However, the agendas of trade and competition politics have moved increasingly toward domestic and regional regulation; and the interest of civil society has moved ever nearer to the existing economic tools of the state. It is at this point that the consensus on the greater good of freer trade and freer markets runs up against the consensus on the greater good of social protection, cultural values and protective, rather than protectionist, regulation. As trade policy appears to have run into the sands of domestic regulation a new orthodoxy has emerged. Central to that orthodoxy, alongside the need to overload the trading system with all manner of social democratic objectives held dear only in Europe, is that civil society has a rightful place at the heart of trade policy-making. At the same time competition policy has found the public interest arguments, long thought dead, making a comeback in important areas of their oversight. The new orthodoxy across economic policy that civil society must be closely involved is starting to move from the trade to the competition regime. However, while this orthodoxy has some important truth to it, it has three major drawbacks.

Civil Society and Economic Politics

The greatest opponents of the WTO tend to come from civil society groups in developed countries. This is not to say that those in developing countries are supportive. This is more a statement about resources and profile. Part of the argument of these groups is that trade policy and the WTO are undemocratic. As a result there is demand for greater access and openness in the trade system to allow civil society to have more influence on talks.

There are a number of core problems with this argument. Firstly, the WTO is an organisation of states. As argued above, the WTO was established without effective legislative mechanisms and without a powerful executive. The power in the WTO thus rests entirely with its membership. Prior to the Seattle WTO meeting of late 1999, this effectively meant the Quad members (United States, European Union, Japan and Canada), a couple of middle ranking developed countries and a few large developing ones. Most other countries were observers only. The lack of representation on the part of developing countries can be viewed as either a profound structural problem in the WTO or as a failure of those countries to take advantage of the powers that they had. It would appear, first from Seattle and then from the Doha WTO meeting of 2001, that the developing countries are increasingly using the powers that they do have. From a blocking stance at Seattle they have already moved to a more proactive stance in demanding policies. This would tend to suggest that the problem is more attitudinal than structural. This is not to suggest that there are not real resourcing issues at stake, particularly in Geneva, but it does indicate that the solution to the 'democratic deficit' at the WTO is more in the hands of members than previously argued.

A second problem with the demands of some vocal elements of civil society for greater involvement in trade policy is the issue of democratic accountability itself. It has to be noted that some of the NGOs most critical of the 'undemocratic' nature of trade policy are hardly models of democratic accountability themselves. NGOs range in their accountability mechanisms enormously. Some are market driven with their accountability coming from their ability to extract money from subscribers. Some are relatively safely funded by large (usually corporate funded) foundations and have relatively few active supporters. Many of the foundation funded groups tend to operate on a principle close to the old democratic centralism manner of organisation – the centre controls and directs and the members follow. Others still are little more than one person bands.

It has to be said that this is not meant to be an attack on the provenance of NGOs per se, nor is it meant to be an attack on the structure of those organisations. Very often the manner of organisation best suits the function of that body. A purely single issue campaigning organisation with a clear target does not need to engage in a good deal of internal debate to know what to do. The observation is more meant to indicate two things. Firstly, anyone raising the issue of democratic accountability or democratic deficits does so at their peril. The old adage about people in glass houses not throwing stones comes to mind. If you raise the issue of someone else's accountability then you have to accept that someone will eventually ask you about your own. Secondly, there is a significant problem of groups acting on 'behalf' of others. This is particularly true for those that seek to 'represent' the voices of developing country peoples. Assuming democratic governance, then the most obvious representative of those people is the government negotiating on their behalf at trade rounds. If one looks at the policy stances of some NGOs that seek to 'represent' the views of the developing world, then one often finds that policies are advanced that act against the interests of those countries. For example, a number of groups seek, on the one hand, to claim that the developing world is not listened to enough while, on the other, promoting policies like a social clause that those very countries oppose wholeheartedly.

The third reason why one needs to be at least sceptical about all demands for greater access relates to the very reason why democratically elected politicians sought to distance trade policy from themselves. Client and interest group politics dictates that those that seek protection will have the greatest incentive to advance their interests and probably the best resources to do so. The buffers and pressure valves have at least managed to channel that demand for protection down certain administrative alleys. Opening up the entire process and handing control back to elected politicians displays a worrying naivety on the part of those seeking to protect the public good. Ironically the best way of advancing the public good is to control the process of access and accountability to insulate the system from the forces of protectionism. In the same manner that one would not want the economic regulation of the telecommunications, water or gas markets voted on by members of parliament on a regular basis, so one should not have the economic regulation of trade controlled on a day to day basis by those in whose private interests it would be to undermine that system.

While competition policy shares two of the above problems, the lack of accountability of civil society groups and the need to remove politicians from the regulatory process, it does not have the issue of national members to deal with. Each system of competition regulation tends to be vested in a body, or number of bodies, with some degree of autonomy from the state. While some degree of political control is ensured through appointment processes and budgetary rounds, many authorities enjoy a significant degree of political autonomy.

Resolving Economic Policy Politics

Given that the evolving orthodoxy about the 'democratic deficit' in the trading and competition regulation system appears to be both naive and ahistorical, one has to ask how one resolves the issue satisfactorily. The question must be answered at both the national and international level.

At the national level it has to be recognised that the system for making trade policy has to be reformed, rather than totally restructured. The buffer and pressure valve mechanisms have to be slowly reformed to make the former stronger and the latter weaker. However, the job of defining the public interest has to be, in the main part, the job of the political class. The elected political class has the ability, through election and through parliamentary scrutiny, to decide if the consensus on trade policy is the right one or not. The direction and scope of trade policy is best influenced through this process. Artificially created 'consultation' processes are rarely productive and tend to promise more than they can deliver. The established governmental mechanisms of policy consultation and parliamentary scrutiny should certainly form the core of future deliberations. The problem here lies in those countries without any formal process of consultation at all. Here national mechanisms must be a priority and their establishment should be a key objective for the post-Doha world.

For competition policy new mechanisms have to be established to allow the 'public interest' to be expressed or taken care of, without undermining the functioning of the competition policy system itself. Trade policy has, for many years, had to deal with such a problem and has developed a series of 'flanking policies' that it can use to deflect protectionist tendencies. It has to be noted that many of these flanking policies are simply other areas of government policy that can be repackaged to appear to be part of a joined-up system of governance to alleviate a wider concern. However, there are also policy areas, like anti-dumping and countervailing duty processes that can be used to divert protectionist forces into complex and time consuming investigations; and areas like trade adjustment assistance and regional aid policy that can be used to buy room for trade policy to make deals that would otherwise be unpopular. In competition policy regulators are left with a limited range of options that force them to respond to demands for wider action with a metaphorical shrug of the shoulders – 'it's outside my competence'. This can work well in areas with limited externalities from a decision or sector. For example, a simple merger in an intermediate goods industry may throw up few transition issues for the sector and few societal impacts. However, mergers in the supermarket sector, or accusations of the abuse of a dominant position, may have spillovers in terms of access for consumers in rural areas, buyer power and the difficulty of firms accessing shelf space. Many of these concerns will have solutions that lie beyond the scope of the competition regulator and at present, that regulator can only point that out. For the sanctity of the system a mechanism, or a number of mechanisms, must be developed to allow competition regulators to keep their limited focus while at the same time providing a route to those unhappy with this limited view to take their concerns elsewhere. There also needs to be greater coordination across regulators to work together to deal with particular problems. Currently regulators place greater priority on avoiding treading on each others' regulatory toes rather than on cajoling each other to solve difficult problems.

At the international level the solution for the WTO is actually pretty straightforward. First, one has to accept that there is a realm of transnational decision-making that requires greater legitimacy and interaction with representative organisations of civil society. Secondly, one has to accept that civil society, in the enlightenment meaning of the term, includes the business community. Thirdly, one has to accept that for transnational accountability very strict rules will have to be adopted about those seeking enhanced consultative status. Here there are lessons from other international organisations. The WTO could easily develop the rules used by the UN for Category 1 status before them.

Here, firstly, organisations have to have proper internal mechanisms of democratic accountability and financing. Secondly, they have to have true representative status in a number of different regions of the world. Third, they have to have an interest in and be supportive of the organisations that they seek to influence. At present there are only around forty or so organisations with Category 1 status. Not all of these will have sufficient interest in trade to wish to apply for an equivalent status at the WTO.

Competition policy has a slightly easier international problem to deal with, mainly because no-one has noticed their international gatherings that much. However, at an international level bodies like the International Competition Network have to spend a good deal more time and effort working on best practice guidelines for dealing with civil society and should begin a workstream on how to deal with flanking policies to support effective competition enforcement.

Conclusion

The relationship between trade policy and democratic accountability has rarely been a straightforward one. When it was, it was disastrous for the world economy and the stability of global politics. Democratically elected politicians the world over have tended to place buffers and pressure valves between themselves and trade policy. This has been done with the best intentions, so as to avoid returning to petty protectionism and losses in world welfare. Demanding that these mechanisms are dismantled to allow greater 'democratic' control are dangerous. When these demands mean that trade policy will be handed back to those who wanted it as far away from them as possible, then the recipe is for disaster or instability. When the demand is really for unelected non-governmental organisations to be given greater control, then demands must be made of those groups to explain their own democratic legitimacy.

The WTO has seen the legitimacy of the GATT stretched beyond breaking point. The first solution to this problem is for the developing world to be given, and to take, the power that they have always had on paper. This is starting to happen, as the events of Seattle and Doha indicate. This has to be helped through real funding of offices for developing countries in Geneva and by developing countries themselves prioritising trade policy within their administrative budgets. However, it can also be aided by establishing very tight criteria for non-governmental groups to seek greater access at the WTO itself. Such groups should be given special access and rights to be heard before panels, but not the right to engage in negotiations. In a contract based organisation only those that will be bound by rules should be able to write those rules.

In the longer term the real legitimacy of the WTO will need to come under scrutiny. The 'democratic deficit' in trade policy is there for a good reason; the trick is to ensure that the forces of protectionism are not unleashed in the quest for a democratic nirvana; the good must not be sacrificed on the altar of the perfect. Reform must be made to bring the system into line with the new demands of the trade agenda; however that reform must be done progressively and slowly to ensure that it is not misused.

In the longer term also the deeper problems of the WTO system will have to be addressed. One has to ask whether a judicial system is appropriate for a diplomatically structured round of negotiations. The proper realm of decision-making in trade policy and economic regulation has not been settled by the creation of the WTO; if anything it has been confused further. Here the experience of the European Union holds out some hope. The experience of European integration has been one of increasing harmonisation accompanied by greater devolution and the establishment of opt-outs, carve-outs and pressure valves. If such a system can operate in the region with the greatest economic integration, why can't it be applied globally?

The problems faced by the trade community should be studied closely by the competition world. The forces that have contributed to a slowing of the trade agenda are wheeling around to look more closely at issues of competition regulation. The twin desires to restrict the activities of transnational corporations while at the same time turning their power to the service of social and environmental agendas are starting to cut across competition policy. While the peculiar nature of the competition agenda and language has insulated it from many of the troubles faced by trade policy this immunity from oversight is starting to wear off. There is an urgent need for the competition community to begin developing mechanisms to allow them to deflect wider societal concerns from their immediate regulatory work by establishing bridges to flanking policies that can help manage the greater interest. If it does not do this the paralysis of the trade world may spread to competition and thence to other forms of economic regulation. For the good of the world economy and its contingent nation states, this must be avoided at all costs.

References

Bhagwati, J. and Srinvasan, T. (1982), 'The Welfare Consequences of Directly Unproductive Profit-seeking (DUP) Lobbying Activities: Price *Versus* Quality Distortions', *Journal of International Economics*, Vol. 13, No. 1, pp. 33–44.
Wilson, J.Q. (ed.) (1980), *The Politics of Regulation*, Basic Books, London.
Zajac, E.E. (1995), *Political Economy of Fairness*, MIT Press, Cambridge, MA.

Chapter 9

Multi-level Economic Diplomacy: The Case of Investment

Stephen Woolcock

This chapter introduces the concept of multi-level economic diplomacy. In earlier chapters we have seen that a central feature of economic diplomacy is the interaction between the domestic and international levels. The Putnam two-level game metaphor for negotiations is one of the analytical tools for assessing this interaction. But when one takes a closer look at both the domestic and the international levels it is clear that they are themselves made up of different levels.

Within domestic decision-making there is a hierarchy of actors – government and non-government, national and subnational – that interact among themselves. These have been examined in Chapters 4 and 5 above. In international contexts negotiations likewise take place on different levels or in different fora. Negotiators may opt for bilateral, regional, plurilateral or multilateral levels and institutions. In particular, governments (and other actors) make strategic use of the interaction between these levels in their negotiating strategies, to conduct multi-level economic diplomacy.

This chapter is divided into two main parts:

- The first part identifies the main features of the different international levels. It explains how multi-level economic diplomacy seeks to take advantage of the interaction between them.
- The second part illustrates how negotiators conduct multi-level diplomacy by using the case of international investment agreements. The chapter provides an overview of the issues involved in investment agreements and how these have evolved over time.

Identifying the International Levels of Economic Diplomacy

But what does it mean to speak of the different international levels of economic diplomacy? What do these levels consist of? What do they have in common and how do they differ? The first task is to differentiate between the four levels – bilateralism, regionalism, plurilateralism and multilateralism – so as to create a simple taxonomy.

Taxonomy of the Levels

The simplest level is *bilateral* economic diplomacy, practised between just two parties, usually single states. *Multilateral* economic diplomacy, as practised in institutions of global membership, like the IMF, the WTO or the UN, is the most complex. Though these two levels are at the extremes, they have one thing in common. They are open to all countries. Any state can conduct bilateral economic diplomacy. All states can belong to multilateral economic organisations and most of them do. There are still a few exceptions to this – Russia is not yet in the WTO, for example – but essentially the multilateral system is now fully global.

The two intermediate levels are the *regional* and the *plurilateral*. Here there are distinct criteria for taking part – not every country can play. Regional economic agreements are between neighbours, so that the criteria are based on geography. South Africa, though active in the African Union, can never be a member of Asia-Pacific Economic Cooperation (APEC) or the EU. At the plurilateral level the criteria may be wholly objective: only oil-exporters can be members of the Organisation of Petroleum Exporting Countries (OPEC). Or they may be more subjective: only industrial democracies can be members of the OECD, though this term allows for a flexible definition. These intermediate levels can accommodate groups of varying size, from NAFTA with three members to the Commonwealth with over 50; but they are all exclusive in a sense that the IMF or UN can never be.

Two more propositions can be advanced about what differentiates the four levels, though neither can be seen as an absolute rule. The first proposition is that all the levels except the bilateral require a degree of organisation and shared responsibility. This can range from elaborate institutions with independent secretariats, like the World Bank or OECD, to arrangements for rotating chairmanship in an informal group with few members, like the 'Quad' of trade ministers; but it cannot be escaped altogether. Of course, bilateral relations can be organised too and embodied in treaties. But if they only concern two national governments they can be very fluid and informal.

The second proposition is that the intermediate levels – the regional and the plurilateral – especially appeal to medium-sized countries. The solidarity and common purpose provided by these levels enables medium powers to combine either to resist their more powerful neighbours or to emulate them. In contrast, very large and powerful countries see less need to combine with others and less advantage in doing so; bilateralism appeals to them. Small ones, on the other hand, may be more wary of negotiating with stronger states unless these can offer clear economic benefits.[1] They may also feel that their limited resources are better deployed in a multilateral context, where they will go further. As a result, every country, however small, seeks to be in the United Nations and other multilateral

---

1   The increase of free trade agreements in recent years has, however, seen a growing number of smaller economies agreeing to bilateral FTAs, mostly as part of a strategy of attracting foreign direct investment.

institutions. (They cannot always ensure a physical presence there, but that is for other reasons.)

It is now possible to establish the basic taxonomy of the four levels in a simple matrix, as set out in Figure 9.1.

	Bilateral	**Regional**	**Plurilateral**	**Multilateral**
Open to all countries:	x			x
Selected countries only:		x	x	
Requires organisation:		x	x	x
Large countries favour:	x			
Medium countries favour:		x	x	
Small countries favour:				x

Figure 9.1   Basic taxonomy of the levels

Defining the Levels

The four international levels will be defined below and analysed in greater detail in Chapters 10, 13 and 15 of this book. But before doing so, it is worth disposing of a fifth level – *unilateralism* – which might be considered the 'zero option' of economic diplomacy.

Unilateralism would seem to be irrelevant to economic diplomacy, as it does not involve negotiation. Unilateral action, for example in trade liberalisation or protection, is a domestic policy decision. But unilateral liberalisation or protection clearly has an impact on other economies, by expanding or restricting access to the market concerned for investors or exporters from other countries. This can lead to a political response, in the form of imitation or retaliation. There are many examples of countries taking unilateral actions, without agreeing with, consulting or even informing others in advance, which have evident effects on the international system and require others to react. One notorious example is President Nixon's decision to break the dollar's link with gold in August 1971; Nixon deliberately decided to act unilaterally instead of with consultation and negotiation (Kenen 1994; Odell 2000).

Unilateral actions in economic diplomacy are usually signs of weakness or signs of strength. Weak actions are taken when countries do not feel able to enter into commitments with others, or where they know that others would take no notice. Ecuador's dollarisation of its currency is an example of this; the Ecuadorians have no illusions that the US will change its monetary policy because they have adopted its currency. Strong unilateral actions are taken by countries that are convinced they have chosen the right course. Many countries over the last two decades have undertaken programmes of unilateral trade or investment liberalisation, independent of GATT, WTO or OECD negotiations. They believed this would bring them benefit, even if others did not open their markets too. The United States often acts unilaterally, as its great economic strength enables it to act where other countries cannot. The same unilateral actions may betoken either strength or weakness. Threats by Russia, early in 2001, not to service its debts were a sign of strength. But Argentina's debt default at the end of that year indicated weakness, as it was unable to pay.

Bilateralism

Bilateral relations still form a major part of economic diplomacy, whether this consists of informal dealings between countries on a range of issues, or formal bilateral trade or investment treaties. Bilateral economic diplomacy is the simplest technique, which makes it easy to explain to domestic interests. But it gives advantages to the stronger partner and can easily become confrontational. Bilateral deals also contribute to building up more complex agreements on a regional or global level. Indeed, some scholars tend to argue that all negotiations are in fact bilateral; multilateral deals only result from adding up a series of bilateral ones.[2] There is, however, a different dynamic to bilateral economic diplomacy conducted within a wider regional or multilateral context, as compared with bilateral diplomacy conducted on its own account and for its own sake. For example, bilateralism can be important in determining how regional or multilateral rules should be interpreted.

Regionalism

The regional dimension in economic diplomacy is of growing importance at present, because of doubts about the effectiveness of the multilateral system. Regional economic agreements, although often politically motivated, also offer a more rapid way of opening markets. Economic liberalisation may be easier for national interests to accept when it occurs within a regional grouping of countries with broadly the same levels of development and similar policy preferences. For business interests, access to a larger regional market may be seen as a substitute for wider markets, or as a stepping stone to international competition. Regional agreements often involve legally binding commitments and dispute settlement. They may even involve the pooling of sovereignty in order to have a greater impact in international negotiations or over the power of global markets.

Plurilateralism

The plurilateral level of economic diplomacy attracts less attention than either regionalism or multilateralism. But plurilateral bodies, like the OECD, the G8 and the Commonwealth, serve two important purposes in economic diplomacy. First, they can provide a forum where national governments seek to reconcile domestic and international economic objectives, most frequently by a process of voluntary cooperation. Second, they enable like-minded governments to develop

---

2   This view emerges from Odell 2000. Most of his case studies are of bilateral negotiations involving the United States.

agreed positions which they can then advance in wider multilateral contexts and use as the basis for multi-level diplomacy. The OECD has been the forum in which discussion and dialogue has led to the development of norms and standards that have, for example, provided the foundation for agreements on services, investment and agriculture at other levels. More informal plurilateral groupings have attached themselves to multilateral institutions, like the G24 (of developing countries) at the IMF and the Cairns Group (of agricultural exporters) at the WTO.

Multilateralism

Finally, multilateral economic diplomacy provides for the involvement of all countries, though this makes it cumbersome. It incorporates regimes such as the WTO, the IMF and World Bank and the economic work of the United Nations, as well as a wide range of specialist organisations. Multilateral economic diplomacy is well suited for rule-making and there were great advances here in the 1990s, especially in the trade and environmental fields, as noted in Chapter 1. But this has led the multilateral institutions into controversy: NGOs attack them as opaque and undemocratic; developing countries complain that the multilateral system puts them at a disadvantage; even developed countries find it hard to come to terms with the increasing encroachment of international rules into domestic policy. So while the prizes are high in successful multilateral economic diplomacy, the risks are high also.

Multi-level Economic Diplomacy: Choice and Interaction of Levels

All four levels interact and the simpler ones, especially bilateralism, contribute to the more complex. The operations of the European Union illustrate this well. For example:

- in the *multilateral* WTO, the countries of the *regional* EU combine so as to negotiate as one;
- when the EU negotiates a free trade agreement, say with Mexico, the European Member States operate at the *regional* level, while Mexico follows the *bilateral* level;
- within the *regional* EU there is an active network of diplomacy at the *bilateral* level. This may be systematic, as in the regular contacts between France and Germany; or occasional, as when the Presidency summons each Member State in turn to a 'confessional' during a European Council meeting.

More generally, during any multilateral gathering there will be an immense number of bilateral contacts, and often these will provide the foundation for any wider agreement reached.

In economic diplomacy governments seek to take advantage of the different levels and the interaction between them in various ways. First of all, countries may identify different levels as suitable for specific policy issues. For example:

- *regional* agreements will suit neighbouring countries seeking the benefits of integrated markets for trade and investment;
- *plurilateral* understandings will suit policy issues, such as export credit policy, which cannot command the support of enough countries for multilateral rules to be agreed;
- *multilateral* treaties are used, for example in global environment issues, where the involvement of all countries is necessary.

In addition, the availability of different levels means that governments, as well as non-state actors, will shop between them, seeking to make progress wherever it looks most promising. An analysis of economic diplomacy in any policy area will often show how norms or models developed at one level can find application in the others. For example, plurilateral work in the OECD can form the basis for regional agreements such as NAFTA. The regional agreements will generally take the principles developed within the OECD further, both in terms of the coverage and the binding nature of the agreements. Regional agreements may in turn provide the model for multilateral agreements; or they may set regulatory norms or standards that have an influence beyond the region itself, for example, standards of food safety in North America or Europe. In short, agreements reached at one level will have implications for other levels of policy-making. Seldom do negotiations occur in a vacuum. There are normally models or precedents that can be found in other agreements.

The interaction between levels can be analysed in terms of motivation, as follows (Woolcock 2006, 20–21):

- *Synergistic interaction.* This occurs when economic diplomacy on different levels interacts in an iterative, two-way process. Techniques or approaches developed at one level are applied on other levels and improved upon, as when work on services in the OECD was successfully introduced into the GATT and WTO.
- *Liberal forum shopping.* This occurs when countries switch between levels to overcome obstacles to open policies and broad commitments. For example, if negotiations are blocked at multilateral or plurilateral level, progress can be sought at other levels between fewer participants. This has happened with investment, as explained later in this chapter.
- *Mercantilist forum shopping.* This occurs when countries switch levels so as to further or protect their narrow national or sectoral interests. For example, the United States has withdrawn from multilateral commitments of climate change, preferring to work through a plurilateral group of Asia-Pacific countries.
- *Exporting domestic rule-making.* This applies when a country uses bilateral or regional levels to extend a domestic regime. When globalisation results in tension between domestic regulations and those in other countries or regions, the least-cost route is to export one's own domestic rules. This option, however, has hitherto only been available to major powers like the United States or the European Union.

The Case of International Investment

Investment provides an excellent case study to illustrate the different levels of economic diplomacy and the interaction between them. Investment is a key to understanding economic interdependence, because it involves foreign firms penetrating the domestic economy and becoming embedded there. For this reason international investment agreements have generated considerable controversy over the years. The investment provisions in the International Trade Organisation (ITO) Charter of 1948 were a major reason for its demise and thereafter developed and developing countries sought, in vain, to find a consensus on the issue. In the last decade the controversies surrounding the OECD's so-called Multilateral Agreement on Investment (MAI – in fact a plurilateral instrument) and the inclusion of investment in the WTO's Doha Development Agenda (DDA) have provided an important litmus test of views on globalisation. Yet though more ambitious projects have failed, a patchwork of bilateral, regional and plurilateral agreements, as well as some investment rules in the WTO's General Agreement on Trade in Services (GATS), have created a form of de facto international investment regime.

After summarising the content of investment agreements, the chapter looks at the economic diplomacy involved in three stages: up to the mid-1980s; the next decade, occupied by the Uruguay Round in the GATT and the NAFTA negotiations; and the period to the present day. It illustrates the role of the different levels in the process of negotiation and shows how precedents set at one level have shaped rules on other levels. It also shows how negotiators have used the interaction between levels strategically to further their policy objectives.

Elements of Investment Agreements

To explain how economic diplomacy functions in the case of investment, this section sets out the potential scope of investment agreements.[3] The key components are:

- *Definitions.* There are three major types: foreign direct investment (FDI); portfolio investment; and other assets such as intellectual property or licences.
- *Coverage.* This is determined by *positive listing*, where only named sectors are included, or *negative listing*, where everything is included except for specified 'sensitive' sectors. Negative listing produces a more liberal outcome.
- *National treatment.* This is central to investment agreements, which may grant *pre-investment* national treatment, giving effective right of establishment, or *post-investment* national treatment, which allows the host state to control entry.

---

3   An extensive discussion of the typical elements of investment rules can be found in UNCTAD (2004).

- *Liberalisation measures.* These can involve: the right of establishment; removal of investment controls; prohibiting performance requirements; prohibiting investor incentives; right of entry for key personnel.
- *Transparency.* This facilitates investment and can aid liberalisation by drawing attention to restrictions, thus resulting in pressure for their removal.
- *Investment protection.* This can include: protection against 'classic' expropriation, with full compensation; the right to transfer funds; and protection against regulations equivalent to expropriation.
- *Dispute settlement.* This takes two main forms: state-to-state settlement, where only governments can bring cases; and investor-state settlement, where firms can challenge host governments direct. Both systems may use international arbitration bodies: the International Centre for Investment Disputes (ICSID) and the UN Centre on Investment and Trade Law (UNCITRAL).

From the Nineteenth Century to the Mid-1980s

Negotiation on investment dates back over a hundred years. Capital importers generally supported the Calvo doctrine, named after the Foreign Minister of Argentina in the 1870s, according to which investment was to be solely governed by the national laws of the host countries. After widespread nationalisation in the 1920s and 1930s, the League of Nations debated the case for 'fair, prompt and effective' compensation in cases of expropriation, but to no effect.

From the end of World War II investment became a subject for negotiation at all levels, starting at the most ambitious end.

Multilateral

The United States sought to have investment covered by the multilateral institutions that it pioneered in the late 1940s. But American negotiators were prepared to settle for weak investment provisions in the projected International Trade Organisation (ITO). Articles 11 and 12 of the 1948 Havana Charter granted capital importing states rights to screen and restrict ownership and impose other 'reasonable requirements'. The weakness of the rules on investment was a key reason why US international business did not support the ITO, a fact that contributed to its demise (Diebold 1952). The General Agreement on Tariffs and Trade (GATT) had a narrow trade focus and did not cover investment.

Investment returned to the multilateral level in the 1970s, but with no better success. The US proposed a 'GATT for investment', but failed to get support from developing countries. Instead, the UN General Assembly debates on the rights of states in the 'New International Economic Order' (NIEO) proved more attractive to capital importing developing countries (Vandevelde 1998). They sought to use the UN negotiations, in which they had a built-in majority, to reorient investment rules in the direction of the Calvo doctrine. They succeeded in having the 1974 UN Charter of Economic Rights and Duties of States (UNGA Res 3281 (XXIX) 1974) adopted, but this was not a binding agreement (UNCTAD 2004). These moves were resisted by the developed capital exporting countries, for which the UN was not the forum of choice.

Plurilateral

In the light of these multilateral failures, the plurilateral OECD, created in 1961 as the successor to the Marshall Plan, emerged as the main vehicle for agreeing liberalised investment regimes among its members (Snyder 1963). Binding codes on Liberalisation of Capital Movements and Current Invisible Operations (OECD 1987) were adopted in 1964 that provided for a ban on investment controls. In practice all governments made exceptions to this prohibition, so that transparency measures combined with peer pressure were used to promote liberalisation. Once barriers to investment were identified, reviews of national schedules in the Committee on International Investment and Multinational Enterprises (CIME) were used to get them removed. A 'ratchet' provision precluded any reintroduction of controls once they had been discarded.

A decade later, the OECD adopted its 1976 Declaration and Decisions on International Investment and Multinational Enterprises, which provided for national treatment for investment (OECD 1993). But European governments would not commit themselves to a binding of national treatment that would prevent them introducing new laws that discriminated against foreign investors. In the late 1970s and early 1980s the United States, followed by the UK and other European countries, unilaterally removed investment controls and the 'ratchet' mechanism of the OECD Codes made this liberalisation irreversible. This slow, quiet work of the OECD continued while debates at the multilateral level were more heated.

Regional

The first important regional move was the Treaty establishing the European Economic Community (later the European Union) in 1957. Article 56 prohibited restrictions on the freedom of establishment, through agencies, branches and subsidiaries, by European firms throughout the Community. But in practice these provisions were not applied throughout all the Member States until the 1980s. The European Community stimulated widespread imitation, so that common markets and customs unions with investment provisions were launched in Africa, the Arab world, the Caribbean, South America and South-East Asia in the 1960s and 1970s. But none of these investment regimes survived the economic turmoil created by the first oil crisis, being neither fully implemented nor adequately enforced (Reiter 2006, 218).

Bilateral

While the OECD was preferred for investment liberalisation in a limited circle, bilateral investment treaties (BITs) began to be used for the protection of investment worldwide. The first BIT was negotiated between Germany and Pakistan in 1959 and most early treaties were initiated by individual European countries, reaching a total of about 250 by 1980 (UNCTAD 2000). Though investment within the European Community was covered by the founding treaty, international investment, unlike international trade, remained in the competence of the Member States. The BITs concluded on the European model provided for protection from expropriation, the right to compensation, free transfer of payments and state-to-state dispute settlement supplemented by international arbitration. They offered limited liberalisation, in the form of post-investment national treatment (Reiter 2006, 210–11). All the obligations fell on the capital importing states, but many of them saw the conclusion of a BIT as a means of attracting investment.

The 1980s saw a more rapid growth – nearly 400 BITs in the decade – and the arrival of the United States, which signed its first BIT in 1982. The US model BIT was more demanding than the European. It embraced liberalisation measures (pre-investment national treatment and prohibition of performance requirements); investment protection (regulatory as well as classic expropriation); and effective enforcement (investor-state dispute settlement) (US Senate 1982). The model BIT would shape the later US approach to negotiations at all levels.

Multi-level Diplomacy to the Mid-1980s

Three attempts to conclude a multilateral agreement during this period all ended in failure, for different reasons. Capital exporters, blocked at multilateral level, concentrated on building up a regime for investment liberalisation in the plurilateral OECD – an example of liberal forum shopping. A parallel regime for investment protection was developed bilaterally, through the use of BITs. This regime started independently of attempts at liberalisation, but later the United States employed synergistic linkage to bring elements of the OECD's regime into its model BIT. Meanwhile regional diplomacy provided for some far-reaching treaty commitments, but implementation was slow in Europe and ran into the sand elsewhere.

The Uruguay Round and NAFTA – Mid-1980s to Mid-1990s

Multilateral

In the preparations for the Uruguay Round in the GATT (1986–1994) the United States pressed strongly for investment to be on the agenda. The US sought stronger GATT rules to help American companies seeking to expand overseas in the information technology and pharmaceutical sectors.[4] This pressure was resisted by India and Brazil, backed by other developing countries, in the run up to the

---

4   Investors in other sectors such as extractive industries were already established in many markets and had 'paid the entry fee' in terms of accepting performance requirements to do so. These companies were therefore not motivated to make it easy for new entrants to their overseas markets. This partially explains why the European multinationals did little to press the EU for an inclusion of ambitious investment rules in the Uruguay Round.

launch of the Round. The EU assumed an intermediate position, favouring the prohibition of a short list of five performance requirements, compared to the 14 targeted by the US. Some of these, such as local content requirements, were arguably already covered by the GATT. Japan and the Newly Industrialising Countries (NICs) argued for a confirmation that the GATT already covered certain aspects of investment. A compromise was found to the effect that trade related investment measures (TRIMS), but not investment policy per se, would be included in the Round (Crome 1999).

To back up the US negotiating position Congress included investment in the aggressive unilateralist provisions of Super 301 in the 1988 Omnibus Trade and Competitiveness Act. As the US had no general controls on investment, other countries' controls were viewed as 'unfair' and thus targets for trade retaliation. Unilateral action thus offered a BATNA (best alternative to a negotiated multilateral agreement) for the United States (Odell 2000). India and Brazil were threatened with trade sanctions if they did not agree to liberalise investment, though in fact these were never applied.

By the Dunkel text of 1991 the shape of the TRIMS agreement was already clear, though final acceptance had to await the conclusion of the Round late in 1993. This would require all TRIMS contrary to the GATT to be notified. TRIMS that fell into this category included local content, export and trade balancing requirements and foreign exchange restrictions. Developed countries had to eliminate these by 1997, developing countries by January 2000 and the least developed by 2002. Any dispute was subject to the general state-to-state dispute settlement provisions of the WTO. From the point of view of those like the US seeking a comprehensive settlement, the TRIMs agreement was inadequate and did little more than prohibit measures already contrary to the GATT.

The Uruguay Round, however, did agree more substantial investment provisions in the context of the General Agreement on Trade in Services (GATS). This provided a framework for liberalising trade in services according to four 'modes of supply', which included not only cross-border trade but also 'commercial presence', in other words investment. The framework would be filled in by sector negotiations, for example in telecommunications and financial services, in which WTO members would offer market access and national treatment in chosen areas, following a 'positive listing' approach. By 2005 developed countries had made investment commitments in nearly 80 per cent of services sectors, though only 30 per cent were without conditions; for developing countries the figures were 45 per cent and only 14 per cent. The conclusion must be that GATS commitments are mainly being used to lock in unilateral liberalisation rather than to open new markets. Even so, the GATS provides a valuable multilateral regime for services investment, with potential for expansion (Reiter 2006, 215–16).

Plurilateral

In 1990–1991 there was a review of the OECD instruments with a view to agreeing a binding National Treatment Instrument (NTI) (OECD 1992). But negotiations failed due to US/EU differences over the inclusion of subfederal level government (sought by the EU), provisions on regional preferences (sought by the US) and the scope of national security exemptions. After the 1991 talks failed, work continued in the OECD on a 'wider investment instrument' that would shape the negotiations on a Multilateral Agreement on Investment (MAI) – see below.

Regional

Even as the multilateral negotiations began in the GATT, the US was negotiating the Canada/US Free Trade Agreement that included comprehensive investment provisions at a high standard, including removal of investment controls, a ban on performance requirements and investment protection against 'regulatory expropriation.' The negotiations were concluded in 1988, but failed to provide a model for investment rules in the GATT, as the US had hoped. Given the limited nature of any likely GATT provisions the United States would have to look elsewhere for higher standards. In March 1990 the initial soundings began for what became the North American Free Trade Agreement (NAFTA) between the US, Canada and Mexico.

NAFTA contained detailed investment provisions based on the US model BIT. It provided for:

- pre-investment national treatment at the central government and state/provincial level and thus right of establishment, subject to the negative listing of sensitive sectors;
- prohibition of 12 performance requirements;
- protection against 'regulatory taking' or de facto expropriation and unrestricted transfer of funds;
- investor–state dispute settlement and detailed implementing rules including the use of international arbitration procedures through ICSID and UNCITRAL.

The American desire for higher standards was reflected in most elements of the NAFTA rules. NAFTA's investor-state dispute settlement regime, contained in Chapter 11, embodies the US preference for private actions in cases of non-compliance. Half of the 39 articles in the chapter are concerned with setting out the procedures for investor-state actions. It is worth noting that any investor within NAFTA can benefit from the provisions of Chapter 11, including investors from third countries, provided these have 'substantial business activity' within a NAFTA party. These NAFTA rules would provide the model for the investment provisions in a new type of US bilateral Free Trade Agreement, especially in the 2000s.

Regionalism in the European Union took quite a different direction. From 1988 to 1992 the EU pursued its campaign to complete the single market, to ensure free movement of goods, services, people and capital among all the member states. This finally brought into effect, by Directives such as the 1988 Investment Directive, the liberalisation of investment promised in the founding treaty. Once the single market campaign was over, the EU turned its attention to absorbing the ex-communist countries of Central Europe into membership. These countries had to accept existing EU regimes – the *acquis communautaire* – including all the provisions on investment.

Bilateral

While the main attention in this period was on other levels, the negotiation of BITs continued to accelerate. By the middle of the 1990s about 200 new BITs were being signed every year and the number of signatory countries almost doubled during the decade. By then less than half of the BITs then in force were between developed capital exporters and developing importers. The rest were concluded among emerging market and transitional economies. But the contents of these agreements still followed a standard pattern, with the US model being more demanding than the European.

Multi-level Diplomacy to the Mid-1990s

The United States was the most active player in investment negotiations during this period. It made a strong pitch for a strong, comprehensive agreement of worldwide application through the GATT. But when the results on offer multilaterally were inadequate, the US turned again to forum shopping, seeking to make progress through NAFTA.

By contrast, the European Union and its members were inactive on most levels and hardly practised interaction at all in this period. They took little interest in the GATT investment negotiations, though European countries continued to conclude BITs. Their highest priority was in rather inward-looking regional measures, first to complete the single market and then to engage their Central European neighbours.

The MAI, the WTO and the Shift to Bilateralism: Mid-1990s to Mid-2000s

Once the Uruguay Round was over and the WTO was in place, there was a widely held view in the international investment policy community (both government officials and private sector experts) that 'investment could provide the next great boost to the world economy, following the powerful impulse given by the removal of trade barriers during the Uruguay Round'.[5] But there were differences over the best forum for negotiation. The EU preferred the WTO, for reasons explained below. The US pressed for negotiations in the OECD, on the grounds that only a plurilateral setting of like-minded countries could negotiate the kind of high standard agreement it sought. Developing countries were clearly not going to support comprehensive investment rules in the WTO anywhere near those the US had negotiated with Canada and Mexico in NAFTA. By building on past OECD work the US believed a high standard agreement could be concluded

---

5   This was the view of the EU Trade Commissioner, Sir Leon Brittan. See his *Smoothing the Path for Investment Worldwide* speech in Washington, January 1995.

and then opened to non-OECD countries to sign (US Council for International Business, 1995). In the end both plurilateral and multilateral routes were taken, but the OECD came first.

Plurilateral

The May 1995 OECD Ministerial Meeting launched the negotiations for a Multilateral Agreement on Investment (MAI) and set 1997 as the target date for completion (OECD 1995). The view in the OECD at the time, reflecting business sentiment, was that there had to be an ambitious agenda to make the MAI exercise worthwhile (Henderson 1999). The mandate for the MAI was to negotiate a comprehensive and fully binding agreement at the highest standard in every respect.

Progress was made up to 1997, when the draft negotiating text included:

- a broad, asset-based definition of investment;
- pre-investment national treatment;
- coverage of all sectors and all levels of government (subject to reciprocity);
- tighter controls on performance requirements, privatisation and monopolies;
- protection against *de facto* expropriation;
- investor – state dispute settlement.

But during 1997 opposition from a coalition of trade unions, environmental NGOs and finally development NGOs began to grow.[6] This opposition had not been anticipated (Henderson 1999). Neither ministers nor chief executives sought to frame the public debate on the MAI. The officials and business experts involved assumed that as in the past there would be little or no public interest. The coalition of NGOs was therefore able to frame the public debate unopposed and depicted the MAI as an attempt to undermine organised labour and environmental regulation, while exploiting poor developing countries. The NGO campaign found resonance in public opinion and the political masters of those negotiating the MAI began to question the benefit of the agreement if it meant losing votes. In an attempt to defuse the opposition, concessions were made and wording on environmental and labour interests was inserted into the draft agreement. This had no impact on the NGO's principled opposition to the MAI, but it weakened the agreement and thus diminished business support.

These factors combined to bring negotiations to a halt in the spring of 1998. A six month pause was agreed, during which opposition only grew. In the end the French government, under strong public pressure, withdrew from the negotiations

---

6   This NGO coalition first came together in opposition to NAFTA. Emboldened by its success over the MAI, it went on to cause mayhem at the WTO Ministerial in Seattle. See Walter 2000.

just before they were due to resume in October 1998 and thus effectively killed the MAI.[7]

Multilateral

The European Union advocated investment negotiations in the WTO, on the grounds that most barriers to EU investors were in developing countries. It was unrealistic to expect developing countries to sign up to a *fait accompli* negotiated in the OECD (European Commission 1994). The EU considered that the completion of its single market, which was largely open to non-European investors, gave it a good basis to negotiate investment concessions from other WTO members.[8] The Europeans proposed an agenda based on transparency, national treatment and MFN as well as state-to-state dispute settlement.

The WTO Working Group on Trade and Investment (WGTI) was established at the 1996 Singapore WTO Ministerial. But its work between 1996 and 1999 provided little by way of convergence of views between those seeking a high standard agreement and developing countries, which were more reticent. In the preparations in Geneva for the Seattle WTO Ministerial in December 1999, the EU called for the inclusion of investment in the proposed new round (European Commission 1999). But the US Administration was explicit in its opposition. In a pre-election period it had little to gain from provoking US labour, environmental and anti-globalisation NGOs by seeking an agreement which US business was convinced would not be worth the paper it was written on.[9] Some leading developing countries, such as India and Brazil, continued to actively oppose including investment in the WTO agenda; others simply had more pressing objectives in the WTO negotiations, such as improving market access to developed country markets. In Seattle the EU, together with Hungary, Japan, Korea and Switzerland, tabled a common paper aimed at getting developing country support for a multilateral framework for investment. This proposed: a clarification of the relationship between the WTO rules and those of the OECD, regional and bilateral agreements; progressive liberalisation using a positive list approach; no investor-state dispute settlement; and special account to be taken of developing country needs. These proposals led nowhere, however, as the Seattle meeting broke in disarray.

---

7   A report by a French Member of the European Parliament argued for more modest aims if the negotiations were to be resumed, based on a narrow definition of investment (excluding portfolio investment and asset based definitions), an abandonment of the 'ratchet', limits on the coverage to TRIMS, no de facto expropriation, no investor-state dispute settlement and opening negotiations to developing countries (Lalumière 1998).

8   Negotiating within the WTO would also give a boost to the prospects of extending EC competence to investment, as the European Commission was by convention the sole negotiator in the WTO.

9   For a summary of the US aims in the round see 'Toward Seattle: The Next Round and America's Stake in the Trading System', speech by Charlene Barshevsky at the Council on Foreign Relations, New York, 19 October 1999.

The EU continued to push for the inclusion of investment in the Doha Development Agenda (DDA), as one of the four so-called Singapore issues: the others were competition (also promoted by the EU), transparency in government procurement and trade facilitation. At the 2001 WTO Doha Ministerial meeting these efforts were still being resisted by several developing countries led by India. Investment and the other Singapore issues were put on the agenda; but the decision to negotiate was postponed until the next ministerial meeting in 2003, to be taken, on India's insistence, on the basis of an explicit consensus.[10] By the time of Cancun in 2003 a larger number of developing countries were opposed to including the Singapore issues, apart from trade facilitation. Equally important, there was no US support, since the US government and business interests still held the view that multilateral investment agreements were a lost cause. Investment was therefore taken off the agenda of the DDA at the Cancun meeting.

Regional

As noted above, the EU failed to take advantage of its regional integration in investment at the multilateral level. Its own focus continued to be on negotiating with its Central European neighbours, ten of whom (together with Malta and Cyprus) had become members by 2007, adopting the existing EU regime on investment, as well as other issues, in the process. From 1996 the EU also gave priority to renewed economic links, including investment, with its Mediterranean neighbours under the Barcelona process; but this was slow to produce results.

The process of regional integration begun with NAFTA was originally intended by the United States to be extended to other Latin American countries. This, however, never happened, as Congress refused President Bill Clinton the necessary negotiating authority. The United States instead became active players in two wider regional initiatives: the Free Trade Area of the Americas (FTAA), covering the whole Western Hemisphere; and Asia-Pacific Economic Cooperation (APEC), going all round the Pacific rim. But neither initiative had a substantial investment component and both had run out of steam by the mid-2000s. The only other regional grouping that engaged the US was the Central America Free Trade Agreement (CAFTA). Instead, the main impact of NAFTA was felt in a new generation of bilateral trade agreements initiated by the US, which incorporated strong investment provisions.

Bilateral

The NAFTA Chapter 11 provisions and associated NAFTA rules have provided a model for all subsequent investment rules in the Free Trade Agreements (FTAs) negotiated by the US. The investment provisions in US FTAs with Singapore, Chile and others are more or less identical to NAFTA, except for some of the

---

10 The WTO and the GATT before it worked on the basis of a consensus defined as no country present and actively opposing any decision. An explicit consensus meant that all WTO members even the smallest would have to support.

scheduling of coverage. Having established such high standards at the bilateral and regional (NAFTA) level, the US negotiators and US business interests had a clear alternative to the multilateral (WTO) or plurilateral (MAI) level. They had little incentive to make concessions at those levels. If the WTO or OECD standards turned out to be lower than those in the NAFTA/BIT model, there was a danger that the weaker standard might prevail.

The NAFTA model has also been emulated by a number of leading developing countries. NAFTA investment rules have provided the model for a series of bilateral FTAs negotiated by Canada and Mexico throughout Central and South America. Chile has done the same in its FTA negotiations. With the expansion of US centred FTAs beyond the western hemisphere, the NAFTA model has also found even wider application. For example, the US-Singapore FTA provisions on investment replicated the NAFTA rules. Singapore, the most active negotiator of FTAs in Asia, has adopted the NAFTA investment rules as its own model, except where its negotiating partners, like Japan and Australia, have resisted such extensive commitments (Reiter 2006).

In comparison the investment provisions in FTAs negotiated by the EU have been very much more modest. These are often little more than token statements and do not go beyond the existing OECD or WTO provisions (TRIMS and GATS). There are no investment protection rules and no specific rules on performance requirements.[11] Nor does the EU include investor–state dispute settlement in any of its FTAs.

The EU's lack of ambition on investment in its FTAs is linked to the issue of community competence. The European Commission explicitly favoured multilateral negotiations on investment from the mid 1990s to their collapse in 2003. This was not only to engage developing countries, but to enable the Commission to act as the EU negotiator. In bilateral contexts, however, the Member States are attached to the BITs they have already negotiated, even though they hardly extend beyond classic investment protection. They do not want to see them replaced by trade agreements negotiated by the Commission. This has inhibited the EU from negotiating investment liberalisation provisions in its FTAs, although the investment provisions in the EU – Chile FTA may signify a change towards more ambitious aims in EU FTAs.

Given the opposition from developing countries to the inclusion of investment in the WTO, why do they sign up to FTAs including investment rules? Smaller developing countries, such as those in Central America, seek to gain 'first mover' advantages in attracting foreign direct investment because investors get access to the huge US market through bilateral FTAs and CAFTA. Small countries cannot otherwise expect to compete with the larger emerging markets like China and India. Larger or more developed economies, such as Chile or Singapore, conclude FTAs with investment rules so as to become a hub for MNC activity. Companies might be attracted to work from such hubs if they are linked to a range of other countries by FTAs including suitable investment rules. This helps

---

11 However, anti-subsidy rules in the competition provisions in FTAs concluded by the EU may have some bearing on performance requirements linked to benefits.

to explain FTAs such as Singapore – Jordan, which would otherwise appear to have little economic rationale.

Multi-level Diplomacy to the Mid-2000s

There were two serious attempts to use synergistic interaction to achieve an effective worldwide regime for investment. The United States mobilised earlier work in the OECD, its model BITs and the rules developed in NAFTA as the foundation for a comprehensive plurilateral regime through the MAI. The hope was that this would attract non-OECD subscribers and thus become accepted as the worldwide standard. This made progress at first, but failed because the opposition from NGOs was stronger than the support from business, so that governments got cold feet. The EU then tried to build on its success in regional integration to achieve a more modest multilateral investment agreement in the WTO. This effort survived for several years but also came to nothing, being opposed by developing countries and unsupported by the US.

After these setbacks, the US again turned to forum-shopping, making the NAFTA rules the model for the investment provisions in its bilateral FTAs worldwide, plus a modest regional advance in Central America. There was also an element of exporting domestic rule-making in these FTAs, in that America's partners in practice had to accept the investment regime that prevailed in the United States. Even so, this model of FTA proved very popular, being adopted by Canada and Mexico, the other NAFTA parties, in their bilateral agreements; by other Latin American countries like Chile; and by active Asian negotiators of FTAs, especially Singapore. In contrast, the EU could not pursue parallel forum-shopping, as competence in investment rested with the individual Member States, not the Commission. With few exceptions, EU efforts were confined to its neighbours in Central Europe and the Mediterranean.

Conclusions

This case study has shown how the different international levels of economic diplomacy have all been used to negotiate agreements on investment. To take each in turn:

- *Multilateral* The United States three times sought an open, liberal investment agreement in the ITO and the GATT; the European Union did so once in the WTO. Back in the 1970s the developing countries sought a more restrictive regime in the United Nations. But the only positive result was the limited regime achieved in TRIMS and the GATS in the Uruguay Round.
- *Plurilateral* The OECD was used to promote cumulative investment liberalisation up to the 1980s and again in the more ambitious MAI negotiations in the 1990s. But after the conspicuous failure of the MAI the OECD has fallen out of favour.

- *Regional* The European Union made great advances in integrating the investment regimes of its members, especially through the single market campaign. But the regional level has hardly been replicated elsewhere. NAFTA is the striking exception, but with only three members it is the minimum size of regional grouping.
- *Bilateral* Throughout the period, Bilateral Investment Treaties have become increasingly popular. By the end of 2004 there were over 2,250 BITs in force. Their provisions have expanded and tightened, moving from the limited European model to the more demanding US model. BITs are now being replaced by FTAs with even wider investment provisions, based on NAFTA.

The United States has also used *unilateral* action, for example threatening to impose sanctions on developing countries like India and Brazil if they would not liberalise investment through the GATT. But this tactic proved more effective in trade related intellectual property rights than on investment in the Uruguay Round. In TRIPs the Americans were able to convince developing countries that their unilateral approach offered a strong BATNA (best alternative to a negotiated agreement), so that the TRIPS agreement was much stronger than TRIMS.

All the main players used the interaction between levels in their efforts to make progress. The Americans were the most active. They used synergistic interaction to try to drive agreement at multilateral and plurilateral levels, feeding in their experience from BITs and NAFTA into the Uruguay Round and the MAI. But when these efforts failed, forum shopping drove them back to the bilateral level, which they enriched from synergistic interaction from NAFTA and used as a means to export domestic rules. The EU tried to draw synergy from its achievements at the regional level to make progress multilaterally in the WTO. But when this too failed, the EU was unable to copy the American move to the bilateral level because of the divided competence between Commission and Member States. The developing countries no doubt thought nostalgically of the regime agreed in the UN during the 1970s. But those who seriously wanted to attract investment adopted the bilateral level, concluding BITs and later FTAs not only with developed partners but also among themselves.

Alongside the varying fortunes of these negotiations, policy towards international investment has moved steadily in a liberal direction. Up to the 1970s the Calvo doctrine largely prevailed. But the unilateral liberalisation of investment controls by developed countries took off during the 1980s, underpinned by the OECD regime. In the course of the next two decades almost all developing countries also opened up to foreign direct investment. In 2006 flows of FDI reached $1,200 billion, of which nearly $400 billion went to developing countries.[12] In these conditions it is surprising that there is such resistance to multilateral or even plurilateral rules.

The answer must lie in the fact that investment is more deeply imbedded in domestic policy than other economic activities like trade or financial flows. There

---

12 See Williams 2007, quoting UNCTAD sources.

is a greater risk of conflict between international economic benefits and domestic political anxieties. This is not just in developing countries. During 2006 France, Belgium and Luxemburg tried in vain to stop an Indian company taking over a large steel firm, while the United States prevented a Chinese company from buying an American oil firm and a company based in the Gulf from taking control of some American ports. In these conditions governments hesitate to bind themselves into broad multi-party agreements where they do not feel fully in control. They are happier with bilateral deals where they can more easily determine the pace and scope of negotiations, even where their partner is the powerful United States. This illustrates the difficulty of reconciling the major tension of economic diplomacy – between international and domestic pressures – in conditions of advancing globalisation.

References

Crome, J. (1999), *Reshaping the World Trading System: A History of the Uruguay Round*, 2nd edition, World Trade Organization, Geneva.

Diebold, W. (1952), 'The End of the ITO', *Essays in International Finance No. 16*, Princeton University, Princeton, NJ.

European Commission (1994), Directorate General for External Economic Relations, Unit of Analysis and Policy Planning, 'Trade and Investment', Discussion Paper, December 1994.

European Commission (1999), Submission from the European Communities 'EC Approach to Trade and Investment' to the World Trade Organisation, Document WT/GC/W/245 of 9 July 1999.

Henderson, D. (1999), *The MAI Affair: A Story and its Lessons*, Royal Institute of International Affairs, London.

Kenen, P. (1994), *Managing the World Economy: Fifty Years after Bretton Woods*, Institute for International Economics, Washington.

Lalumière Report (1998), *Report by Catherine Lalumière and Jean-Pierre Landau on the Multilateral Investment Agreement*, English translation available at http://www.geocities.com/w_trouble_o/lumiere.htm.

Odell, J. (2000), *Negotiating the World Economy*, Cornell University Press, Ithaca, NY.

OECD (1987), *Introduction to the OECD Codes of Liberalisation*, Organisation for Economic Cooperation and Development, Paris.

OECD (1992), *The OECD Declaration and Decisions on International Investment and Multinational Enterprises*, 1991 Review, Organisation for Economic Cooperation and Development, Paris.

OECD (1993), *Foreign Direct Investment: Policies and Trends in the OECD Area During the 1980s*, Organisation for Economic Cooperation and Development, Paris.

OECD (1995), *A Multilateral Agreement on Investment*, Report by the Committee on International Investment and Multinational Enterprises (CIME) and the Committee on Capital Movements and Invisible Transactions (CMIT), Document OECD/GD(95)65, Paris.

Reiter, J. (2006), 'International Investment Rules', in Woolcock, S. (ed.), *Trade and Investment Rule-making: The Role of Regional and Bilateral Agreements*, UN University Press, Tokyo, pp. 208–40.

Snyder, E. (1963), 'Foreign Investment Protection: a Reasoned Approach', *Michigan Law Review*, Vol. 61, No. 6, pp. 1087–124.

UNCTAD (2000), *Bilateral Investment Treaties 1959–1999*, United Nations, New York.

UNCTAD (2004), International Investment Agreements: Key Issues, Volume I, Document UNCTAD/IIE/IIT/2004/10 of 10 December 2004.

US Council for International Business (1995), *The Multilateral Agreement on Investment; the Next Challenge for Global Interdependence*, United States Council for International Business, New York.

US Senate (1982), US-Panama Bilateral Investment Treaty, Senate Treaty Document 99–14, 99th Congress, 2nd Session, 27 October 1982.

Vandevelde, K. (1998), 'The Political Economy of a Bilateral Investment Treaty', *American Journal of International Law*, Vol. 92, No 4, pp. 621–41.

Walter, A. (2000), 'Unravelling the Faustian Bargain: Non-State Actors and the Multilateral Agreement on Investment', in Josselin, D. and Wallace, W. (eds), *Non-State Actors in World Politics*, Palgrave, Basingstoke.

Williams, F. (2007), 'Global Flows of Foreign Investment hit $1,200 Billion', *Financial Times*, 10 January.

Woolcock, S. (ed.) (2006), *Trade and Investment Rule-making: The Role of Regional and Bilateral Agreements*, UN University Press, Tokyo.

Chapter 10

Bilateral Economic Diplomacy: The United States

Nicholas Bayne

This chapter is about bilateral economic diplomacy, especially as practised by the United States. It builds on the distinctions established in Chapter 9. The main part of the chapter aims to do three things:

- to identify the main features of bilateralism;
- to apply the features of bilateral economic diplomacy to the United States, showing how well they satisfy its needs;
- to conduct a comparison with Canada, as a country for which bilateralism is much less suited.

The conclusions look more widely at the use made by the United States of the other international levels, especially under Presidents Bill Clinton and George W. Bush, relating these to the tensions of economic diplomacy.

The Main Features of Bilateralism

Bilateralism is the most common and most basic form of economic diplomacy. Within every regional, plurilateral and multilateral negotiation, there is a network of bilateral contacts among the parties. Often more elaborate agreements begin with a central bilateral bargain, such as the Franco-German deal at the heart of the European Community, later European Union, since its foundation in the 1950s. Yet in contrast to the attention given to the more advanced forms of economic diplomacy, the dynamics of bilateral relations have received very little study.[1] The process is considered so elementary as to be taken for granted, rather as Molière's *Bourgeois Gentilhomme* spent his life speaking prose without being aware of it.

In order to isolate *bilateral* economic diplomacy, as distinct from the more advanced levels, it is necessary to identify the main features of bilateralism. Eight such features can be distinguished.

---

1 Kishan Rana's *Bilateral Diplomacy* (2002) is a notable exception.

The Traditional Level

Bilateralism is the traditional level for diplomacy of all kinds and by far the most ancient. There is evidence of bilateral economic diplomacy going back to 2500 BC, with a trade treaty between the Pharaoh of Egypt and the king of Babylon.[2] The bilateral level was developed at a time when far fewer countries were engaged in international dealings and when they were much less exposed to external competition than they are now. It remains the natural level for inward-looking countries with low international dependence. Outwardly oriented countries are likely to favour more complex forms. Similarly, new international issues like the environment, which require the engagement of all countries, are hard to handle bilaterally and need more elaborate structures.

Simplicity

Bilateral diplomacy is simple. With only two parties involved, as noted in Chapter 9, no formal organisation is required to fix agendas or conduct relations. Though pairs of countries often find it useful to develop joint machinery and to conclude bilateral treaties, for example to lock in rules for investors, none of this is essential. It is also simple to find out about the other party's international position and to perceive how it relates to domestic interests. Bilateralism provides plenty of scope for 'two-level games', where one party tries to influence internal opinion in the other.

Ease of Explanation

Bilateral diplomacy is easy to explain to others. Where agreement is reached, the provisions are likely to be clearer and freer from ambiguity than in more complex negotiations. In countries where the demands of domestic accountability are high, this is a considerable advantage. Members of the legislature, for example, are likely to respond well to accounts of bilateral economic dealings, as the links to national interests are easily perceived. In contrast, they are often suspicious of complex multilateral agreements.

Ease of Control

Bilateral diplomacy is easy to control. It is easier to determine the pace and scope of any negotiation if it only depends on one other party. This will appeal to a country that is concerned to preserve its independence or is worried about potential loss of sovereignty. Such countries will tend to prefer bilateralism, as they can more readily draw back from undue commitments than they can in a multi-partner negotiation. Even small countries may prefer the risk of an unequal deal with a single partner to getting trapped as the weakest member of a wider network.

---

2   This is quoted in Winham 1992.

Favours the Strong

Bilateral diplomacy will tend to favour the stronger party. There is no scope for smaller parties to offset their weakness by combining with others. Usually the stronger party will stand to lose less by the failure of the negotiations and can thus drive a harder bargain; it will enjoy a wider range of BATNAs (best alternatives to a negotiated agreement) in economic dealings (see Odell 2000, 27–8). Bilateral economic diplomacy is therefore the easiest level to analyse according to realist theories, which give most weight to power relationships.

Confrontational

Bilateral diplomacy tends to be confrontational. As the balance of advantage will tend to be clearly perceived, there is a strong pressure to get a better deal than the other party. It is easy to think of diplomacy in the terms or the imagery of competitive sport, or even of war, when it is between only two parties. Bilateral economic diplomacy therefore encourages value claiming negotiating strategies. One party may well end up with a worse deal than the other, but still accept it because it has no effective BATNA. In contrast, when three or more parties are involved, it becomes easier to find a balance where everyone looks like a winner. This favours value creating or package deals.

Allows Differentiation

The bilateral level readily allows for differentiation. When several deals are negotiated on the same issue with different partners, it is possible for a country to favour its allies and penalise its rivals. But such differentiation carries the risk of alienating those who are offered worse terms than other parties. It is an effort to ensure that a network of bilateral agreements or relationships is kept in consistent balance.

Laborious

Bilateral diplomacy is labour-intensive and time-consuming, especially in a world with many active participants. It is difficult to operate an international economic system based wholly on a network of bilateral relationships. It was done in the nineteenth century, with fewer players, but it is hard to imagine now. In sectors where bilateral networks persist, like investment (see Chapter 9) or civil aviation, there is recurrent pressure for wider arrangements. Where separate bilateral deals have to be struck with each partner, this requires a lot of time and resources. Only very well endowed countries can afford an active economic diplomacy based mainly on bilateral dealings.

These features of bilateral economic diplomacy are summarised in Table 10.1.

Table 10.1   The main features of bilateral economic diplomacy

1	The *traditional* level, natural for inward-looking countries.
2	*Simple*, needs no organisation.
3	*Easy to explain*, especially to domestic interests and legislature.
4	*Easy to control*, to protect independence.
5	*Favours stronger party*, as weaker ones cannot combine.
6	Often *confrontational*, as each party seeks the better deal.
7	Allows *differentiation*, though also risks inconsistency.
8	*Laborious* in a system with many active players.

Why Bilateralism Suits the United States

The next section of this chapter examines the proposition that the bilateral level of economic diplomacy is particularly attractive to the United States. This is, of course, not a complete explanation of US economic diplomacy, nor is the United States unique. Bilateralism is attractive, for different reasons, to many other countries, such as Brazil, France, India and Switzerland. The United States, like all other countries, makes widespread use of the regional, plurilateral and multilateral levels, as will appear later in this chapter.

Indeed, the United States has been the creator and promoter of many of the existing multilateral and plurilateral regimes, both the Bretton Woods institutions of the 1940s and others since. So it may seem odd to argue that the US is an instinctive bilateralist. But there is evidence to show that, even within multilateral institutions, the United States prefers to act bilaterally; and that it is always a struggle for internationalist impulses to overcome these bilateral instincts. American economic diplomacy during the Clinton and Bush presidencies (1993–2007) illustrates this well. By the end the US pressures for economic diplomacy through multilateral institutions or regional groupings had shrunk to low levels and bilateral initiatives had gained priority.

An examination of the features of the bilateral level identified earlier reveals how well they fit with the United States.

The Traditional Level

Bilateral economic diplomacy is likely to be the preferred level for a country whose size and natural resources provide almost all its needs and which does not depend much on the outside world. These factors fit the United States precisely. Though its dependence on the outside world has greatly increased over the last 50 years, it is still much less than most of its other partners.

Simple and Easy to Explain

The political structure of the United States strongly favours a level of diplomacy that is simple to conduct, without much organisation, and easy to explain and justify, to domestic interests or the legislature. In the US, domestic interests are able to impose unusual constraints on the conduct of its economic diplomacy (Cohen 2000, 145–72). The US Congress maintains very close control over many areas of economic decision-making, especially in trade policy, and often reflects quite narrow local interests (Destler 2005). While monetary policy is rather more independent, it is still at the mercy of Congress for the voting of funds, for example for IMF quotas. The need to engage Congress means policy-making is very transparent and gives openings to other domestic forces, such as private business. In the US the domestic board in the two-level game is so complex that there is a clear preference for keeping the game simple on the international board.[3]

Easy to Control

Bilateralism appeals to countries that want to preserve their freedom of action and are concerned about any loss of sovereignty. This too applies very powerfully to the United States, which shows a strong reluctance to being subject to any rules imposed from outside. This is based both on a long historical tradition of independence and defence of civil liberties and on a deep conviction that the way the United States does things is the best way.[4] The United States, for example, is the only major country to apply its laws extra-territorially, not accepting the jurisdiction of others.

These arguments suggest that it is difficult for the United States to accept any international rules at all. This can often be achieved only where the international rules are in fact the same rules as the US practises itself; and because the US is economically so strong, this is often what happens (Nye 2003, 124–32). Clearly, if the rest of the world will adopt American rules, that will help to make the US overcome its scepticism about international regimes. But in circumstances where the rest of the world can agree on something that is different from what the United States does, for example in accounting standards or measures against global warming, the Americans do not feel the same pressure to join the consensus as other countries would.

Favours the Strong

Since the United States is, by virtually every measure, economically the strongest single state in the world, this gives bilateralism an obvious attraction. By the same argument, the United States would have little incentive to take part in the more complex levels of economic diplomacy, which would allow other countries to combine against it. This, however, seems to go against the observed facts. The US manifestly is very active in various international institutions. Indeed, as noted in Chapter 2, hegemonic stability theory argues that multilateral regimes can only

---

3   Paarlberg 1995 gives a perceptive analysis of the domestic origins of US economic diplomacy, which became especially relevant again after Bush succeeded Clinton.

4   An excellent historical analysis of this is in Kagan 2006.

work properly if there is a dominant power, as the United States was at the end of World War II. This issue clearly requires more analysis.

The US and multilateralism   The historical evidence suggests that the conditions at the end of World War II had an exceptional effect on US policy-making. Both the devastation caused by the struggle against Nazism and the impending threat from Soviet communism generated strong internationalist impulses within the United States, which overcame its normal bilateral instincts. These impulses were political more than economic, coming from leaders like Cordell Hull and George Marshall, but they used economic instruments like the Bretton Woods institutions and the Marshall Plan (Gardner 1980; Marjolin 1989). The Americans thus became subject to two powerful influences which combined to counter their bilateral instincts. First, as the creators of these multilateral and plurilateral instruments and the great advocates of the non-discriminatory economic system, the Americans long felt an obligation to defend and observe them, setting an example to the rest of the world. Second, both the multilateral trade and monetary system and the Marshall Plan proved very successful and satisfied American objectives better than earlier bilateral arrangements had done (Kenen 1994).

That accounted for the initial impulse towards multilateral and plurilateral institution-building and for its persistence over several decades. But as American post-war economic dominance declined, the balance of perceived advantage shifted. The US was still the strongest single power, but now other states could sometimes combine against it and oblige it to accept decisions in wider institutions which it judged to be less favourable than what it could have got bilaterally. The Americans began to fear getting trapped or surrounded in international institutions. They also convinced themselves that they gave more than they got, for example in multilateral negotiations on trade liberalisation. The consequence was that the United States, as far as it could, favoured those economic institutions where it could operate closest to the bilateral level. That meant ensuring that American views could prevail, if necessary, against the combined weight of all the other members.

This has led to a differentiated attitude to international institutions:

- The IMF and the World Bank are the preferred institutions, because the weighted voting system means the US very seldom finds its views do not prevail, as Nigel Wicks explains in Chapter 17 below. On the rare occasions where that does happen, the US may act unilaterally, as Nixon did in 1971. Under Robert Rubin and then Lawrence Summers as US Treasury Secretary, the Clinton Administration was energetic in promoting 'new financial architecture' in the Fund and Bank (Kenen 2001). The Bush Administration, however, has taken far fewer initiatives in these institutions and has preferred to pursue its financial problems with China through a bilateral 'strategic economic dialogue'.[5]

---

5   See 'Paulson's China Task', leader in *Financial Times*, 11 November 2006.

- Institutions like the WTO and the OECD, which operate by consensus, are the next favoured. Consensus means that the US can never be obliged to accept anything it does not want. Since the US is so large an economic power, few agreements that it does not accept can come into effective operation. So far the United States has always respected the judgements of WTO panels. But in case they should be unsatisfactory, the US retains trade legislation which can be applied bilaterally. Clinton was able to conclude the Uruguay Round negotiations and ratify the agreements, but later tried in vain to use multilateral trade policy for non-trade objectives. Bush began well, promoting the launch of the Doha Development Agenda (DDA) and securing 'trade promotion authority' from Congress. But by his second term the Americans were giving priority to negotiating bilateral Free Trade Agreements (FTAs), with Singapore, Chile, Australia and South Korea.[6]
- Finally, the institutions of the United Nations family, which can adopt majority votes that can go against the United States, are the least favoured. Except in the Security Council, it is very difficult for the United States to feel in control of UN activities. Though votes are rarely used in the UN's environmental discussions and the subject demands the widest possible participation, the US emerges as a reluctant participant from the UNCED conference of 1992 onwards. It held back from subscribing to the UN Biodiversity Convention and its Cartagena Protocol. It became a party to the UN Framework Treaty on Climate Change and signed its Kyoto Protocol, which was adjusted to facilitate American participation. But Clinton was unable to get the Kyoto Protocol ratified by Congress. Bush soon came out in total opposition to it and has continued to refuse any binding US commitment to reduce greenhouse gas emissions.

The US and regionalism   This analysis may explain how the US operates at the multilateral level. What about the regional level? Why should the United States want to combine with its neighbours, rather than dealing with them bilaterally? For very many years the United States indeed showed no interest in regional integration, either on a close or a wider scale. This changed quite suddenly in the early 1990s, with the creation of NAFTA in North America and APEC round the Pacific – followed by the initiative for a Free Trade Area of the Americas. This change was due to a realisation by the Americans that, as their relative power declined, even they could gain by joining forces with others. But they took precautions against being encircled even in regional groupings.

In the Western Hemisphere NAFTA was seen as a regional counterweight to the EU, at a time when it looked as though the Uruguay Round might fail. The Americans regarded it mainly as a framework for their bilateral relations with Canada and Mexico. The intention had been that NAFTA would steadily add new members, but Congress declined to grant negotiating authority to Clinton and the idea lapsed. When Bush took office early in 2001, he promised early

---

6   Bergsten 2001, Bergsten 2004 and Garten 2005 offered advice to incoming administrations, but not much of it was followed.

priority to US links with Latin America and pressed for the completion of the Free Trade Area of the Americas (FTAA). But this impetus has since run out of steam, leaving a new Central American Free Trade Agreement (CAFTA) as its only legacy.

In the Asia-Pacific region APEC was not originally intended by the Australians, who invented it, to include the Americans. But the US could not tolerate being left out of a pan-Pacific grouping and Clinton sought to raise its political profile (see Chapter 11). In practice APEC has been constrained by its large and varied membership and its reliance on voluntary cooperation. Bush has used APEC itself mainly for political purposes, for example, in terrorism, and has given priority to the bilateral level for economic diplomacy. All the bilateral FTA negotiations noted earlier are with individual APEC members (Schott 2003; Woolcock 2006).

In short, the US prefers those regional, plurilateral and multilateral contexts where it can simulate bilateral dealings. It came to favour regional integration more as its relative economic power declined. But by the closing years of the Bush administration, bilateral economic dealings emerged as the preferred method, while multilateralism and regionalism were scaled back.

Often Confrontational

Returning to the features of bilateral economic diplomacy, after that long digression, there is a strong tendency for American economic diplomacy to be confrontational and 'tough'. This is often in contrast to the 'softer' approach of the Europeans or the Japanese. American diplomats regularly reproach their European colleagues for leaving them unsupported in economic negotiations to drive a hard bargain and incur the odium, though the Europeans would come in afterwards to take advantage of the new arrangements. Since EU member states have usually had to devise value creating strategies or package deals so as to achieve a common position, they always try at least to appear value creating to their other negotiating partners. In contrast, the Americans do not shrink from value claiming strategies. Americans also worry about 'free-riders' taking advantage of the economic system – but there are no free riders at the bilateral level.

There are two reasons underlying this approach. The first concerns attitudes to the law. Many Europeans are legalistic in that they want everything tied down in precise legal formulae; this reflects their experience of decision-making in the EU, as explained in Chapter 13 below. Americans, on the other hand, draw on their national tradition of litigiousness in taking a forensic attitude to their economic diplomacy. They expect economic diplomacy to deliver judgements *for* them and *against* the other party, like those given in a court of law. That is inevitably confrontational.

The second reason is linked to the basic motives for countries to engage in economic diplomacy at all. Many countries negotiate about the removal of barriers to their economies because of the improved efficiency such opening can bring them. But the Americans – rightly or wrongly – believe that their economy is the most open in the world already and that they are providing much better standards of market access and transparency than Japan or the EU or their other negotiating partners. This means that their main motive in economic diplomacy is usually to get other countries to lower their barriers to access for US trade or investment or capital flows. This attitude also adds a confrontational tone to American economic diplomacy and leads them to favour the bilateral approach.

Allows Differentiation but Laborious

The last two features of the bilateral level can also be traced very clearly in US economic diplomacy. The post-war multilateral economic system, based on *non-discrimination*, was created largely on US initiative. But there has been a gradual American retreat from this ideal. Already in the Uruguay Round, the Americans became reluctant to endorse non-discrimination for trade in services. In the late 1990s it was the European Union, not the United States that was pressing for another ambitious multilateral round of trade negotiations. The US under Clinton became more interested in using trade measures to enforce labour and environment standards (Bayne 2000). This was reversed under Bush, so that his first US Trade Representative, Bob Zoellick, combined with EU Trade Commissioner Pascal Lamy to promote the new Doha Development Agenda in the WTO. But on specific issues, such as anti-dumping, the United States resists any tightening of the multilateral rules which reduces its ability to act bilaterally. Bilateral trade agreements are also used to obtain commitments from individual countries, for example on investment and capital market opening, that are not available multilaterally. The US practises a 'competitive liberalisation' strategy of negotiating bilateral FTAs, aiming to ratchet up commitments from different partners (Evenett 2007).

Even for the United States, however, the bilateral level is laborious and it cannot give the same attention to every country in the world, great or small. The Americans are most at ease and get the most satisfaction in pursuing bilateral economic diplomacy with their major partners. This avoids the entanglements of multilateral diplomacy and the risk of others 'ganging up on them'. It provides them with some worthy negotiating partners, who are large enough to have something serious to offer, but are still not as powerful as the United States itself. This explains the high priority given to bilateral economic dealings with Japan, China and the European Union (Goodman 2003; Hughes 2005; Chapters 11 and 13 below).

The dynamics of relations between the United States and the European Union are very curious. In principle, and on general grounds, it suits both sides very well for the US to deal with the EU as a single entity. For the Europeans, it enables them to mobilise their combined strength. For the Americans, it avoids the tedium of having to negotiate with each Member State separately and gives them a serious partner to deal with. But in practice, and on detailed issues, EU-US relations often run into serious difficulties. Both the domestic policy process in the United States and the collective decision-making process among EU Member States – explained in Chapter 13 – place severe constraints on American and

European negotiators. These constraints operate in such different ways that it is hard to find the balance between the two sides and misunderstandings easily creep in. So the two largest economic powers, who have every incentive to agree with each other, often fail to do so.[7]

Why Bilateralism Does Not Suit Canada

Bilateralism suits the United States, for the reasons given above. But it does not suit other countries so well. The next section applies the features of bilateralism (as in Table 10.1) to Canada and shows that they do not fit Canada well at all (Cooper 1997). Canada is included here, so that Chapters 10, 11 and 13 of this book can reflect the economic diplomacy of all the members of the G7.

The Traditional Level

Bilateralism does not suit countries with high dependence on the outside world. Because it has so large an area in relation to its population and internal communications are so difficult, Canada has always had to look outwards for markets and economic links.

Simple and Easy to Explain

The second and third features of bilateralism – simplicity and ease of explanation – hold no special attractions for Canada. The federal government's powers over most parts of international economic policy are beyond dispute. There may be disagreements between Ottawa and the provinces over aspects of policy, which may increase as economic diplomacy reaches more issues in provincial jurisdiction. Even so, Ottawa usually holds most of the cards and its powers are hard to challenge. So the Canadian government has not been constrained by the domestic context of decision-making from pursuing the more elaborate forms of economic diplomacy.

Easy to Control and Favours Stronger Party

The fourth and fifth features of bilateralism come to the heart of the difference between Canada and the United States and require fuller explanation.

Canada has been nervous of bilateralism – and even of regionalism – precisely because the US is both so strong and Canada's only close neighbour. This meant that in bilateral dealings with the US, Canada was likely to come out worst, as being so much the weaker party. But Canada could not easily combine with its

---

7   Useful analyses of recent US-EU economic and environmental relations are in Baldwin and others 2003, Bodensky 2003 and Pollack and Shaffer 2001. See also Woolcock 1999 for a pre-Bush view.

regional neighbours against the United States, because any such combination must include the US itself.

Canada and multilateralism   In consequence, Canada's traditional preference has always been to pursue its international economic relations through multilateral or plurilateral institutions. Multilaterally, Canada's attachment to the UN is well known. It has also always been active in the IMF, the World Bank, the GATT and the WTO. Plurilaterally, Canada attaches a lot of importance to its membership of the OECD, the Commonwealth and especially the G8. These institutions provide opportunities for Canada to form alliances with like-minded countries and steer their decisions in favourable directions. The advantages of this outweigh any sense of loss of sovereignty. This approach makes Canada inclined to favour value creating over value claiming strategies.

Canada and regionalism   However, much as America's policy shifted, so did Canada's. By the mid-1980s plurilateral and multilateral institutions were no longer adequate to satisfy Canada's interests. While politically Canada could perform on a wider stage, economically it was becoming ever more closely tied to the United States. This determined Prime Minister Brian Mulroney to reverse all previous trends and conclude a bilateral Free Trade Agreement with the United States.

This was a tremendous risk to take, but Mulroney judged the balance of advantage correctly. Economically, the Canadian economy was just competitive enough to survive alongside the American giant and profit from access to this much larger market. The dispute settlement arrangements, where both countries sat as equals, helped to protect Canada as the weaker party.[8] Politically, Canada soon got the chance to convert this risky bilateral arrangement into a series of regional links of a kind not available before. The emergence of NAFTA and the FTAA in the Western Hemisphere and APEC in the Pacific were highly advantageous to Canada, in enabling it to offset undue dependence on the United States.[9]

Often Confrontational

After another digression, it is time to return to the sixth feature of bilateralism. It may suit the US to be confrontational, but it does not suit Canada. Canadians are natural conciliators – it is an aspect of the national character that is emphasised so as to be different from the United States. In the context of their multilateralist tradition and the pursuit of value creating strategies, Canadians have cultivated

---

8   This did not prevent persistent trade disputes with the US, for example over softwood lumber. But Canada was even worse off without the agreement – it did not have an effective BATNA.

9   Canada also took the initiative in the late 1990s in proposing a Trans-Atlantic Free Trade Area with the United States and European Union. Neither the EU nor the US was interested at the time, but see note 12 below.

many gifts that make them respected members of wider institutions and enable them to derive advantage from them.

Allows Differentiation but Laborious

The prospect of discrimination in economic diplomacy has few attractions for a country like Canada. It has no need to reward or penalise different partners; non-discrimination suits Canada well. It has every advantage in conducting its international economic relations collectively and on equal terms with groups of partners, organised regionally or in wider institutions.

Conclusions: The Impact of Accountability on US Economic Diplomacy

More than in any other country, American economic diplomacy is dominated by the Administration's obligation to be accountable to Congress. This not only inclines the United States to bilateralism, as argued earlier, but also affects its use of the other available levels. It casts a particular shadow over US decision-making at electoral periods, so that new Presidents, like Bill Clinton and George W. Bush, usually start their term in office by stating that they will give priority to domestic issues over international ones.[10] Clinton was further constrained by a loss of Congressional support after his first two years. The Republicans retained control for most of Bush's Administration, but he ended, from 2007 onwards, facing Democrat majorities in both Houses. These conclusions examine the implications of this for the United States' use of all the levels in reconciling the tensions of economic diplomacy.

Tension between Economics and Politics

It is often easiest for the Administration to win Congressional support for measures of international economic cooperation when these serve clear political objectives (Mandelbaum 2002). In the period after World War II, the aim of avoiding future wars brought support for the IMF, World Bank and GATT, while the need to contain the Soviet threat ensured backing for the Marshall Plan, which led to the OECD. In the early 2000s, Bush's justified his early promotion of the FTAA as a means of reinforcing democracy in Latin America and this was generally agreed at the Quebec summit of April 2001. His need for international support in the fight against terrorism after 11 September 2001 facilitated agreement on a new trade round in the WTO and stimulated his pledge of $5 billion of additional aid at the UN Financing Conference in Monterrey in March 2002.

In all these examples, the United States pursued its aims at regional, plurilateral or multilateral levels. Yet the Americans often subordinate these wider levels to

---

10 Clinton's attitude emerges from Christopher 1998, the memoirs of his first Secretary of State.

their bilateral strategy for reconciling economics and politics, with an eye to gaining Congressional support. After the end of the Cold War, for example, the US did not give consistent support to new collective economic measures to help Central and Eastern Europe. While it suggested the European Commission could coordinate bilateral assistance and pushed for action by the IMF and World Bank, initially it opposed the new European Bank for Reconstruction and Development (EBRD), which was an EU initiative. The US was most concerned to develop a privileged bilateral relationship with Russia – first Clinton with Yeltsin, later Bush with Putin.

Recent US measures in favour of Africa show a similar trend. Clinton proposed that Africa should be a leading subject of the 1997 G7 summit at Denver, to focus attention on his own visits to African countries. His aim was also to encourage the passage of the Africa Growth and Opportunity Act through Congress, though this in fact took him till early 2000. The new aid announced by Bush at Monterrey was to be spent through bilateral 'Millennium Challenge Accounts', which were opened for individual countries that met the Administration's standards of good governance.[11] But Bush was reluctant to say at the 2002 Kananaskis summit that half of this could go to Africa, as part of the G8's Africa Action Plan, for fear that this would stimulate Congress to attach conditions to the new aid spending (Bayne 2005, 31–2, 127–41).

Tension between Domestic and International Pressures

Members of the US Congress often reflect narrow local interests, which can lead them to press for unilateral economic measures. The powers given to the states, that are insulated from international pressures, can also incline them in the same direction. The Administration has to find ways of channelling or diverting these unilateralist pressures in its economic diplomacy.

One method is to show the United States as always in charge of the international process. This not only favours bilateralism (as argued above) but encourages the practice of building up plurilateral and multilateral agreements from a series of bilateral deals between the US and its main partners. In trade policy, this goes back to the pre-war Reciprocal Trade Agreements Act, which was the foundation for the early tariff-cutting rounds in the GATT. During the Uruguay Round, the US struck bilateral deals with the EU on agriculture (the Blair House accord) and on services, which formed the basis for the multilateral agreements embodied in the WTO. The same practice has been followed between the US and Europe in public procurement, leading to a plurilateral agreement, and in mutual recognition agreements on a range of goods and services. The

---

11 In a critique of US policy, Jeffrey Sachs (Sachs 2005) recognises that American aid has risen sharply under Bush, but points out that most of it is spent on humanitarian programmes or in the US itself. Little goes to economic development programmes in the recipient countries.

idea of a transatlantic economic agreement has been revived in 2007 by German Chancellor Angela Merkel and found a receptive hearing in Washington.[12]

Congressional opinion, being domestically motivated, regards US practice as the best in the world and therefore expects international rules to conform to American standards. This too affects the choice of approaches to economic diplomacy, for example the American preference for a network of bilateral investment agreements, as explained in Chapter 9. Even so, the US is a frequent user of the dispute settlement mechanism of the WTO as a useful means of obliging other countries to accept the same standards of openness and transparency as its own. So as to preserve the integrity of the WTO mechanism, the United States has hitherto respected all panel judgements, even those that have gone against it. When domestic pressures obliged the US in 2002 to introduce new tariffs on steel and Canadian timber and to adopt a law expanding subsidies for agriculture, the Administration sought to defend these moves as being in line with its WTO obligations.

Finally, the Administration has developed methods to deter Congress from adding unwelcome conditions to international economic agreements and measures. When 'fast-track' trade negotiating authority is given to the Administration, that means that Congress undertakes either to accept or reject an agreement, but not to amend it. Clinton was unable to persuade Congress to grant such authority after 1994; Bush was more successful in winning 'trade promotion authority' to cover WTO and FTAA negotiations in 2002, but this involved a long, hard struggle and major concessions to domestic interests, including the steel tariffs and farm subsidies noted in the previous paragraph. In the event, neither set of negotiations could be completed within the original five-year lifetime of this authority, which expired in June 2007, largely because of declining US interest in them.

Tension between Government and Other Forces

In its dealings with Congress, the Administration looks for allies who will advocate outward-looking, cooperative policies to offset the Congressional preference for domestically motivated unilateralism. Its most frequent ally is international business, which has thus become increasingly integrated into decision-making. Throughout most of the period since the 1940s the Administration relied on manufacturing industry to press for multilateral trade liberalisation. When their support flagged in the 1980s, the Administration turned to the food and financial services sectors and to knowledge-based industries like pharmaceuticals and electronics. This brought agriculture, services and intellectual property onto the agenda for the Uruguay Round. In contrast, the Doha Development Agenda, with its focus on development issues, aroused little interest in US business circles.

---

12 See, for example, the interview with Chancellor Merkel reported in Benoit and Peel 2007. This provoked favourable comment from Canadians – see Emmott and MacLaren 2006.

This absence of business pressure has made it harder for the Bush administration to take the tough domestic decisions needed to complete the DDA.

But reliance on the support of business interests can have a distorting impact on US approaches to economic diplomacy. American advocacy of capital market liberalisation through the IMF and their approach to financial rescues of countries like Mexico in 1995 and Korea in 1997 have been attacked for favouring the interests of large US banks more than those of the countries concerned (Stiglitz 2002). Several of the cases brought by the United States in the WTO, for example against the EU on bananas and Japan on photographic film, were brought at the behest of American firms. US firms often want the Administration to press for the removal of practices in other countries which they consider put them at a competitive disadvantage. Thus, because the US has strict anti-corruption laws, it pressed vigorously and successfully for an international agreement with matching provisions to be introduced in the OECD.

NGOs can have a comparable influence on US decision-making, especially in electoral periods. Pressure from trade unions and 'green' NGOs, traditional Democrat supporters, induced Clinton to speak out in favour of trade sanctions to enforce labour and environmental standards at the WTO meeting in Seattle late in 1999, as the presidential election campaign was beginning (Bayne 2000). The US has also sought GATT and WTO panels on behalf of environmental interests, on fishing practices endangering dolphins and turtles. However, NGOs are less integrated into decision-making than they are in Europe. Obstructive protests at economic meetings, organised via the internet, began in the United States, at Seattle and Washington, before they spread to Europe and reached their lowest point at the Genoa G8 summit of 2001.

US attitudes to climate change show a very unusual combination of attitudes as between Administration, Congress, states, private firms and NGOs. Under Clinton the Administration backed the Kyoto Protocol, but Congress was highly sceptical and the Senate voted against its ratification by a wide margin. This emboldened Bush, under pressure from the large energy firms based in his native Texas, to reject the Kyoto Protocol outright. He denied the evidence for man-made global warming and declared any restrictions on greenhouse gas emissions contrary to America's economic interests. This extreme attitude naturally made Bush very unpopular internationally and among environmental NGOs, but over time it also turned all sectors of US domestic opinion against him. American scientists came to lead the international consensus arguing that global warming was man-made and required urgent action; the general public worried that natural disasters, like the hurricane that struck New Orleans in 2005, were linked to climate change; firms outside a small group of oil companies looked for greater predictability in regulating the problem; important states, led by California (under its Republican Governor, Arnold Schwarzenegger) introduced their own measures to limit emissions; a number of senators and congressmen, Republican as well as Democrat, urged the introduction of mandatory limits nationwide and closer international cooperation. All these groups have recognised the drawbacks of

Bush's unilateralist approach, so that US policy seems bound to change when he leaves office, if not before.[13]

In short, the United States employs all the available approaches to economic diplomacy, in addition to bilateralism, though each of them is coloured by the need for Congressional endorsement. Yet there is a bias in favour of bilateralism and an instinctive resistance to wider international commitments that has been well demonstrated in the Clinton and Bush presidencies. The remaining chapters of this book will contain more examples of how both the United States and other countries make choices between the different levels and seek advantage from the interaction between them.

References

Baldwin, M., Peterson, J. and Stokes, B. (2003), 'Trade and Economic Relations', in Peterson, J. and Pollack, M. (eds), *Europe, America and Bush: Transatlantic Relations after 2000*, Routledge, London, pp. 29–46.

Bayne, N. (2000), 'Why Did Seattle Fail? Globalisation and the Politics of Trade', *Government and Opposition*, Vol. 35, No. 2, pp. 131–51.

Bayne, N. (2005), *Staying Together: the G8 Summit Confronts the Twenty-first Century*, Ashgate, Aldershot.

Benoit, B. and Peel, Q. (2007), 'Relations with US Top Agenda as Germany Takes on EU Presidency', *Financial Times*, 3 January.

Bergsten, C.F. (2001), 'America's Two-Front Economic Conflict', *Foreign Affairs*, Vol. 80, No. 2, pp. 16–27.

Bergsten, C.F. (2004), 'Foreign Economic Policy for the Next President', *Foreign Affairs*, Vol. 83, No. 2, pp. 88–101.

Bodensky, D. (2003), 'Transatlantic Environmental Relations', in Peterson, J. and Pollack, M. (eds), *Europe, America and Bush: Transatlantic Relations after 2000*, Routledge, London, pp. 59–68.

Christopher, W. (1998), *In the Stream of History*, Stanford University Press, Stanford.

Cohen, J.E. (2000), *Politics and Economic Policy in the United States*, 2nd edition, Howard Mifflin Co., Boston.

Cooper, A.F. (1997), *Canadian Foreign Policy: Old Habits and New Directions*, Prentice Hall, Scarborough, Ontario.

Destler, I.M. (2005), *American Trade Politics*, 4th edition, Institute of International Economics, Washington.

Emmott, B. and MacLaren, R. (2006), 'Why a Transatlantic Trade Pact Can Work', *Financial Times*, 20 December.

Evenett, S. J. and Meier, M. (2007), 'An Interim Assessment of the US Trade Policy of "Competitive Liberalisation"', available at http://www.evenett.com.

Gardner, R. (1980), *Sterling-Dollar Diplomacy in Current Perspective*, Columbia University Press, New York.

Garrahan, M. (2007), 'Legacy Issue: How Bush is Preparing an About-Turn to Tackle Climate Change', *Financial Times*, 23 January.

---

13 See Garrahan 2007.

Garten, J.E. (2005), 'The Global Economic Challenge', *Foreign Affairs*, Vol. 84, No. 1, pp. 37–48.

Goodman, M. (2003), 'An Overview of US-Japanese Economic Relations', in Bayne, N. and Woolcock, S. (eds), *The New Economic Diplomacy: Decision-Making and Negotiation in International Economic Relations*, 1st edition, Ashgate, Aldershot, pp. 181–96.

Hughes, N.C. (2005), 'A Trade War with China?' *Foreign Affairs*, Vol. 84, No. 4, pp. 94–106.

Kagan, R. (2006), *Dangerous Nation: America's Place in the World from its Earliest Days to the Dawn of the Twentieth Century*, Atlantic Books, London.

Kenen, P.B. (ed.) (1994), *Managing the World Economy: Fifty Years after Bretton Woods*, Institute of International Economics, Washington.

Kenen, P.B. (2001), *The International Financial Architecture: What's New? What's Missing?*, Institute of International Economics, Washington.

Mandelbaum, M. (2002) 'The Inadequacy of American Power', *Foreign Affairs*, Vol. 81, No. 5, pp. 61–73.

Marjolin, R. (1989), *Architect of European Unity: Memoirs 1911–1986*, Weidenfield and Nicholson, London, translated by William Hall from *Le Travail d'une Vie*, Robert Laffont, Paris, 1986.

Nye, J. (2003), *The Paradox of American Power: Why the World's Only Super-power Can't Go it Alone*, Oxford University Press, Oxford.

Odell, J. (2000), *Negotiating the World Economy*, Cornell University Press, Ithaca, NY.

Paarlberg, R. (1995), *Leadership Begins at Home: US Foreign Economic Policy after the Cold War*, The Brookings Institution, Washington.

Peterson, J. and Pollack, M. (eds) (2003), *Europe, America and Bush: Transatlantic Relations after 2000*, Routledge, London.

Pollack, M.A. and Shaffer, G.C. (2001), *Transatlantic Governance in the Global Economy*, Rowman and Littlefield, Lanham, MD.

Rana, K.S. (2002), *Bilateral Diplomacy*, DiploFoundation, Malta and Manas Publications, New Delhi.

Sachs, J.D. (2005), 'The Development Challenge', *Foreign Affairs*, Vol. 84, No. 2, pp. 78–90.

Schott, J. (ed.) (2003), *Free Trade Agreements: US Strategies and Priorities*, Institute of International Economics, Washington.

Stiglitz, J. (2002), *Globalization and its Discontents*, Allen Lane, London.

Winham, G.L. (1992), *The Evolution of International Trade Agreements*, University of Toronto Press, Toronto.

Woolcock, S. (1999), 'The United States and Europe in the Global Economy', in Burwell, F.G. and Daalder, I.H. (eds), *The United States and Europe in the Global Arena*, Macmillan, London, and St Martin's Press, New York, pp. 177–207.

Woolcock, S. (ed.) (2006), *Trade and Investment Rule-Making; the Role of Regional and Bilateral Agreements*, UN University Press, Tokyo.

Useful Websites

Office of the US Trade Representative: http://www.ustr.gov.
US Department of State: http://www.state.gov.
US Treasury Department: http://www.ustreas.gov.

Chapter 11

When the Twain Meet: US Economic Diplomacy towards Asia

Matthew Goodman

Introduction

'Oh, East is East, and West is West, and never the twain shall meet.' This famous first line of Rudyard Kipling's *The Ballad of East and West* is often interpreted to mean that there is little scope for mutual understanding between Asia and the West. In fact, the poem as a whole makes precisely the opposite point: while separated by geography, Asians and Westerners are more alike than not and can make common cause where their interests align. Such an alignment clearly exists in the realm of economic affairs.

The nations of East Asia and the Pacific – a region defined here to encompass the 21 economies of the Asia-Pacific Economic Cooperation (APEC) group – account for over half of the world's gross domestic product and more than 40 per cent of global trade.[1] Since this dynamic area includes some of the world's fastest-growing countries, these figures are likely to grow in the years ahead. Indeed, it is not a bold prediction to say that what happens in the Asia-Pacific region will do more to shape global economic trends over the next several decades than developments in any other part of the world.

As the largest country in the region, the United States plays a central role in its economic affairs. America absorbs most exports of other Asia-Pacific countries, provides these countries with technology and management know-how, and is the principal destination for both their direct and portfolio investments. Moreover, of particular relevance here, policy decisions taken in Washington on matters of trade, investment, and finance shape government actions and market outcomes throughout the Asia-Pacific region.

This chapter offers an overview of US economic diplomacy towards Asia from both a historical and present-day perspective. Asia, in this context, means the East Asian members of APEC, not the entire continent.

---

1   The members of APEC are: Australia; Brunei Darussalam; Canada; Chile; China; Hong Kong, China; Indonesia; Japan; Republic of Korea; Malaysia; Mexico; New Zealand; Papua New Guinea; Peru; Philippines; Russia; Singapore; Chinese Taipei; Thailand; United States; Vietnam.

Why Asia Matters to the United States

Americans living in New York, Boston, or Washington often overlook the fact that the United States is a Pacific nation. Some 7,600 miles of its shores are lapped by the Pacific Ocean, more than three times the length of the Atlantic seaboard. To be sure, America's history and culture are dominated by Atlantic influences, and events in Europe and Africa today remain a central focus of American foreign policy. However, America's *interests* – be they military, economic, or otherwise – are increasingly tied to developments in the Asia-Pacific region.

Security Interests

The United States fought four wars in the Asia-Pacific theatre in the three-quarters of a century between 1898 and 1975.[2] In addition, many key 'battlefields' of the Cold War were in Asia. Largely as a legacy of these conflicts, some 100,000 American troops remain deployed in the Pacific, most of them in Japan and South Korea.

The US military presence is a vital source of stability in a region fraught with unresolved historical tensions and potential future conflicts. These include the continued division of the Korean Peninsula between an isolated, communist North and a rapidly emerging South; the struggle between Beijing and Taipei for sovereignty over greater China; and the potent mixture of historical resentment and growing political competition between Japan and China on one hand, and Japan and Korea on the other. The United States is an indispensable 'balancer' in all of these disputes.

Economic Ties

Roughly $800 billion worth of goods and services flowed back and forth across the Pacific in 2006,[3] representing the lifeblood of US-Asian economic relations. For the United States, trade with Asia accounts for over one-third of its total trade. Five of America's top 10 trading partners are in Asia. This robust trade is driven, on one hand, by the voracious appetite of American consumers for competitively produced goods from Asia, from toys to automobiles; on the other, by Asian demand for American capital equipment, agricultural produce, healthcare products, and financial services.

Foreign direct investment (FDI) also binds the United States to Asia. As of the end of 2005, American companies had an accumulated stock of some $376 billion invested in factories and other operations in Asia.[4] China in particular has become a major destination for American FDI, as companies move to exploit

---

2   The Spanish-American War (1898), World War II (1941–1945), the Korean War (1950–1953) and the Vietnam War (1965–1975).

3   US Department of Commerce, Bureau of Economic Statistics (http://www.bea.org).

4   Ibid.

cost efficiencies and/or a growing Chinese domestic market. FDI also flows heavily in the other direction: Japanese companies from Toyota to Toshiba have become major producers in the United States, driven by the desire to be closer to their customers and to skirt American protectionism. In recent years, Chinese companies have begun to follow the Japanese lead in this area.

America's financial well-being is also increasingly tied to Asia. Led by China and Japan, Asian countries hold over \$1 trillion worth of US Treasury securities, some 25 per cent of total outstanding issuance.[5] These holdings reflect the fundamental macroeconomic symmetry between surplus Asian savings searching for a profitable place to invest and America's need to finance its excess consumption. This financial interdependence, more than any other fact, underscores the enormous stakes in US-Asian economic relations.

Other Interests

In addition to security and economics, a wide array of other interests draws the United States to Asia. Washington depends on its closest ally in the region, Japan, to support it on global initiatives from fighting terrorism to addressing poverty in Africa. Increasingly, the US government faces the challenge of channelling China's growing power towards similarly constructive ends, while ensuring that Beijing – with its veto power in the United Nations Security Council and its growing economic and diplomatic links with emerging countries in Asia, Latin America and Africa – does not undermine Washington's political objectives around the world.

Indonesia, with the largest Muslim population in the world, is a vital actor in the Bush Administration's 'global war on terror'. Longstanding Muslim insurgencies in Thailand and the Philippines are obstacles to political stability in those US-friendly countries. And the repressive military regime in Burma (Myanmar) presents a serious challenge to American human rights policy.

The SARS and avian influenza epidemics were reminders that the Asian region is a potential incubator for global health crises that would both directly affect the United States and require American leadership around the world. Similar Asia-based challenges exist in the areas of environmental degradation, narcotics trafficking, and illicit finance.

In sum, Asia matters tremendously to the United States and demands substantial policy attention from the US government across a plethora of issues.

History: From Black Ships to Open Regionalism

To put current US economic diplomacy towards Asia in perspective, it is worth briefly reviewing some historical highlights of American engagement in the region during the past 150 years. Over this period, pursuit of economic interests

---

5   US Treasury Department (http://www.ustreas.gov), as of end-March 2007.

has evolved from being the primary *objective* of US policy – with military force applied if necessary to support that objective – to being an important *tool* of broader foreign policy.

1850–1900: Opening the Door

The beginning of significant American diplomatic engagement with Asia can be dated to July 1853, when four 'black ships' under the command of US Navy Commodore Matthew Perry sailed into Edo (Tokyo) Bay. Perry had been sent to Japan by President Millard Fillmore with a two-part mission: to open the Japanese market to trade, and to allow America's commercial whaling fleet to call at Japanese ports for refuelling and resupply. By the time Perry returned to Japan eight months later, in the spring of 1854, a traumatised Japanese government was ready to sign a 'peace and amity' treaty with the United States.

The opening of Japan marked one of the first significant projections of American power beyond the young nation's immediate sphere of influence. It was driven first and foremost by commercial considerations, as America's sprint for economic development drove it westwards, first across the continent and eventually across the Pacific, in search of new resources and markets. US military might was exercised in support of these commercial objectives, rather than to extend America's political reach or ensure its physical security.

The next major milestone in US economic diplomatic history occurred at the end of the nineteenth century. With the Chinese empire in decay, the major powers (Britain, France, Germany, Italy, Russia, and Japan) were vying for strategic influence in the Middle Kingdom. In late 1898, US President William McKinley publicly called for an 'open door' that would allow all powers equal trading rights in the Chinese market. The following year, McKinley's Secretary of State, John Hay, tried to formalise the Open Door policy through a series of diplomatic notes among the major powers.

While hiding behind the rhetoric of defending China's territorial integrity, McKinley and Hay were in fact primarily seeking to protect America's commercial interests. The United States had become an Asian power through its acquisition of the Philippines from Spain in 1898 but had no sphere of influence of its own in China. In constructing the Open Door policy, McKinley and Hay were trying to prevent the other major powers from partitioning China and excluding American investors and traders from that sizeable market.

World Wars I and II: From Protectionism to Reconstruction

The Open Door policy would mark the high-water mark for constructive application of US economic diplomacy for the next half century. Following World War I, isolationist sentiment took hold in America, a mood reinforced by the stock market crash of 1929 and the onset of the Great Depression. In international economic policy, the result was protectionism, with the infamous Smoot-Hawley Tariff Act of 1930 sharply raising tariffs on over 20,000 imported goods. This precipitated a downward spiral of protectionism that plunged the global economy into depression and contributed to the onset of World War II.

While the tariff hikes of 1930 had been largely reversed by the middle of that decade, Washington began to apply another tool of international economic policy to Asia in the run-up to World War II: trade and financial sanctions. In response to Japan's occupation of Indochina, the Roosevelt Administration in 1940 imposed an embargo on US iron and steel exports to Japan, and the following year froze Japanese assets in the United States. The latter action amounted to a de facto ban on oil exports to Japan, since the Japanese did not have the wherewithal to pay for desperately needed energy supplies. This series of sanctions is widely viewed as the precipitating factor behind Japan's attack on Pearl Harbor and America's entry into World War II.

Following the Japanese surrender in August 1945, the United States began a seven-year occupation of Japan. Given the brutality of the Pacific campaign, it might have been expected for the United States to use its dominant postwar position to thwart Japan's meaningful recovery. Instead, anticipating the coming Cold War confrontation with the Soviet Union, Washington chose to invest heavily in the economic and political rebuilding of Japan, to ensure that the country became a bulwark against communism and a stable base for the forward deployment of US troops in the Pacific.

The years immediately following World War II were arguably the 'golden age' of US economic diplomacy. As the sole power to emerge largely unscathed from the war, Washington used its dominant position to champion the institutional architecture that would govern global economic affairs throughout the postwar period, notably the creation of the Bretton Woods institutions: the International Monetary Fund (IMF), World Bank and General Agreement on Tariffs and Trade (GATT). These institutions invested in the reconstruction of war-ravaged countries in Europe and in the economic development of the poor nations of Asia, Africa, and Latin America; provided resources and technical advice to promote global financial stability; and encouraged the liberalisation of international trade in goods and services. While these policies were not targeted at any particular region, a history of US economic diplomacy towards Asia would be incomplete without reference to the profound impact that the postwar institutional architecture had on the Asian region.

1970s and 1980s: Growing American Insecurity

By the early 1970s, the United States was no longer the confident superpower it had been in the immediate postwar period. Bogged down by an expensive war in Vietnam, and facing serious economic dislocations at home, the Nixon Administration announced in August 1971 two major policy moves that rocked the global economy: it suspended the convertibility of the US dollar against gold and imposed a 10 per cent surcharge on all imports into the United States. Given the heavy dependence of the Japanese economy on exports to the US market (and on a weak yen), these moves – together with the President's announcement earlier that summer that he would travel to Communist China – are known in Japan as the 'Nixon shocks' and still haunt Japanese policy-makers today.

The oil shocks of the 1970s had other significant effects on the course of US economic diplomacy. First, they prompted Washington to join with other advanced industrialised nations in attempting to coordinate management of the international economy, through the so-called 'Group of Seven' or G7 (now G8). From the beginning, Washington used this forum to influence the exchange rate and other macroeconomic policies of Japan, the only Asian member of the group. There have been growing calls in recent years for China to be admitted as a full member of the G8, including by architects of US international economic policy who see the forum as a tool to shape Chinese financial policies.[6]

Second, the burgeoning of the US trade deficit prompted Washington to become more aggressive in its trade relations with surplus nations, notably Japan. Thus began in the late 1970s two decades of virtually non-stop, often contentious trade negotiations, as Washington demanded that Tokyo open its market to American exports of everything from agricultural products to automobiles and financial services. However, despite intense rhetoric and Congressional passage of hostile trade legislation, the US government only once over this period imposed retaliatory tariffs against Japanese imports.[7] Haunted by the memory of Smoot-Hawley, successive administrations of both parties did everything they could to avoid overtly protectionist actions, including through creative – if questionable, in GATT terms – use of 'voluntary export restraints' to limit Japanese automobile sales in the United States.

Mid-1990s to Today: Towards Asian Regionalism

By the mid-1990s, with the Japanese economy floundering and the United States more economically confident, the Clinton Administration began to move away from its early use of aggressive trade policies, particularly aimed at Japan, to a more cooperative approach to trade relations with Asian countries generally. In 1993, the Administration upgraded the Asia-Pacific Economic Cooperation forum from ministerial to head-of-government level, with President Bill Clinton himself hosting the Leaders Meeting that year. Washington also committed itself to APEC's long-term goal of becoming a free trade area, based on the principle of 'open regionalism'.

The Clinton Administration also abandoned its initially hostile rhetoric on trade with China and successfully persuaded Congress to grant 'permanent normal trade relations' (formerly 'most-favoured-nation treatment') to that rapidly emerging power. And at the very end of his term, President Clinton announced

---

6   See, for example, O'Neill and Hormats 2004. I have argued the case in Goodman 2004, while O'Neill has returned to the theme in O'Neill 2007.

7   In 1987, the Reagan Administration briefly imposed 100 per cent duties on $300 million worth of Japanese imports in retaliation for Tokyo's alleged violation of a bilateral semiconductor agreement.

a free trade agreement with Singapore, a harbinger of a significant shift in US economic policy towards Asia in the coming years.

The Administration of George W. Bush substantially built upon these initiatives. Under the leadership of President Bush's first US Trade Representative, Robert Zoellick, Washington launched a series of bilateral FTA negotiations with Asian countries, including Singapore, Thailand, Korea, and Malaysia. The Bush Administration in 2001 also completed negotiations on China's accession to the WTO, a landmark event in the integration of China into the world economy. As for APEC, President Bush not only attended all of the group's summits on his watch but, at the 2006 event in Vietnam, actively championed a 'Free Trade Area of the Asia-Pacific', encompassing all 21 APEC members. (Washington's FTA, China, and APEC strategies are all discussed in more detail later in this chapter.)

As this brief historical overview has shown, US economic policy towards Asia has evolved over the past 150 years from the era of 'gunboat diplomacy', when Washington sent warships to open markets on behalf of American trading interests, to an approach today that is based on a more complex mix of commercial, political, and security considerations. The following section will review the main drivers of the present-day approach, and the process by which economic policy towards Asia is designed and executed.

Key Characteristics of US Asian Economic Policy Today

Domestic 'Push' and Strategic 'Pull'

As mentioned in the previous section, when President Fillmore sent the Black Ships to Japan in 1853, US commercial interests were foremost in his mind. He was responding to pressure from American trading concerns that had crossed the Pacific in search of new sources of supply and markets. Yet Fillmore was also thinking strategically – not about expanding American territory or political influence, but about enhancing the young nation's economic prosperity. Thus, from the beginning, US international economic policy has been driven by both the 'push' of domestic political forces and the 'pull' of strategic considerations.

One can clearly see these dynamics at work today. Commercial interests still lie behind most of Washington's international economic policies. When USTR presses America's trading partners for open markets or a predictable foreign investment climate, it is advancing the interests of US corporations wishing to export to or invest in those markets. Similarly, when the US Treasury seeks exchange rate flexibility in China, one of its goals is to ensure American trade competitiveness. Washington's demands for enhanced labour rights in developing countries, meanwhile, reflect concerns of American workers about their global competitiveness.

On occasion, the 'push' factor in international economic policy stems from non-commercial sources. The US government may be seeking to modify offensive behaviour by a foreign government, such as violations of human rights or environmental degradation. When they are serious enough, human rights concerns may impel Washington to impose trade or financial sanctions; two Asian nations, Burma and North Korea, are currently targets of such sanctions. Meanwhile, USTR now routinely seeks tough environmental provisions in the trade agreements it negotiates.

Yet it would be misleading to portray US international economic policy as purely reactive, driven merely by the domestic 'push' factors discussed above. As with Fillmore and the Black Ships, there is almost always a more proactive, strategic dimension that 'pulls' Washington to engage with other countries. The strategic objectives can be either economic in nature, or related to broader national security concerns, or both.

Even when ostensibly driven by narrow commercial concerns, most US international economic policies are aimed at enhancing American prosperity more broadly. Consider macroeconomic policy. Since the early 1970s, successive administrations have pressed Japan to pursue 'domestic demand-led growth', and this is now part of Washington's 'mantra' in its discussions with China. By encouraging the Japanese and Chinese to rely more on domestic consumption, and less on exports, for growth, Washington has sought to reduce the large and persistent current account imbalances across the Pacific. This is partly a response to domestic politics, but there are also broader economic interests at stake: promoting more balanced American growth, and ensuring financial stability by avoiding over-reliance on foreign savings to finance US deficits.

A similar mix of motivations is involved in the US government's pursuit of trade liberalisation. Reducing tariff and non-tariff barriers abroad not only directly benefits US export interests but also generates substantial economic gains for countries undertaking the liberalisation, in turn raising global economic growth and benefitting Americans more broadly. Again, these potential gains are particularly sizeable in Asia, given its large share of global trade and GDP.

Moreover, there is another strategic consideration at work in US trade policy: Washington must keep the 'bicycle' of international trade liberalisation moving forward or risk falling into the protectionist ditch. Despite its economic logic, free trade is a difficult concept to sell to domestic political audiences, given the transitional pain it can inflict on less competitive companies and workers. Hence it is critical that the broader gains from trade be constantly demonstrated through market opening abroad that expands US export opportunities. Again, this consideration has been especially important in American trade policy towards the large surplus nations of Asia that have been the focus of most domestic political concern: Japan in the past, China today.

In addition to these economic forces, US international economic policy is often 'pulled' by broader strategic considerations. This can be seen in a number of aspects of present-day policy towards Asia. Arguably, America's overriding long-term national security interest in Asia is ensuring that China emerges as a stable, confident but not aggressive, and ultimately democratic country. To this end, since Beijing launched its opening to the world in 1979, successive US Administrations have sought to integrate China into the global rules-based system, to give it a greater stake in that system, and to encourage it to play by the rules – rules that, for the most part, were written by the United States and other

Western powers. Facilitating China's accession to the World Trade Organization has been the primary vehicle for pursuing this strategic objective. In addition to opening China's borders to trade, WTO accession, completed in December 2001, prompted or accelerated a wide range of domestic institutional reforms in China. By encouraging not only economic efficiency but also the rule of law in China, and subjecting Beijing to global standards of economic behaviour, the US government has sought – with considerable success – to make China a more 'responsible stakeholder' in the region and the world.[8]

Other examples from Asia of economic policy in the service of broader foreign policy objectives include the Bush Administration's use of targeted aid programmes to expand economic opportunities for the large Muslim populations of South-East Asia, which is ultimately aimed at bolstering US counter-terrorism strategy in the region. Washington's negotiation of a network of free trade agreements in South-East Asia, meanwhile, is designed in part as a 'hedge' against China's growing political influence in the region.

In sum, while it is easy to take a cynical view of the US government's economic diplomacy as primarily designed to serve narrow commercial interests, in reality there are almost always broader strategic considerations at play, related both to promoting America's overall economic welfare and to enhancing its national security.

The Policy-Making Process

International economic policy-making in the United States is like a Rube Goldberg machine, a complex contraption with ramps, wheels, pulleys, and switches. The machine has multiple operators inserting balls into various openings, and when and where the balls will emerge is highly uncertain. However, it is possible to describe a few general characteristics of the policy-making process that shed light on how the US government designs and carries out economic policy towards Asia.

First, international economic policy-making is highly decentralised. The US Constitution divides power over foreign economic affairs between the executive and legislative branches: while the President has the prerogative to 'make treaties' (Article II, Section 2), Congress has the power to 'regulate commerce with foreign nations' (Article I, Section 8). The awkwardness of this division of labour is most clearly seen in the area of international trade negotiations, where Congress must periodically delegate so-called 'trade promotion authority' to the administration through specific legislation.[9]

---

8   The term 'responsible stakeholder' was coined by Robert Zoellick, then US Deputy Secretary of State, in a September 2005 speech to the National Committee on US-China Relations.

9   Under this delegated authority, formerly known as 'fast-track', Congress retains the power to approve or reject negotiated deals on an up-or-down vote, but cannot alter the terms of the agreement the Administration lays before it.

Decision-making on international economic policy is further diffused within each branch. The House of Representatives and Senate each has several committees with some jurisdiction over international economic policy, including Ways and Means, Financial Services, and Commerce in the House; and Finance, Banking, and Commerce in the Senate. A similar division of labour exists within the executive branch, where at least a dozen federal agencies have significant responsibility for international economic policy-making: the Treasury Department for foreign exchange, macroeconomic and financial issues; the US Trade Representative for trade negotiations; Commerce for enforcement of anti-dumping and countervailing duty laws; and so on. In theory, all of this is coordinated through inter-agency meetings managed by the staff of the President's National Security Council, but in practice each of the executive agencies has considerable authority to design and implement policies in its own jurisdiction.

In the open American political system, this diffusion of authority means that industry associations, think tanks, non-governmental organisations, and other interest groups have a multitude of channels through which to get their voices heard on policy. This tends to accentuate the domestic 'push' factor in international economic policy described earlier. (It also explains why US policy can be somewhat incoherent at times, and inconsistent *over* time.)

The decentralisation of policy-making authority also has its advantages. As intended by America's founding fathers, it creates a system of 'checks and balances' to ensure that government policy does not become captive to a narrow set of interests. It also gives Washington useful leverage in negotiating with other nations, through a kind of 'good cop/bad cop' routine in which the administration's trade negotiators can cite an unruly and demanding Congress as the force behind their tough negotiating positions.

A second salient feature of US international economic policy is that it tends to follow a cyclical pattern over time. Like the moon's gravitational pull on the oceans, the US political calendar sets the rhythm of the policy-making tide, while domestic growth and employment are the atmospheric conditions determining the intensity with which the policy waves crash up on shore.

Coming into office, an administration is typically at the peak of its energy, talent, and political capital; thus it is no surprise that most new policy initiatives are launched during the first year or two of a four-year Presidential term. In the area of international economic policy, the first major event of the year, the G8 Summit, typically comes a convenient six months into the new President's term and thus becomes a focal point for key initiatives. For Asia, the equivalent annual event is the APEC Leaders Meeting in the autumn, which often drives policy towards that region.

By year three of a President's term, the policy energy has typically been spent, and the administration's focus has shifted to the politics of the next election cycle. In the case of politically sensitive policy issues, however, a new dynamic then takes hold. With the Presidential election looming, these issues often draw heightened media attention as candidates attempt to differentiate themselves from their competitors. Trade policy is one such issue. Challengers from both parties in recent years have tended to disparage the incumbent as 'soft' on trade and to portray themselves as the true champion of American workers. This has often forced an incumbent administration to launch new trade initiatives – a bilateral negotiating process, or a WTO filing against an 'unfair' foreign trade practice – to demonstrate its 'toughness' on trade and avert possible protectionist legislation in Congress.

Macroeconomic conditions in the United States can intensify or smooth out these cycles of policy engagement. During periods of slow growth, when unemployment is high or workers feel insecure about their jobs and living standards, political sentiment can easily turn against import competition as the source of America's economic woes. This can force the administration to take a more aggressive policy stance vis-à-vis its major trading partners. On the other hand, where economic conditions at home are generally sound, an administration can often ride out domestic political pressure with toughened rhetoric but few substantive policy responses.

The rhythm just described is clearly apparent in US economic policy towards Asia, particularly Japan in the past and China more recently. In the 1980s and early 1990s, Japan's large trade surpluses with the United States made it the focal point of political attention and policy action. This activity peaked around the 1988 and 1992 Presidential elections, when anxiety about America's economic decline relative to Japan was running at its highest. In addition to a plethora of trade negotiations, this period was punctuated by the imposition of retaliatory sanctions against Japan in 1987 (mentioned earlier); passage of tough new trade legislation in 1988; and a disastrous trade mission to Japan by President George H.W. Bush in early 1992.[10]

Since the late 1990s, China has replaced Japan as the principal external source of American economic anxiety. Again, policy has proceeded according to a predictable rhythm, intensifying during election cycles and when economic conditions in the US are weak.

A third characteristic of US policy-making that is particularly relevant to a discussion of economic diplomacy towards Asia is the dearth of regional expertise in the US government. Due to the American system of political appointments to top policy-making positions, it is rare for senior officials to have relevant language skills or in-country experience. At the time of this writing (end of 2006), there is not a single foreign policy official in the US government at the level of Assistant Secretary or above (that is, at the key policy-making tiers) who has proficiency in an Asian language, and only two or three who have significant experience working in the region.

Even in the career bureaucracy, there is no more than a handful of true Asia experts; most of these are at the State Department, and few are economic specialists. With the deepening of business and cultural ties with Asia, the

---

10 Among other problems, the White House first postponed the trip for domestic political reasons, then rescheduled it to occur during Japan's near-sacred New Year's holiday; during the trip, the President was accused of being 'salesman in chief' for having invited a group of automotive executives to accompany him; and he famously fell ill during the State Dinner thrown in his honour by the Japanese Emperor.

number of relevant experts in the US government is growing but remains small in comparison with the number of Europe experts – let alone with the size and growth of economic interaction across the Pacific.

This expertise gap has significant implications for US economic policy towards Asia. It means that most senior officials tend to be preoccupied with priorities in other parts of the world and to pay too little regular attention to Asia. As a result, Washington may overlook emerging risks from Asia, or miss new opportunities for engagement. When problems do arise that demand policy-makers' attention, the lack of familiarity with the region can result in misguided responses. Critics blame this expertise gap for causing the Clinton Administration early in its term to underestimate Japan's resistance to 'managed trade' proposals, or the Bush Administration to mishandle the North Korean nuclear crisis, insofar as the views of most senior officials responsible for the issue were shaped by European Cold War experience.

The Importance of Leverage

Despite all of the quirks and inadequacies of the policy-making process, US economic diplomacy towards Asia has been remarkably effective over the past several decades. For the most part, Washington has managed to win more open markets for its exporters and investors, to promote domestic reforms and the rule of law among America's trading partners, and to give all players in the Asia-Pacific area a greater economic stake in regional peace and security.

The success of all diplomacy ultimately comes down to leverage, ie the carrots and sticks that a country wields to persuade other countries to do what it wants. In the case of US economic diplomacy in Asia, this leverage stems from two main sources. The first is America's security posture in the region. Washington no longer has to rely on the crude 'gunboat diplomacy' of the nineteenth century to get its way. Instead, most countries in Asia want the United States to remain engaged in the region as a 'balancer' in various disputes, as mentioned earlier. If listening to economic entreaties is the price of keeping Washington happy and involved in the region, Asian governments are generally willing to play along. Even China – the principal source of other Asian countries' concern about regional 'balance' – probably recognises that an economically satisfied United States serves its own interests as it pursues its 'peaceful rise'.

The other source of Washington's leverage is, of course, the purely economic carrots and sticks the United States can hold out to Asia. Foremost among these is the large and generally open American market. As mentioned earlier, most export production in Asia is geared towards final consumption in the United States, and maintaining access to the US market is therefore a matter of highest priority for most Asian countries. The credible threat of closing off that market – whether through relatively narrow tools such as anti-dumping actions or broader protectionist measures – gives Washington a powerful hand in economic negotiations with its Asian counterparts.

Other economic carrots include the capital, technology, and management know-how that the United States has to offer Asia. As long as these incentives and the large American market remain important to Asian countries, Washington will retain powerful tools of economic diplomacy in the region.

US Asian Economic Diplomacy in Action: Three Examples

Having discussed some of the general characteristics of US international economic policy-making, we turn to three current examples of America's economic diplomacy towards Asia, all of which have been touched upon above: Washington's support for regional integration through APEC; its pursuit of a network of free trade agreements in Asia; and its efforts to manage bilateral economic friction with China. These examples are at the core of Washington's approach to the region in recent years and are likely to remain so over the medium term. In addition, they highlight the three levels of US engagement with Asia – regional, sub-regional, and bilateral.

Supporting Regional Integration through APEC

The Asia-Pacific Economic Cooperation forum was established in 1989, when Australian Prime Minister Robert Hawke invited foreign ministers from 12 Asia-Pacific countries to Canberra to discuss ways of strengthening regional economic ties. The United States was a founding member of the group, but it was not until 1993, when the new Clinton Administration was looking for ways to revive the flagging Uruguay Round of multilateral trade negotiations, that APEC moved to the core of Washington's regional strategy. President Clinton invited fellow Asia-Pacific leaders to the first head-of-government level summit on Blake Island near Seattle, Washington, in November 1993, and Leaders Meetings have been held every year since as the pinnacle of the APEC year.

The US government's enthusiasm for APEC has waxed and waned in the years since Blake Island. The Clinton Administration initially used the forum to press an ambitious agenda of regional economic integration, brokering the so-called Bogor Goals in 1994, which committed APEC economies to 'free and open trade and investment' in the region by 2010 (2020 for developing economies). But efforts to put the Bogor Goals into practice soon bogged down, and Washington became distracted by other issues in the latter half of the 1990s. In particular, the Asian financial crisis of 1997–1998 took the wind out of APEC's sails – not only by diverting most members' attention to more pressing challenges, but also by undermining US leadership in the group, since Washington's response to the crisis was poorly received in the region.

APEC assumed new prominence in the George W. Bush Administration's Asia strategy, although this was based more on security considerations than on an interest in regional economic integration per se. President Bush's first APEC meeting, in Shanghai in October 2001, came in the immediate aftermath of the attacks of 11 September, and he used the event to press for regional cooperation in the fight against terrorism. The focus on security objectives continued through the 2006 summit in Hanoi, when Washington signaled renewed interest in APEC's original goals of regional trade and investment liberalisation by pressing for endorsement of a 'Free Trade Area of the Asia-Pacific' (FTAAP).

Washington's on-again-off-again approach to APEC reflects its views of the effectiveness of the organisation in promoting US priorities. In this context, it is useful to dissect APEC into the three levels at which it effectively operates: at the bottom is an array of working groups and technical cooperation efforts; in the middle, 'headline' policy initiatives, such as regional trade and investment liberalisation; and at the top, the Leaders process. Senior US policy-makers have little time for the bottom tier but acknowledge that the work done there on business facilitation, technical standards, capacity building, and so on, are vital to long-term regional development and integration. In fact, it is at this level that most of the US government's resources and energy are consistently dedicated to APEC matters.

At the other end of the spectrum, the annual Leaders Meeting creates frustrations of its own for senior US officials: the ratio of ceremony to substance is too high, the meetings are too long, and there are too many people around the table for constructive debate. However, Washington recognises that the APEC summit is the only occasion during the year when leaders from this vital region come together to discuss issues of regional and global concern. This creates opportunities to develop personal bonds, to address bilateral issues on the margins of the formal meetings, and, most important, to align other APEC governments with Washington's broader foreign policy goals. Hence both the Clinton and Bush Administrations have devoted intensive effort to getting APEC leaders to publicly endorse US policy priorities of the day – from reviving global trade talks to combatting terrorism and nuclear proliferation.

It is the middle tier of APEC that has been most disappointing to supporters and detractors of the forum alike. With 21 members at vastly different stages of economic and political development – ranging from the United States to Papua New Guinea – it is not surprising that the group finds it difficult to agree and follow through on comprehensive trade liberalisation measures within meaningful timeframes. Most APEC pronouncements on core matters of regional economic integration – such as the Bogor Goals – have turned out to be little more than aspirational, and the broader economic benefits of the grouping have yet to be realised.

Even here, however, the US government still finds APEC a useful tool serving its foreign policy objectives. The Bush Administration's campaign at the 2006 Leaders Meeting to win approval for the FTAAP concept may have been motivated less by the pursuit of real economic gains in the near term than by a desire to demonstrate the US commitment to Asia in the face of growing Chinese influence in the region. For want of another grouping in which Washington can pursue such political ends, APEC is likely to remain the centerpiece of US regional level diplomacy in Asia.

Building a Regional Network of Free Trade Agreements

Free trade agreements (FTAs) have been part of US international economic policy since the early 1980s, when President Ronald Reagan announced his willingness to negotiate such regional or bilateral deals as a means of sparking a new round of multilateral trade talks. The Reagan, first Bush, and Clinton Administrations negotiated or proposed a handful of FTAs – the North American Free Trade Agreement (NAFTA) of 1992 being the most significant – but it was George W. Bush's government that first put FTAs at the heart of its international economic policy, and particularly its strategy towards Asia.

Bush's first US Trade Representative, Robert Zoellick, was the champion of the new strategy. In addition to their intrinsic value in opening markets to US exports, Zoellick saw bilateral FTAs as a catalyst for 'competitive liberalisation' that would in turn galvanise multilateral efforts to reduce trade barriers – where the real economic gains for the United States (and the world) lay. Zoellick had political and security considerations in mind as well: FTAs would help both lock in domestic reforms in counterpart countries and strengthen US relations with key allies and friends.

All of these considerations had a particular significance in Asia. For one thing, as mentioned before, the region accounted for the bulk of global trade and included several of the fastest growing economies in the world. Moreover, the rapid emergence of China offered both opportunities and risks for US interests in the region: on one hand, China was a source of economic growth, markets, and potential constructive cooperation on issues of mutual concern; on the other, it was an economic and political competitor – and a potential security threat. China had already launched a series of trade initiatives with South-East Asia that sharpened Washington's focus on the need for a counterbalancing strategy.

Thus the Bush Administration in 2001 launched a series of FTA negotiations with Asian trading partners. By the middle of the second Bush term, agreements had been signed with Singapore and Australia, active negotiations were underway with Korea and Malaysia, and Thai talks had been launched but suspended following a coup in Bangkok in September 2006.[11] Meanwhile, the Administration in August 2006 signed a Trade and Investment Facilitation Agreement with the Association of South-East Asian Nations – following moves by China, Japan, and Korea to launch their own agreements with the strategically important ASEAN bloc. And by late 2006, the first serious discussion of the biggest of all possible FTAs – between the United States and Japan – was beginning to be heard in Washington and Tokyo.

Measured by the number of negotiations underway, the Bush Administration's FTA strategy in Asia can clearly be deemed a success. Yet many questions have been raised about making bilateral or regional trade negotiations a centerpiece of international economic policy. Economists complain that the agreements reached under this approach are discriminatory to countries outside the free

---

11 The Korean negotiations were concluded, right against the deadline, in April 2007.

trade area, with the 'trade diversion' costs of these agreements outweighing their 'trade creation' benefits. Furthermore, critics claim that such bilateral or regional deals deflect energy from, rather than galvanise, multilateral trade negotiations. Jagdish Bhagwati of Columbia University has famously criticised the proliferation of FTAs as creating a 'spaghetti bowl' of preferential trade arrangements that undermine global economic welfare (Bhagwati 1995).

Moreover, there are other costs associated with an active FTA strategy. Negotiating trade agreements is a labour-intensive process, and the US government has had to divert substantial resources to the plethora of bilateral talks with countries in Asia and other regions of the world. Between an over-stretched USTR and the growing challenge of winning Congressional approval for new trade deals, the energy behind the Bush Administration's FTA strategy had clearly petered out by the middle of the second term.

Nevertheless, FTAs have become a key element of Washington's international economic policy toolkit, and, given its size and importance, Asia is likely to remain a prime target of FTA efforts by US Administrations in the future.

Managing Currency Friction with China

As discussed earlier, successive American Presidents have pursued a policy of economic engagement with China since that country launched its reforms in 1979. Yet increased interaction with China has inevitably brought with it a rise of friction as well. This has forced the US government to perform a careful balancing act between aggressively pursuing American commercial interests vis-à-vis China and preserving its strategic objective of coaxing China into deeper integration with the global rules-based system.

The large and growing trade imbalance between the US and China has become the main lightning rod for bilateral friction. China's trade surplus with the US grew sharply beginning in the late 1990s and by 2006 was well over $200 billion.[12] However economically insignificant the bilateral trade imbalance may be, in political terms it produced an outcry from a broad array of US manufacturing and labour interests threatened by Chinese competition. A leading complaint of these groups was that Beijing manipulated its currency, the renminbi, to gain unfair advantage in trade.

Beginning in mid-2003, currency concerns moved front and centre in US-China relations. Armed with calculations from respected economists that the renminbi was undervalued by as much as 15-40 per cent,[13] Congressmen from both sides of the aisle submitted a slew of more or less protectionist legislation designed to pressure the Bush Administration to end China's currency 'manipulation'. In early 2004, a coalition of manufacturing interests filed a Section 301 trade petition with the US government seeking negotiations with China to raise the value of

---

12 US Department of Commerce, Bureau of Economic Affairs (http://www.bea. gov).

13 See, for example, Goldstein and Lardy 2003.

the renminbi, backed by the threat of retaliatory tariffs against Chinese imports into the United States if Beijing refused to move.

The Administration was forced to respond to this intense pressure with an aggressive, multi-pronged strategy. On the home front, it firmly rejected the Section 301 petition, argued against most of the proposed legislative remedies, and declined to label China a currency 'manipulator', while reassuring Congress that it was working assiduously to persuade Beijing to amend its currency policies. The White House and Treasury also tried to shift the focus of debate from currency *rates* to the exchange rate *system* – a more important target in the long run, and more appropriate as a subject for inter-governmental dialogue. Eschewing public calls for the Chinese to revalue the renminbi, Administration officials instead developed the public mantra that US policy was aimed at promoting 'free trade, the free flow of capital, and flexible, market-based exchange rates'.[14]

Meanwhile, the Administration stepped up its efforts to persuade Beijing to introduce greater flexibility into its exchange rate system. Accepting the conventional wisdom that the Chinese do not respond well to foreign pressure, Washington used a number of private channels to urge Beijing behind the scenes to move in this direction. Beginning in the late summer of 2003, US Treasury Secretary John Snow and other senior officials travelled frequently to China for meetings on this subject with their Chinese counterparts, and Treasury launched a 'technical dialogue' in early 2004 to help the Chinese authorities learn from US experience in managing a market-based exchange rate system. Currency issues later became a centrepiece of the US-China Strategic Economic Dialogue initiated in late 2006 by Treasury Secretary Hank Paulson, who had long experience of dealing with China in his earlier business career.

As of the end of 2006, the Bush Administration's strategy for managing currency friction had succeeded in both encouraging the Chinese Government to modernise its exchange rate system (and even to revalue the renminbi modestly) and staving off protectionist legislation in Congress. However, the Administration was fortunate to have a relatively benign macroeconomic environment in the United States to moderate political sentiment on the issue; were US growth to slow significantly, it is likely that domestic pressure on Chinese currency matters would rise again. There is also a considerable risk of renewed friction in the run-up to the Presidential elections in 2008 – campaigning for which will be at fever pitch just as the Beijing Olympics are being broadcast 24 hours a day on American television screens.

The US government's management of currency issues with China is a good example of both 'push' and 'pull' factors at work in American economic diplomacy. Washington was clearly responding to commercial and political interests in raising these issues with Beijing. At the same time, strategic considerations were never absent. To the extent that its encouragement of a more flexible, market-based exchange rate regime contributed to integrating the Chinese economy into the global rules-based system, Washington was also

---

14 See, for example, Treasury Secretary John Snow's testimony before the Senate Committee on Banking, Housing and Urban Affairs, 30 October 2003.

advancing its strategy of making China a 'responsible stakeholder' in that system, with all the economic, political, and security benefits that was expected to bring.

Conclusion

US economic diplomacy towards Asia over the past century and a half has been driven by a variety of motives and carried out through a disjointed, sometimes incoherent process. Yet in the last 25 years it has been remarkably effective in promoting American economic, political and security interests and in reconciling any tensions between them. By creating new export opportunities and keeping the US market open to cheap and plentiful imports, it has contributed to a steadily rising prosperity for Americans. It has also helped raise living standards for Asians, who have benefitted from US-driven market opening and domestic reforms in their own countries. This has not only produced economic benefits for both Americans and Asians, but has helped to keep a volatile region largely at peace and friendly to the United States. US national security has also been enhanced, as any potential threat from the rise of China has been averted and the United States has been able to combine with regional powers to check the dangerous policies of North Korea. American foreign policy and economic policy have thus successfully reinforced each other.

Given the breadth of its interests in Asia, especially its deep economic ties, the United States is likely to maintain an active economic diplomacy towards the region for the foreseeable future. Indeed, there is good reason to believe that Washington will be required to 'step up its game' in coming years, in the face of fresh demands. China is becoming established as a major political and economic power not only in the region, but in the world at large. Rivalry is clearly growing between Japan, as an established regional leader, and China, as the newcomer. US policy towards East Asia needs to be meshed with its approach to India, the third emerging power on the continent (not covered in this chapter, but see Chapter 12 below). To meet all these new demands, the United States will have to be even more creative and persuasive than before in exercising its leadership in the region. Its formidable economic and political assets in fact give Washington all the tools it needs. But it will require the sustained focus and attention of successive US administrations if they are to rise to this challenge.

References

Bergsten, C.F. (2005), *The United States and the World Economy: Foreign Economic Policy for the Next Decade*, Institute for International Economics, Washington.
Bhagwati, J. (1995), 'US Trade Policy: The Infatuation with FTAs', in Bhagwati, J. and Kreuger, A. (eds), *The Dangerous Drift to Preferential Trade*, AEI Press, Washington.

Blustein, P. (2001), *The Chastening: Inside the Crisis that Rocked the Global Financial System and Humbled the IMF*, Perseus Books Group, Cambridge, MA.

Destler, I.M. (2005), *American Trade Politics*, 4th edition, Institute for International Economics, Washington.

Ellings, R. and others (eds) (2003), *Strategic Asia 2003–04*, National Bureau of Asian Research, Seattle.

Frankel, J. (2001), 'The Crusade for Free Trade: Evaluating Clinton's International Economic Policy', *Foreign Affairs*, Vol. 80, No. 2, pp. 155–61.

Goldstein, M. and N. Lardy (2003), 'A Modest Proposal for China's Renminbi', *Financial Times*, 26 August.

Goodman, M. (2004), 'The G8 Should Start Opening to China', *Financial Times*, 3 June.

Hufbauer, G.C., Wong, Y. and Sheth, K. (2006), *US-China Trade Disputes: Rising Tide, Rising Stakes*, Institute for International Economics, Washington.

Lincoln, E. (1999), *Troubled Times: US-Japan Trade Relations in the 1990s*, The Brookings Institution, Washington.

Malloy, M. (2001), *US Economic Sanctions: Theory and Practice*, Aspen Publishers, New York.

Murphy, R.T. (1996), *The Weight of the Yen: How Denial Imperils America's Future and Ruins an Alliance*, W.W. Norton & Co., Inc., New York.

O'Neill, J. (2007), 'The Brics Economies Must Help Form World Policy', *Financial Times*, 23 January.

O'Neill, J. and Hormats, R. (2004), 'The G8: Time for a Change', Global Economics Paper 112, Goldman Sachs, accessible at http://www.gs.com.

Schoppa, L. (1997), *Bargaining with Japan: What American Pressure Can and Cannot Do*, Columbia University Press, New York.

Useful Websites

Asia-Pacific Economic Cooperation: http://www.apec.gov.
Bureau of Economic Analysis, US Department of Commerce: http://www.bea.gov.
Office of the US Trade Representative: http://www.ustr.gov.
US Department of State: http://www.state.gov.
US Treasury Department: http://www.ustreas.gov.

Chapter 12

Economic Diplomacy: The Experience of Developing Countries

Kishan S. Rana

Some developing countries have mastered their interactions with the external world to the point where they actively pursue international economic opportunities, be it in trade, investments, technology-driven business partnerships, tourism, off-shore banking and a whole range of services. These countries regard globalisation in benign fashion and are active participants in an interdependent world, be it at the World Trade Organization (WTO) or the World Economic Forum's annual big-splash gathering at Davos, Switzerland. At the other extreme are the developing states that either confront severe inadequacy of resources, or are torn by internal conflict and poor governance, leaving them woefully dependent on foreign aid. The globalisation process does nothing for them. In between are located the majority of states, scrambling for the right mix of structure, policy and method, to take proactive advantage of the external environment.

Economic diplomacy is the process through which countries tackle the outside world, to maximise their national gain in all the fields of activity, including trade, investment and other forms of economically beneficial exchanges, where they enjoy comparative advantage; it has bilateral, regional and multilateral dimensions, each of which is important. No longer the monopoly of state entities, the official agents – the foreign and economic ministries, the diplomatic and commercial services, plus their promotional agencies – now engage in dynamic partnerships with an array of non-state actors. Indeed, such domestic collaboration is a sine qua non for effective external outreach; abroad, in mirror fashion, the actions similarly address a wide field of foreign stakeholders. In recent years multilateral economic diplomacy has gained in prominence, leading some to assert that this form is 'more important' than the bilateral. In reality the relationship between pairs of states is the building block in the composite process, where multilateral arrangements are more vital today than ever before.[1]

---

1   A good introduction to economic diplomacy can be found on the website of the DiploFoundation (http://www.diplomacy.edu). Its portal on economic diplomacy is http://textus.diplomacy.edu/textusBin/BViewers/oview/EconomicDiplomacy/oview.asp.

The Foundations of Economic Diplomacy

Globalisation has expanded and accelerated economic interdependence among states. The striking feature of the response of developing states is its remarkably uneven nature, to the point where some countries have moved to the forefront, and others have stagnated, or slid backwards to become the victims of globalisation. Diplomacy is an expression of the governance that a country dispenses to itself in its external relationships. As with the other forms of governance, it is rooted in the vision, efficacy, organisation and motivation of its people and institutions, including the leaders, the officials, and civil society at large. Why some countries perform better than others is an enigma, to which political scientists grope for answers. Take the example of the textile preferences that the European Community (EC) extended to the Africa, Caribbean and Pacific (ACP) countries in the Lomé Convention of 1976. On the basis of the levels of transformation achieved in these underprivileged countries, the EC extended the facility of quota-free and duty-free entry.[2] In the late 1980s the World Bank noted that while the generous ACP preferences were available to almost 70 countries, the island-state of Mauritius with a population at the time of barely 1.1 million accounted for almost 90 per cent of the textiles that entered the EC under this umbrella. The other countries had simply not got their act together to take advantage of this concession, while Mauritius made it the central plank of its development strategy.

Let us consider the key ingredients for successful economic diplomacy. First, economic engagement abroad involves more than the ministries of foreign affairs, commerce and industry; it is the business units of the country, associations of industry and chambers of commerce, the financial sector, business schools and think tanks, the tourism industry and a host of domestic actors that are both the stakeholders and the prime movers. The state agencies need to take initiatives to create viable, innovative public–private partnerships. Some countries have proactively reached out to these non-state actors and have co-opted them for the advancement of economic interests abroad, through formal and informal mechanisms. Examples are: advisory groups composed of businessmen to guide external economic outreach and FDI mobilisation; official bilateral joint commissions that are actually driven by associations of business and industry; joint eminent person groups and CEO panels to brainstorm on new opportunities; think tanks and scholars working with business leaders to advise on free trade negotiations. We find that the countries that pursue inclusive home partnerships also tend to work well with non-state actors in foreign countries.

In a few developing countries the foreign ministry is marginalised when other agencies, be it the defense and security establishment or the economic ministries, gain ascendance in foreign policy decision-making. One direct consequence is

---

2   The EC used this formula in lieu of the more common percentage of domestic value addition, no doubt because this was convenient in the textile industry; cotton to yarn represented a level of transformation, another was yarn to textiles, while textiles to garments also represented a level of transformation.

that the country's network of overseas representation is often not utilised to its capacity for the advancement of national interests.

Second, the structures of foreign affairs and external economic management need to be integrated or harmonised. This is broadly handled in three ways. Some twenty countries have combined foreign affairs with external trade. This is practiced in the Caribbean (Barbados, Dominica, Grenada, St Lucia), Scandinavia (Denmark, Finland, Iceland, Norway, Sweden), the South Pacific (Fiji, Marshal Islands, Samoa, Solomon Islands, Vanuatu), and a few other countries (Australia, Brunei, Canada, Mauritius, New Zealand, South Korea and Swaziland). South Africa actively considered integrating foreign affairs and international trade in 1997–1998. The proposal was dropped, but harmonised arrangements of work have been implemented.

Some developed countries, such as Australia, Canada and New Zealand, make a distinction between trade policy issues (which are combined with foreign affairs), and trade promotion activity, which is handled by a separate agency, outside the foreign ministry orbit. In contrast, the Scandinavian countries completely integrate trade and investment promotion, as also trade policy and external aid management, into the foreign ministry; a single set of officials handle all these tasks, and their embassies are similarly charged with the full range of work.[3] A second method is to establish a special coordination mechanism to handle external economic work, such as 'joined-up' oversight as practiced by the UK, or through entrusting trade and investment promotion to dedicated agencies, as in the case of Singapore.

A different integration method, especially for small states, is through a joint foreign trade negotiation mechanism, as established by the 15-member Caribbean Community (Caricom); their single negotiator at the EU, who also handles issues relating to preferences, delivers considerable value. It is interesting that other small countries, such as the island states of the South Pacific, have not similarly banded together. The obstacle for these small states, members of the Pacific Islands Forum, is perhaps that they are separated by vast distance and do not share economic commonalities. The small countries of other regions, such as Southern Africa or West Africa, have also not pursued the Caricom option.

Countries that do not harmonise foreign affairs and trade expend a great deal of effort on turf disputes, on bilateral economic issues and even more on multilateral tasks such as WTO affairs; they also fail to utilise their overseas diplomatic network in the best way possible for the exploitation of foreign trade and investments. No large or medium-sized developing country has combined foreign affairs and trade. One reason may be the institutional weight of traditional systems that blocks experimentation. Another factor may be that in these countries the commerce ministry fulfils a vital domestic trade management function, and this makes a joint ministry less appealing.

---

3   Japan follows Scandinavian practice in aid management. In contrast, the UK and the US separate aid management from foreign affairs; it is hard to believe that this contributes to efficiency.

Third, the twin immediate priorities of economic diplomacy are export promotion and mobilisation of inward foreign investment. A range of options is available for pursuing these tasks, which are distinct, but interconnected. Export promotion involves helping home commercial enterprises to seek out foreign markets; market studies, visits by business delegations, participation in international trade fairs, and buyer-seller meets are among the standard devices for helping exporters, where the official agencies can play a facilitator role. Embassies and commercial offices can especially play a key role in reaching out to new markets and developing outlets for new export products. In contrast, mobilising FDI involves, first of all, sensitising potential foreign investors on the opportunities in the home country, and thereafter undertaking targeted promotion; the former produces the catchments of potential foreign investors, and the latter works to translate intention to action. Such 'salesmanship' activities by the official agencies, of course, always hinge on close harmonisation with business associations and individual enterprises. An advanced form of FDI promotion is assistance to one's own enterprises to invest abroad.

Fourth, the regulatory framework is squarely the responsibility of governments – assisted by business chambers, think tanks and scholars – which aim to create the conditions needed to advance trade and investments. The home economic agencies and the diplomatic network have to proactively identify the priority areas, and negotiate the required agreements, keeping in view the mutuality of interests. The instruments available include: free trade and preferential trade agreements, on a bilateral and regional basis; agreements that tackle non-tariff obstacles (such as phytosanitary regulations); shipping and other transport agreements; and investment protection and facilitation accords. A recent trend is to address a range of such areas, usually through mutual trade-offs among the contracting parties, through 'comprehensive' economic cooperation accords. These aim at better synergy through simultaneous handling of related subjects, which also facilitates the trade-offs between contracting parties.

Here too, smooth cooperation between the economic ministries and the foreign ministry is a prerequisite. The countries that have combined their foreign affairs and external trade departments are at an obvious advantage, but those that feature effective joined-up and other collaborative formats also do well. In addition to these institutional arrangements at home, if the diplomatic network also plugged into the process, economic advocacy and negotiations are handled optimally.

Fifth, we should distinguish between the economic diplomacy as it operates out of the home capital, and the field, that is, through the network of embassies and consulates.[4] The majority of developing states have some way to go in optimising their diplomatic networks to deliver full value. While these networks are exhorted to implement a 'whole of government' mindset in their work, it is the foreign

---

4   The role of consulates has shifted from consular protection and visa facilitation (as provided in the 1963 Vienna Convention on Consular Relations), to the wider promotional jobs of subembassies, engaged in almost everything but hard political work, and sometimes even some of that. In takes the consulate back to its original commerce facilitation and representational roots of the thirteenth and fourteenth century.

ministry that is their immediate master, and thus in the best position to mobilise them. Consequently, countries that marginalise their foreign ministries in their economic diplomacy outreach handicap themselves from the start.

Sixth, while almost all countries today recognise the value of economic diplomacy, what varies is their effectiveness in actions taken. Usually, a weakness in this sector is part of a general lack of drive in the country's entire diplomatic mechanism. 'A diplomatic service that is well resourced and above all well staffed … give(s) a state a significant increment of power and influence' (Berridge, Keens-Soper and Otte 2001, 3). Singapore demonstrates how a small state can harmonise its diplomatic machinery to punch much above its weight class. This lesson holds lasting value.

Three Phases of Economic Diplomacy: an Indian Example

The organisation of economic diplomacy in India is both traditional and modern. From its inception in 1947, the Indian Foreign Service has been an integrated entity, handling political as well as economic and other forms of diplomacy.[5] I believe this is functionally rational; the different elements in external work interact with one another, and require unified handling. My subjective view is that such services (for example, also in Brazil, UK) are more efficient than the ones that treat commercial diplomacy as a separate professional branch, handled by specialists from other agencies (for example, in China, South Africa, Thailand).[6] A possible gain in specialisation is more than offset by the fact that economics is now part of the centre stage that all diplomats must master and relate to all other work areas.

A major Indian weakness is institutional disharmony, in the shape of turf battles between the Ministry of External Affairs (MEA) and the economic ministries, though on major issues these agencies are able to put aside their differences. For instance, MEA swaps some posts abroad with the Commerce Ministry in exchange for a several placements in that ministry for its officials; those holding commercial assignments abroad are answerable to both ministries. The permanent secretary heading Commerce serves on the MEA personnel board that selects officials for subambassador level assignments abroad. But WTO issues are handled primarily by Commerce, which also appoints the envoy handling this subject in Geneva. MEA's Economic Division (actually a full department with four divisions handling Indian aid and technical cooperation with foreign countries, plus external economic promotion and multilateral economic work) receives less

---

5 Prime Minister Jawaharlal Nehru personally drafted the 1946 cabinet note that created the Foreign Service, on the basis that it should perform all categories of diplomatic work. But it was not until 1966 that the Ministry of External Affairs set up its Economic Division.

6 The US State Department, operating the world's largest diplomatic network, now has five 'cones' within which officials perform different roles, but this model is not used by anyone else. The US also has a separate commercial service, a product of that country's complex decision-making process that led to the 1946 Foreign Service Act.

than fulsome cooperation from the Ministries of Commerce and Industry. [7] The Finance Ministry's Department of Economic Affairs, which handles inbound aid as well as the interface with the World Bank and the IMF, has even less to do with MEA. It does not help matters that MEA practices a closed-shop policy, receiving no in-placement at its headquarters from the economic ministries. [8] In 2005 Prime Minister Manmohan Singh created a cabinet level 'Trade and Economic Relations Committee' which he chairs, for apex-level coordination; this top-down process is powerful, but it does not substitute for better ground-level harmonisation.

In consequence, the Indian embassy network is utilised far less than it should be, both in relation to FDI mobilisation and export promotion. India laments that approved investment proposals are often not implemented, producing a large shortfall. [9] As the embassies are the only external investment promotion agency, they should be utilised more intensively. Unlike in China or Brazil, the volume of FDI inflow – $6 billion in 2005, up to around $10 billion in 2006 – is still not high enough to go on autopilot!

In a December 2005 interview a Thai diplomat described the evolution in economic work in his service. Their ambassadors had moved from the conventional political discourse, to a situation in the 1980s when they were asked to become salesmen; now their assigned task was to function as 'managers'. I would expand on that evolution to speak of three distinct phases in economic diplomacy, using the Indian example. [10]

Economic Salesmanship

India grasped the economic diplomacy nettle in the early 1970s, as a response to the first 'oil shock' by the OPEC cartel, which almost overnight quadrupled crude oil prices. As a 'non-oil' developing country, India was forced into heroic actions to raise foreign exchange resources, with primary focus on the Gulf region. By good fortune, my first ambassadorship was in Algeria (1975–1979), in that initial *economic salesmanship* phase. In essence, India leveraged its political connections with the Arab countries to win turnkey projects, consultancy

---

7   The Indian Ministries of Commerce and Industry are separate entities, but since 2001 they have been placed under a single cabinet minister, while they retain their distinct identity.

8   MEA has traditionally apprehended such placement, fearing that these officials would demand assignments abroad. A simple way exists to square this circle: pre-select the dozen odd non-MEA officials serving abroad (against posts earmarked for them), and deploy them in MEA for a couple of years before they go abroad; that would also shed MEA's image of exclusivity.

9   Typically, 30 to 40 per cent of approved projects are implemented (this is necessarily an evolving figure); a variety of reasons underlie such a low rate, where inadequate Indian follow-up is one element. The current Indian effort is to shift the bulk of FDI to the automatic approval route, by simplifying procedures.

10   My observations on India's diplomatic system, and examples drawn from personal experience with economic and other forms of diplomacy are narrated in *Inside Diplomacy* (Rana 2000).

assignments and contracts for skilled as well as advanced technical manpower. In Algeria, India's technology expertise was unknown, but we took advantage of opportunities to help Indian companies, public sector and private, to sign their first 12 industrial and consultancy contracts in 1975–1979. We also sent over 800 doctors, besides dozens of professors and engineers. That story was replicated in Libya and elsewhere, with the difference that many thousands of skilled workers went out. Today, the Gulf region has a total of over three million Indian skilled workers, besides tens of thousands of Indian professionals; they are the principal contributors to an inflow of over $24 billion received as remittances from the Indian diaspora. That same salesmanship mode was deployed to help the Indian software industry gain its first wins in Silicon Valley and other parts of the US in the late 1980s (during my three years as consul general in San Francisco). Many of our embassies played a similar role.

A feature of this phase was the country's heavy dependence on foreign aid; the annual meetings in Paris of the 'Aid India Consortium' were a major event, and considerable effort was expended via summit level diplomacy to maximise the commitments announced by the major donors and the international financial institutions. Through much of the 1980s, the Finance Ministry, directly supervised by the Prime Minister's Office, handled this vital diplomatic effort, while MEA was relatively isolated.[11]

Economic Networking and Advocacy

By the time I reached Germany in 1992–1995, on my final assignment, India had matured into the second, *economic networking and advocacy* phase, though salesmanship continued; on the ground, the two phases telescoped into one another. India launched economic reforms in 1991, which many have viewed as no less than a second independence movement, freeing the economy from self-imposed shackles of statism and the 'license raj'. These gave salience to efforts to maximise exports, mobilise FDI, and assist Indian companies to access technology, besides improving the flows of inward aid and of foreign tourists. This involved reaching out to the new diplomacy actors, both the agencies of government as well as the non-state actors, at home and abroad. Indian economic diplomacy is better in its coordination with the latter, that is, the non-state agents: the principal business organisations, notably the Confederation of Indian Industry (CII),[12]

---

11 I observed this first-hand as a member of Prime Minister Indira Gandhi's staff in 1981–1982.

12 The full story of the extraordinary role played by this industry association is yet to be told, though see Kantha, 2006. In the 1980s, the pre-reform phase when an external drive commenced, CII regularly took delegations of top industrialists to lobby US and other counterparts on the opportunity presented by India. Jack Welch of GE has spoken of how he was wooed over several years. This spurred its longtime rival association, the Federation of Indian Chambers of Commerce and Industry (FICCI), to reinvent itself in the 1990s. The third major business player is the Associated Chambers of Commerce (ASSOCHAM).

as well as the economic think tanks, the NGOs that are active on international economic issues, and the media. While MEA regained for itself a central role in external economic diplomacy, coordination among official agencies remained patchy. When good collaboration takes place, it hinges on individuals, rather than institutional arrangements. Thus India's strong negotiation posture at the WTO is not sufficiently backed with matching advocacy at the key bilateral capitals; nor is investment promotion activity sufficiently harmonised, producing the 'approved but not implemented' limbo described above.

Regulatory Management and Resource Mobilisation

The third and latest priority is *regulatory management and resource mobilisation*, that is, negotiation of FTAs, energy access agreements, and regional diplomacy via innovative new groupings. One characteristic of this phase is an awareness of the country brand, leading to efforts to build an image of modernity. These tasks require domestic coalition building, where the competence of each agency, official and private, is respected, to work together to advance economic interests abroad. India does not have, as yet, 'public diplomacy boards' where the foreign ministry takes the lead in *suggesting* unified action to autonomous agencies, such as those covering the public media, culture, education and tourism.

The associated home task is to reach out to the varied partners and harmonise their sectoral interests with national priorities. Such coordination cannot be imposed by right or dictate; it emerges when the other agencies see the foreign ministry as bringing value to their direct interests. The foreign ministry is the logical centre point of such efforts, because it has no sectoral agenda of its own. The forte of the foreign ministry is its control of the totality of the external inter-state dialogue, of course, under the oversight of the head of government and his staff.

An outstanding example is India's very first bilateral FTA, signed with Sri Lanka in 1999 (Rana 2004, 66–70). Up till then India had an 'ideological' bias that viewed regional and bilateral FTAs as a derogation from the principle of multilateral universality of trade liberalisation under the GATT/WTO formula. But the Sri Lanka FTA has been a singular economic and political success. India has since signed similar agreements with Thailand and Singapore and is negotiating other FTAs, including one with ASEAN.

In contrast, in relation to other trade regulation arrangements, the inter-ministry coordination has been uneven, and sometimes notably absent. India shows the complexity of economic management; with policy-making fragmented, and the Ministry of External Affairs confined to a small role, the operation of economic diplomacy is not always in synch with political objectives.[13] Yet, positive

---

13 In December 2005, on the eve of the first enlarged 'East Asia Summit' (where Australia, India and New Zealand joined the ASEAN + 3 leaders), the Indian Commerce Minister presented the first draft of India's negative list for the ASEAN-India FTA that is under negotiation. The list of items that were to be kept out of the free trade regime ran to 1,414 items, and as the Malaysian Trade Minister pointed out, included toilet seats; it became clear that the list had not been screened by either the Ministry of External Affairs

examples also exist; in the search abroad for energy sources, Indian embassies have frequently played a proactive role in helping state and private enterprises in pursuing opportunities (Rana 2004, 68).

At the same time, new initiatives in regional economic arrangements have come from MEA. A few of these show considerable promise. In 1997 Thailand and India set up a cross-regional network with Bangladesh, Myanmar and Sri Lanka (BIMSTEC), later joined by Bhutan and Nepal, aiming to create a free trade area. IBSA (India, Brazil and South Africa) came into existence in 2003, when the three countries decided to build on their proximity on international economic issues, to develop closer trade and transport links; it held its first summit meeting in Brasilia in October 2006. But IOC-ARC, a group of Indian Ocean rim states that want to expand mutual cooperation, seems to have lost steam, though it has a secretariat in Mauritius. MEA is the lead coordinator on each of these, marshalling cooperation with other agencies, state and non-official.

Other National Examples

Let us turn to some other examples – in alphabetical order – to reflect on the manner in which economic diplomacy operates in different situations.

A number of medium and small countries in *Africa* and *Asia* with fragile economies have remained mired in conventional diplomacy, some of them observing the forms of international discourse, but without coherent pursuit of national objectives. Appointments as envoys are seen as sinecures for failed politicians and retired generals.[14] Professional diplomats are under-trained, and when sent on assignment overseas are often demoralised and inactive. A change factor in some of these countries is the public sector reform imposed by the IMF and the World Bank, as part of the 'structural adjustment programme', in the highly indebted countries facing default in their international payment obligations. Episodic evidence suggests that performance management norms and business plan systems brought into foreign ministries may produce superficial changes without improving the management of diplomacy or external projection.

The tiny, reclusive Himalayan kingdom *Bhutan* (population 675,000)[15] would hardly come to mind as notable for its economic diplomacy. But it is of interest

---

or other agencies. Yet, safeguarding the interests of domestic industry and agriculture is a vital issue, one that has to be handled with finesse and sensitivity, without over-pitching one's demands; by early 2007 differences had narrowed and an agreement is under finalisation.

14 A few years back, out of nearly a score of Ugandan ambassadors abroad, only one was a professional from the foreign ministry. Several Central American countries also reserve the majority of envoy appointments for those connected politically. In contrast, a law in Brazil requires that only professionals from the foreign ministry be appointed as envoys abroad.

15 This is the official figure based on a 2005 census, though other estimates place the total population much higher, at about 2 million.

on two counts. One of its few resources is its latent hydropower capacity. Since 1974, it has utilised its privileged relations with India to implement three major hydro projects, Chukha I, Chukha II and Tala (completed in 2006), producing nearly 2000 MW of power, all sold to electricity deficient India, earning for the country over 50 per cent of its GNP. Contrast this with *Nepal*, with a potential hydropower capacity of over 80,000 MW. Since the controversial Kosi project of the 1950s, it has not added a single kilowatt of new power export capacity, owing to inhibitions in its relationship with India.[16] Bhutan is also notable for the measured pace at which it has opened itself to high-end tourism, with a strict quota on the numbers permitted entry, to avoid disruption to its traditional cultural and societal fabric.

In *Brazil,* the Ministry of External Relations, still known by its old location name in Rio de Janeiro, Itamaraty, enjoys a primacy that counterparts in most developing countries envy. Itamaraty has always monopolised external negotiations; the professional competence of its diplomats, their mastery of foreign languages and their experience have served as mutually reinforcing elements. As new subjects entered the international dialogue, it added new departments; observers have called its economic diplomacy 'surprisingly agile and dynamic' (Lampreia and da Cruz 2005, 108). The increasing technicality of subjects has prompted the Itamaraty to hand over some responsibilities to the Commerce Ministry specialists and shift its economic diplomacy management to a multi-agency mode. A Trade Council based in the Presidency carries out policy harmonisation. In the early 1990s, when Mercosur was established as the regional integration mechanism and WTO replaced GATT, Itamaraty was reorganised in consonance with this regional and global economic paradigm (it handles all FTA negotiations). Brazil is one of the few countries represented at WTO by its foreign minister. The diplomatic service handles commercial work abroad.

China presents a very different picture. Until its breakup in 2002, the powerful Ministry of Foreign Trade and Economic Cooperation (MOFTEC) handled all external economic activities (its successor is the Commerce Ministry plus other agencies). As before, the Foreign Ministry does not handle field level external economic promotion, which is carried out by a separate commercial cadre. Coordination is implemented through the party mechanism, which is very effective on strategic issues; a series of thematic 'leading small groups', under the supervision of the Politburo, bring together top party leaders and the key ministers for decision-making. Paradoxically, in relation to the issues of detail the system is less efficient. Inter-ministry coordination takes place primarily at the level of vice-minister; inter-ministry meetings at varying lower levels, the norm elsewhere, are unknown. Overseas, while the Commerce Ministry specialists handle trade promotion, economic policy remains with the diplomats. Chinese embassies are

---

16 Many Nepalese have rightly seen the trans-border multipurpose Kosi project as grossly unbalanced in its distribution of benefits. That legacy, plus a suspicious mindset toward India, has inhibited progress on any other hydro project, despite countless rounds of discussion, summit encounters, interim accords and memoranda. For India this represents a huge failure of its diplomacy.

now moving to active advocacy on behalf of their companies, borrowing the methods that the others have long pursued.

The tiny island state of *Mauritius* has been surprisingly innovative on external economic issues affecting its vital interests (for example, combining foreign affairs and trade and promoting textiles exports, see above). In the 1970s it played a leading role in working out the sugar preferences given to the ACP countries by the European Community under the 1976 Lomé Convention; this has brought windfall gains to the producing states of Africa, the Caribbean and the Pacific.[17] Having achieved middle-income country status with a per capita income of over $3000, rising labour costs have eroded the competitive advantage of Mauritius in textiles and sugar. It is now adopting targeted mobilisation of FDI focused on the service industry, value-added manufacture, and offshore banking, while shifting its textile industry investments to neighboring countries such as Madagascar.

In the mid-1980s Mauritius persuaded India (originally home to 70 per cent of its inhabitants) to give it exceptional treatment in a double taxation avoidance agreement, exempting Mauritian registered companies from capital gains tax. After the launch of India's economic reforms this has provided a bonanza, with around 20 per cent of the FDI flowing into India using the 'Mauritius route', to minimise tax liability. Mauritius also persuaded China (home to 3 per cent of its population) to sign a similar treaty.[18]

Singapore has harnessed economic diplomacy as a major instrument in its transformation from a sleepy entrepôt in 1965 at the time of its separation from Malaysia and independence, devoid of a hinterland or resources, to a thriving economy, enjoying Asia's highest per capita GDP. Singapore's legendary Economic Development Board (EDB) has played a key role; together with its Irish counterpart it is arguably the best among investment mobilisation agencies, specialising in targeted pursuit of investors (Chan Chin Bock 2002). A comparable role in promoting exports of products and services has been played by International Enterprise Singapore (IES, formerly known as TDB, the Trade Development Board). Singapore's hallmark has been: an inclusive approach that mobilises all stakeholders on a 'team Singapore' formula; long-term vision and thinking outside-the-box (witness its investments in technology parks in China, India and elsewhere, and its 'growth triangles' with Malaysia and Indonesia, utilising their hinterland); astute regional and trans-regional diplomacy (for

---

17 In the 1970s, when sugar prices reigned higher than the guaranteed price offered by the EC, Mauritius played a key role in persuading the producing countries to take a long view; in consequence these countries have enjoyed high profits in the ensuing years of much lower world prices for this commodity. The preferences are now under phase-out, under the WTO regime.

18 The Indian tax authorities have long attempted to close this loophole (especially to block domestic investors who illegally route investments through Mauritius in 'round-tripping' deals), but the island state has blocked this on the basis of kinship and close political ties. It was reported in January 2007 that the Chinese have pushed through a partial revision of this concession, and India is attempting the same.

example the ASEM dialogue linking ASEAN and the EU); and an exploitation of best practices in diplomacy and human resource management (Rana 2006).

Thailand's economic diplomacy, like its international profile, looks unspectacular, even conventional. But as befits its centrality in South-East Asia – as a country never colonised, sharing 4863 km of land frontiers with four neighbours – it has specialised in regional diplomacy. ASEAN came into being at its initiative in 1967, at a time when most of the five original members had irredentist claims against one another. Thailand has since moved ahead with concrete regional economic actions. The 1992 Greater Mekong Subregion (GMS) brings China into collaboration with Cambodia, Laos, Myanmar, Thailand, and Vietnam, with scores of projects funded by the Asian Development Bank and other agencies totaling over $10 billion, to improve transport infrastructure and trade. BIMSTEC was launched with India in 1997 – see above. The ambitious Ganga-Mekong Project, still largely on the drawing boards, aims to develop transport and other linkages between the basin states of these two great river systems.

In 2004 Thailand advanced the concept of the 'CEO ambassador', first as a pilot project and thereafter passed into law, which mandates that its envoys abroad are to exercise full control over all the representatives of ministries and agencies located abroad, to function as chief executives to advance Thai interests. Initially limited to six embassies, this is now standard policy and resembles the US system of designating ambassadors as heads of 'country teams', to get all official agencies to work together under united leadership. But it is unlikely that a related move, to impose a unified budget for the entire gamut of offices abroad, to be controlled by Thai envoys, will be implemented. Other countries will watch the dénouement with interest.

Looking to the collective experience of the 130 developing countries of the G77, a rough economic diplomacy typology – set out in Table 12.1 – finds them in several clusters: those that are moored in conventional methods, only implementing slow change; those that have identified a niche, to focus actions on that chosen sphere; those that have adapted themselves to new opportunities with structural changes and clear actions; and those that have moved to the forefront with cutting edge techniques and continual reform. Of course the real world does not respect such neat categorisation, but this approach allows us to focus on the points along the learning curve where these countries are located.

Economic Diplomacy Management

We observe that many developing states a progression has taken place in the diplomatic process, with countries moving up the value chain and improving performance in the economic and other arenas. Let us consider the principal ingredients of this change.

Table 12.1 Economic diplomacy typology

	Traditional	Niche-focused	Evolving	Innovative
External economic management	Handled by the trade and economic ministries; little involvement of MFA	Promotion concentrates on the identified niche	Some coordination between trade and foreign ministries; contestation also likely	Joined-up and other cooperative arrangements
Policy management	Limited role for MFA, frequent turf battles	Good internal coordination	Inter-ministry or cabinet level coordination; tending towards improvement	Institutionalised management, strong teamwork
Role of non-state actors	Episodic, depends on personalities	Variable	New procedures, strong networking	Harmonisation with all stakeholders
Economic Aid: Recipient	Handled by economic agencies, seldom coordinated with MFA	Limited coordination	Networking between the aid management agency and MFA	'Graduated' out of aid receipt, or close to that stage
Economic Aid: Donor	Unlikely to be an aid donor	Unlikely to be an aid donor	Modest program, usually covering technical cooperation	Expanding programme, run by MFA in harmony with trade promotion agencies
Trade promotion	Often handled by a commercial cadre, outside MFA control	Limited focus on commercial promotion, outside the niche area	Cooperative arrangements, often integration of political and economic work	Well-coordinated activities, role model in range of activities
Investment promotion	Handled by domestic agencies, limited role of the diplomatic system	Active use of embassy network	MFAs and embassies work actively with home agencies, often at individual initiative	Strong team effort, based in institutional arrangements
Regional diplomacy role	Usually reactive	Focused on preferred niche area	Active	Innovative, exploitation of potential

Process of Decision-Making

First, the external economic *decision-making process* is more plural and often better coordinated than before; some countries are more efficient at this than others. We saw this in the examples given above. The city-state Singapore, consistently managing to punch above its weight class, shows how much mileage sound policy management can produce (Leifer 2000; Rana 2006). Several devices are available:

- In and out personnel placements are valuable; the diplomatic establishments working as hermetically sealed establishments are the losers. It also makes sense to send officials to work in business enterprises, and demystify the perception of these partners towards the official agencies.
- Transparent networking with all the home partners is needed, on the premise that the foreign ministry and its overseas network is at their service, for the advancement of their agendas. The foreign ministry becomes an external coordinator not by right or decree, much less by self-proclamation; it has to earn that recognition. Embassies abroad need a 'whole government' mindset in the way they handle their tasks.[19] This is far harder this than it sounds; it is the foreign ministry's partners that will make the judgment.
- Lateral entry, where people join and leave the foreign ministry at different levels, is becoming customary in postmodern countries where job rotation is the norm. But as the UK saw a few years back while trying to recruit consuls general for the US, even top economic jobs do not attract the needed high grade talent. Developing countries do not face job churn, and for them lateral entry is even less workable. What can be borrowed from the West is another concept – better use of locally engaged staff. Singapore and Australia have shown the way.[20]
- Finally, cabinet level coordination is fine, but it is at working levels that decisions are implemented. Barring exceptions, this is often a weak point.

Management of Trade Policy

Second, trade policy management now brings a range of concerned non-state actors into the process, beyond the trade chambers and industry associations (the obvious, often very vocal, stakeholders); these include the domestic think tanks, academics, NGOs and even the media. Policy choices become easier

---

19 This was one of the conclusions of the March 2005 Wilton Park workshop on diplomacy; a fine report on the conclusions of that workshop is available on the Wilton Park website (Wilton Park 2005).

20 Recently Australia replaced their trade commissioners in the US with local staff, on the premise that Americans would know how best to sell to their own market; developing countries might reason that besides local knowledge, the commercial secretary would also need knowledge of the home country. But the general case for better use of local staff is incontestable.

when autonomous public policy think tanks exist in sufficient numbers; in most developing countries they are growing, in spread and competence. This is especially visible on the issues relating to WTO; regional and bilateral FTAs require the participation of business, as stakeholders directly affected by the decisions taken by the government representatives. For instance, Indian officials now recognise that they hastily accepted some arrangements during the Uruguay Round in the early 1990s, without fully grasping the implications, because business partners and the industry associations were absent. Developing countries have been unenthusiastic over alliances with the international NGOs that seemingly support the developing world, but do not always understand the complex motivation, and the dynamics, in these countries.

Capacity Building

Third, even in the relatively advanced countries, capacity building remains an issue. Few foreign ministry or commerce officials have been trained in negotiation technique, though this is beginning to change. A similar situation is encountered in the middle tier of developing states. This needs careful handling, since foreign ministries and trade ministries are sensitive to external advice. In many developing countries there is need to give greater weight to economics in induction training in the diplomatic services, as well as more, high-quality mid-career training programmes for officials from the foreign ministry and its economic counterparts. Training programmes conducted jointly for officials of the foreign and economic ministries, where representatives of business also join, are ideal, covering international negotiations, intercultural management skills and other craft skills.

Regional Diplomacy

Fourth, the regional diplomacy practiced by some of these countries is remarkable. In China, the provinces are important actors in regional diplomacy, addressed at the countries that adjoin them (Lampton 2001). Thus, Liaoning and Shandong provinces play the lead role in relation to South Korea; Yunnan does the same with the Greater Mekong Subregion project (GMS), as noted above. China addresses a different cluster – Bangladesh, India and Myanmar – through the putative group BCIM, which it is also actively promoting. China is currently a member of some 40 regional and neighborhood networks, most of them with an economic focus. We noted above the regional diplomacy practiced by Thailand, as well as the transcontinental entity IBSA, covering Brazil, India, and South Africa.[21] In most regions similar integration in trade and other fields is driven by economic logic, with anticipated political and security benefits.

---

21 IBSA plans to double mutual trade in four years to reach $10 billion, and is pursuing a free trade agreement. Such an FTA would effectively link Mercosur with SACU, the customs union that covers several countries in Southern Africa, and India (the South Asia FTA is still under implementation).

One interesting dimension of this new diplomacy is that foreign ministries often lead it, acting in concert with trade and other economic ministries; we observe this in relation to the developing country members of Asia-Pacific Economic Cooperation (APEC), as well as in other groupings. Indirectly this inculcates 'transgovernmentalism', that is, the system's capacity to work jointly.

Role of Subnational Entities

Fifth, subnational entities emerge progressively as autonomous external economic actors. We noted above the role of Chinese provinces in regional diplomacy. In addition, most inward FDI approvals are handled by Chinese provincial governments. In India, the recent shift to automatic investment approval has produced a like effect, with competition among states to attract big ticket projects. Similarly, the large developing countries (for example, Brazil) send out increasing numbers of provincial level business delegations. The next step would be for some of them to establish their own marketing offices abroad, following the lead of developed states such as Canada, Germany and the US. Some Indian states have ventured to establish 'partner state' relations with foreign counterparts.[22]

Economic Promotion in the Field

Economic promotion carried out in the field by large and medium sized developing countries shows congruent features.

Foreign Direct Investment (FDI)

First, FDI investments for many of the large developing countries now take on a two-way character, though inflows remain much larger than the outflows. (In India 2005 saw about $5 billion as inflows, and almost $2 billion as outflows, as investments in oilfields abroad, manufacturing, and IT services; during 2006 FDI outflows jumped to nearly $7 billion.) China's foreign investments, especially in Africa, have attracted even greater notice, in hydrocarbons as well in some technology-dominated sectors. Further, inflows into Brazil and China have matured to the point where the work of mobilising new investments is less important than facilitation, working with investors to overcome obstacles. India, which has lagged behind in FDI inflow volume, remains concerned with investment mobilisation; this is a high priority activity for its embassies.

Investment promotion remains a key task for embassies, regardless of the stage of economic development. Of course, the work content evolves, but in the best systems the entire embassy team, including the ambassador, is engaged in

---

22 China has been relaxed in permitting such external activity by its provinces, but in India such actions push the envelope of centre-state relations; economics is thus also helping in shifting the federal power balance.

this activity. Other sectoral work – science and technology, education, media promotion and even culture – feeds into and interacts with economic outreach.

Trade Promotion

Second, trade promotion also remains a high priority, with the difference that in addition to a search for new markets and the promotion of new export products, the embassy networks are also engaged in policy issues, for example, potential trade agreements and FTAs, and the related anti-dumping negotiation tasks.

Some question whether the embassy networks of the larger developing states should persist with promotion work, on the argument that services of consultants and other agencies are more efficient and affordable by most home enterprises. But ground evidence, including the experience of Western countries, shows that while the content of promotion work evolves, embassies remain engaged in such tasks. For the smaller countries basic help with market studies, hosting small buyer-seller meets at the embassy, and reaching out to the economic entities and individual enterprises in the target country remain vital, simply because home exporters lack the means to sustain such actions on their own.

Integration with Mainstream Diplomacy

Third, integrating economics into mainstream diplomacy promotion is easier when a single service handles all the work segments than when commercial work is handled by a separate cadre. It also makes sense to use the entire team in a foreign capital for economic promotion, on a task force basis (Thailand has attempted this with its 'CEO ambassador' policy). The ambassador carries sizable leadership responsibility vis-à-vis official as well as private business representatives in his country of assignment (Rana 2004/5).

Embassies abroad necessarily work with a range of domestic actors in their promotion work in the target country. Through these actions, they become for the foreign ministry a conduit for better links with the economic ministries and with non-state entities. Foreign ministries often underestimate this home role of embassies, in part because this is a new and evolving situation.

Brand Image

The home country's image underpins most diplomatic activities. Wally Olins writes in a brilliant monograph that nations need new images because 'a changing reality is leaving perceptions far behind' (Olins 1999). This is especially true of developing and transition states, which have seen dramatic change, but this is underestimated abroad. Country branding is about 'presenting a nation or region in a powerful, attractive and differentiated way'; however 'branding works when it projects and reinforces a changing reality — but it can be counterproductive if isn't rooted in fact'. The key is to use a central idea that is powerful and simple, capturing the country's unique qualities.

There is no aspect of external relations, bilateral, regional or global, that is not affected by 'image'. Foreign ministries, embassies, and diplomats are considered responsible for the projection of a 'correct' image of their country — even if in reality their capacity to radically or immediately influence their country's image perception abroad is limited. But proactive diplomacy demands that serious and constant attention be paid to the country image. Diplomacy theorist Brian Hocking has written of a survey of 200 US Fortune 500 companies, in which 72 per cent said that national image was significant to external purchase of goods and services, adding that 'company brands interact with national identities in concrete ways' (Hocking 2000).

Consider the way some of these countries have worked. China used image consultants in marketing Beijing as the venue for the 2008 Olympics and Shanghai did the same in presenting itself as a 'world city'. The successful tourism destination countries make focused use of branding. Poland recently invited Olins to help re-fashion its overseas image. South Africa has long been an accomplished practitioner of country branding. Brazil attaches weight to this too, and has a special unit in the office of the minister of foreign relations that oversees image activities. In 2006, Pakistan was reported to be working with foreign advisers to improve its image.

In the mid-1990s India created a 'brand equity fund' of Rs5 billion (then equal to $130 million), only to find that the Commerce Ministry was unable to disburse any money. In 2003 the operational management was handed over to the Confederation of Indian Industry (CII), as a public–private partnership.[23] The India Brand Equity Fund helps Indian companies to build their product image in export markets, and in the process burnish the country image; it also carries out other promotional activities overseas.

Image building is a dimension of public diplomacy; the latter encompasses culture, the media, education and all the different activities through which publics, abroad and at home, are influenced in relation to a country's foreign policy. What is missing in most developing countries is a sustained and coordinated image management effort, mobilising all the agencies that contribute to the way the country is perceived. Developing countries do not as yet have the kind of 'public diplomacy boards' that exist in France and the UK, headed by the chief mandarin of the foreign ministry, which bring together the authorities handling the state media, tourism, education, culture and others that contribute to this image. While this subject takes us quite far from economic diplomacy, suffice it to say that public diplomacy is closely connected with the pursuit of external economic interests.

---

23 Ministry officials were wary of deciding in favor of one or another applicant, in the absence of hard criteria, but found it easier to approve recommendations made by CII, through its autonomous examination. The website of this fund is http://www.ibef.org.

Conclusions

To sum up:

- First, the differences among developing countries in their economic diplomacy partly reflect differences in the evolution of their response to the external environment. Often those that pursue their economic interests poorly also do an inadequate job in their political diplomacy; their foreign ministries are isolated islands, inadequately networked with official and non-state counterparts. Conversely, when the government structure works in unison, with a decision process that is open to inputs from a wide community of stakeholders, we also find the best diplomacy role models.
- Second, sound economic policies at home and effective economic diplomacy go together. Growth produces the capacity to project the country overseas; this virtuous circle operates powerfully, in that expanding attractiveness produces a receptive climate for country marketing. But individual and systemic actions remain equally essential; that explains in part why some countries do better than others.
- Third, combining foreign affairs and foreign trade is a powerful device for synergy; real joined-up arrangements may work almost as well (as in the UK). This is a concept whose time has come.
- Fourth, foreign ministries need to build economic skills into their diplomatic networks and to open themselves to the economic partners, with exchanges of personnel. Training programmes should be run jointly for the functional economic agencies, businessmen and foreign ministry personnel.
- Fifth and last, the economic management systems can benefit from mutual learning, analyzing the best practice models. Traditionally, few foreign ministries have looked to one another, or carried out benchmarking. But this is one of the new tricks that this old profession is now beginning to absorb, adapting to the era of globalised diplomacy.

References

Berridge, G.R., Keens-Soper, M. and Otte, T.G. (2001), *Diplomatic Theory from Machiavelli to Kissinger*, Palgrave, Basingstoke.

Chan Chin Bock (2002), *Heart Work: Stories of How EDB Steered the Singapore Economy from 1961 to the Twenty-first Century*, Singapore Economic Development Board, Singapore.

Hocking, B. (2000), *Diplomacy of Image and Memory: Swiss Bankers and Nazi Gold*, Diplomatic Studies Program Discussion Paper No. 64, University of Leicester.

Kantha, S. (2006), *Building India with Partnership: The Story of CII 1885–2005*, Penguin, New Delhi.

Lampreia, L.F. and da Cruz, A.S. (2005), 'Brazil: Coping with Structural Constraints', in Robertson, J. and East, M.A. (eds), *Diplomacy and Developing Nations*, Routledge, London.

Lampton, D.M. (ed.) (2001), *The Making of China's Foreign and Security Policy in the Era of Economic Reforms*, Stanford University, Stanford, CA.

Leifer, M. (2000), *Singapore's Foreign Policy: Coping with Vulnerability*, Routledge, London.

Olins, W. (1999), *Trading Identities: Why Countries and Companies are Taking on Each Others' Roles*, Foreign Policy Centre, London.

Rana, K.S. (2000), *Inside Diplomacy*, Manas, New Delhi.

Rana, K.S. (2004), 'Economic Diplomacy in India: A Practitioner's Perspective', *International Studies Perspectives*, Vol. 5, pp. 66–70.

Rana, K.S. (2004/5), *The Twenty-first Century Ambassador*, DiploFoundation, Malta and Geneva, and Oxford University Press India, New Delhi.

Rana, K.S. (2006), 'Singapore's Diplomacy: Vulnerability into Strength', *The Hague Journal of Diplomacy*, Vol. 1, No. 1, pp. 81–106.

Rana, K.S. (2007), *Asian Diplomacy: The Foreign Ministries of China, India, Japan, Singapore and Thailand*, DiploFoundation, Malta and Geneva.

Saner, R. and Yiu, L. (2003), *International Economic Diplomacy: Mutations in Modern Times*, Studies in Diplomacy No. 84, Clingendael, The Hague.

Wilton Park (2005), 'Diplomacy Today: Delivering Results in a World of Changing Priorities', http://www.wiltonpark.org.uk/documents/conferences/WP505-4/pdfs/WP505-4.pdf.

Useful Websites

DiploFoundation: http://www.diplomacy.edu.

Indian Brand Equity Fund: http://www.ibef.org.

Professor G.R. Berridge: http://www.grberridge.co.uk.

Singapore Economic Development Board: http://www.edb.gov.sg.

'Studies in Diplomacy' Papers, Clingendael Institute, The Hague: http://www.clingendael.nl.

Chapter 13

Regional Economic Diplomacy: The European Union

Stephen Woolcock

This chapter examines regionalism, as part of the assessment in this book of economic diplomacy on its different international levels – bilateral, regional, plurilateral and multilateral. The greater use of regional institutions has been identified in Chapter 1 as part of the new strategies adopted to meet the growing demands of economic diplomacy. Regionalism made great advances in the 1990s, though the 2000s have seen a shift towards a greater use of bilateral agreements (Mansfield and Milner 1997; WTO 2007). As Chapter 10 illustrates, bilateral economic diplomacy tends to be favoured by the large more powerful countries. Regional economic diplomacy, on the other hand, offers a means for the not so large countries to pool resources in order to enhance their economic wealth and influence in the international system. Cooperation at the regional level with a view to these ends has been the aim of the European Union for many years. It is also the aim of the Mercosur countries, of the Caribbean Community (Caricom), of a number of African regions, which see regional cooperation as means of engaging with the international economy, and of ASEAN which is seeking to develop stronger common policies in order to retain its identity at a time of a proliferation of bilateral agreements in Asia.

Compared to bilateral agreements, which are simple and carry no threat to political sovereignty, regional economic diplomacy implies external solidarity, or the need to maintain common positions in negotiations. This is likely to require a legitimacy for the regional level that comes from economic benefits, such as from internal liberalisation and the positive welfare effects of regional integration. It also requires a balance of membership, with no members being too large compared to the others. Joint institutions are also likely to be needed; these can ensure that the interests of the smaller members are respected and provide the forum for defining common interests and preferences. As regional arrangements require negotiation at the regional level, they tend to foster value creating strategies in economic diplomacy; if value creation at the regional level is seen to be working, it is extended to the international level. On the other hand, regional economic diplomacy can create problems of rigidity if 'domestic' agreements reached after long internal negotiations limit the flexibility of the region in negotiations with others. The complex institutional arrangements required at the regional level can also be opaque and raise problems of accountability.

In the literature regional economic groupings have been divided into four categories, with growing depth of commitment (Bomberg and Stubb 2003, 27–8). The simplest type is a *Free Trade Area*. In this the members have joint rules for trade among themselves, but still deal individually with trade outside the region. They may add other provisions, e.g. on investment. Next comes a *Customs Union*, where both internal and external trade policy is determined collectively. Beyond that is a *Single Market*, which allows for free movement of goods, services, capital and people. The most advanced type is an *Economic Union*, with a single currency and a wide range of other common economic policies, both internal and external. The first two types largely deal with what happens at the frontiers of the member states; the two more advanced types penetrate much deeper into domestic policy. Most regional arrangements now in force are free trade areas, with a few customs unions. The European Union is the only one to move to the higher stages of single market and economic union. This chapter therefore concentrates on European economic diplomacy, in other words the role of the European Union in international economic negotiations. It does so because the EU is the leading, one might say the only real regional actor in economic diplomacy today. By looking at the EU we can assess how the theoretical analysis offered for economic diplomacy in Chapter 2 needs to be viewed when applied to regional economic diplomacy. Above all, as the EU is an important actor in economic diplomacy, it is necessary to understand what factors shape policy and how decisions are taken.

This chapter and the one that follows consider EU policy in the fields of trade, monetary policy and the environment. The definition of European economic diplomacy used is one that is limited to the external role of the EU. EU external policy is of course shaped by domestic policies and structures in the same way as any national economic diplomacy, so there will be reference to domestic policies. The chapter first summarises the evolution of European economic diplomacy from the beginnings of the integration process, showing how the competence for economic diplomacy has shifted from the national to the European level. The chapter then describes how the EU goes about deciding a common position on external trade and monetary relations. Finally, there is an assessment of the factors that shape European economic diplomacy. This examination shows how the scope and structure of European economic diplomacy has been shaped by ideas, systemic and societal factors as well as European institutional arrangements. It draws on the theoretical framework set out in Chapter 2 and suggests some general hypotheses on how European economic diplomacy is distinctive from other equivalent national policies.

The Evolution of the European Dimension in Economic Diplomacy

The signature of the Treaty of Rome 50 years ago set out the aim of creating a customs union among the original six Member States of the European Union. By definition this required the adoption of a common external tariff. Article 113 of the Treaty (later renumbered 133) granted the European Community (EC) exclusive competence for common commercial policy, a somewhat wider concept, but it took some time for a modus operandi for external trade policy to develop. One factor influencing the evolution of policy was the pressure from the United States to negotiate tariff reductions and agricultural liberalisation as part of the Kennedy Round of trade negotiations in the GATT from 1963–1969 (Preeg 1970). At the time building Europe and in particular the establishment of a European preference in trade and common policies such as the common agricultural policy (CAP) were the priority among the EU Member States. A common position vis-à-vis US pressure was therefore essential and helped to establish the European Commission as a single voice in trade negotiations (Woolcock 2005).

The EC contemplated monetary union as early as the Werner Plan of 1969, since this was seen as a potent symbol of European integration. Contemplation turned to action when the fixed but adjustable exchange rate regime of the Bretton Woods system, hitherto supported by US leadership, began to unravel. In the early 1970s floating exchange rates became widespread, encouraged by the US. But the EC countries, led by France and Germany, maintained fixed rates among themselves, within a band of 2.25 per cent margins known as the snake. However, exchange rate policies were still set nationally and the strength given to the Deutsche Mark (DM) by Germany's strict anti-inflation policies put the snake under strain. The British pound and Italian lira were soon obliged to float and even the French franc had to leave the snake for a time.

The 1970s saw an expansion of the trade agenda. Under US pressure new issues, such as subsidies, preferences in government procurement and other non-tariff barriers were added to the agenda in the Tokyo Round of the GATT. In Europe the customs union had been created but not yet a single market. National governments pursued national champion policies, in other words they sought to promote the competitiveness of national industries using the policy instruments the US wished to discipline in the GATT. The EC therefore had to defend the national policy space of the Member States, along with a renewed defence of the CAP. But the expansion of the trade agenda resulted in a de facto extension of EC competence in trade to include the new issues. Although still defensive and reactive to US initiatives, the European Union (EU) nevertheless emerged as part of a de facto duopoly shaping international trade by the end of the 1970s (Winham 1986).

President Valéry Giscard d'Estaing of France, devoted to fixed rates but dissatisfied with German monetary dominance, successfully promoted in 1978 a proposal for a European monetary system (EMS) with an exchange rate mechanism (ERM). Each European currency had to keep within 2.25 per cent of its central rate against the 'ECU' (European currency unit – also an old French coin). When currencies reached their limits, this would trigger debate in the EU Monetary Committee and any changes in central rates had to be agreed by the Council of Finance Ministers (ECOFIN). But this failed to break Germany's power over the system. Currency adjustments were always downwards against the DM, while some Member States, notably the United Kingdom, stayed outside the ERM altogether.[1]

The 1980s saw important changes. The decade again began with renewed US initiatives in trade, to which the EU first responded defensively. But by the middle of the decade there had been a shift away from national champion policies towards the creation of a single European market (SEM) as a means of promoting European international competitiveness. The deepening of integration in the SEM along with the extension of the trade agenda resulted in a further increase in de facto and de jure EC competence in international trade and investment. The SEM also resulted in the strengthening of the *acquis communautaire* (the domestic regulatory framework for market integration). This provided European external trade policy with a common starting point in a range of new policy areas. The removal of internal frontiers also ended any scope for retaining national trade protection in the form of residual quotas for sectors such as textiles and clothing.[2] The liberalisation that resulted from the SEM also reduced the salience of trade policy for Member States. As the EU adopted a generally liberal stance in manufacturing and services, Member State governments were happy to see offensive positions adopted in trade negotiations and gave the European Commission, as the agent for the national principals, more autonomy in many sectors of policy. But this was not the case in agriculture, where the defensive Member States retained their hold over DG Agriculture that continued to negotiate separately from DG Trade. Taken together these effects of the SEM strengthened both the EU's position in trade negotiations and the position of the European Commission as agent or sole negotiator. EU trade policy also approximated to a two-level game, rather than a three-level game in which national trade policies remained a powerful presence alongside the EU level (Woolcock and Hodges 1996).

Across the other side of the Atlantic the US negotiators were under intense unilateralist pressure from the Congress as US macroeconomic policy led to the growth of massive fiscal and trade deficits. In response to this more defensive US position the EU sought to tie the US into multilateralism, or at least counter US unilateralism, by shifting to support a rules-based multilateral order in a fashion it had not in the 1970s.

European economic diplomacy in the early 1990s was significantly shaped by wider strategic developments in a way that had not been the case since the 1960s. The end of the Cold War placed the European Union in the centre of strategic interest. This led to a number of strategic/security motivated economic initiatives. One immediate response to the opening of the Berlin Wall was a debate on the need to re-emphasise the economic underpinnings of the transatlantic alliance. Although earlier calls for a new transatlantic treaty were not heard, the Transatlantic Declaration of 1990 elevated the importance of the EU in that it

---

1   The UK finally went into the ERM in 1990, only to be forced out ignominiously in 1992.

2   Article 115 of the Treaty of Rome provided for these quotas that were euphemistically called 'regional' quotas.

was between the United States and the European Community. This was followed in 1995 by the New Transatlantic Agenda, which sought to deepen transatlantic cooperation, again between the EU and the US rather than the national governments and the US. But it is noteworthy that this stopped well short of the transatlantic free trade agreement advocated by some.[3] Nor was there any real attempt to promote cooperation in international monetary policy.

The EU's role in the post Cold War economic reordering in Europe was confirmed with the decision by the G7 summit in July 1989 to have the European Commission coordinate much of the West's financial support for the transition economies of Central Europe. The role of European economic diplomacy in serving broad strategic goals was also reflected in the Europe Agreements signed by the EU with all the transition economies. These offered market access to the EU market and financial support as a means of promoting economic stability in the transition countries and thus promoting Western, and above all European security.[4] Strategic and security interests were also behind the decision taken in 1995 to negotiate Association Agreements with the North African and Middle Eastern near neighbours of the EU in the Barcelona Process. Similar to the case made for the Europe Agreements, and subsequently for the Stability and Adjustment Association agreements with the western Balkan states, the Euro-Med agreements were seen as means of promoting economic development and thus political stability in the Mediterranean region, so as to counter the potential of 'new security threats' such as terrorism, fundamentalism or organised crime (Aggarwal and Fogerty 2004).

The completion of the Single European Market revived interest in monetary union, which was seen as an essential complement. In 1989 a Committee chaired by Jacques Delors, President of the Commission, agreed a strategy for moving to economic and monetary union (EMU) by stages. The end of the Cold War strongly accelerated the process of European monetary integration. The absorption of the former communist East Germany into the Federal Republic made Germany by far the largest Member State. To counter fears of German domination, Chancellor Helmut Kohl, against the advice of the Bundesbank, agreed to the end of the DM and the creation, by 1999, of EMU based on a common monetary policy and a single currency, the euro.

The Germans drove a hard bargain, insisting on an independent European central bank, charged exclusively to check inflation, and strict fiscal disciplines on Member States. France and other continental Europeans accepted this as the price of a genuine European system, being convinced of the inherent benefits of monetary integration. But outward-looking states of northern Europe – the UK, Denmark and Sweden – were more sceptical and declined to adopt the euro.

---

3   The relevant proposal in 1994 came from Germany, but the UK government had on various occasions favoured such an agreement.

4   There were, however, some less than generous provisions in the Europe Agreements, that excluded 'sensitive' sectors, at least initially, as EU sector interests made their presence felt in the negotiations.

Nevertheless the eurozone came into effect as planned in 1999 and the national currencies of its members disappeared in 2002.

Although European economic diplomacy was actively engaged in policies that served broader strategic interests, the dynamism generated by domestic developments in the shape of the Single European Market initiative resulted in Europe being seen as a model. First the EFTA states, then hot on their heels the Central European and Baltic countries sought accession to the EU, boosting membership from 12 to 27 in a little over a decade. Second, European integration again became a model for countries outside Europe as it had been in the first phase of regionalism in the 1960s. Regional integration initiatives in Latin America, African and to a lesser degree Asia emulated the European model.

This summary of the evolution of European economic diplomacy shows that it has been shaped by a range of systemic and domestic factors as well as ideas. The following section now turns to focus on the institutional framework within which European trade and external monetary policy is decided.

European Trade Policy

By granting the European Community exclusive competence for commercial policy the Treaty of Rome laid the legal foundations for a common European trade policy.[5] The need to aggregate the national preferences of the EU Member States means that EU trade policy is made in a relatively 'dense' institutional structure, relative that is to the institutional structure that exists in nation states. This is of course all the more so now that there are 27 Member States. The community method that comes into play when the EC has competence for trade is broadly as follows. Figure 13.1 gives a graphical presentation of the decision-making process.

It is helpful to distinguish between *de jure* competence according to the Treaties and *de facto* competence in the day to day operation of EU trade policy. De jure competence determines the legal basis for decision making. Exclusive Community competence means the Member States in the Council decide by qualified majority, mixed or national competence means decisions are based on unanimity. In practice a consensus is always sought, but if there is a threat of being outvoted Member States opposed to any policy will be more ready to seek an accommodation, whereas the ability to wield the threat of a veto will strengthen the position of the Member State concerned. The Treaty clearly grants exclusive competence for commercial policy to the European Community, but does not provide an exhaustive definition of commercial policy. The deepening of the trade agenda to include non-tariff barriers, services and other regulatory

---

5   It is important to remember that European Community competence does not mean that the European Commission decides things on its own. Community competence involves a process whereby the Commission and the Member States, working through the European institutions, determine policy.

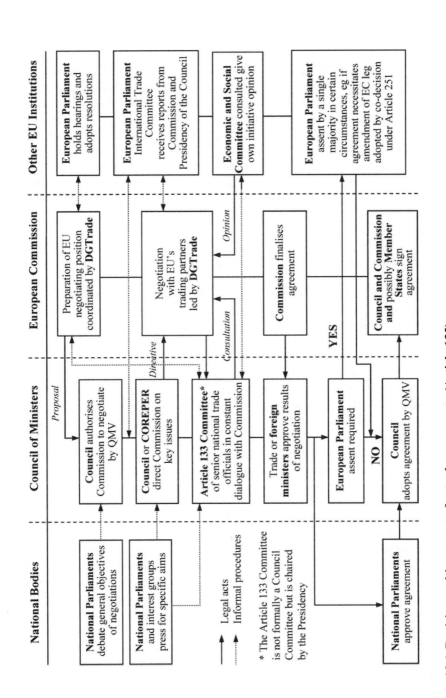

Figure 13.1 Decision-making process for trade agreements (Article 133)

issues has therefore posed the question of whether these should be Community or Member State competence.

In the conduct of negotiations the EU has dealt with this question pragmatically and allowed the growth of de facto competence. Accepting the benefits of the EU speaking with one voice in negotiations that linked Community and Member State competence topics, the Member States have simply allowed the Commission to negotiate on all topics. Only when it has come to ratification has the competence question been contentious, when it has been resolved through political agreement or rulings of the European Court of Justice. When the Treaties have been discussed the Commission has pressed for de jure extension of community competence to include, for example, services and investment, which the Member States have resisted. At the Amsterdam inter-governmental conference an 'enabling clause' (Art 133(5)) was added to allow the Member States to extend Community competence at any time by a unanimous decision. The Constitutional Treaty proposed bringing foreign direct investment under Community competence, so one can expect debates on competence to continue

Agenda-Setting, Consultation and Political Decision

The European Commission makes proposals on the negotiating mandate after consulting the Member State governments through the so called Art 133 Committee, taking on board any opinions of the European Parliament (EP) and soliciting the views of the various interest groups. In this early stage of agenda-setting the Commission has a good deal of autonomy. The European Parliament has no formal powers to grant negotiating authority and can only shape the general climate within which agendas are set through resolutions or through the adoption of reports that are not binding on the EU negotiators. In recent years the EP has become more active in trade and in 2005 a new International Trade Committee was established to provide more focus.

There are informal channels through which interest groups can make representations to the European Commission that are broadly similar to those available in the Member States. Interest groups clearly make their views know to the Commission, especially those that have defensive, protectionist interests. Sectors with offensive interests tend to have more collective action problems, but are also active players. The European Commission favours dialogue with EU-level interests rather than individual companies or national lobbies, which can enhance the Commission's autonomy in that it forces the various national sector associations to find a common position. In finding an agreed position more extreme positions are invariably moderated, as more liberal national lobbies balance out the more protectionist. Again agriculture is an exception to this, in that there is more uniform support for defensive policies in the farming community.

In 1989 the EU introduced a Consultative Forum for non-governmental organisations in the wake of the collapse of the negotiations on the Multilateral Agreement on Investment (MAI) – see Chapter 9 above. But the Consultative Forum brings together business and civil society NGOs. This helps the Commission defend its autonomy as there is plenty of scope for it to define the EU interests somewhere in the middle ground between the range of positions aired by this broad spectrum of NGO opinion.

Within the European Commission it is the Directorate General Trade that leads in trade negotiations, with DG Agriculture negotiating on agricultural trade. Before presenting a draft position to the Member States, DG Trade must first go through inter-service consultation with other Directorates General of the European Commission, such as DG Enterprise, which represents European sectors such as textiles, steel, chemicals and automobiles, DG Market, which is responsible for the internal market liberalisation, DG Environment, DG Development and DG Health and Consumer Protection (which leads on food safety).

But in agenda-setting, as in other phases of negotiation, the Member States provide the most important input in the shape of the Art 133 Committee, which is made up of senior national trade officials. Working together the Commission and Member State officials thus effectively determine the EU preferences. Sector interests are therefore first aggregated at the national level by the Member State governments and then at the EU level. The EU mandate is formally adopted by a qualified majority of the Member States in the General and Foreign Affairs Council (GFAC), but in practice decisions are taken by consensus. In other words if in the preparatory work in the Art 133 Committee it becomes clear that there is significant opposition to the proposed mandate, the Commission reworks the proposal until it can be sure that the proposal will be accepted by the Council. The Commission seeks to maintain as broad a mandate as possible to give it some negotiating flexibility. Member States with specific interests, especially defensive interests, will seek to have these anchored in the mandate. The mandate seldom defines the EU's 'bottom line' in any negotiation as this would preclude any 'middling strategies' by the EU, as the EU's partners would simple take as their starting point the resistance point defined in any explicit EU mandate.[6] Finally, EU mandates in trade negotiations are not time-limited, as for example is the case for trade promotion authority granted by the US Congress. Throughout the Doha Development Agenda negotiations of the World Trade Organisation (WTO) the EU negotiated on the basis of a formal mandate adopted in 1999 in the run up to the Seattle WTO Ministerial, but subsequently modified by decisions taken by the Council.[7]

---

6   A middling strategy is when a negotiator seeks to frame negotiations by setting ambitious targets well beyond what he or she is willing to accept. This enables concessions to be made while still meeting or exceeding the original aims.

7   Although the US negotiators use the deadline set by the limited duration of Trade Promotion Authority to bring pressure to bear on other countries, there has been a history of negotiating authority being extended at regular intervals. The point here is that extending negotiating authority provides the US Congress with a means of shaping the negotiating objectives. This opportunity is not open to the EP or national parliaments in the EU.

Negotiation and Agreement

In EU trade policy the European Commission negotiates 'in consultation' with the Member States (Meunier and Nicholaidis 1999). This means continuous dialogue between the Commission and Member States in the Art 133 Committee in which the Member States retain fairly tight control over the Commission. Again the practice in the Art 133 Committee is not to have votes, although the basis for decision making on issues of Community competence (see above) is a qualified majority. During the course of a negotiation the Council can formally direct the European Commission to adopt a specific position, if there is a major new proposal. But in most cases EU negotiating positions are decided in the Art 133 Committee, or on more politically sensitive issues in the GFAC at ministerial level.

The Member States generally also sit in on formal negotiations but do not speak. For example, before a meeting in the WTO in Geneva the Member State delegates will meet and refine the position the EU should take as negotiations progress. The Commission then takes this negotiating brief into the meeting. At key junctures the responsible ministers from the Member States will also be present. This is by definition the case at WTO Ministerial meetings at which there are often attempts to resolve major issues in multilateral negotiations. In such cases the Commission will consult the Member State ministers at regular intervals.

In other words the Commissioner for Trade in the EU as chief negotiator is under constant, close scrutiny and thus has little agent slack and little scope to determine a negotiating strategy independent of the Member States. This contrasts with the position in other WTO members, such as the United States where the US Trade Representative has more scope to decide on negotiating tactics provided the end result is ratified by Congress. The European Commission also consults the European Parliament and the Consultative Forum of NGOs during negotiations. But neither have any real ability to influence the EU position.

Ratification

As in agenda-setting and during negotiations it is the Member States in the Council that ratify any agreement negotiated by the EU. In cases of exclusive Community competence this is by qualified majority vote. For issues that remain in national competence, such as intellectual property rights, non-cross border services issues, labour standards and investment for example, unanimity is required. In practice, however, consensus is sought. This has a spill back effect on negotiations, because the desire to find consensus among the Member States will tend to strengthen the position of individual Member State governments holding out against an outcome that creates domestic political difficulties for them.

The European Parliament has no real power under the main provisions of the Treaty concerning commercial policy. Indeed in redrafting the Treaty in 1991 Member State governments went out of their way to exclude the EP from a role in trade policy. The Treaty does however provide for the European Parliament to give its assent, by a simple majority of members voting, when any trade agreement has institutional or budgetary implications. These circumstances tend to arise when the EU concludes bilateral Association Agreements because these invariably include EU financial support for the associate, as well as second and third pillar issues, in other words foreign policy or justice and home affairs questions.[8] Association Agreements also generally include provisions on international human rights, a topic in which the EP takes a close interest. EP assent is also required when a trade agreement requires changes in EU domestic legislation adopted by co-decision under Art 251 of the Treaty. Co-decision making means that the Council and European Parliament are responsible for the legislation. With integration more and more issues come under co-decision making.

In the past the EP has in practice given its assent to the outcome of multilateral negotiations, such as the Uruguay Round and bilateral Association Agreements, because these have had 'domestic' implications or because of wider financial or political implications. It remains to be seen whether this will continue to be the case. Multilateral trade negotiations in the DDA have modest scope and are unlikely to have any real impact on EU domestic legislation. The new generation of bilateral agreements the EU is seeking to negotiate may also be pure free trade agreements without any second or third pillar provisions.[9] On the other hand, the growing awareness of trade in public opinion resulting from the advocacy campaigns of the civil society NGOs may require EP assent for broader political reasons.

The EP has never seriously challenged a multilateral trade agreement. Once the outcome has been approved by all EU Member States, for the EP to veto the results would constitute a 'nuclear option' and is not a credible veto power. As a consequence the influence of the EP during negotiations is limited. Ratification by national parliaments has in the past been rather a rubber stamping exercise in which national governments present the findings for ratification.

Up until the early 2000s national parliaments have not generally been very active on EU trade issues. There are a number of reasons for this. Few members of national parliaments have much interest in the detail of trade policy, unless they have in their constituency an industry that is threatened by liberalisation. Major regional concentrations of employment and wealth creation, such as steel, shipbuilding and to a lesser degree textiles, have been progressively reduced in most EU member states. Agriculture remains over represented in most national parliaments. Even if national parliamentarians have an interest it is not easy for them to follow the detail of negotiations that are taking place at two steps removed from national parliaments, namely first in the EU and then in the level I negotiations between the EU and its trading partners. This lack of political input is something that governments have not gone out of their way to rectify, as it helps them keep protectionist forces at arm's length. Civil society advocacy

---

8   This three pillar structure dates from the Treaty of European Union adopted after the Maastricht intergovernmental conference in 1991.

9   The Commission is making the case that general cooperation agreements including political issues already exist with countries such as India and Korea, so that there is no need to conclude Association Agreements.

has however, raised awareness of trade and led to a greater interest on the part of members of parliament.

European Monetary Policy

The common commercial policy has been in force for 50 years. The common monetary policy has operated for less than a decade. The chief instrument is the European Central Bank (ECB), which is charged with the fundamental tasks of checking inflation, ensuring monetary stability, setting interest rates and issuing and managing the euro (Bomberg and Stubb 2003, 63 and 147; McNamara 2005, 149–54).

European Decision-Making

In agenda-setting and consultation the ECB – the lead agency for monetary policy – has far greater autonomy than the Commission has in trade policy. For example, there are no arrangements for taking into account the views of private interest groups, like the commercial banks. There are contacts at working level with central banks in eurozone countries and with the Commission. But there is no formal consultative machinery comparable with the Art 133 Committee in trade or the Monetary Committee in earlier years.

For all its autonomy, however, the ECB is only an agent. It draws its authority from its Governing Council (also called the 'Eurosystem'), composed of the central bank governors of the eurozone countries. The Council members have every incentive to reinforce the autonomy of the ECB, to underline their own independence from national government or parliamentary pressures. A Commission representative and the President of the 'Eurogroup' of eurozone finance ministers can attend the Governing Council, but only as observers. The President of the ECB regularly reports to the European Parliament, but the EP has no leverage to bring about changes of policy. The process thus allows for very limited accountability.

This austere process is constrained by two factors. First, this regime only applies to the 13 Member States out of 27 that have adopted the euro. Three of the pre-2004 EU members – UK, Denmark, Sweden – still keep their own currencies, as do all the new members except Slovenia. A few other new Member States are close to adopting the euro, but most are far from meeting the necessary standards. Member States outside the eurozone still keep control of their national monetary policies.[10]

Second, the ECB is only responsible for monetary policy. Budgetary and fiscal policy remains with EU finance ministers, even though certain macroeconomic standards are conditions for adopting the euro. National macroeconomic policies

---

10 Central bank governors from outside the eurozone join their euro using colleagues in the General Council of the European System of Central Banks (ESCB). But the only function of the General Council is to validate decisions taken in the Eurosystem.

are coordinated in the Council of Finance Ministers (ECOFIN), for the whole EU, and in the Eurogroup for eurozone members. The ministers seek to agree on objectives for growth and employment and to coordinate policies to achieve these objectives. But the ECB has resisted pressure to take these objectives into account, insisting that the control of inflation is its sole aim.

International Negotiation

While the EU pursues economic diplomacy in trade on all levels, from bilateral FTAs to the multilateral WTO, in monetary matters it does so only in the IMF and the bodies dependent on it, like the G7 and G20 finance ministers. In contrast to the domestic powers given to the ECB, the EU's international monetary competence is ill-defined and disputed (McNamara and Meunier 2002).

The Maastricht Treaty of 1991 gave the ECOFIN Council responsibility for deciding on formal exchange rate regimes, by a qualified majority vote. This was clarified in 2000 to the effect that the ECB would be 'solely competent' for the euro exchange rate on the basis of an understanding with the Eurogroup on the 'strategic direction' of policy. There is some ambiguity here, but it is not a real problem. With floating universal, the euro has no formal exchange rate regime against other currencies.

More seriously, there is no European agreement on a single figure who would speak for the EU, or even the eurozone, in the IMF and related contexts. The ECB has observer status at the IMF and the ECB President (with the Eurogroup President) attends some G7 meetings, but not all (Padoa-Schioppa 2004, 226–7). Yet the finance ministers of the EU Member States, including those in the eurozone, maintain their existing positions both in the G7, where Germany, France, UK and Italy are members, and in the IMF structure, where power is based on national quotas. Germany, France and the UK have their own seats on the IMF Executive Board; all the other Member States are grouped in 'constituencies' shared with non–EU countries. In fact, seven out of the Board's 24 seats are occupied by EU members, but they do not act collectively.[11]

The consequence is that while the EU can take far-reaching initiatives in international trade contexts, it cannot do so in international monetary contexts. This puts it at a disadvantage compared to the United States, where the US Treasury, despite strict accountability to Congress, is able to launch new proposals to which the EU can only react defensively. Even in responding to problems as they arise in the IMF, such as the financial crisis in Argentina, EU and eurozone members are quite likely to disagree among themselves. There are various suggestions for reorganising the EU's representation in the IMF to avoid these problems, but these have not got far (see Kenen and others 2004, 93–5 and Chapter

---

11 At present Belgium, Netherlands, Italy, and Finland are spokesmen for their constituencies, in addition to the seats held by Germany, France and UK. Spain, Poland and Ireland are in constituencies where they are the only EU country. The European Commission has no status at all on the Executive Board.

17 below). The EU's inability to take the lead in international monetary issues is a weakness in its economic diplomacy.

Application of the Theoretical Analysis

The final section of this chapter assesses the factors that shape European economic diplomacy and whether the theoretical frameworks discussed in Chapter 2 of the book need to be modified when applied to the rather special case of the EU. The analysis looks first at the role of ideas, which are especially important for the EU; examines systemic and domestic factors and the links between them, as explained by Putnam and Odell; and considers how far rationalist and constructivist theories can be applied.

Ideas

The European Union owes its success to two powerful ideas, both of which use economic instruments to achieve political goals. The first is that progressive integration and the removal of barriers to competition would promote not only prosperity but also political stability and offer a better alternative to communism. This is clearly a liberal concept. The second is that common economic policies applied by supranational central institutions would guarantee peace in Europe, embedding all members (and especially Germany) in a network of wider obligations. This concept gives priority to regulation. The two ideas sometimes worked together and sometimes conflicted.

The case of trade policy illustrates how building Europe within a regulatory framework was the predominant idea in the early years of the European Union. In the 1980s this changed with the progressive strengthening of liberal ideas. The liberal paradigm was the dominant idea in the economic diplomacy of most countries during the 1980s. In the EU it went hand in hand with internal liberalisation and contributed to a shift towards a consensus within the EU for greater support for a liberal, rules-based international order.

Within the EU the liberalising impulse later ran out of steam, as shown by the difficulties in implementing the Lisbon Agenda of 2000. But more widely the success of the European initiatives in the 1980s also led to the re-emergence of Europe as a model.[12] The EU was seen as the model for the EFTA states that joined in the mid 1990s and especially for the transition economies of Central and Eastern Europe that soon followed in seeking accession. Beyond the EU's near neighbours the integration process was also seen as a model. Regional integration initiatives were revived in Africa and Latin America, as well as in ASEAN and between Australia and New Zealand. Even the North American Free Trade Agreement (NAFTA) might be seen to have been influenced by the European model. To some extent the EU sought to export this model to other regions

---

12 The success of the initial Common Market programme in the 1960s had provided a model for other regional integration initiatives at that time.

through the region-to-region approach to trade and association agreements that emerged in the 1990s. Therefore if the EU has 'soft power' in the international system it is because it provides a model for economic and political integration, which is clearly distinct from the realist concept of nation states condemned to compete using all means.

Two more ideas became important during the life of the EU. Some Member States, especially the founder members, became convinced that the political merits of closer integration were so great that it was not necessary to demonstrate its economic benefits; integration was by definition a good thing. Other members, drawn from those who joined later, were more open-minded about integration and needed to be convinced that it would really produce the advantages claimed. This division of ideas strongly influenced attitudes to EU monetary policy and is still unresolved, leading countries like the UK to stay out of the eurozone.[13]

Systemic Factors

Structures of relative power have been influential in shaping European economic diplomacy. The evolution of EU trade policy appears to have been significantly shaped by the way the EU responded in a common fashion to the US initiatives. This external pressure may well have contributed to the desire for cohesion in the EU approach. The expansion of the trade agenda also tended to increase EC competence over national competence as the EU was asked to negotiate on new issues in successive rounds of trade negotiations. The growth of US economic power and competitiveness regularly stimulated the EU to respond, first by the single market campaign and later by the Lisbon agenda. This raises the question of the relative importance of such external factors compared to the internal deepening of the integration agenda. But there seems to be evidence of an important systemic influence on the scope of European trade policy. Much the same could be argued for monetary policy. Efforts to develop European monetary union only began when the Bretton Woods system began to weaken. Certainly a leading motivation behind EMU was a desire to promote European monetary stability and to make Europe more independent of the impact of US fiscal and monetary policies.

But the EU did not just react to the power of others. It soon began to exert its own power internationally. It used its network of trade agreements to extend its influence worldwide, seeking to maintain – in a more acceptable way – the power formerly exercised by its members through their empires. After a long period on the defensive in multilateral trade contexts, the EU became active in binding the US into a stronger legal regime in the Uruguay Round and then tried to pioneer its own ideas for a 'Millennium Round'. Trade agreements provided clearer evidence of the EU's collective impact, political as well as economic, than the common foreign and security policy, which was often undermined by divisions among the Member States. Another important systemic factor shaping European trade policy

---

13 The contrast between the 'existential' and the 'instrumentalist' view of integration is well analysed in 'Existential Dreaming', *The Economist*, 24 March 2007.

has been wider strategic considerations. These had a particularly direct impact with the end of the Cold War and the addition of a range of trade agreements with Central and East European and Mediterranean states to the EU's portfolio of preferential agreements.

Power relationships within the EU also had an impact, which is especially visible in monetary policy. While Germany sought to maintain the independence of its monetary policy, which made the DM the dominant currency, France tried to bind the Germans into European arrangements that would give more influence to the other Member States. This power struggle was only resolved with the introduction of the euro, replacing the DM.

Societal Factors

Domestic societal factors combined with systemic factors to bring about a general liberalisation of European trade policy in the 1980s. There is strong evidence that it was the desire of the business community to end the fragmentation of the European market through non-tariff and other barriers, that was the catalyst for the single European market programme in the 1980s. This was in response to a perceived (and real) loss of competitiveness vis-à-vis Japan and the United States. The combination of such market led factors with the political initiatives pursuing European integration provided the force for change that brought about the 'domestic' liberalisation within Europe in the 1980s. This more than external pressure appears to have had the greatest impact on liberalisation.

Domestic policy shapes European international trade and monetary policies like any nation state. But in the case of the EU domestic policies are increasingly the product of common European policies codified in the *acquis communautaire*. The single European market and economic and monetary union have considerably increased the scope and thus importance of these common policies. In many respects the aggregation of national policy preferences in any given policy area has therefore already occurred at the EU level, thus providing the EU negotiators with both a stronger starting position and a fairly narrow 'win-set' that reduces the European negotiators flexibility in negotiations.

State Centred Factors and Institutions

Domestic state centred factors must also be considered. This is especially the case for the EU where common European preferences need to be defined and common policies developed among the 27 Member States. The discussion of the decision-making process in trade suggested that the aggregation of sector preferences at first the national level and then at the EU level tends to blunt sector lobbies and strengthen the hand of officials in determining policy. Compared to the model of a classical nation state government maximising utility, the EU process is more complex. Member State governments reach a view on national priorities based on their national utility function. But this then feeds into the common European discussions in which national officials make important judgements.

This does not mean that sector interests cannot shape EU policy, as the case of agriculture shows.

The relative strength of bureaucratic actors in European economic diplomacy is also aided by the fact that the main channels of accountability and democratic control run through the national governments and the Council of Ministers rather than through legislative bodies. National parliaments have become remote from the policy process and the European Parliament has not yet established a credible role in shaping European trade and much less monetary policy.

In a classical nation state context a relative strong bureaucracy would tend to suggest a greater degree of policy autonomy. Political forces are more easily held at arm's length and legislatures are not able to intervene directly in the process of economic diplomacy. In the EU, however, the close control exercised by the Member States over the Commission, at least in trade policy, means that a stronger bureaucracy does not necessarily mean a greater degree of autonomy or agent slack for negotiators. The almost day-to-day surveillance and control by the Member States means that the Commission cannot exercise much discretion in how it goes about negotiations. In the case of external monetary policy the ECB has considerable autonomy thanks to the guarantees of its independence. In addition, neither the Member States through the Eurogroup or the European Parliament have yet developed effective scrutiny of the ECB.

Interaction between Levels: Putnam and Odell

The theoretical approaches that seek to link the international and domestic can be very helpful in explaining the process of European economic diplomacy

Two-level games In Putnam's two-level game model, as applied to EU trade policy, there is a clear asymmetry between the actors. For the Commission, level I (international) is the WTO or a foreign partner and level II (domestic) consists of European institutions involving the Member States. But for the Member States, the European institutions comprise level I, while national entities – ministries, pressure groups, etc – make up level II. This double process is inevitably more cumbersome than decision-making in nation states, even those with federal structures (some EU members are also federations, like Germany). It means that the EU will always have a small win-set and be a tough negotiator, even when it does not want to be. The EU does not offer a two-level game in monetary matters, however, as the ECB has no access to the international level, while the Member States have no purchase on the ECB.

In trade policy the EU is skilled at using Putnam's 'reverberation', i.e. using international pressures to gain domestic advances and vice versa. International pressure mobilised through the Uruguay Round helped to promote European reforms in services and investment, thorough the single market campaign, and even in agriculture. Once the European reforms were secure, the EU replayed them to induce others to move in the GATT or to get new subjects onto the WTO agenda.

The EU seeks to use reverberation in process also. Decision-making within the EU proceeds by formal commitments that are binding on the Member States. This makes the EU prefer legally-based treaties in its external relations. It prefers to conclude trade and other economic agreements, where a nation state would be content with informal relations based on voluntary cooperation. In the WTO, while most other countries give priority to market opening, the EU is also interested in rule-making.

Value claiming and value creating The concepts of value claiming and value creating, as used by Odell and others, are also instructive in EU contexts. When the Commission seeks agreement from the Member States on a new proposal, it will always adopt a value creating strategy or seek to construct a package deal. This will be essential to achieve unanimous support, which is the convention even where qualified majorities are the formal rule. Value claiming is thus not an option. But the position is reversed when the Commission or certain Member States are trying to modify previously agreed positions. Here the unanimity rule permits a minority of Member States – sometimes only one – to preserve the status quo and thus claim value at the others' expense. This accounts for the long resistance to reform of the Common Agricultural Policy, which French President Jacques Chirac managed to hold up, sometimes single-handed, throughout his twelve years in office.

In international contexts the EU will always wish to present itself as value creating, because that is the way it has reached its negotiating position. But its partners may have a different view. Because the EU is so tough and inflexible in negotiation, it is often perceived as value claiming at the expense of others.

BATNAs and the role of markets Odell demonstrates that the United States deliberately uses BATNAs to put pressure on its negotiating partners, by showing it has little to lose if the negotiations fail. By contrast, the European Commission, as EU negotiator, always prefers to reach a negotiated agreement, as that is the way the EU extends its power. But the Member States do not necessarily share this view, so that in practice the EU also may have to fall back on its BATNA, especially as its win-set is small.

The negotiations for a financial services agreement in the GATT and WTO illustrate this – see Chapter 3 above. At first the EU was ready to accept any agreement, however weak; but the US preferred its BATNA and the negotiations twice failed. Then the banking and insurance industries in the US and EU got together: they persuaded the Commission to press for a stronger agreement and convinced USTR that this was worth having. The agreement was finally concluded in December 1997.

Likewise, the EU has always recognised the value of markets, as being integral to one of its founding ideas, and the present President of the Commission, José Manuel Barroso, is a strong advocate. But while the US may be happy to let the market take charge, the EU will want to be sure that the market is properly regulated.

Rationalist versus Constructivist Approaches

Much of the discussion above on the importance of institutions suggests a need to qualify rationalist assumptions of utility maximisation within European economic diplomacy. To this one must add the fact that the EU is clearly much less of a unitary actor than any single government. In the case of individual governments it is already a rather heroic assumption to suggest that governments are unitary actors. But in the case of the EU this is clearly not the case, with EU trade policy determined by a community process involving the Commission and Member States.

The way the domestic *acquis* is developed in internal negotiations clearly provides scope for negotiation leading to the emergence of common norms and expectations. So that one could say that European economic diplomacy is shaped by agreed norms and standards. When it comes to defining the specific EU position on a trade issue for example, there is also dialogue and discussion within the Commission, in the Art 133 Committee and the Council of Ministers. In the European context all these bodies function to a considerable degree as colleges in which persuasion and argument over extended periods of time can be expected to shape policy. To give just one example, some members of the Art 133 Committee have held that post for over ten years. This long term institutional memory can be expected to elevate the importance of argument and agreed norms higher than would be the case when short term political appointees are making trade policy within the context of sector lobbies working through the US Congress, which in the case of the House of Representatives is shaped by elections every two years.

In other words the kind of rationalist arguments developed in US political science and applied to international relations are likely to require some considerable qualification when applied to European economic diplomacy. In contrast constructivist approaches that stress the importance of argument and persuasion in developing norms may well prove a useful analytical tool.

Conclusions

Broadly speaking the theoretical analysis summarized in Chapter 2 can be applied to the EU. *Ideas* have been very influential, providing political motives for economic measures. European economic diplomacy has clearly also been shaped by *systemic factors* outside the EU at various times. Indeed, one could argue that systemic factors have been as important in shaping European economic diplomacy as domestic developments within the EU. As regards *domestic factors*, European economic diplomacy is made in a pretty dense institutional framework that shapes the autonomy or agent slack of the EU negotiators, although this clearly varies between policy areas. It has been suggested here that institutions are relatively more important in the EU than in other equivalent powers and that the impact of sector or societal interests is more muted as a result. The *two-level games* linking international and domestic are complex and asymmetrical, but can yield results in both substance and process. *Value creating* dominates new decision-making, but defending existing positions permits *value claiming*. *BATNAs* are never sought intentionally. Finally, *constructivist theories* may be more helpful than *rationalist theories* in explaining the complexities of European decision-making.

References

Aggarwal, V. and Fogerty, E. (2004), *EU Trade Strategies: Regionalism and Globalism*, Palgrave Macmillan, Basingstoke.

Bomberg, E. and Stubb, A. (2003), *The European Union: How Does it Work?*, Oxford University Press, Oxford.

Kenen, P.B., Shafer, J., Wicks, N. and Wyplosz, C. (2004), *International Economic and Financial Cooperation: New Issues, New Actors, New Responses*, Geneva Reports on the World Economy, No. 6, International Centre for Monetary and Banking Studies, Geneva.

Mansfield, E. and Milner, H. (1997), *The Political Economy of Regionalism*, Columbia University Press, New York.

McNamara, K. (2005), 'Economic and Monetary Union', in Wallace, H., Wallace, W. and Pollack, M.A. (eds), *Policy-Making in the European Union*, 5th edition, Oxford University Press, Oxford, pp. 141–60.

McNamara, K. and Meunier, S. (2002), 'Between National Sovereignty and International Power: What External Voice for the Euro?', *International Affairs*, Vol. 78, No. 4, pp. 849–68.

Meunier, S. and Nicholaidis, K. (1999), 'Who Speaks for Europe? The Delegation of Trade Authority in the EU', *Journal of Common Market Studies*, Vol. 37, No. 3, pp. 477–501.

Padoa-Schioppa, T. (2004), *The Euro and its Central Bank: Getting United after the Union*, MIT Press, Cambridge, MA.

Preeg, E. (1970), *Traders and Diplomats: An Analysis of the Kennedy Round of Negotiations under the GATT*, The Brookings Institution, Washington.

Winham, G.R. (1986), *International Trade and the Tokyo Round Negotiations*, Princeton University Press, Princeton, NJ.

Woolcock, S. (2005) 'European Union Trade Policy', in Kelly, D. and Grant, W. (eds), *The Politics of International Trade in the Twenty-First Century*, Palgrave, Basingstoke, pp. 235–51.

Woolcock, S. and Hodges, M. (1996), 'The European Union in the Uruguay Round: The Story behind the Headlines', in Wallace, H. and Wallace, W. (eds), *Policy-Making in the European Union*, 3rd edition, Oxford University Press, Oxford, pp. 301–24.

WTO (2006), *The Changing Landscape of Regional Trade Agreements*, World Trade Organization, Geneva.

Useful Websites

European Central Bank: http://www.ecb.org.
European Commission: http://www.ec.europa.eu.
European Union: http://www.europa.eu.

Chapter 14

Making EU International Environmental Policy

Matthias Buck[1]

Seen from outer space, life on planet earth appears as a thin belt of activity on the planetary crust. At closer inspection, this thin belt of activity reveals itself as a complex system, sustained by energy from the sun, which has evolved over millions of years into an abundance of interrelated organisms, species and ecosystems that interact with, drive and sustain global chemical, biochemical and atmospheric cycles. While natural science still fails to understand life in all its forms, complexities and interrelations, there is clear recognition that the web of life itself ensures that planet earth remains a habitable place (Lovelock 1972; Lovelock 2006; Wilson 2006).

The human species is one small part in the web of life. However, its rapid expansion and the increasing impacts of its activities are profoundly altering the conditions for life on earth. Signs are mounting that life as such is coming under threat. The so-called Millennium Ecosystem Assessment found that 'over the past 50 years, humans have changed ecosystems more rapidly and extensively than in any comparable period of time in human history, largely to meet rapidly growing demands for food, fresh water, timber, fibre and fuel. This has resulted in a substantial and largely irreversible loss in the diversity of life on Earth'.[2] The massive scale of this impact on the web of life can only be properly understood by placing it into the history of the earth as such: human pressure on ecosystems has triggered the sixth period of mass extinction in the life of planet earth; the last occurred about 65 million years ago (probably when earth was hit by a huge meteorite) and is best known for the sudden disappearance of the dinosaurs.

Human societies and their economies are to a very large extent based on services provided by natural systems. According to the Millennium Ecosystem Assessment, approximately 60 per cent (15 out of 24) of the ecosystem services examined are being degraded or used unsustainably, including fresh water, capture fisheries, air and water purification, and the regulation of regional and local climate, natural hazards, and pests. One particular issue that has recently

---

1 The author currently works as policy officer for international biodiversity and biosafety issues in the Environment Directorate General of the European Commission. The views expressed here are the author's only.

2 For comprehensive information on the Millennium Ecosystem Assessment see http://www.maweb.org.

received major public attention is human induced climate change (IPCC 2007). If natural systems are less productive or collapse entirely, it has immediate and potentially grave implications for the stability of societies and for local and regional security. In some parts of the world the consequences of such developments can be witnessed today (Carius and Lietzmann 1999; Kaplan 1996; Diamond 2005). Most prominently, conflicts arise over increasingly scarce fresh water resources.

This short and admittedly bleak introduction seeks to show that environmental policy today is about much more than protecting some endangered species or about setting aside some wilderness areas. Tackling the root causes of environmental degradation requires drastic reductions in the pressure put by humans on natural systems. This can only be achieved through mainstreaming environmental considerations into all areas of human and economic activities: energy production, transport and mobility, human settlements and food production systems to name but a few. Concerns about safeguarding the natural environment will therefore increasingly appear centre stage on the political agenda. Human induced climate change is only the first prominent example in this regard. Industrialised countries have a special responsibility to lead the way towards an environmentally sustainable future. This responsibility arises not only from their historic contributions to environmental degradation, but more importantly from the fact that the per capita ecological footprint of industrialised societies today by far exceeds those of poorer societies. Industrialised countries also have privileged access to the scientific, technical and financial means for reducing the ecological footprint of human activities.

The following section briefly explains why international cooperation efforts are increasingly important in tackling the global environmental crisis. The chapter then discusses the policy-making processes of the EU, before describing in more detail and by way of concrete examples the practice of EU international environmental policy-making.

Why is International Cooperation on Environmental Problems Important?

All concerns about environmental degradation can be related to specific human activities 'on the ground.' Most environmental problems are also local in character, restricted to local ecosystems and may or may not affect local livelihoods. Some cases of environmental degradation have, however, more far-reaching effects. This is the case when local environmental resources of international importance (for example, native forest or certain species) come under threat, when the affected environmental resources lie outside of national boundaries (for example, fish stocks in the high seas) or when localised activities have transboundary (for example, acid rain) or even global environmental consequences (for example, depletion of the stratospheric ozone layer, human induced climate change).

International environmental cooperation plays a role in addressing all of the above mentioned types of environmental degradation. Solving transboundary environmental problems frequently requires international cooperation between those causing and those affected by environmental degradation. The protection of the environment outside national boundaries, in so-called 'open access' resources like the high seas, presupposes coordination between the main contributors to the environmental problem. Multilateral and bilateral cooperation also plays an important role in transferring necessary technical and financial resources to countries that lack domestic capacity. The internationalisation of environmental issues is also driven by increasingly globalised trade and investment activities that impact on domestic patterns of production and consumption and, in the absence of sound domestic environmental policies, often stimulate over-exploitation of natural resources. In addition, high levels of debt in many poor countries mean that international financial institutions such as the World Bank, regional development banks or the International Monetary Fund play an important role in designing public spending programmes, including environmental programmes.

Institutional Foundations of EU Participation in International Environmental Affairs

The European Union is a unique player in international environmental affairs. No other group of countries in the international system has achieved a comparable level of unity in external representation. The unified representation of the interests of the Member States makes the EU one of the most influential players in international environmental affairs. No deal can be struck without the EU supporting it.

The EU's negotiating partners are clearly aware that this influence is based on the EU's effective coordination of the often diverse views of the Member States and the European Commission. Frequently, however, they are puzzled to see that sometimes it is the EU Presidency that takes the floor to speak on behalf of the EU and its Member States, sometimes it is the European Commission and sometimes negotiators from different Member States represent EU interests on specific subjects.

This diversity in external representation follows from the provisions of the EC Treaty (henceforth TEC) on the external policy-making of the European Community in general and on environmental policy in particular. The treaty provisions do not provide a clear picture of how the EU and its Member States are to address the diversity of situations encountered in international environmental affairs. On the one hand the TEC and the case law of the European Court of Justice grant the European Community competence to engage in international environmental affairs. On the other hand competence for environmental policy is shared between the Member States and the European Community and both can negotiate in international fora and conclude international agreements.

In order to understand the practice of EU international environmental policy-making it is necessary to have some knowledge of the institutional framework within which decisions are made. The next subsection briefly summarises this framework. This is followed by a discussion of the practical challenges arising from shared competence in international environmental policy and a description of EU international environmental policy-making.

The EC's External Order of Competence in Environmental Affairs

Legally speaking, it is not the European Union (EU) that participates in international environmental affairs, but the European Community (EC). Cooperation between Member States and the European Institutions in the framework of the European Community constitutes the so-called 'first pillar' of EU-cooperation.[3] The first pillar has its origin in the European Economic Community that was founded 50 years ago by the Treaty of Rome. First pillar issues include, for example, the internal market, competition policy, state aid, external trade or agriculture and fisheries policies. In all these areas, Member States have transferred substantive competencies to the European level. As discussed in Chapter 13 the EC has exclusive competence in policy areas such as external trade policy. This means that Member States have completely given up their own ability to regulate. In other areas Member States can only regulate where no EC legislation exists (for example, internal market) or they have to seek prior approval from the European Commission before enacting national measures (for example, state aid).

In matters falling under the TEC, cooperation within the EU has many features of 'supranationalism'.[4] The European Community has legal personality. It also has the monopoly right to propose legislation or policies and a strong role in supervising proper implementation of existing legislation by the Member States. The European Parliament, together with the Council of Ministers, is co-legislator in approximately 75 per cent of legislative acts adopted under the TEC and the European Court of Justice is the sole adjudicator in disputes relating to the proper interpretation or application of EC law. Article 281 TEC provides the European Community with legal personality, but it does not empower the European Community to engage in international negotiations.[5] All competences of the European Community are 'derived' from the Member States. This means that all activities of the European Community need to be based on specific competencies granted by Member States to the Community in the TEC.

---

3   The second pillar is the Common Foreign and Security Policy and the third pillar the Cooperation in Justice and Home Affairs.

4   A consolidated version of the EC Treaty, incorporating amendments from the Treaty of Nice, is found in the Official Journal of the European Communities, C 325 of 24 December 2002, pp. 33–184 (European Union 2002).

5   Legally, this provision applies only to the EC and its Member States. As regards third countries and international organisations, the legal personality of the European Community has, however, been recognised through long-standing practice and through the acknowledgement of full party status of the EC in a number of international organisations, instruments and processes.

The TEC provides for explicit external competences of the Community only in the areas of external trade (Article 133) and for the conclusion of association agreements (Article 310). However, since its judgement in the AETR-case, the European Court of Justice has held that there is a general parallelism between the internal and the external competencies of the Community (ECJ 1971). In areas in which EC legislation has been established internally, the European Community also acquires external competences. Furthermore, at least in the area of environment, implicit external competences of the EC also exist in areas in which the Community would, in principle, be competent to legislate internally, but has not yet done so. Therefore, cases may exist in which the conclusion and ratification of an international environmental agreement constitute the first activities of the European Community in a new subject (ECJ 2006).

Title XIX of the TEC concerns protection of the environment. Article 175.1 provides the EC with competence to regulate in environmental matters and thus also to participate in international environmental affairs. The EC competence to engage in international environmental affairs is reinforced by Article 174.1, which identifies the promotion of 'measures at international level to deal with regional or worldwide environmental problems' as one of the objectives of EC environmental policy. Article 174.4 TEC further holds that EC participation in international environmental affairs 'may be the subject of agreements between the Community and the third parties concerned'.

Today the EC is a party to about 40 multilateral environmental agreements (MEAs), including major international accords like the UN Framework Convention on Climate Change and its Kyoto Protocol or the UN Convention on Biological Diversity.[6] Commitments set out in MEAs and the politically binding decisions adopted by meetings of Conferences of the Parties have a major impact on EU environmental law.

Public international law is primarily a law between sovereign nation states. Therefore, international agreements generally only allow states to become parties to an agreement. Since the EC is not a state, its ability to join an international agreement with full party status requires the insertion of a special provision that allows Regional Economic Integration Organisations to become parties. The 'REIO' clause in Article 22.1 of the UN Framework Convention on Climate Change, for example, simply provides that '(t)he Convention shall be subject to ratification, acceptance, approval or accession by states and by regional economic integration organizations.' If the participation of REIOs is allowed in principle, states will ensure that upon ratification an REIO provides clarification of the specific extent of its competence and of the relationship between it and its members that may also join as full parties. For example, the UN Framework Convention on Climate Change provides that:

---

6   Further information and a detailed table listing the international environmental agreements to which the Community is already a party or a signatory are accessible at http://ec.europa.eu/environment/international_issues/agreements_en.htm.

- Any regional economic integration organisation which becomes a Party to the Convention without any of its Member States being a Party shall be bound by all the obligations under the Convention. In the case of such organisations, one or more of whose Member States is a Party to the Convention, the organisation and its Member States shall decide on their respective responsibilities for the performance of their obligations under the Convention. In such cases, the organisation and the Member States shall not be entitled to exercise rights under the Convention concurrently (Art 22.2).
- In their instruments of ratification, acceptance, approval or accession, regional economic integration organisations shall declare the extent of their competence with respect to the matters governed by the Convention. These organisations shall also inform the Depositary, who shall in turn inform the Parties, of any substantial modification in the extent of their competence (Art 22.3).

If an international agreement allows for the participation of a REIO, it will also include some language on the distribution of voting rights between a regional organisation and its members. Such provisions do not make much difference in practice as decisions in international negotiations are generally taken by consensus, even if an agreement provides for qualified majority in specific instances. This applies mostly to the amendment of technical annexes, such as the listing of new species under the Washington Convention on International Trade in Endangered Species (CITES) or modifications to the schedules for phasing out ozone depleting substances under the Montreal Protocol on Substances that Deplete the Ozone Layer.

The EU faces some real challenges in its participation in some 'old' MEAs, such as the 1971 Ramsar Convention on Wetlands of International Importance or the 1973 CITES. According to its internal order of competence the EC would be competent to participate in these, but the agreements do not include a REIO clause and consequently do not allow the EC to join as a party.

The EC Treaty offers two procedures to formalise EC participation in international meetings. One is set out in Article 300.1 TEC and applies when the outcome of a negotiation may be the 'conclusion of agreements between the Community and one or more States or international organisations'. In such situations, the EC Treaty foresees that the Commission makes recommendations to the Council on how it intends to approach the negotiations. The Council will then authorise the Commission to conduct the negotiations in consultation with representatives of Member States and, if deemed appropriate, also issue negotiating directives. In the field of environment, the Council will generally act by qualified majority.[7] The EC Treaty does not foresee a formal role of the European Parliament at this stage. However, since the European Parliament has to be consulted before the ratification of an international agreement and will in certain cases be able to veto the outcomes of international negotiations, the Commission has undertaken in an Inter-Institutional Agreement with the

---

7   Unanimity in the Council is required if matters under negotiation fall under one of the subject matters listed in Article 175.2 TEC.

Parliament to provide early and clear information to the Parliament both during the phase of preparation of agreements and during the conduct and conclusion of international negotiations.[8]

The second procedure to formalise EC participation in international meetings is found in Article 300.2.2 TEC. The scope of this provision was significantly expanded through the Treaty of Nice. Now, it applies to all situations where a decision 'having legal effects' is adopted by a 'body set up by an agreement'. A typical trigger for the use of the Article 300.2.2 procedure is the recommendation by a subsidiary body of an international environmental agreement that a future Conference of the Parties (COP) should adopt specific amendments to an agreement's technical annexes. The potential scope of application of Article 300.2.2 is, however, much broader, since many decisions adopted by a COP to an international environmental agreement may have a 'legal effect' on EC legislation, irrespective of the formal status of such decisions under international law. In cases, in which Article 300.2.2 TEC applies, it foresees that the Commission proposes to the Council a decision establishing the position to be taken by the European Community during the international meeting on the issue under consideration. As in the case of Article 300.1 TEC, the Council will generally act by qualified majority. The European Parliament 'shall be immediately and fully informed'.

Finally, Articles 300.2 and 300.3 TEC foresee specific procedures for the EC to join an international agreement as a party. The decision on ratification or accession is usually undertaken in parallel with the development of implementing legislation. Significantly for the field of international environmental cooperation, the assent of the European Parliament is required when implementation of the international agreement under consideration necessitates amendments to an act adopted under the co-decision procedure. This applies not only to all acts adopted under the environment competence of the Treaty (Article 175) but also to acts adopted under Article 95 TEC harmonising Member State legislation with relevance to the internal market, which is frequently used to harmonise product-related environmental standards.

Shared Competence – Challenges for EU Policy-Making

According to Article 174.4 TEC, the Community and Member States shall cooperate 'within their respective spheres of competence' with third countries and competent international organisations. This shall be without prejudice to Member States' competence to negotiate in international bodies and to conclude international agreements. The main provision indicating these respective spheres of competence is Article 176 TEC. According to this provision, the adoption of EC

8   Article 300.3 TEC stipulates that the assent of the European Parliament is required for the conclusion of Association Agreements based on Article 310 TEC, as regards the conclusion of agreements establishing a specific institutional framework of cooperation, agreements with significant budgetary implications and agreements necessitating amendments to an act adopted under the co-decision procedure (Article 251 TEC).

environmental legislation does not prevent any Member State from maintaining or introducing more stringent protective measures. While the above-mentioned provisions are not an example of legal clarity, they are generally interpreted to mean that in international environmental affairs Member States maintain a competence to act in parallel with the EC insofar as they seek to go beyond existing EC legislation. In other words the EC and Member States can both be competent at the same time.

This does not imply that Member States can exercise their own competence in international environmental matters independently from the Community. Whenever both Community and Member States are competent, Member States are bound by the principle of loyal cooperation with the Community which, in external affairs, obliges them to make their best endeavours to achieve unity in the external representation of the EC and its Member States. EU participation in international environmental affairs can therefore best be characterised as an area of 'shared competence'. Shared competence means that both Member States and the EC will participate in the negotiation of new MEAs, both may become party to the same MEA and both will participate in the work undertaken within the institutional framework established by such agreements.

In situations of shared competence the question arises as to whether the representative of the EU Member State holding the Presidency of the EU or the Commission will speak for the European Community and its Member States in international negotiations. It is increasingly the practice that the European Commission will take a leading role on issues of predominantly community competence, when EC legislation is extensive and covers essentially all aspects. The Commission will also lead in areas of exclusive community competence. The latter includes, for instance, all environmental agreements or provisions of such agreements that are closely related to international trade.

The issue of Community versus Member State competence in international environmental matters is also one of the reasons for recurring differences of opinion between Commission and Council on the proper legal basis for the conclusion of international environmental agreements by the EC. When there is doubt, the Commission will push for Article 133 TEC, the exclusive Community competence in international trade matters, whereas the Council will opt for Article 175, the environmental competence. This institutionalised conflict of interests has resulted in a stream of case law by the European Court of Justice on the proper legal basis for concluding international agreements with an environmental component.[9]

---

9   See Opinion 2/00 [2001] *European Court Reports* (ECR) I-9713, on the legal basis of the ratification of the Cartagena Protocol on Biosafety (ECR 2001); Case C-281/01 ECR [2002] I-12049 on the legal basis to conclude the EC-United States agreement on the coordination of energy-efficient labelling programmes for office equipment (Energy Star Agreement) (ECR 2002); Case C-94/03 ECR [2006] I-1, on the legal base for the ratification of the Rotterdam Convention on the Prior Informed Consent Procedure for certain hazardous chemicals and pesticides in international trade (ECR 2006).

The Practice of EU Participation in International Environmental Affairs

International environmental cooperation is still a relatively young area of international affairs, but one that has evolved rapidly. Its evolution since the 1970s has mostly been driven by multilateral environmental agreements (MEAs) that focus on specific issues of international concern and by a growing body of decisions taken by the parties to such MEAs.

The conclusion of a MEA typically marks the first major step of international cooperation on an issue. At a minimum, a MEA will establish a common understanding of the underlying problem, overarching objectives for cooperation and general principles to guide international and domestic action. Article 2 of the United Nations Framework Convention on Climate Change, for instance, establishes that the ultimate objective of cooperation in this framework is a stabilisation of greenhouse gas concentrations in the atmosphere at a level that would prevent dangerous anthropogenic interference with the climate system. A number of important principles of modern international environmental law underpin most MEAs. These include the precautionary principle (that is, the notion that under conditions of uncertainty states shall act prudently), the avoidance of harm to the environment, the principle of common but differentiated responsibilities of industrialised and developing countries and the 'polluter pays' principle. Frequently, the agreement will also include obligations on parties to evaluate the effectiveness of existing commitments and to engage in further negotiations on more specific commitments, including the adoption of additional international instruments. The Kyoto Protocol to the UN Framework Convention on Climate Change is a good example in this respect as is the Cartagena Protocol on Biosafety to the UN Convention on Biological Diversity.

The dynamic evolution of international environmental law is supported by the establishment of MEA-specific institutional arrangements. Parties to an MEA meet at regular intervals, mostly every one to three years, during the Conference of the Parties (COP) or Meeting of the Parties (MOP). These are the supreme decision-making bodies of an MEA. COPs and MOPs serve to review existing commitments in light of new scientific knowledge and experience with national implementation. Normally, further decisions will be adopted that establish new commitments, refine existing ones and, importantly, channel financial support to national implementation efforts by developing countries.

Decisions taken at COPs and MOPs are usually prepared through a series of inter-sessional meetings. Some MEAs, such as the UN Framework Convention on Climate Change or the UN Convention on Biological Diversity have set up permanent subsidiary bodies that are tasked to provide scientific or technical advice, to review and support national implementation efforts or to deal with cases of non-compliance. Further commitments are mostly negotiated in specialist working groups. Additional support is also provided by ad hoc meetings of technical experts who take stock of the latest technical and scientific developments and provide negotiators with factual information on agreed topics.

The growing body of international environmental agreements has resulted in a proliferation of international meetings. The two week long session of the COP of one major MEA, such as the UN Convention on Biological Diversity, for instance, is prepared by about 12 weeks of inter-sessional meetings. Adding to this are regional preparatory meetings as well as expert workshops organised by think tanks such as the Royal Institute for International Affairs in London. As a consequence, international environmental governance today is characterised by an almost uninterrupted stream of international negotiating meetings on different, but often related topics.

From the perspective of the parties to such agreements and for the individuals working in national governments and representing their countries, this means that there is a constant cycle of preparation and participation in negotiations proper, debriefing on the results to colleagues responsible for domestic implementation and further preparation for subsequent meetings. Often, international negotiators will service more than one negotiating stream at any given time, particularly when substantive issues are taken up in different negotiating fora at the same time. Forest issues, for instance, are currently negotiated in the UN Forum on Forests, in the UN Convention on Biological Diversity, in the UN Framework Convention on Climate Change discussions on a post-Kyoto agreement, in the International Tropical Timber Trade Organization and, increasingly, in bilateral and regional negotiations that seek to reduce the trade in forest products or products from illegal logging.

EU Preparations in the Run-Up to International Negotiations

As explained above, shared competence in international environmental affairs does not mean that the Commission and Member States are free to express their own views in international environmental negotiations. The duty of loyal cooperation and the obligation to ensure unity in the external representation of the EU requires that positions on all matters related to Community competence are discussed and agreed within the EU before they are communicated to the outside world.

Achieving unity in international representation of the EU is often burdensome and time-consuming. EU internal preparations will therefore start well in advance of upcoming international meetings, at times months before any official agendas and supporting documents are made available.

EU positions are discussed and decided upon in the Council. Most of the work in this regard is done at the level of Council Working Groups. To cope with the increased workload due to the active role of the EU in international environmental negotiations, the Council has established several formations of the Working Party on International Environmental Issues to cover issues such as climate change, biodiversity, biosafety, forests etc. Preparations for international environmental negotiations may also be taken up in other Council Working Groups that normally discuss the development of EC internal environmental policy and law.

The number of meetings of a specific Council Working Group depends on its scheduled workload and will be determined by the EU Presidency in cooperation with the Council Secretariat, usually after consultation with the Commission. The various formations of the Working Party on International Environmental Issues generally meet every three to five weeks.

Meetings of Council Working Groups are always chaired by the respective EU Presidency. In meetings of the Working Party on International Environmental Issues, Member States are represented mostly by staff from their respective capitals. Generally, only the leading ministry at national level will be represented; in case of cross-cutting issues or internal conflicts representatives of one or more national ministries may also attend to follow the discussion. Small Member States, or those with low interest in a specific issue, are sometimes represented by staff from their permanent representation to the EU.[10]

EU internal discussions in the run-up to international environmental negotiations frequently touch upon issues of competence. One of the first practical questions that arises between Presidency and Commission when planning for negotiations, is whether the Commission intends to ask for a negotiating mandate based on Article 300.1 or whether it will make a proposal for a Council decision based on Article 300.2.2 EC Treaty.

In cases in which the Commission indicates that it will not initiate one of the formal procedures under Article 300 TEC, the Presidency and Commission need to decide whether EU coordination is needed and if so, who should develop a first draft of an EU position. On issues where coordination appears necessary, the Commission will normally lead on matters of exclusive or predominant Community competence, whereas the Presidency will lead on all other issues. The exact distribution of work will be decided pragmatically on the basis of the availability of staff and technical expertise. Big Member States holding the EU Presidency will often seek to do almost all of the work, whereas small Member States holding the EU Presidency will look to the Commission to do most of the work or seek support from other Member States. Although the Commission is the only player with a permanent formal role in EU international environmental policy-making, its involvement will vary from issue to issue and from one Presidency to the next.

Commission recommendations under Article 300.1, proposals under Article 300.2.2 TEC and draft EU position papers are presented to and discussed in the relevant formation of the Working Party on International Environmental Issues or, at times, in another environment-related Council Working Group. Over the course of two or three 'readings', discussions will move from general political considerations to the drafting of specific texts. Once the EU position has been more or less finalised, it is the practice to develop speaking points for the first and perhaps second round of official EU statements on an issue under negotiation.

---

10 Permanent representations of Member States to the EU are not called 'embassies', since the EU is not a state, but they fulfil the same functions as an embassy in a third country. Given the important role of EU policy and law for Member States, permanent representations tend to be well staffed, with up to 250 Brussels-based personnel in the case of big EU Member States. The post of ambassador to the EU is one of the most respected positions in a successful foreign affairs career.

During international meetings, such statements are almost always delivered by the EU Presidency.

The open discussion during EU preparations for international negotiations is perhaps its greatest source of influence and leadership in international environmental affairs. As a group of 27 democratic states with different legal traditions, environmental problems, and economic capabilities, internal EU discussions reflect a range of interests and viewpoints comparable to that at the international level. For many Member States economic and employment implications tend to be a major concern. The ten new Member States generally are keen to keep an eye on potential administrative and budgetary implications of any agreement. Member States such as Denmark, Sweden and the Netherlands traditionally have a genuine commitment to consider the interests of developing countries. All this is conducive to the development of negotiating positions that third countries perceive as relatively balanced. There is also a real exchange of views and arguments on contentious issues. Regardless of the outcome, such exchanges help to underpin EU positions with well-reasoned arguments. They also raise consciousness about the strengths and weaknesses of the EU position and about potential alternative approaches. All these are positive assets for a successful negotiation, with one or the other providing the potential to break a deadlock or identifying the last minute compromise in international negotiations.[11]

Discussions on the distribution of competence between the EC and Member States are a recurring feature during the internal preparations for international negotiations, particularly in the case of formal Commission recommendations or proposals. However, such discussions in the Council Working Group are rarely conclusive and indeed issues of competence do not fall within the remit of working group experts but must, like all institutional questions, be dealt with by the Committee of Permanent Representatives (COREPER).

In the case of Commission recommendations based on Article 300.1 or a Commission proposal based on Article 300.2.2 TEC the Presidency will decide when expert discussions in the Working Party on International Environmental Issues have been exhaustive and put the draft decision on the agenda of an upcoming Council meeting. If some aspects of the draft decision are still contentious, an effort will be made to find a solution at the level of the COREPER. If this is not successful, the issue will be addressed by Ministers in the Council. Normally, this will be a meeting of the Council of Environment Ministers, where decisions of this nature can generally be adopted by qualified majority. However, to expedite proceedings and if it is not contentious a decision can also be adopted as an 'A' Point by any meeting of the Council.[12]

---

11 See the classics of negotiation literature, Fisher, Ury and Patton (1991) and Lempereur and Colson (2004).

12 Although it is commonplace to refer to a meeting of the 'Environment Council,' the 'Fisheries Council', the 'Agriculture Council' etc, institutionally there is only one Council of the European Community (see Articles 202ff. TEC) that meets in different formations according to policy domains. The Council endorses 'A' Points without discussion.

The formal adoption of Community positions through Council decisions based on Article 300 of the Treaty clearly constitutes the exception. In most cases, EU positions for international environmental negotiations are 'adopted' in the respective Council Working Group by simple agreement on the relevant position papers. To raise the level of political commitment on agreed EU positions, there is a general practice to adopt Council conclusions that reflect the main political lines the EU will take during a negotiation. This practice is not foreseen in the Treaty and has the clear disadvantage that Council conclusions are adopted by consensus and therefore may be less ambitious than a decision taken by qualified majority under Article 300. From the perspective of the European Commission, Council conclusions have two further institutional deficiencies. First, although they touch upon matters of Community competence, they are not based on a Commission proposal and thus undermine the Commission's right of initiative. Second, they do not establish a clear role for the Commission in the negotiations, which is at odds with the general notion of the Treaty that the Commission should represent the European Community in external affairs. In some cases, the adoption of Council conclusions instead of a Council decision based on Article 300.2.2 TEC may also undermine the right of the European Parliament to be 'immediately and fully informed'.

The EU during International Negotiations

Typically EU delegates have a relatively relaxed start into an international negotiating meeting, provided the Council decisions or conclusions are adopted in good time and the necessary positions and speaking points finalised before travelling to the country hosting the negotiations. If complications occur, additional EU internal negotiations may be needed to enable the EU to effectively participate in an international meeting. With this in mind, the EU Presidency will reserve a suitable meeting room for EU coordination meetings at or close to the premises where the actual negotiations are taking place. The first EU coordination meeting is typically convened in the afternoon or evening before the official start of a negotiating session. Subsequent coordination meetings are typically held at 0830 or 0900 in the morning, before negotiations are officially resumed at 1000. EU coordination meetings are normally preceded by so called 'troika' meetings of the current EU Presidency, the incoming Presidency and the Commission.

Depending on the course of negotiations, the EU will hold ad hoc coordination meetings to reflect on developments and if necessary revise its agreed position. Mostly, it is possible to hold such EU coordination meetings during lunch break or in the evening while the official negotiations are formally interrupted. At times, and particularly during the final hours of a meeting, however, EU delegates will simply huddle in a corner of one of the negotiating rooms to briefly exchange views before going back to work.

Who negotiates for the EU can vary from case to case. If the Commission has obtained a negotiating mandate, it will lead the negotiations on behalf of the European Community and its Member States, on all issues covered by its mandate. In this way, the Commission negotiated at the Second and Third MOPs of the Cartagena Protocol on Biosafety that led to international obligations concerning the identification of GM content of internationally traded agricultural commodities such as wheat, maize or soya. In cases in which an EU position has been established by a simple agreement in the relevant Council Working Group (possibly reinforced by Council conclusions) and in cases in which the EC position has been fixed through a Council decision based on Article 300.2.2 TEC, the EU negotiator will be determined by discussions between Presidency and Commission, and possibly some Member States.

Generally, the respective EU Presidency will deliver the agreed EU speaking points during plenary sessions and the 'first reading' of an issue in the working group of the international negotiation'. When discussions move to informal groups and to an 'open mode' of negotiation often requiring quick reactions, for example, to counter a draft text proposed by other parties, the EU negotiator is generally an individual selected for the task. On issues of exclusive or predominant EC competence, this will usually be someone from the European Commission. But it may also be an individual from a Member State not holding the Presidency. In the area of climate change, for example, the current practice is for the same people to be the EU negotiators on specific issues for several years, regardless of which Member State currently holds the EU Presidency. Under normal circumstances, delegations from other EU Member States will not take the floor, but simply monitor the work of the Presidency, the Commission or whoever is the lead negotiator.

Structure of International Environment Negotiations

In a UN context, negotiations typically unfold in a cascade of settings:

- The *plenary* appoints a chair of the meeting, adopts the agenda and the final decisions of a meeting, generally by consensus.[13]
- *Working Groups* are established by the Plenary to work through specified agenda items. Working Groups are attended by all parties to a meeting and, in the UN framework, are generally open for the participation of observers from states that have not ratified an agreement and representatives of non-governmental organisations. Often, observers are allowed to make statements or even to circulate papers. Discussions in Working Groups aim at identifying areas of consensus and points of contention that exist on specific issues.
- If necessary, the chair of a Working Group will appoint one or two well-respected negotiators to chair a *Contact Group* on one contentious issue

---

13 A few multilateral environmental agreements foresee that decisions on specific issues can be adopted by qualified majority, mostly to amend technical annexes. Prominent cases are amendments of technical annexes to the Montreal Protocol for the protection of the stratospheric ozone layer or to the Washington Convention on International Trade in Endangered Species. However, in practice voting is normally avoided. The 'threat' of being outvoted provides additional incentives to all delegations to arrive at a consensus.

that will foreseeably consume a lot of negotiating time. Contact Groups are open to all parties that regard themselves as having a stake in the issue under discussion. Contact Groups meet as often and long as necessary. In some MEAs observers are allowed to participate also in contact groups, but not to make statements.

- If discussions come to a crunch point, the chair(s) of a contact group will invite a small number of key delegations to nominate someone for a *Friends of the Chair* group. Friends of the Chair groups are closed to observers. Only invited delegations are allowed to enter the room. This is the setting in which real negotiations take place, often for many hours without a break. If need be, even smaller *drafting groups* will be established to develop passages of compromise text. *Bilateral consultations* frequently take place at the sidelines.

If a compromise is found in a Friends of the Chair group, it will be proposed to the Contact Group as the basis for further negotiation. Depending on the reception, negotiations in the Contact Group may move on or the issue will go back to a friends of the chair setting. The chair of the Working Group will push delegations to come up with compromise solutions before the scheduled final meeting of the Working Group. It frequently happens that the Working Group will not be able to recommend a decision for adoption by the Plenary, particularly on the main issues of contention. Negotiations will then continue in parallel to the final plenary. If there seems to be a chance for finding a last-minute compromise, the chair of the meeting will 'stop the clock' at 1800 on the last official day of the meeting to allow for negotiations to continue as if the scheduled meeting time was not yet exhausted. Frequently, compromises on difficult issues are only found in these final hours of a meeting, when negotiators are physically exhausted after one or two weeks of work. At times the conference facilities are being dismantled while negotiations continue. If a last minute compromise is found, the final plenary will formally be resumed to adopt the compromise decision and close the meeting.

When negotiations move to Friends of the Chair groups, it is general practice to invite both EU Presidency and the Commission into the room given the EU's importance in international environmental affairs. The lead EU negotiator from a Member State not holding the Presidency will be offered one of the EU places available. Other Member States are normally not invited. During these phases of the negotiation, EU coordination meetings also serve the important purpose of keeping the whole of the EU informed and for those doing the negotiations to regularly check with EU colleagues on whether an emerging compromise would be acceptable. Where the EU has internal differences, this may mean the opening of a second line of EU internal negotiations. These EU internal negotiations may consume considerable time and energy. In the final hours of the Kyoto Protocol negotiations, for example, the EU spent so much time in internal negotiations, that it became known for its 'bunker mentality'. On at least one occasion the EU was still discussing issues internally that in the meantime had already been decided in the official negotiations (Oberthür and Ott 1999, 86–7).

Conclusion

The EU is today one of the key players in international environmental affairs. In part, this is based on the privileged access of EU Member States to material sources of influence, such as control over raw materials, over sources of capital and markets, access to technology and finance as well as a competitive advantage in the production of highly valued goods (Keohane 1984, 32–3; Strange 1996, 7–12). However, to a considerable extent this influence is based on the ability of the 27 states that constitute the EU to speak with one voice in international environmental affairs. Achieving such unity is not an easy task and constitutes a permanent challenge.

Due to the open and discursive nature of EU internal discussions in the run-up to international environmental negotiations, core EU positions and sometimes first and second fall-back positions may be known to other interested delegations prior to or during international meetings. Still, EU positions and proposals very often constitute the nucleus of a final compromise, since the diversity of interests within the EU tend to result in positions that are perceived as relatively balanced by the outside world. This balance in substance compensates to some extent for the EU's relative inflexibility to change agreed positions, particularly on politically sensitive issues that have been subject to long internal debate.

Greater clarity in the EU's external order of competence would further add to the EU's ability to exercise leadership in international environmental affairs. The draft EU Constitution had promised to provide significant advances in this regard, but failed to find public support in both France and the Netherlands. In 2007 the German Chancellor Angela Merkel, as EU Presidency, eventually found support from EU heads of state and government to discontinue work on the Constitution and to launch negotiations on a much more limited 'Reform Treaty'. The European Council in June 2007 established political agreement on the cornerstones of this new treaty. It seems, however, that the Reform Treaty will not substantively change the current practice of EU participation in international environmental affairs.

References

Carius, A. and Lietzmann, K.M. (eds) (1999), *Environmental Change and Security*, Springer, Berlin.

Diamond, J. (2005), *Collapse: How Societies Choose to Fail or Succeed*, Penguin Books, London.

European Community (2002), Treaty establishing the European Community, Official Journal C325 of 24 December 2002.

ECJ (1971), European Court of Justice Judgment of 31 March 1971, Commission/ Council – *AETR*, Case 22/70.

ECJ (2006) European Court of Justice Judgment of 30 May 2006, Commission/ Ireland – *Mox Plant Sellafield*, Case C-459/03.

ECR (2001), Opinion 2/00 (2001) European Court Reports I-9713.

ECR (2002), Case C-281/01 (2002) European Court Reports I-12049.

ECR (2006), Case C-94/03 (2006) European Court Reports I-1.

Fisher, R., Ury, W. and Patton, B. (1991), *Getting to Yes*, Houghton Mifflin & Co., Boston, MA

IPCC (2007), The Fourth Assessment Reports of the Intergovernmental Panel on Climate Change, accessible at http://www.ipcc.ch/.

Kaplan, R.D. (1996), *The Ends of the Earth. From Togo to Turkmenistan, from Iran to Cambodia – a Journey to the Frontiers of Anarchy*, Vintage, New York.

Keohane, R.O. (1984), *After Hegemony. Cooperation and Discord in the World Political Economy*, Princeton University Press, Princeton, NJ.

Lempereur, A.P. and Colson, A. (2004), *Méthode de Négociation*, Dunod, Paris.

Lovelock, J. (1995), *Ages of Gaia*, 2nd edition, Oxford University Press, Oxford.

Lovelock, J. (2006), *The Revenge of Gaia*, Penguin Books, London.

Oberthür, S. and Ott, H. (1999), *The Kyoto Protocol: International Climate Policy for the 21st Century*, Springer, Berlin.

Strange, S. (1996), *The Retreat of the State: The Diffusion of Power in the World Economy*, Cambridge University Press, Cambridge.

Wilson, E.O. (2006), *The Creation: An Appeal to Save Life on Earth*, W.W. Norton, New York.

Useful Websites

European Commission: http://www.ec.europa.eu.
Intergovernmental Panel on Climate Change: http://www.ipcc.ch.
Millennium Ecosystem Assessment: http://www.maweb.org.

Chapter 15

International Institutions: Plurilateralism and Multilateralism

Nicholas Bayne

This chapter is about how governments use international institutions in economic diplomacy. It elaborates on one of the principal strategies in the new economic diplomacy identified in Chapter 1. It covers the ground often described by the term 'global governance'. But the study of global governance usually puts the *institutions* at the centre of the enquiry. In contrast, this chapter is mainly about what *governments* do, as members of international institutions, and how they try to make the institutions serve their national purposes, domestic as well as external.

The chapter begins with a general analysis of what governments want from international economic institutions in conditions of advancing globalisation. These arguments apply mainly to industrial democracies, but they are also relevant for developing and ex-communist countries.[1] This general analysis embraces the use made of both plurilateral and multilateral institutions. As explained in Chapter 9, *plurilateral* institutions are composed of like-minded countries, spanning several regions; they often embrace a wide variety of subjects. *Multilateral* institutions are universal in membership, though they may require tests on entry; they are likely to focus on a single subject, like finance or trade.[2]

The main body of the chapter contains separate assessments of plurilateral institutions, focusing on the OECD, the G8 summit and the Commonwealth, and of multilateral ones, concentrating on the WTO, the IMF and World Bank and the environmental work of the UN. These are all examined and compared in relation to their contribution to economic diplomacy, using a method based on the analytical framework set out in Chapter 1. Several of the practitioner case studies in this book, such as the treatment of the G8 in Chapter 6, have already looked at individual institutions from this selection. The three remaining case studies, by Joan MacNaughton in Chapter 16, Nigel Wicks in Chapter 17 and Roderick Abbott in Chapter 18, expand on this examination with reference to the International Energy Agency (co-located with the OECD), the IMF and World Bank and the WTO.

---

1   The thesis set out here was originally formulated in Bayne 1997, though it has since been adjusted in the light of later developments.

2   Every rule, however, has its exceptions. So there are also single-issue plurilateral institutions, like OPEC, and many-faceted multilateral ones, like the United Nations.

What Governments Want from the Institutions

The argument of this chapter is that governments want international economic institutions to do four things for them:

1) to reinforce their current economic policies – their most desired objective;
2) to share their burdens;
3) to extend their reach;
4) to give good value.

Each objective will be examined in turn.

Reinforcing Current Policies

With a few exceptions, governments value the endorsement of international institutions like the IMF and World Bank, the WTO and the OECD. Despite much criticism, internal as well as external, these are still the institutions that set the standards in the international economy. Their endorsement impresses trading partners, foreign investors and financial markets and may be necessary to release flows of funds, from both public and private sources. Governments do not like to go against them.

On the other hand, sovereign governments want to be making their own decisions and to have 'ownership' of their economic policies. These policies are unlikely to be effective if they are clearly imposed from outside. That looks weak and exposes the government to popular and parliamentary criticism, especially with the rise of the anti-globalisation movement. So the ideal is if the policies already chosen by the government are endorsed without change by the institutions. Governments thus get the best of both worlds.

Governments therefore have an incentive to anticipate what the institutions will recommend and do it before they are asked. Those departments within government that are closest to the institutions will invoke them in policy arguments. Thus finance ministries will argue the need for IMF endorsement when they promote policies of economic and monetary rigour and oppose ambitious spending plans from other ministries, which would enlarge the budget deficit. Departments responsible for international trade will invoke the WTO when arguing for competition and open markets against those who want more protection. As already noted in Chapter 3, members of these departments can come to feel greater solidarity with their foreign colleagues, whom they see at IMF or WTO meetings and regard as their allies, than they do with people from other ministries at home, whom they regard as their rivals.

So the institutions act as the *conscience* of governments, in helping to make them internationally minded. At the same time, the institutions realise that their public intervention may not be helpful to the government. They often therefore supply the government with ideas they can pretend they thought of themselves.

Sharing their Burdens

Reinforcing current policies, though desirable, may not be sufficient or sustainable. Governments realise that economic policy changes may be necessary and that these changes will be unpopular. In these conditions, it can be helpful to a government if it can share its burdens with the institutions and their other members. For example, it may be able to demonstrate to its people that it is not suffering alone. Other countries are also having to introduce painful or unpopular measures; there is a sort of 'equality of misery'. For example, G8 members, like the UK under Prime Minister Margaret Thatcher, have in the past used their annual summits for burden-sharing of this kind (Thatcher 1993, 290 and 586–7).

This burden-sharing is especially valuable in GATT or WTO trade negotiations, which operate on the basis of reciprocity. It may be economically advantageous for a country to open its market unilaterally, as many have done in recent years. But it is politically helpful if this market opening is matched by similar actions by other countries, so that no one gets something for nothing.

In some cases, when painful change is inevitable, governments may seek to make the institutions the *scapegoat* for unpopular measures. This often happens with IMF programmes. If a government is obliged to introduce unpopular measures to get access to IMF and related funds, it will be happy if popular discontent is directed against the IMF rather than against itself. But if the IMF programme restores prosperity, then the government will take the credit.

Of course, this strategy depends on the IMF medicine working and this does not always happen. During the Asian crisis of 1997–1998 the IMF was blamed for prescribing the wrong policies. The IMF largely defended itself, but did admit some mistakes, eg in Thailand. This put the Thai government in an embarrassing position, since the IMF's admission of error suggested that Thailand had been wrong to put so much trust in IMF advice (Blustein 2001; Stiglitz 2002). The IMF was blamed again for the collapse of Argentina late in 2001, because the Fund went on supporting the government's risky policies for too long (Blustein 2005). More generally, countries often do not identify themselves with policies agreed with the Fund. They follow IMF guidance for long enough to get the finance required and then relapse until they need a new fix from the Fund. It is important that countries take full ownership of their economic strategy and do not become dependent on the IMF. This has become a key component of the Poverty Reduction Strategies agreed in the context of the Heavily Indebted Poor Countries (HIPC) programme of debt relief (Addison, Hansen and Tarp 2004).

Extending their Reach

The first two objectives show governments making use of international institutions to advance their domestic policies. This third objective, in some respects, relates more to their external interests. Governments try to use the institutions in order to gain access to markets or to get their debts paid. Rather than exerting direct pressure, governments shelter behind the institutions, which have the advantage of being highly reputable and relatively anonymous. In particular, smaller governments can sometimes use the institutions as a check on the abuse of power by major powers like the United States and the European Union. For example, several countries, including the tiny Caribbean state Antigua, have brought cases against the US in the WTO and have won them. But this depends on the institutions being regarded as sufficiently independent of its larger members and able to stand up to them.

Governments also use the institutions to extend their reach in a different, more domestic way. This is done so as to compensate for loss of power at home. Many states have conducted programmes of privatisation and deregulation, which move responsibility away from national government towards the private sector. As long as activities remain under their own control, governments tend to resist international rules. This explains why international negotiations on agriculture are so difficult. But privatisation and deregulation at home make governments seek better rules internationally. Thus the WTO has been able to conclude agreements on trade in services, like telecommunications; and the IMF, in developing new financial architecture, has paid more attention to improved international supervision of financial markets.

Getting Good Value

These activities – serving as conscience or scapegoat for governments, sharing their burdens and extending their reach – create lots of extra work for the institutions, for which they seek extra resources. But here governments make clear their desire to get good value. Domestically, many governments have reduced their spending to balance their budgets. They have shifted tasks to the private sector. Governments that are spending less on themselves are reluctant to spend more on international institutions. Those institutions, like the IMF and World Bank, that can generate their own income, are sheltered to some degree. But those that rely on contributions from their members, like the OECD, the WTO and the UN, are becoming severely squeezed. There must be doubt if they can continue to do all the extra things that governments want; and if the quality of their work falls, their authority declines too.

Classifying and Comparing Institutions

This analysis has so far examined the general objectives of governments in making use of international institutions. The remainder of this chapter looks more closely at how specific institutions are used. It first develops a method of assessing and comparing institutions for their contribution to economic diplomacy. It then applies this method to selected plurilateral and multilateral institutions.

How Institutions Contribute to Economic Diplomacy

This section sets out a method of classifying international institutions in the light of their contribution to economic diplomacy. The method is derived from the three tensions of economic diplomacy identified in Chapter 1. The performance of economic institutions – both plurilateral and multilateral – will be judged against a range of indices based on these three tensions, as set out in Table 15.1.

Table 15.1   International institutions: Economic diplomacy indices

1	Political/economic
2	Departmental intensity
3	Domestic/external
4	Rules/voluntary
5	Accountability
6	Business friendly
7	Transparency
8	Staff or member driven
9	Multi-level activity

There are nine indices in all. The first one explicitly relates to the first tension of economic diplomacy. The next four cover issues arising from the second tension, between domestic and international pressures. Two more indices (nos 6 and 7) relate to the third tension, between governments and other forces. The last two indices are concerned with the shape and purpose of the institution itself.

- *Political/economic* Index no. 1 assesses how far the institution reconciles economics and politics, in its objectives and methods.
- *Departmental intensity* The second index considers how many parts of government are involved in the institution's work.
- *Domestic/external* The third index examines whether the institution covers only international issues or whether it becomes involved in domestic policy.
- *Rules or voluntary cooperation* The fourth index examines whether the institution is based on voluntary cooperation or embraces rule-making and enforcement.
- *Accountability* The fifth index assesses how far the institution serves all its members and is accountable to its members' governments and citizens.
- *Business friendly* The sixth index considers how far the institution is accessible to private business firms and seeks to cooperate with them.
- *Transparency* The seventh index assesses whether the institution is open to the outside world, including NGOs.
- *Staff or member driven* Index no. 8 takes account of the wide variations between institutions in their staff resources. Some are very well endowed with staff, who can take on ambitious tasks, while others have slender staff resources and have to rely much more on their members.
- *Multi-level activity* Finally, index no. 9 assesses whether the members' benefits are limited to the institution itself, or whether it also helps them to pursue their objectives in wider contexts. In short, does the institution facilitate multi-level economic diplomacy, as defined in Chapter 9?

This completes the list of indices. The only point to add is that institutions change over time and may look different today against many of the indices than they did ten years ago.[3]

Assessing Plurilateral Institutions

These nine indices provide a basis for analysing the three sample plurilateral institutions – the OECD, the G8 summit and the Commonwealth. The passages that follow will go through the indices for each of the institutions – not in any fixed order – so as to assess how they contribute to economic diplomacy.

The OECD

The Organisation for Economic Cooperation and Development (OECD) looks like a supremely *economic* institution. It covers all the economic subjects of interest to governments, from agriculture to transport and including education and employment, but none of the political ones – no defence, law and order, culture or sport. Even so, the OECD's underlying motivation is *political*, to support the open democratic system. It developed out of the regional Organisation for European Economic Cooperation (OEEC), which applied the Marshall Plan in 18 European countries, with the political aim of checking the spread of communism. This role was continued by the plurilateral OECD, which settled at 24 members over a long period: the 18 original Europeans, plus Finland and five non-Europeans – US, Canada, Japan, Australia, New Zealand.[4] For them the OECD was the standard-bearer of the West in the contest of economic systems in the Cold War. When the Cold War ended, the OECD shifted again to helping bring ex-communist countries and others into the open economic order. In the process it has added six new members – Poland, Hungary, Czech Republic, Slovakia (all now also in the EU), Mexico and South Korea – but is having some difficulty in finding a distinctive role for the 2000s (Woodward 2006).

The OECD is of interest to all economic departments and so scores highly in *departmental intensity*; that is a great part of its value. It goes deeply into *domestic policy-making*. It can assess the impact of one policy, such as environment policy, on a range of others. Its method of work is based on a network of expert committees – trade, industry, economic policy, environment and so on – formed of national representatives. This committee structure means that, although the staff are numerous and highly intelligent, the OECD is not as highly *staff-driven* as one might expect; the *members* are still in charge (Henderson 1993; Wolfe 2007).

---

3   The first edition of this book attached numerical scores to the indices for each institution reviewed. But this grading was rather subjective and has been abandoned.

4   Fifteen of the 19 European members of the OECD also joined the European Union. None of the four still outside – Iceland, Norway, Switzerland and Turkey – are likely to join the EU soon, though Turkey has begun negotiations.

The OECD pursues mainly *voluntary cooperation.* Countries are persuaded – never forced – to adjust their policies by the supply of better information or by peer pressure. It operates very tactfully and unobtrusively, encouraging governments to take ownership of the ideas the institution supplies. This voluntary cooperation is what the OECD does best. It is still the favoured institution in many economic areas where its members seek higher standards or closer cooperation than are attainable in multilateral contexts, for example in employment and social policies, export credit (Ray 1995), official aid policy, tax cooperation and money laundering.

The OECD does less in *rule-making*, and does it less well, because it has no powers of enforcement. Its rule-making ambitions suffered a serious setback with the collapse of the Multilateral Agreement on Investment (MAI) in 1998 (Henderson 1999 and Chapter 9 above). The impact of other rule-making ventures, such as a treaty to counter corrupt practices, is limited by the lack of enforcement machinery.[5]

The OECD seems very *accountable*, as it is consensus-based and its member governments must answer to their electorates; very *business friendly* in that private firms usually welcome its policies; and very *transparent*, as it publishes a huge amount. But all this needs some qualification. The OECD is accountable and business friendly and transparent in output rather than input. It has its Business and Industry Advisory Council (BIAC) and Trade Union Advisory Committee (TUAC), but they are kept at arms length. Since the OECD promotes voluntary cooperation, rather than formal agreements, very little of its work actually has to go to parliaments. Hardly anyone gets into the meetings where deals are struck except government officials (or sometimes ministers) and OECD staff. This is not unusual in international institutions, but it did make the OECD vulnerable when NGOs attacked its secretiveness over the MAI.

In terms of *multi-level* activity, the OECD is formally self-contained, working for its members. But though it rarely makes rules itself, its well-researched work is often used as the basis for rule-making in bilateral, regional and multilateral contexts. Principles on investment worked out by the OECD (before the failed MAI) have been used both in bilateral investment treaties and in NAFTA. It has had a special impact in trade negotiations, where the OECD can compensate for the weakness in resources of both the old GATT and the new WTO (Cohn 2002). The concepts that underlie the agreements on agriculture and on services concluded in the Uruguay Round were originally worked out at the OECD (Drake and Nicolaides 1992; Wolfe 1998). The main constraint in multilateral contexts is that the OECD has to work indirectly or by stealth. Developing countries resent having measures openly imposed upon them by the OECD; this has emerged clearly from its attempts to discipline tax havens (Persaud 2001; Wechsler 2001). This factor limits the OECD's usefulness in multi-level economic diplomacy.

---

5 For example, though the UK strongly backs action to cut back corruption in developing countries, it has not brought any cases against British firms and abandoned an enquiry into bribery by BAE, an armaments supplier, over a contract with Saudi Arabia, citing security concerns. See Adams, Peel and Burns 2007.

In short, the OECD is a wide-ranging, unobtrusive institution relying wholly on its powers of persuasion.[6]

The G8 Summit

As an institution, the G8 summit (originally G7), looks like the inner circle of the OECD – same subjects, fewer people. In fact it is quite different. President Valéry Giscard d'Estaing of France, who invented it, insisted it was a wholly *economic* instrument and tried to prevent non-economic subjects being discussed at the summits. But both the method and the motivation were in fact *political.* Giscard realised that in the mid-1970s the greatest threat to the West came not from the Soviet Union but from the confused response to the economic crisis provoked by the first oil shock. His answer was to invoke political leadership instead of bureaucracy: leadership by the most important countries and the most important people in them (Putnam and Bayne 1987). Political issues soon crept in, against Giscard's wishes. The summit added a parallel agenda of foreign policy topics, like terrorism and non-proliferation, and admitted Russia for political reasons from 1998, thus becoming G8. In the 2000s it deliberately chose themes that combined economic and political aspects (Bayne 2005).

Originally the heads of government were supported only by their foreign and finance ministers. But over time so many other G8 ministerial and official groups have sprung up that the heads of government have detached themselves from this apparatus and now meet on their own (Hajnal 2007). But some things have not changed. The G8 still has no written rules, no headquarters and no staff. Everything is *member-driven*, led by the host country for the year – Russia for the first time in 2006, Germany in 2007.

The G8 has high *departmental intensity.* It can potentially involve as many parts of government as the OECD – even more – though in practice it does not. It cannot do everything at once and has to be selective. Only the most intractable problems find their way up to summit level. The G8 members have become accustomed to treating them on an iterative process; if they fail once, they try again. The G8 does have great capacity to treat *domestic and external* issues together, especially at summit level. That was the second reason – political leadership being the first – for involving heads of government. As explained in earlier chapters, heads of government can reconcile domestic and external pressures better than ministers with more limited authority. They also tend to have good democratic legitimacy and to be clearly *accountable* to the concerns of their people. The G8 therefore scores strongly against all these indices, though its achievements have often fallen short of its promises and its potential.

The G8 only conducts *voluntary cooperation*. Rule-making would not make sense in such a small group. At first the summit was self-contained, focusing on economic coordination among themselves. But it has always pursued *multi-level* activity, as it relies on other bodies to get its decisions implemented. At first, in

---

6   I have in the past called it the Cinderella of economic institutions, as compared with its ugly sisters the IMF and World Bank (Bayne 1987).

their dealings with international institutions, the summit leaders would throw stones into the pool but then stand back. In some areas they set up their own parallel channels, which weakened established organisations. But this approach changed, as the G7 lost both its dominance in the world economic system and became more active below summit level. From the mid-1990s the summit leaders took a conscious decision to work more directly and more persuasively at steering multilateral institutions. The G8 has also sought more legitimacy by inviting the leaders of major developing countries to summit meetings and associating them with the decisions taken. A meeting with the 'Plus-5' countries – Brazil, China, India, Mexico and South Africa – has become a standard element of every summit, with more formal consultation introduced in 2007.

The summit has adapted slowly to the shift from state to non-state actors. For most of its life the G7 was *business friendly* in substance, but not in procedure, like the OECD. From 2000 onwards, however, the G8 has involved business leaders in both preparation and follow-up of selected topics, adopting a 'multi-stakeholder' approach (Hart 2005). It has also become more accessible to NGOs, after the summits of the late 1990s were the target of some massive lobbying over debt relief. The violent demonstrations at the Genoa summit of 2001 were a severe shock and drove the summits into seclusion for several years. By Gleneagles in 2005 and St Petersburg in 2006, however, mass peaceful involvement by civil society had been restored. Yet despite these changes the G8 remains almost totally *non-transparent*. Nothing gets out, except agreed statements and other documents interpreted at national press briefings.

In short, the G8 summit is a highly select, member-driven institution, aiming to provide political leadership and to reconcile external and domestic pressures in economic policy-making (Bayne 2005).

The Commonwealth

The Commonwealth is very different from the other two institutions. With 54 members, it is much larger and more varied. G8 and OECD members are all 'high-income' countries. Commonwealth members range from the richest to the very poorest. G8 members are large countries. The Commonwealth includes some of the smallest countries on earth. The factors which have kept Commonwealth members together and determine new admissions are *political* rather than *economic*: the use of English; similarities in legal and political systems; more recently, standards of democracy and human rights. The Commonwealth economic preferences which prevailed from the 1930s to the 1960s are long gone and have left hardly any legacy.[7]

Yet the Commonwealth has a distinctive impact on the international economic system. It is largely *member-driven*, as the Commonwealth Secretariat is small and has limited resources. It engages only a few departments so far – education, finance, environment, trade – so that *departmental intensity* is fairly low. Apart

---

7   A recent, though controversial, assessment of the Commonwealth is in Srinavasan 2005, which has provoked comment in McIntyre and others 2007.

from work on education, especially distance education, its economic work is focused on *external* issues more than *domestic* ones and it involves *voluntary cooperation* only. While the Commonwealth seeks to develop activities for its own members, like encouraging intra-Commonwealth trade, these are less influential than the Commonwealth's *multi-level* activities, especially those focused on multilateral institutions.

The clearest example is in debt relief for low-income countries. Every year the Commonwealth finance ministers meet together in the week before the IMF/World Bank annual meeting. On three occasions – in 1991, 1994 and 1997 – Britain, with Canada in support, launched a debt relief initiative in the Commonwealth as the springboard for getting agreement in the G7 and the IMF. Having support from Commonwealth members, who were so numerous and so varied in size, development and geographical spread, greatly strengthened their negotiating hand. It took two to three years to move from Commonwealth initiative to IMF endorsement and required help from other quarters too, but it worked every time (Bayne 1998).

There was similar evidence from the international environment. The Commonwealth contributed greatly to assessing the consequences of global warming in causing higher sea-levels, because this would endanger so many Commonwealth members, such as Bangladesh, the Maldives and small Pacific states. Commonwealth cooperation enabled members to launch joint initiatives during the1990s in the UN on forests: Britain with Malaysia, Canada with India. Commonwealth environment ministers now meet regularly, for example to discuss climate change.[8]

Trade was more difficult for many years, as Commonwealth trade ministers did not meet regularly. Britain's trade policy was tied up with the EU. Commonwealth markets showed great variations in their degree of openness, from Singapore to India. Yet Commonwealth members have realised that, if they could agree among themselves, they could exert a powerful influence both on the agenda for a new trade round and the course of such a round. In Durban in 1999, Commonwealth heads of government listened to the Commonwealth Business Council when they presented the report cited in Chapter 3, prepared by their LSE academic advisers. Many Commonwealth trade ministers were active at the WTO meetings at Seattle, Doha and Cancun, while the Commonwealth Secretariat helped its members to negotiate (Mbirimi and others 2003). But the Commonwealth was not always united, with India often taking a more reserved line than others. By the time of the Hong Kong WTO ministerial in 2005, however, there was much stronger convergence and the Commonwealth could present a united front.

The Commonwealth Business Council is a move to make the Commonwealth more *business friendly*, though it is a fairly new body, launched in 1997. In *accountability* and *transparency* the Commonwealth looks quite different from the OECD or the G8. In addition to democratic standards for each state, the members are linked by the Commonwealth Parliamentary Association. The Commonwealth

---

8 However, Australia has followed the US in not accepting the Kyoto Protocol (Barnsley 2006).

also has an easy and confident relationship with NGOs and does not fear upsets like those of the OECD or WTO. It clearly helps that the economic activities of the Commonwealth are part of a much wider whole with political content. Yet for all this apparent transparency, the real decision-making at Commonwealth Heads of Government Meetings is done in an exclusive 'retreat'.

In short, the Commonwealth is a very broad-based and varied institution, with strong potential to influence global economic organisations (Bayne 1997a).

Interim Conclusions on Plurilateral Institutions

That completes the assessment of the three sample plurilateral institutions. The main conclusions about international institutions will come at the end of this chapter, but three initial points can be made about these plurilateral bodies:

- all these institutions have a stronger *political* content than may appear at first sight;
- all are better adapted for *voluntary cooperation* than rule-making;
- all are giving increasing attention to *multi-level* activities. They try to help their members in multilateral contexts, while plurilateral voluntary cooperation can also provide the content for tighter rules at bilateral or regional level.

Assessing Multilateral Institutions

The same method of analysis will now be applied to four sample multilateral institutions. Those chosen are the WTO; the IMF and World Bank, taken together; and United Nations bodies concerned with the global environment.

The WTO

The World Trade Organization (WTO), like the OECD, looks like a wholly *economic* institution, both in its instruments and in its purpose, which is the expansion of international trade. In some respects politics are separated out; for example, where security interests predominate, WTO rules do not apply. Yet *political* elements are at work in the WTO in various ways. The methods it uses to promote trade liberalisation, such as non-discrimination and reciprocity, are political methods. The deeper the WTO gets into rule-making affecting domestic policy, the more it impinges on politics. This is especially evident where members want the WTO to go beyond the scope of trade, into intellectual property rights, food safety rules or labour standards.

The old GATT, without agriculture or services, was largely the concern of specialised trade negotiators, based in economics or foreign ministries or dedicated agencies like USTR. But as a result of the Uruguay Round negotiations (see Chapter 4 above) the WTO involves many more departments – agriculture, finance, environment, transport, development – so that it is almost as *departmentally intensive* as the OECD. It is penetrating deeper and deeper into *domestic policy*, such as regulation of services, industrial subsidies and agricultural support programmes.

The WTO is almost entirely a *rule-based* institution, devoted to drawing up, implementing and enforcing trade rules. Its principal activity consists of negotiating the removal of trade barriers; the results of these negotiations are formal obligations on members, subject to binding dispute settlement. There is some *voluntary cooperation*. The Trade Policy Review System, which examines the trade policies of individual members, does not lead to binding recommendations. But this is only a minor part of the institution's work. In fact, the WTO supervises the tightest rule-based regime in the multilateral economic system (Croome 1999).

The attacks mounted by hostile NGOs from the 1999 Seattle ministerial meeting onwards portray the WTO as remote, unaccountable and the creature of predatory multinationals (Bayne 2000). The NGO critics were right to recognise an instinctive lack of *transparency* in the WTO. The WTO is a negotiating body, and, as was said in Seattle, 'negotiators are not good communicators'. That is because, as explained earlier, negotiation is like courtship, not easy to conduct in public and the WTO continues to negotiate in private, as its members insist. In the 2000s, however, there have been increasing efforts to open up the rest of the WTO's activities, both by taking in outside advice and making the results of its work more widely known. It is also true that the WTO is *business friendly,* in that the removal of trade barriers favours efficient, well-resourced and internationally oriented firms. But the WTO can be a defence against aggressive multinational companies. When the US, pressed by Kodak, brought a case against Japan over the marketing of photographic film, the WTO found in favour of Japan.

The WTO is also firmly *accountable* in many senses. It is a consensus-based institution; decisions require the assent or acquiescence of all participating members. Each formal agreement has to be ratified by all the members, who normally have to submit it to their legislatures, and the agreement does not enter into force until this process is complete. This should give an important protection to all the members, big or small. Nevertheless, the great debate in the WTO in the 2000s has been over whether it is equally accessible to its poorer, developing members as it is to its rich industrial ones. When developing countries complained over unequal burdens imposed open them by the Uruguay Round agreements, the WTO agreed to launch the Doha Development Agenda in 2001 to redress the balance (Odell 2006, 1–38). But it has proved very difficult to bring the DDA to a fruitful conclusion. Larger developing countries, like Brazil and India, have successfully combined in the G20 to promote and defend their interests (Narlikar and Tussie 2004). But countries with limited resources, because of their size or their poverty, find it hard to handle complex negotiations or to profit from dispute settlement; many of them are not present at Geneva at all (Page 2003). The WTO is also short of resources, in staff or funds. The WTO in fact has to be a *member-driven* institution, because its staff is so small (Nordström 2005). That can sometimes be a source of strength, if it gets national delegations more deeply involved and committed. But it means the WTO has to rely on its member governments for help in increasing the capacity of small or poor countries to benefit from their WTO membership.

The WTO provides plenty of scope for *multi-level* diplomacy. It includes a few plurilateral agreements to which not all members subscribe, the most important being on government procurement. The regional European Union always negotiates collectively, with the Commission as spokesman, though it is not a WTO member. Plurilateral groups, like the G20 and the Cairns group, are increasingly active. When agreement proves elusive in the cumbersome, slow-moving WTO context, the same issues can be pursued among members in smaller groups at other levels; the bilateral level was especially favoured in the early 2000s.

In short, the WTO is devoted to rule-making, democratic but not instinctively transparent and increasingly intrusive into domestic policy (Hoekman and Kostecki 2001).

The IMF and World Bank

The International Monetary Fund (IMF) and the World Bank will be assessed together, though sometimes their indices diverge. They are again fundamentally *economic* institutions, seeking to promote financial stability and economic development. But there are definite *political* influences at work as well. Sometimes the grant or the refusal of Fund or Bank lending has been used as a political weapon for or against countries: for example, to encourage reform in Russia, or to punish China after the Tiananmen Square shootings. This is strictly against the rules, but it happens. The World Bank and even the Fund have gone beyond the strictly economic sphere into institution-building, standards of governance and especially checking corruption, while Paul Wolfowitz was President of the Bank in 2005–2007. Finally, the policy adjustment associated with major Fund or Bank programmes has inevitable political consequences.

The activities of both Fund and Bank go deeply into *domestic policies:* the Fund into monetary and fiscal policy and increasingly financial regulation; the Bank into every aspect of development from agriculture through education and health to transport systems. But their *departmental intensity* is very low. In general, finance ministries have a near monopoly hold on the Fund and Bank, which they share with central banks and occasionally with development ministries, but not wider.

It is not easy to strike the balance between *rule-making* and *voluntary cooperation*, as regards the Fund and the Bank. The IMF used to define and enforce the rules for exchange rates, but that function is almost wholly eroded. By the mid-1990s the Fund and Bank had largely gone over to voluntary cooperation and the provision of information (James 1996). Since then, however, as part of the new financial architecture developed since the Asian crisis, rule-making has revived. The Fund has developed codes of good practice in supplying economic data and in the openness of monetary and fiscal policy, while there is a parallel code on social policy for the Bank. The Fund is also stimulating international disciplines in financial regulation. But not all of this is binding and none of it is enforceable (Kenen 2001). For countries borrowing from the Fund and the Bank there are often conditions requiring policy adjustment. These conditions had become especially complex in the Fund and when Rodrigo Rato became IMF Managing Director in 2004, he moved to simplify them. This conditionality is certainly more than the wholly voluntary cooperation seen in the OECD, though well short of the rule-making practised in the WTO.

The Fund and the Bank are *accountable* to their members, but they are less democratic than the other institutions examined so far, because they have a system of weighted voting which favours the rich members. Rich countries that lend have more power than poor countries that borrow; the poor countries tolerate this because they need the funds on offer. Over the years this division has increased between the rich countries, who treat the Fund and Bank as if they were shareholders, and the poor countries, who are more like consumers of the services they provide. But this division is now under challenge. Major developing countries like China and others in Asia have less need to borrow from the institutions and are challenging the basis for allocating votes. In 2006 the IMF launched a process designed to reform the basis of quota allocation with a two-year deadline – see Chapter 17 below.

The Fund and the Bank have developed very close links with private suppliers of finance and are *business friendly* in this sense. Their annual meetings every autumn gather crowds of bankers and investors, keen to meet the finance ministers coming from all over the world. Private financiers often wait for the approval of a country's policies by the Fund or Bank before releasing funds or agreeing to reschedule debt. They tend, however, to resist the idea that they should share responsibility for the financial rescue operations of the Fund and Bank (Eichengreen 1999). As regards *transparency*, the Bank has been ready to engage in dialogue with development NGOs, especially during James Wolfensohn's decade as President from 1995 to 2005, and has at times adapted its policy strategy to their views (Mallaby 2004). This openness of the Bank is in contrast to the Fund. The IMF is the guardian of financial stability, which is all too easily upset by rumour and speculation. So the Fund has been traditionally sparing in its public statements and gained a reputation for being tight-lipped and sometimes arrogant. But this is now changing, so that the IMF too publishes more and explains itself more.

As indicated earlier in this chapter, the Fund and Bank finance themselves from their lending operations and that has given them an advantage over those institutions that rely on subscriptions from their members.[9] This has enabled both to have large and active staffs, especially the Bank. Since only a small number of delegations actually sit on the Executive Boards, that gives more power to the staff. So the Fund and the Bank are strongly *staff-driven*; though the staffs do try to work for the entire membership, to offset the dominance of the rich countries on the Boards.

---

9   The IMF began worrying in 2006, however, that a decline in major borrowings would affect its resources and commissioned a report on its future financing (Crockett 2007).

There is scope for *multi-level* activity in both institutions, especially the IMF. There is very little interaction with the regional level, as Chapter 13 showed over the EU. But plurilateral groupings are active, such as the G7 finance ministers, the G20 finance ministers (not to be confused with the G20 in the WTO) and the Financial Stability Forum. Most of the measures adopted in the Fund and Bank originate from initiatives taken at the plurilateral level.

In short, the IMF and World Bank, driven by their staffs and dominated by finance ministries, are moving tentatively back into rule-making, with rich countries as shareholders and poor ones as consumers (Woods 2006).

United Nations Work on the Global Environment

The United Nations (UN) is the last multilateral institution to be considered. This will be only a limited sampling of the UN's contribution to economic diplomacy, concentrating on its environmental activities. It leaves aside all that the UN does in humanitarian or technical assistance activities, as well as the work of UNCTAD and agencies like the Food and Agriculture Organisation (FAO) and World Health Organisation (WHO).

The United Nations is both a *political* and an *economic* institution. It employs more staff on economic activities than political ones and spends more funds on them, except at the height of peace-keeping operations. But in the founding Charter the UN's political role is clearly defined, including its mandatory powers, while its economic role is left vague and ill-focused. Some features are common to all UN work: universality, equitable geographic distribution of staff and decisions by 'one member, one vote'. Much of the UN's economic activity over the years has been *voluntary cooperation,* based on non-binding resolutions or technical assistance programmes financed by unreliable national contributions. The results of this have tended to be disappointing.

However, the UN has developed a method of getting round these drawbacks. It has moved into *rule-making* by the negotiation of binding international conventions that the members ratify formally and bring into force collectively. This has been done, for example, with the law of the sea and the control of narcotic drugs. In the 1990s this method was widely adopted for global environment issues, which depend on worldwide participation such as the UN can provide. The earliest instrument in this area was the Montreal Protocol on the ozone layer. The two most important treaties originated from the UN Conference on Environment and Development (UNCED) in 1992. They are the UN Framework Convention on Climate Change and its associated Kyoto Protocol; and the UN Convention on Biological Diversity with its Cartagena Protocol (Grubb and others 1993). There are less prominent UN conventions on deserts and oceans, while there has been much discussion of a convention on forests, though no agreement. This global environment work engages a growing *departmental intensity*, going well beyond environment ministries. It penetrates deeply into *domestic policy*, as countries have to take measures, for example, to cut back on their national use of CFCs or greenhouse gases.

The rule-making attempted by these conventions and protocols is not as advanced as that offered by the WTO and problems have arisen over *accountability*. The work is democratically accountable in the conventional sense, in that it is agreed by consensus and must be endorsed by national parliaments. The main dispute is over the distribution of commitments between the parties to the treaties. In the Kyoto Protocol of 1997 developed countries made commitments to reduce greenhouse gas emissions over a set timetable (Grubb, Vrolijk and Brack 1999). But developing countries did not, arguing that the industrial states' policies had caused global warming and that reducing emissions would damage their development prospects. In the event, the United States first failed to ratify the Kyoto Protocol and then rejected it outright. With the US uncommitted, developing countries became even more reluctant to make international commitments, though many are taking unilateral action. The position over biodiversity is even less promising, as the US has not even signed the underlying Convention and sought to undermine the Cartagena Protocol negotiations (Ball, Falkner and Marquand 2002). Even those developed countries that have agreed to take action, like the EU member states, often have trouble in implementing their commitments.[10] There is no dispute settlement mechanism, which explains why some environmental disputes have gravitated to the WTO instead. For these reasons, UN environment work has not met early expectations.

Much of the impetus for work on the global environment came originally from NGOs. As one might expect, this UN work leaves plenty of openings for NGO activity and is widely *transparent*. There are lessons here that other institutions could learn: Reinhard Quick demonstrates this in Chapter 7, when he compares the open and orderly access for NGOs in UNEP with the more opaque regime in the WTO. The attitude to *business* is better integrated than in other institutions. Some firms, especially in conventional energy sectors, have regarded international environmental discipline as a threat and have tried to undermine it. For example, they have cast doubt on the scientific work that underpins it, since the environment is an area where epistemic communities of meteorologists and other scientists are highly influential. But other firms have recognised that conservation and lowering pollution make economic sense and governments have sought to take advantage of this trend. The system of tradable permits in greenhouse gas emissions was developed to make environmental discipline market friendly and so encourage business to take part. By the mid-2000s business firms and NGOs were combining with individual US states (like California) and members of Congress (of both parties) to put pressure on the Bush Administration to accept mandatory reduction of greenhouse gases.

Much of the UN's other economic work is staff-driven, for example in UNCTAD. This is less true of the environment work. Scarcity of resources, as well as the choice of Nairobi as the site of the United Nations Environment Programme

---

10 The EU introduced an Emissions Trading Mechanism in 2005, to induce European firms to cut back in their carbon emissions. But the initial allocation of tradable permits was set too high, so it had the opposite effect. See Grubb and Neuhoff 2006.

(UNEP), puts the staff at a disadvantage. In addition, the UN's environment work is fragmented through a number of different bodies. So environment work is *member-driven*, depending on the initiative of the participating governments. Finally, there is only limited scope for *multi-level* activity, though the regional EU does work together, as Chapter 14 has shown. It is recognised that action on global environment problems, like climate change, requires universal participation; action below multilateral level has limited attractions.

In short, the United Nations has developed a method for rule-making in the global environment that is transparent and democratic. It has potential worldwide reach, but there are problems about getting countries to sign up and ensuring commitments are met.

Conclusions

The system of indices used in this chapter enables comparisons to be made between these institutions, from which conclusions can be drawn about their contribution to economic diplomacy. These conclusions, which incorporate the interim conclusions from earlier in the chapter, are as follows:

1) All these institutions are actively engaged in reconciling *economics and politics* and political influences are growing. This is obviously true of the Commonwealth and the UN, which are political as well as economic institutions. But even in institutions that appear wholly economic, like the OECD, WTO and IMF/World Bank, the political content is surprisingly high.

2) Most of these institutions are engaging an increasing range of departments within government. This growing *departmental intensity* is a consequence of advancing globalisation. The near monopoly control of the IMF and World Bank by finance ministries is a striking exception.

3) Nearly all of them are likewise are going deeper into *domestic policy-making*. This is recognised as an essential feature of economic diplomacy, as international economic cooperation moves within the border.

4) Plurilateral institutions concentrate on *voluntary cooperation,* while *rule-making* is pursued in multilateral bodies. There is plenty of evidence of a general move from voluntary cooperation towards greater rule-making during the 1990s. But much of this has proved controversial, leading to blockages or even reversals in the 2000s.

5) Most of these institutions are visibly *accountable* to all their member governments and to their electorates. But the OECD, by its focus on unobtrusive voluntary cooperation, largely escapes scrutiny, while in the IMF and World Bank rich countries have more power than poor ones. In the WTO and the UN's environment work there is tension between industrial and developing country members.

6) While all these institutions emerge as moderately *business-friendly*, hardly any of them have gone far in involving the private sector in their work.

The exception is the environment, where governments' concern to engage the private sector has influenced the design of agreements, eg on carbon trading.

7) All the institutions are trying to become more *transparent* to the outside world and accessible to NGOs, even those, like the WTO and IMF, that were previously tight-lipped. Those institutions have done best which are not just economic institutions but combine both political and economic responsibilities, like the UN and the Commonwealth.

8) There is an adverse correlation between *high staff levels* and rule-making. Though the WTO and the UN environment bodies do most rule-making, they are starved of resources, as compared with the Fund and Bank, and rely heavily on their *members*. It suggests that governments are reluctant to entrust rule-making to independent staffs.

9) *Multi-level activities* are frequent and expanding, except in the environment. Plurilateral institutions seek to help their members in multilateral contexts, while multilateral bodies often rely on initiatives from the plurilateral level. Bilateral agreements and regional groupings both benefit from plurilateral cooperation in their rule-making and provide input to work in the WTO and UN, though not the Fund and Bank.

From these conclusions one final question arises: are international economic institutions becoming more powerful (Reinalda and Verbeek 1998)? This is the basic assumption of hostile anti-globalisation protesters, demonstrating against the WTO in Seattle or the G8 in Genoa. The idea may be encouraged by the growing study of 'global governance', which concentrates on what the institutions do to manage the international economic system. But the analysis in this chapter does not support the conclusion that institutions, whether plurilateral or multilateral, are expanding their power to act on their own. It rather suggests that, while member governments are making much greater use of the institutions, for domestic as well as external purposes, they want the institutions to advance their national objectives, rather than operate autonomously.

References

Adams, C., Peel, M. and Burns, J. (2007), 'OECD to Question Scrapping of Arms Inquiry', *Financial Times*, 18 January.

Addison, T., Hansen, H. and Tarp, F. (eds) (2004), *Debt Relief for Poor Countries*, Palgrave Macmillan, Basingstoke.

Ball, C., Falkner. R. and Marquand, H. (eds) (2002), *Cartagena Protocol on Biosafety: Reconciling Trade in Biotechnology with Environment and Development*, Earthscan, London.

Barnsley, I. (2006), 'Dealing with Change: Australia, Canada and the Kyoto Protocol', *The Round Table*, No. 385, pp. 399–410.

Bayne, N. (1987), 'Making Sense of Western Economic Policies: the Role of the OECD', *The World Today*, Vol. 43, No. 1, pp. 4–11.

Bayne, N. (1997), 'What Governments Want from International Institutions and How They Get It', *Government and Opposition*, Vol. 32, No. 2, pp. 361–79.

Bayne, N. (1997a), 'Globalization and the Commonwealth: International Economic Relations in the Post-Cold War World', *The Round Table*, No. 344, pp. 473–84.

Bayne, N. (1998), 'Britain, the G8 and the Commonwealth', *The Round Table*, No. 348, pp. 445–57.

Bayne, N. (2000), 'Why Did Seattle Fail? Globalisation and the Politics of Trade', *Government and Opposition*, Vol. 35, No. 2, pp. 131–51.

Bayne, N. (2005), *Staying Together: The G8 Summit Confronts the 21st Century*, Ashgate, Aldershot.

Blair, D. (1993), *Trade Negotiations in the OECD: Structures, Institutions and States*, Kegan Paul International, London and New York.

Blustein, P. (2001), *The Chastening: Inside the Crisis that Rocked the Global Financial System and Humbled the IMF*, Public Affairs, New York.

Blustein, P. (2005), *And the Money Kept Rolling In (and Out): Wall Street, the IMF and the Bankruptcy of Argentina*, Public Affairs, New York.

Cohn, T. (2002), *Governing Global Trade: International Institutions in Conflict and Convergence*, Ashgate, Aldershot.

Crockett, A. (Chairman) (2007), *Report of the Committee to Study Sustainable Long-Term Financing of the IMF*, accessible at http://www.imf.org.

Croome, J. (1999), *Reshaping the World Trading System: a History of the Uruguay Round*, 2nd edition, World Trade Organization, Geneva.

Drake, W.J. and Nicolaides, K. (1992), 'Ideas, Interests and Institutionalization: "Trade in Services" and the Uruguay Round', *International Organization*, Vol. 46, No. 1, pp. 37–100.

Eichengreen, B. (1999), *Toward a New International Financial Architecture: A Practical Post-Asia Agenda*, Institute for International Economics, Washington.

Grubb, M., Koch, M., Thomson, K., Minson, A. and Sullivan, F. (1993), *The 'Earth Summit' Agreements – a Guide and Assessment: an Analysis of the Rio 1992 UN Conference on Environment and Development*, Earthscan, London.

Grubb, M. with Vrolijk, C. and Brack, D. (1999), *The Kyoto Protocol: a Guide and Assessment*, Royal Institute of International Affairs, London.

Grubb, M. and Neuhoff, K. (eds) (2006), *Emissions Trading and Competitiveness: Alllocations, Incentives and Industrial Competitiveness under the EU Emissions Trading Scheme*, Earthscan, London.

Hajnal, P. (2007), *The G8 System and the G20*, Ashgate, Aldershot.

Hart, J.A. (2005), 'The G8 and the Governance of Cyberspace', in Fratianni, M. Kirton, J.J., Rugman, A.M. and Savona, P. (eds), *New Perspectives on Global Governance: Why America Needs the G8*, Ashgate, Aldershot, pp. 137–52.

Henderson, D. (1993), 'International Economic Cooperation Revisited', *Government and Opposition*, Vol. 28, No. 1, pp. 11–35.

Henderson, D. (1999), *The MAI Affair: A Story and its Lessons*, Royal Institute for International Affairs, London.

Hoekman, B.M. and Kostecki, M.M. (2001), *The Political Economy of the World Trading System*, Oxford University Press, Oxford.

James, H. (1996), *International Monetary Cooperation Since Bretton Woods*, International Monetary Fund, Washington.

Kenen, P. (2001), *The International Financial Architecture: What's New? What's Missing?*, Institute for International Economics, Washington.

Mallaby, S. (2004), *The World's Banker*, Yale University Press, New Haven, CN.

Mbirimi, I., Chilala, B. and Grynberg, R. (2003), *From Doha to Cancun: Delivering a Development Round*, Commonwealth Secretariat, London.

McIntyre, W.D., Mole, S., Ashworth, L.M., Shaw, T.M. and May, A. (2007), 'Whose Commonwealth? Responses to Krishnan Srinavasan's *The Rise, Decline and Future of the British Commonwealth*', *The Round Table*, No. 388, pp. 57–70.

Narlikar, A. and Tussie, D. (2004), 'The G20 at the Cancun Ministerial: Developing Countries and their Evolving Coalitions in the WTO', *World Economy*, Vol. 27, No. 7, pp. 947–66.

Nordström, H. (2005), 'The World Trade Organization Secretariat in a Changing World', *Journal of World Trade*, Vol. 39, No. 5, pp. 819–53.

Odell, J.S. (ed.) (2006), *Negotiating Trade: Developing Countries in the WTO and NAFTA*, Cambridge University Press, Cambridge.

Page, S. (2003), *Developing Countries – Victims or Participants: their Changing Roles in International Negotiations*, Overseas Development Institute, London, accessible at http://www.odi.org.uk.

Persaud, B. (2001), 'OECD Curbs on Offshore Financial Centres: A Major Issue for Small States', *The Round Table*, No. 359, pp. 199–212.

Putnam, R.D. and Bayne, N. (1987), *Hanging Together: Cooperation and Conflict in the Seven-Power Summits*, Sage, London.

Ray, J.E. (1995), *Managing Official Export Credit: the Quest for a Global Regime*, Institute for International Economics, Washington.

Reinalda, B. and Verbeek, B. (eds) (1998), *Autonomous Policy Making by International Organisations*, Routledge, London.

Srinavasan, K. (2005), *The Rise, Decline and Future of the British Commonwealth*, Palgrave Macmillan, Basingstoke.

Stiglitz, J. (2002), *Globalisation and its Discontents*, Allen Lane, London.

Thatcher, M. (1993), *The Downing Street Years*, HarperCollins, London.

Wechsler, W. (2001), 'Follow the Money', *Foreign Affairs*, Vol. 80, No. 4, pp. 40–57.

Wolfe, R. (1998), *Farm Wars: The Political Economy of Agriculture and the International Trade Regime*, Macmillan, London.

Wolfe, R. (2007 forthcoming), 'From Reconstructing Europe to Constructive Globalisation: the OECD in Historical Perspective', in Mahon, R. and McBride, S. (eds), *The OECD in Global Governance*, University of British Columbia Press, Vancouver.

Woods, N. (2006), *The Globalizers: the IMF, the World Bank and their Borrowers*, Cornell University Press, Ithaca, NY.

Woodward, R. (2006), 'Age Concern: the Future of the OECD', *The World Today*, Vol. 62, No. 8–9, pp. 38–9.

Useful Websites

Commonwealth Secretariat: http://www.thecommonwealth.org.
G8 Research Group, University of Toronto: http://www.g8.utoronto.ca.
International Monetary Fund: http://www.imf.org.
Organisation for Economic Cooperation and Development: http://www.oecd.org.
United Nations Environment Programme: http://www.unep.org.
World Bank Group: http://www.worldbank.org.
World Trade Organization: http://www.wto.org.

Chapter 16

Cooperating on Energy Policy: The Work of the International Energy Agency

Joan MacNaughton

The profile of energy issues, and particularly international energy policy issues, has recently become much higher after many years of relative obscurity. But those years, rather than the last few when energy has scarcely been off the front pages, should perhaps be regarded as exceptional. In the 1970s, when the International Energy Agency was established, few would have expected the periods of minimal public interest in energy questions, such as have been seen over the last decade or so. Renewed interest recently has been driven by concerns over energy security and the part energy plays in climate change.[1]

The international energy scene is dominated by two plurilateral institutions, while global bodies, like the UN, play only a minor part. The oldest is the Organisation of Petroleum Exporting Countries (OPEC), founded in 1960. It now has twelve members, all developing countries and seven of them Arab states.[2] The second is the International Energy Agency (IEA), founded in 1974, the main subject of this chapter. As of the end of 2006, there are 26 states in the IEA, all developed countries and members of the OECD: Australia, Austria, Belgium, Canada, Czech Republic, Denmark, Finland, France, Germany, Greece, Hungary, Ireland, Italy, Japan, Korea, Luxembourg, Netherlands, New Zealand, Norway, Portugal, Spain, Sweden, Switzerland, Turkey, United Kingdom and United States.[3] Nearly all are net oil importers, though the list includes some current and former oil exporters, like Canada, Norway and the UK.

This chapter is organised as follows:

---

1 In writing this chapter I have relied extensively on Richard Scott, *IEA – the First 20 Years* (Scott 1994) and Craig S. Bamberger, *IEA – the First 30 Years* (Bamberger 2004) for material prior to 2002. I am indebted also to Christine Goodwin for typing my manuscript.

2 The current members of OPEC are Algeria, Angola, Indonesia, Iran, Iraq, Kuwait, Libya, Nigeria, Qatar, Saudi Arabia, United Arab Emirates and Venezuela. Angola only joined in January 2007. Indonesia has become an honorary member, as it is no longer a net oil exporter. Ecuador and Gabon have been members in the past.

3 Currently Poland and Slovakia are working towards accession to the IEA, which it is hoped will take place in 2007.

- it begins with a brief account of the creation of the IEA and its original remit;
- the central part examines the work of the IEA in the early 2000s. This covers the emergency response to Hurricane Katrina, the Agency's broader policy goals, the process of decision-making and the IEA's involvement with the G8;
- a third section analyses the IEA's external relations, especially with OPEC.

The chapter's conclusions explore the future challenges the IEA needs to address.

The Establishment of the IEA and its Original Remit

In October 1973, Arab members of OPEC began to reduce oil supplies generally and to target particular countries through embargo action with the aim of inducing change in their policies towards Israel. This led to a decision by the whole of OPEC to introduce a fourfold increase in the price of oil. The industrial oil importing countries were caught napping. They lacked information to implement mitigation policies, effective machinery to collaborate in responding to supply shortfalls and – until that point – real awareness of the vulnerabilities stemming from their huge reliance on oil and oil products, and consequently no, or very underdeveloped, policies to lessen their dependence on oil. Existing voluntary arrangements in Europe for the holding and release of oil stocks in an emergency proved impossible to use. They required unanimity and some countries that had escaped OPEC's selective targeting were concerned lest they offend OPEC by taking action.

The failure to take any action, stemming from both the lack of information and analysis and the unsuitability of such machinery as did exist, led during 1973 and 1974 to much heart searching about the lessons to be learnt. Henry Kissinger, then US Secretary of State, called together a conference in Washington. This evolved into an 'Energy Coordination Group' which led to the IEA being set up, by an agreement among 16 of the then member countries of the OECD. Other countries were to join later as their national politics allowed: most notably France, the only G7 country not among the founding members, which with Finland acceded in 1992.[4]

The International Energy Programme Agreement

It was decided to found the IEA on the basis of an Agreement on an International Energy Program (IEP Agreement), given effect in November 1974 (IEA 1974). This embodied in an international treaty legally binding commitments on

---

4   A detailed account of the origins of the IEA is in Scott 1994, vol. 1. This draws on the analysis by Ulf Lantzke, the IEA's first Executive Director, in Lantzke 1975, one of the articles in a special issue of *Daedalus* devoted to the oil crisis of 1973–1974 (*Daedalus* 1975).

emergency oil stocking and sharing arrangements, the limitations of the previous voluntary arrangements having been painfully obvious during the oil crisis. With this approach would come monitoring of oil markets and of members' compliance with their stockholding obligations by the new agency. This would also help in remedying the dearth of information which impeded an effective policy response to OPEC's selective disruption of supplies.

The IEP Agreement went wider, however, than just the response to oil supply disruptions, notably including a commitment by the programme's signatories to engage in long term cooperation to reduce their dependence on oil. From the outset, the IEA was intended to enhance international collaboration generally and in particular to work to reduce members' vulnerability to future oil shocks (and thus to price spikes, though by reducing oil dependence not by attempting to manipulate oil prices). The IEP Agreement fully reflected member countries' realisation that they had a great deal to do on diversifying energy sources, on increasing energy conservation and efficiency, and on developing new sources of sustainable energy, through the provisions it set out in a 'Long Term Cooperation Programme'. This enjoined members to 'undertake national programmes and promote the adoption of cooperative programmes' under four headings:

- first, ways of reducing the growth of energy consumption through conservation;
- second, the development of alternative sources of energy such as domestic oil supplies, coal, natural gas, nuclear and hydro-electric power;
- third, research and development 'including as a matter of priority cooperative programmes' on for example coal technology, solar energy, waste heat utilisation and several aspects of nuclear energy – radioactive waste management, nuclear fusion and nuclear safety;
- fourth, collaboration on uranium enrichment.

While the unifying theme was how to attain the objective of secure energy supplies and, towards that, how to reduce oil dependency, the inclusion of nuclear related issues in the sections on development of alternative sources of energy and on energy research and development is entirely understandable. The section on uranium enrichment was perhaps more puzzling. But in 1974 there was much optimism about the rate of growth of the role of nuclear in power generation, and concern over the then relatively limited reserves of uranium.

Cooperation on the development of alternative sources of energy was also to include, in the words of the IEP Agreement, the 'criteria, quality objectives, and standards for environmental protection'. This probably meant the control of pollution and the impact of the extractive industries on the environment, rather than climate change. Climate change as an international policy issue, and one bearing very significantly an international energy policy, was not to come to prominence for some years.

The IEA at Work in the Early 2000s

Thirty years on from its foundation, the IEA has clearly adapted extensively from its initial role, but certain aspects remain constant. This main section of the chapter analyses the work of the IEA today, drawing on my experience as Chair of the Governing Board and of the UK as a participating member country.

IEA Emergency Response: After Hurricane Katrina

Preparing for and responding to oil supply disruptions lies at the heart of the IEA's original role, and it is worth looking at how well the arrangements have worked and whether they might need to be further improved in the future. The emergency response arrangements have been activated only twice: in 1991, in response to the crisis in the Gulf and, most recently, in 2005.

On 29 August 2005, Hurricane Katrina swept through the Gulf of Mexico (GOM) and Louisiana. Apart from the tragic impact on New Orleans and other residential areas, the hurricane laid waste to refineries, oil transport infrastructure, and offshore platforms. On 30 August, the IEA estimated that 1.375mbpd (million barrels per day) of oil production (over 90 per cent of GOM production), and 8.2 billion cubic feet per day of gas (over 80 per cent of GOM production) was shut in, along with 2.35mbpd (about 30 per cent of GOM) of refining capacity. In addition the LOOP (Louisiana Offshore Oil Port) import terminal was closed, shutting in 1mbpd. These figures should be seen in the context of total US oil consumption figures in August 2005 of just under 22mpbd.

Early on Friday 2 September, the United States updated the IEA with their view of the situation. Because an IEA member had suffered oil supply disruption of 7 per cent or more, the Executive Director invoked the emergency procedures, as he was empowered to do. He proposed to the Governing Board members a release of oil stocks to the market to compensate for the disruption. This followed telephone consultations between the Executive Director and the Chair of the Governing Board and, subsequently, by the IEA Secretariat executives with all members of the Governing Board. Release of stocks to the market had come to be preferred over arrangements for oil sharing among governments and reflected the increasing emphasis in IEA member countries on market based ways of delivering energy supplies. The oil companies were engaged through the Industry Advisory Board, 'the framework for consultation with the oil companies [in member countries]' envisaged in the IEP Agreement.

In the United Kingdom (to look at an example of how an individual member country responded) officials briefed ministers and secured their agreement to the stock release. They convened a meeting with industry representatives who bear the responsibilities for holding reserve stocks (unlike in some other countries, where stocks are held by or on behalf of governments) and, with their full cooperation, were ready to act by the time of the IEA announcement at 1900 hours Paris time on 2 September (1300 hours Washington time). This reported the decision to offer stocks of crude oil and oil products equivalent to 60 million barrels of oil for an initial period of 30 days, and came very promptly after the US President's announcement, at the noon closure of the American markets for the Labor Day holiday, that he had requested the IEA to act.

The IEA's action had an immediate and calming effect on the markets. The upward price pressure eased and, indeed, on 2 September alone the price of oil (one-month Brent) fell by nearly $2 per barrel from the intra-day high, and by another $4 over the next ten days. This was a rational response to the price pressures deriving from expectations of shortage, which the stock release had just confounded. Reducing prices had not, however, been the object of the stock release and the IEA does not take action in order to reduce prices.

What lessons do we draw from this, only the second stock release in the IEA's more than thirty-year history? I suggest five:

- First, the Agency showed itself capable of acting very quickly, vindicating the founders' strategy to vest decision making powers in the Governing Board (predominantly comprising senior experts from their governments' energy policy functions) and the right to take steps to initiate consideration of emergency action in the Secretariat. These experts would of course seek their respective governments' approval for this and other significant decisions by the Governing Board. But, compared to some international organisations, the IEA has, certainly until recently, tended to operate with a relatively low political profile and with little overt political intervention, as discussed further below.
- Second, the procedures allow for – but do not require – a request from an affected member country. It might suit an individual country not to invoke the procedure, yet others could well be seriously impacted. Nevertheless, a request for assistance, as was received in this instance from the US, sends a clear signal of that country's view of the justification for acting, which may well help with speedy decision-making and certainly did in this instance. It is interesting to ponder whether, with a less clear cut set of circumstances, the September 2005 speed of decision-making could be matched in the future.
- Third, the Agency was careful to keep key producers (such as OPEC and Russia) informed of its intention to act and of the rationale for doing so, which not only helped relations but probably contributed to the producers' willingness to keep pumping oil as fast they could.
- Fourth, the action achieved its intended effect of cushioning the impact of a fall in supply, albeit in a market well supplied overall (from both production and global stocks). Moreover, following the hurricane, US demand was significantly restrained by several factors: policy action, the price impact, and consumer restraint at a time of national crisis (consumption fell by 1.6mbpd between August and September 2005, or over 7 per cent).
- Fifth, in giving effect to the decision to offer stocks to the market in the weeks following 2 September, a few member countries did not fully comply with their obligations. In the event this did not undermine the objective of the stock release, as other countries committed to offer a total of 63 million barrels and the market in fact stabilised before the stocks offered for sale were fully taken up. Some member countries relied on the argument that they had

imposed demand restraint measures and these had had the effect of freeing up oil and oil products, thus contributing to the overall supply demand balance. But other members were unconvinced by this line of reasoning and the post hoc evaluation showed that some countries' claims on demand restraint could not be substantiated.[5]

The Three 'E's and the Shared Goals

Beyond emergency response, the IEA's work today on broader collaboration and reducing vulnerability to future shocks derives from the encapsulation of the IEA's goals – energy security, environmental protection and economic growth – known as 'the three E's'. These were set out by IEA Ministers in their Communiqué of 2003, which also reaffirmed the IEA's Shared Goals of energy policy, though they had originally been identified a decade earlier. In June 2005 the Governing Board again reaffirmed the Shared Goals, as follows:

1) *Diversity, efficiency and flexibility within the energy sector* are basic conditions for longer-term security: the fuels used within and across sectors and the sources of those fuels should be as diverse as practicable. Non-fossil fuels, particularly nuclear and hydro power, make a substantial contribution to the energy supply diversity of IEA countries as a group.
2) Energy systems should have *the ability to respond promptly and flexibly to energy emergencies.* In some cases this requires collective mechanisms and action – IEA countries cooperate through the Agency in responding jointly to oil supply emergencies.
3) *The environmentally sustainable provision and use of energy* is central to the achievement of these goals. Decision-makers should seek to minimise the adverse environmental impacts of energy activities, just as environmental decisions should take account of the energy consequences. Government interventions should where practicable have regard to the Polluter Pays Principle.
4) *More environmentally acceptable energy sources* need to be encouraged and developed. Clean and efficient use of fossil fuels is essential. The development of economic non-fossil sources is also a priority. A number of IEA members wish to retain and improve the nuclear option for the future, at the highest available safety standards, because nuclear energy does not emit CO_2. Renewable sources will also have an increasingly important contribution to make.
5) *Improved energy efficiency* can promote both environmental protection and energy security in a cost-effective manner. There are significant opportunities for greater energy efficiency at all stages of the energy cycle from production to

---

5   The original decision setting up the emergency mechanism had allowed for a contribution from demand restraint and from increased production from member countries' own resources.

consumption. Strong efforts by governments and all energy users are needed to realise these opportunities.

6) Continued *research, development and market deployment of new and improved energy technologies* make a critical contribution to achieving the objectives outlined above. Energy technology policies should complement broader energy policies. International cooperation in the development and dissemination of energy technologies, including industry participation and cooperation with non-member countries, should be encouraged.

7) *Undistorted energy prices* enable markets to work efficiently. Energy prices should not be held artificially below the costs of supply to promote social or industrial goals. To the extent necessary and practicable, the environmental costs of energy production and use should be reflected in prices.

8) *Free and open trade* and a secure framework for investment contribute to efficiency energy markets and energy security. Distortions to energy trade and investment should be avoided.

9) *Cooperation among all energy market participants* helps to improve information and understanding, and encourage the development of efficient, environmentally acceptable and flexible energy systems and markets worldwide. These are needed to help promote the investment, trade and confidence necessary to achieve global energy security and environmental objectives (IEA 1993).

There are interesting differences of emphasis in these Shared Goals compared with the provisions in the IEP Agreement of 1974 on long term cooperation. There is much in common: the emphasis on diversification of supply, on research and development into new technologies, and on the efficient use of energy. But there is more in the Shared Goals on effectively functioning markets and free trade in energy, including cooperation among what are described as 'all energy market participants', and much more in them on environmental issues. In Goal 3 on 'the environmentally sustainable provision and use' of energy and Goal 4 on the need to encourage and develop 'more environmentally acceptable energy sources', there are references to the need to minimise adverse environmental impacts, with adherence to the Polluter Pays Principle, to use fossil fuels cleanly and efficiently and to the potential contributions from renewable sources and nuclear power.

However, the qualified reference to nuclear energy – 'a number of IEA members wish to retain and improve the nuclear option for the future ... because it does not emit CO_2' – stands in marked contrast to the prominence of nuclear in the long term cooperation provisions of the IEP Agreement. (This is the only reference to CO_2 in the Shared Goals.) The absence of any substantive reference to nuclear in recent ministerial communiqués illustrates the growing resistance to nuclear by some IEA member countries.[6]

The last three goals address market issues. Goal 7, on the need for undistorted energy prices which 'enable markets to work efficiently', also featured the

---

6   The bland reference in the 2003 communiqué was only agreed after much debate, and the word 'nuclear' did not feature in the 2005 communiqué.

environmental issue. Prices should not be held below the costs of supply to promote social or industrial goals, but where possible should reflect the environmental costs of production *and* use of energy. Goals 8 and 9, on 'free and open trade' and 'cooperation among all energy market participants' mention the need to promote investment in order to help achieve energy security (and, in the case of Goal 9, global environmental objectives). The emphasis on suitable conditions for investment has continued to grow, culminating in the conclusion in the World Energy Outlook of 2005 that consuming countries could not assume that the $16 trillion investment required by 2030 (updated to $20 trillion in 2006) would be forthcoming (IEA 2005). The implications would be profound. This is a good example of how, by the quality of its analysis, the IEA can guide government thinking into the areas which need attention. It builds on much work over the last few years aimed at the complex question of how governments individually and collectively construct the right policy frameworks within which energy market participants can act to develop and deliver energy resources in an efficient and environmentally sensitive way.

Decision-Making in the IEA: Ministers, Officials and the 2005 Brainstorming

The main collective input from IEA Ministers comes from what are described as 'Meetings of the Governing Board at Ministerial Level', which generally take place at two yearly intervals. This arrangement in principle enables ministers to give a steer on the priorities they would like to see the IEA addressing, in a flexible way. But, as with many such gatherings, there is a risk of officials (the Governing Board representatives and the IEA Secretariat) over-preparing the agenda to the extent that ministers feel a degree of frustration at being used as a rubber stamp. Thus it was in May 2005, when the discussions culminated in ministers reworking the draft communiqué they had been offered by officials. Their main intent was to replace a somewhat general conclusion with a firm steer to the Agency on where the priorities for its work programme should lie, pointing, as they did so, to 'the importance of clear and measurable outcomes' for the IEA. The communiqué stated that the priorities for the work programme should be:

- improved transparency and analysis of energy markets;
- improved engagement with key non-member countries;
- the pursuit of energy efficiency, particularly in the transport and building sectors;
- research and development of cleaner combustion technologies and carbon dioxide capture and storage;
- encouraging an improved investment environment to meet the challenges of future energy demand, much of which will occur in the developing world;
- further work on economic growth and CO_2 reduction (IEA 2005a).

Official representatives on the Governing Board had, prior to the Ministerial Meeting, already agreed to hold a strategic brainstorming to look at the medium and longer term priorities for the IEA and how it should tackle them. This was timed for June 2005, in order to be able to take on board the outcome from the Ministerial Meeting.

In initiating the brainstorming, as Chair of the Governing Board, I had been struck by the tendency of individual member countries to regard the Shared Goals as a menu from which to cherry-pick subjects dear to their own hearts. The challenge for the IEA was how best to focus its efforts, yet many on the Governing Board were growing increasingly concerned at the seeming inability to identify topics which should be given lower priority: when everything is a priority, nothing is a priority. Surely the official representatives of the Governing Board could simply have taken the list of ministerial priorities and mapped the IEA work programme onto them, downgrading activities which did not appear in the ministerial communiqué? The problem with this approach was that the ministerial list had been prepared 'on the hoof', during the meeting, and was driven by the ministerial chair and a few others. It was perceived as a somewhat selective approach to the agenda. It was not the subject of consultation with all member countries. If few participants in the meeting registered any reservations, that was perhaps because the list of priorities did not have the status of a binding remit to the Governing Board but rather that of a signpost as to the preferred direction of travel.

One subject on which all would have signed up was energy efficiency. This has been consistently present throughout the IEA's existence – seen, first, as a way to reduce oil dependency, then, later, seen also as making an important contribution to tackling climate change. But consistent emphasis on the value of energy efficiency (or energy conservation – the terms have tended to be, but probably should not be, used interchangeably) has not consistently translated into performance improvements in this area, either geographically or over time. The muted impact on economic growth of the sudden and large price rises of 2004 and 2005 – with the barrel price peaking at $78 per barrel in 2006 compared to an OPEC price band of $22-$28 a few years earlier – is testament to the earlier efforts of member countries to use oil more effectively and to diversify away from it. IEA analysis helped point them towards such policies: but, frankly, the price shocks of the 1970s and 1980s (when, in 2005 terms, the average annual barrel price peaked at $87.65) were overwhelmingly more important in that regard.

As well as the challenge of setting priorities, there was the issue of using resources efficiently. Some representatives on the Governing Board, in discussions during 2004 and 2005, were of the view that the resource disciplines felt in member countries' own government services seemed to be felt less strongly in the IEA (notwithstanding a wide consensus that the Agency benefits from talented and hard working staff). Was enough being done to exploit fully the efforts of staff, the Governing Board and its Committees, and others associated in various ways with the IEA's work? Given the difficulties in identifying lower priority tasks, it seemed unlikely the IEA would be able to cope with the growing demands across the whole energy agenda without the ability to improve how it used its resources of all kinds. Certainly it had long been clear that few member countries had any appetite for increasing their contributions to the IEA budget: quite the reverse, in fact. Japan for some time had been looking to reduce its contribution and the US had a policy at that time of no growth, even in nominal terms, in its subscriptions to international bodies. This was particularly significant as these two countries alone contribute about 40 per cent of the IEA budget.

In tackling these issues, the 2005 Governing Board brainstorming produced some clear conclusions and some provisional findings requiring further work, covering both what the IEA should do and how it should go about its work. It was agreed that energy security and sustainability were the top priorities; the focus on oil security had to be widened to cover particularly gas and to a lesser extent electricity; energy efficiency, and the link between technology research and policy, both needed a bigger push, with the IEA using its analytical role more proactively to deliver policy solutions. A more strategic approach to the IEA's communications and outreach could also secure greater influence for the IEA, and better exploitation of the products of its analytical work. Agreement on ways of working covered the relationship between the Governing Board and its Committees and how meetings were conducted. Implementation of most of the changes was agreed at the Governing Board meeting in December 2005 – just six months after the brainstorming, representing a good pace of progress for a 26 member, consensus governed, international organisation.[7]

The IEA and the G8

An important opportunity for the IEA to demonstrate how it could have more influence on policy on energy security and sustainability was to come with the UK Presidency of the G8 in 2005 (and later the Russian in 2006) – see Chapter 6 above. During 2004 and 2005, G7 Finance Ministers had been increasingly concerned about high and volatile oil prices and had remitted the relevant international finance institutions and also the IEA to undertake work on the issue. A very significant increase in the IEA's profile overall, however, was to come with the invitation to the Executive Director to be present at the Gleneagles G8 Summit in July 2005.

The UK Prime Minister's decision to make climate change one of the two key priorities for his presidency of the G8 is well known. Less well known, perhaps, was his personal emphasis on putting energy at the heart of how to tackle climate change. UK energy policy officials, in discharging this remit and preparing for Gleneagles, drew on earlier IEA work to identify the key challenges (such as how to encourage China to avoid locking itself into high CO_2 intensity power generation, given the pace and scale of investment there). With input from G8 colleagues a far ranging and practical programme of work was put together. Governing Board representatives from non-G7 countries were consulted about

---

7   There is provision for voting in the IEA, usually requiring both a simple majority of IEA member countries and 60 per cent of the weighted votes which vary from three for the smallest countries to 17 for Japan and 46 for the USA, and which comprise in total 178 votes. But the Governing Board prefers to proceed by way of consensus wherever possible.

the proposal to give the IEA a lead role in delivering this work, which became known as the Gleneagles Plan of Action.[8]

The IEA role was formally discussed and endorsed at a specially convened meeting of the Governing Board in September 2005.[9] The expected push back from some non-G7 members did not materialise – in the author's view, because of the congruence of the work with the general thrust of the IEA's programme, including the Shared Goals, and the growing consensus on the need to address climate change and how best to do it. Many Governing Board members also took the view, as some said at the September meeting, that there would be benefits in bringing energy policy expertise to bear on the development of international policy on climate change.

At Gleneagles President Putin, in a conversation with the Executive Director, also invited the IEA to engage during the 2006 Russian Presidency. The Executive Director was invited both to the G8 Energy Ministers meeting in March and to the St Petersburg summit in July, Russia having tabled 'Energy Security' as a priority topic for discussion during its Presidency. Ahead of St Petersburg the IEA submitted some 'key messages' on both general energy topics and on Russia specific ones. At the general level, the IEA pointed out to G8 leaders the pressing need for them to improve the investment climate; they, and the world as a whole, were under investing in the energy supply chain; not enough was being done to maximise energy efficiency nor to deliver breakthroughs in energy technology. For Russia, there should be greater transparency in its upstream activities; it should tackle the growth in market power of its huge monopolies; seek to establish better relations with its trading partners; and take steps to realise the huge gas and emissions savings available by reducing gas flaring, tackling leakage in transportation structure and giving independent producers access to the Gazprom network. After the problems of the 2005/2006 winter, there are signs Russia may now be taking some steps along the path to reducing gas flaring.

Germany has picked up the energy theme during its 2007 Presidency of the G8 with a strong focus on energy efficiency. Japan is committed to table during its 2008 Presidency a report back on the Gleneagles Plan of Action. The expectation is that the IEA will be invited to participate during both Presidencies. The form which such participation will take will be at the discretion of the host country.

Does all of this constitute 'mission creep' on the part of the IEA, posing a threat to successful discharge of its core remit on energy security? On the contrary, the emphasis on reducing consuming countries' dependence on oil (and by extension hydrocarbons) was, from the time of its foundation, seen as integral to the IEA's objective of contributing to energy security. There is also a growing realisation that energy is at the heart of the climate change agenda, and in particular that policies to tackle climate change will risk having adverse impacts on energy security if those impacts are not assessed at a formative stage.

---

8   The Gleneagles Plan of Action is accessible at http://www.g8.gov.uk or on http://www.g8.utoronto.ca.

9   This meeting fortuitously also allowed the Governing Board to take stock of the situation post-Hurricane Katrina and the stock release, and to agree on the next steps.

Moreover, climate change policies which are not grounded in well informed analysis of the energy security implications will be less likely to gain acceptance or to be sustainable longer term.

The External Relations of the IEA

The Oil Producing Countries

The IEP Agreement (Article 44) recognised the importance of 'cooperative relations' with oil producing countries and other consuming countries, including developing countries. Progress in the early years was disappointing, with the outgoing Executive Director, Ulf Lantzke, saying in 1984 that 'the one area where the IEA has made little progress during the last ten years is in its relations with OPEC'.[10]

This seems to have continued to be the case during the 1980s. But in the aftermath of the IEA countries' joint emergency action at the time of the 1991 Gulf crisis, the IEA held two conferences in 1992 of 'technical experts' from both oil importing and exporting countries. The first had the specific objective of 'increasing market transparency and efficiency'; the second concentrated on projections of oil demand, on developments in exploration and production costs (including environmental costs) and on investment needs. These were followed over time by further meetings of experts called the North–South dialogue, which evolved into a biennial ministerial level meeting, in alternative years to those of the IEA Ministers, called the 'International Energy Forum'. All IEA and OPEC Ministers, as well as Russia and a growing circle of other countries, are invited to these meetings. They are prepared by a permanent secretariat located in Riyadh.

At the most recent Forum, in Doha in April 2006, keynote presentations from the IEA Executive Director and the OPEC Acting Secretary General both covered the situation in the oil market but, while using fairly similar data, they came to somewhat different conclusions. These centred on the likely growth of oil demand and the implications of this for investing in supply. OPEC focussed on the impact of the commitments by consuming countries to cut CO_2 emissions on oil demand growth. In response to this, in a 'Note on Security of Demand' circulated to participants in Doha, the IEA argued that, even assuming effective implementation of all policies currently under discussion to address energy security and environmental objectives, there was relatively little doubt over the level of supply required over the next decade. Admitting to more uncertainty on demand in 2030, the IEA argued that investment decisions for delivering oil supplies in 2030 need not be taken until at least 2015, when the prognosis would be clearer. This note probably did not succeed in persuading OPEC away from their view that demand risks lay predominantly on the downside, but it did represent

---

10 Lantzke made this comment in 1984 on his retirement as Executive Director (Scott 1994, vol. ii, 341).

a timely and well reasoned intervention on behalf of IEA member countries and seems, to some degree at least, to have lowered the temperature of the debate. Certainly the emerging calls in late 2005/early 2006 from producers (Russia as well as OPEC) to consuming countries to give them 'a demand road map' abated during the course of 2006.[11]

After a slow and fitful start, the IEA has proven a useful channel of communication with OPEC for its member countries. It not only can speak to OPEC without the political complications attendant on member countries' own engagement, being able to convey possibly unwelcome messages; it also has the benefit of substantial expertise. IEA analysis of the oil markets is generally recognised as authoritative and objective. The IEA monthly Oil Market Report is keenly awaited and the comments of the Executive Director and other senior IEA officials are clearly influential in financial and policy circles. Although, like many others, it was slow to spot the full extent of the rapid growth in Chinese demand during 2004, it was an early leader in making the case for more, and more reliable, oil market data and far more transparency in oil markets. Over time this work led to the Joint Oil Data Initiative (JODI), now led by the International Energy Forum Secretariat. JODI brings together all major consuming and producing countries, well beyond the IEA membership, and includes six other key international organisations, in an endeavour to assemble comprehensive data on supply, demand and stocks. The IEA has been an important catalyst for this initiative, illustrating the sort of area where the IEA can make progress when an individual member country, or even a group of countries, would find it difficult to gain traction.

In July 2006 the IEA introduced a new annual publication, the Medium Term Oil Market Report (or MTMOMR) which, in looking forward five years, bridges the gap between the Monthly Oil Market Report and the longer term (25 years) material in the IEA's yearly flagship publication, the World Energy Outlook. The MTMOMR, interestingly, draws attention to the lower rate of growth in demand for oil during the high price years of 2005–2007 compared to the low price years of 1995–1997. This perpetuates the difference with OPEC on the impact of prices (and by implication the lack of spare capacity) compared to OPEC's concerns with consuming governments' CO_2 emissions reduction policies. There have, over recent years, also been questions over the activities of speculators in the financial markets whom some (including some OECD members) have argued are driving prices to artificially high levels and contributing to price volatility. In time the IEA must hope that its support of JODI (including its membership of the steering board of the International Energy Forum) will help that initiative regain momentum (it having stalled somewhat during 2005 and 2006). With a better understanding of what is happening to supply, demand and stocks in the oil market, there would be (it is assumed) a more benign environment for the encouragement of the huge investment needed to access oil (and gas) reserves.

---

11   This was probably helped by the joint IEA/OPEC workshop on Global Oil Demand in Oslo in May 2006.

Other Countries and Organisations

The IEA's perception of the importance of outreach has grown throughout
its existence, with the increasing inter-regional trade in sources of energy, the
increasing interdependence among countries in energy usage (for example,
electricity interconnectors and gas and oil pipelines), an increasingly market based
approach to energy, the growth in developing countries' demand for energy, and,
of course, the inherently global issue of climate change.[12] Engagement well beyond
its own membership was, of course, always going to be necessary – if only so that
IEA analysis and publications could continue to be well informed. But as well as
this 'pull' from non-member countries, the IEA was keen to 'push' its key messages,
and to do so by hosting or contributing to events such as country, region or subject
specific conferences, reviews of the energy policies of non-member countries and
ad hoc missions to them. This engagement extended to the biennial Ministerial
Meetings with, for example, the Russian Energy Minister attending much of the
2003 biennial meeting, and the Chinese taking part in 2005, both of them speaking
and engaging substantively. The opportunities (and sometimes the demands) for
outreach are huge. The risk is of spreading a key resource (the time of the small
number of knowledgeable and highly skilled IEA staff) too thinly, with much
activity but perhaps not a commensurate weight of tangible outcomes.

At the June 2005 brainstorming meeting, the Governing Board agreed the IEA
should produce a new outreach strategy. This should cover the IEA's relationships
with relevant international organisations as well as key non-member countries.
The emphasis should be on engagement, not primarily expansion of membership.
And that engagement should be clearly driven by a purpose – the contribution it
could make to fulfilment of the IEA's objectives. During 2006, in follow up work,
the newly agreed strategy focused particularly on Russia, India and China. Indian
and Chinese representatives were invited to take part in part of the December
2006 Governing Board meeting of the IEA (the first held in the APEC region).

Conclusions

The IEA has demonstrated its ability to carry out the tasks at the core of its
original mission in the 2005 action to respond to Hurricane Katrina. Its wider
role in cooperation on energy has been given an additional push with its work for
the G8 on energy policy and climate change. But major challenges lie ahead.

---

12 For example, in their 1999 communiqué IEA Ministers agreed that developing
countries play 'a critical role' in the evolution of energy markets and enjoined the IEA
to widen and deepen engagement with non-member countries, by bringing them into
membership or sharing expertise with them.

Energy Security

It is clear that at some point in the fairly near future contingency planning or emergency response confined to IEA members alone will no longer be sufficient to manage the response to oil supply disruptions. For example, China is on a path to become the world's second largest oil importer before 2011. It is good that China has begun to establish a national oil reserve system, and that the IEA has helped with this process – as the Chinese representative explained to the Governing Board in December 2006. But we are a long way from China – or indeed the other increasingly significant consumers, such as India – being both willing and able to collaborate on how to deal with an oil supply disruption. And the (admittedly minor) tensions which emerged on the 2005 emergency response action suggest that future supply disruptions are unlikely to be straightforward to handle. And what about gas? With gas increasing its share of the energy mix, the IEA must continue with urgency to raise its game on gas, learning the lessons of the last 30 years from oil while recognising that gas poses different, if no less important, challenges.

The IEA's expertise in gas markets is much less well developed than in oil, and, like the need for work on medium term issues, was identified as a priority by the Governing Board's strategic brainstorming of June 2005. The Governing Board now receives as routine at each meeting a gas market update mirroring that on oil, and the Agency's Gas Market Review is making an increasingly useful contribution to understanding. The IEA's gas expertise is building fast; but there is still some way to go. Although the analysis is beginning to tackle the information deficiency in the gas sector – such as data about gas flows across Europe – the dearth of that information constituted a real difficulty in understanding the tight gas market conditions of the winter of 2005/06, and in developing appropriate policy responses to them. The European Commission has been seeking to plug the information gap across the EU and has proposed an analysis of gas storage facilities under the rubric of solidarity between member states, notably in the event of an energy supply crisis. This has undoubtedly been given added impetus by the January 2006 dispute between Russia and the Ukraine, which disrupted gas supplies to Europe.

Given the concentration of gas resources in a few countries and the investment challenges there, the need to move to contingency planning and effective emergency response arrangements in gas should not be left too much longer. The challenge will be for IEA member countries to demonstrate a shared vision, based on the enlightened self interest of its member countries, which will have to entail give and take among them. Such a vision also needs to be persuasive enough to secure buy-in from the big consuming countries who are not currently members. Will that be achieved on gas without the experience of a crisis to galvanise consuming countries into action? It seems doubtful, especially as the global gas market is not as fully developed as that on oil. Also, gas poses more difficult logistical issues, of storage and transport. Perhaps it is inevitable that individual countries will continue to operate on the basis of 'sauve qui peut' to the delight no doubt of the gas producers.

Essential to delivering energy security, as the IEA cogently described in its 2005 World Energy Outlook, is getting adequate investment across the whole energy supply chain – to exploit the hydrocarbons which are still abundant, and to provide the infrastructure to get them to consumers where and in the form required. A market which functions really well in transmitting the signals to facilitate this is some way off (and will not be fully attained any time soon). How can the IEA deploy its expertise to enable governments to address the key market failures – and its member countries to avoid sub-optimal policy responses?

Energy sustainability

On this issue there are tensions evident between the IEA's European and some of its APEC members. The growing realisation in hitherto sceptical countries of the need to tackle climate change – particularly the US and Australia – should help those tensions to attenuate, although neither of those countries appears willing yet to subscribe to CO_2 emissions reduction targets. Their continued faith in the ability of technology breakthrough may prove to be well-founded; but the contrasting European approach, which encompasses targets supported by market based instruments in addition to direct support for new technologies, appears to most commentators, including the author, more cognisant of the urgency of the situation. A key challenge for the IEA as a whole will be to deliver on the Gleneagles Plan of Action notwithstanding the APEC/EU difference of emphasis. In doing so, the IEA will need to engage the 'Plus-5' countries (Brazil, China, India, Mexico and South Africa) in ways they believe respect their national interests. Moreover the IEA needs to drive forward the global debate (and hence progress) on new energy technologies to a level not yet achieved, though the IEA's 2006 publication 'Energy Technology Perspectives' is an excellent first step (IEA 2006). On energy sustainability as on energy security, the IEA has first class expertise to offer. But is it hitting the right buttons with the way it conveys its findings, with governments across the world and other key decision-makers?

Institutional Issues

Can the IEA as an autonomous agency within the plurilateral OECD do enough to engage globally on both energy security and environmental sustainability? Should consideration be given to new arrangements – for example, weakening or even breaking the OECD link so that extending the IEA membership becomes easier? At present OECD membership is a precondition of accession to the IEA, but does this risk keeping out of the IEA countries whose participation would be beneficial? Could the IEA continue to operate effectively as it moves to more than 26 member countries, all entitled to speak individually on any topic on the agenda, or should there be a move towards groupings of members, as happens in some other organisations? How long can voting weights and budgetary contributions continue to be allocated according to oil use (and historic figures for that), no doubt a relevant criterion in 1974, but hardly now?

Any of these changes would require amendments to the Treaty which established the IEA and significant changes might better be achieved through the drawing up of a new Treaty. It would take some years to secure agreement to any Treaty changes, or a new Treaty – and would entail considerable political will. As ever, the appetite for such an exercise is limited until there appears what Americans would term 'clear and present danger'. But by the time that that is generally accepted, it is often too late to escape some painful consequences.

References

Bamberger, C.S. (2004), *IEA – the First 30 Years*, Organisation for Economic Cooperation and Development/International Energy Agency, Paris.

Daedalus (1975), 'The Oil Crisis: In Perspective', Special Issue, Vol. 104, No. 4, pp. 1–294.

IEA (1974), Agreement on an International Energy Program, accessible at http://www. iea.org/textbase/about/iep.pdf.

IEA (1993), Shared Goals of Energy Policy, accessible at http://www.iea.org/textbase/ about/sharedgoals.htm.

IEA (2005), *World Energy Outlook 2005*, accessible at http://www.worldenergyoutlook. org.

IEA (2005a), Communiqué from Meeting of Governing Board at Ministerial Level, 2005, accessible at http://www.iea.org/textbase/press/pressdetail.asp?PRESS_REL_ ID=147.

IEA (2006), Energy Technology Perspective Scenario Analysis, accessible at http://www. iea.org/textbase/papers/2006/scenario.pdf.

Lantzke, U. (1975), 'The OECD and its International Energy Agency', *Daedalus*, Vol. 104, No. 4, pp. 217–28.

Scott, R. (1994), *IEA – the First 20 Years*, Organisation for Economic Cooperation and Development/International Energy Agency, Paris.

Yergin, D. (1991), *The Prize: The Epic Quest for Oil, Money and Power*, Simon & Schuster, New York.

Useful Websites

G8 Research Group, University of Toronto: http://www.g8.utoronto.ca.

International Energy Agency: http://www.iea.org.

International Energy Forum: http://www.iefs.org.sa.

Joint Oil Data Initiative: http://www.jodidata.org.

Organisation of Petroleum Exporting Countries: http://www.opec.org.

UK G8 Presidency: http://www.g8.gov.uk.

Chapter 17

Governments, the International Financial Institutions and International Cooperation

Nigel Wicks

The World of the International Financial Institutions

The men who established the international financial institutions shared a fundamental belief. Put simply, it was that mankind has the capacity through his own actions to be master of his economic fate. He need not be subject to the dictates of either random or deterministic economic forces. Economic policy, properly formulated and implemented, so goes the belief, can improve the economic lot of mankind.

That belief has been subject to periodic challenge during the sixty or so years of the existence of the Bretton Woods institutions, the International Monetary Fund (IMF) and the World Bank. It was challenged by those who believe that iron laws of economics predetermine human progress. Marxism is one form of this belief and Marxist thought was dominant in a large part of the world when the Bretton Woods institutions were establishing themselves in the late 1940s. Ironically, the fall of the Marxist states east of the Iron Curtain provided the Bretton Woods institutions, from 1989 onwards, with a substantial increase in its membership. Another form of 'the iron laws of economics' belief is the belief in the reliance on laissez-faire market capitalism. This belief can lead to a denial of the need for the international financial institutions. Indeed, the institutions could frustrate market forces. Modern day proponents of this belief have provided the ideological capital for an influential school of opponents in the United States of the Bretton Woods institutions. Latterly, the waves of globalisation, especially in the form of the massive cross border flows of private sector capital flicked around the globe at the click of a computer mouse, have strengthened the view of those who believe that the world economy is beyond any human control that is designed to improve the economic lot of the generality of mankind.

If mankind is to be master of his economic fate, in a world of states, it is up to the governments of states to act. To do that governments need instruments. Their main instruments in the field of international finance have been the International Monetary Fund (IMF) and the World Bank. Since the IMF and the World Bank are instruments of government, it follows that those two institutions are not autonomous self-ruling bodies. Of course, staffs working in the Fund and Bank have their own views on economic and development policies. Nor, naturally enough, are they motivated to minimise the role of their own institutions. Even so, it would be unfair to Fund and Bank staffs, as well as a misunderstanding of the essential power relationships, to deny that responsibility for the policy of the two institutions rests with the governments that own the institutions. Since different governments have different levels of shareholding, and therefore influence, in the Bank and Fund, different governments bear different burdens of responsibility.

Yet governments have never found it easy to assume this mantle of responsibility. Governments, in the form of finance ministers and central bankers, have often found the Fund and the Bank to be convenient scapegoats when unpopular decisions have to be taken. Indeed, one of the reasons for establishing the two institutions was to provide a buffer between politics and economics. Individual governments working on a bilateral basis could not do this. The sensitivities of bilateral international diplomacy would blunt the thoroughness of policy appraisal, mute the frankness of policy advice and soften the terms of lending conditions for bilateral loans. Sometimes, rightly or wrongly, the institutions have been perceived as being dominated either by one member state (often in the shape of the United States) or by a group of member states (often in the shape of the Group of Seven major industrialised countries (G7)). Such perceptions can undercut the ability of the two institutions to act on what ideally should be the basis of global consensus or compromise.

Institution Building after World War II

The fundamental belief – the Bank and the Fund are instruments which permit man to be master of his economic fate – was evident from the earliest years of their foundation at the end of World War II. Indeed, the belief in the value of international organisations, economic, political and military, was characteristic of the spirit of the time. Those years saw creative acts of statesmanship in world politics, in international economic policy and in regional military and economic cooperation. In politics, there was the establishment of the United Nations and the settlements granted to the countries defeated in World War II. In international economic policy, there was the creation of the IMF; the World Bank; the General Agreement on Tariffs and Trade (GATT), forerunner of the World Trade Organization (WTO); and the Organisation for European Economic Cooperation (OEEC), the administrator of the Marshall Plan and forerunner of the Organisation for Economic Cooperation and Development (OECD). In regional economic integration in Europe, there was the Treaty of Paris, which established the European Coal and Steel Community (ECSC), the earliest component of what became the European Union. In regional military and political cooperation, there was the founding of the North Atlantic Treaty Organisation (NATO) and the Council of Europe respectively. In short, the global leaders were more successful in their task of reconstruction after World War II than were their counterparts after World War I.

So the five years or so after the end of World War II saw a golden age of creative statesmanship, the like of which the twentieth century had not seen before and was not to see again. Their establishment laid the basis for 50 years of cooperation between governments among the major countries. Sixty years on, these institutions are still the pillars of the international polity. The reason for these initiatives is clear. The post war leaders believed that lessons could be learned from the study of history. They wanted to do everything possible to prevent the recurrence of the economic and political horrors of the interwar years, years which were dogged by boom and slump, trade restrictions and interminable squabbles about debt settlements and war reparations. When the global financial system began to be rocked by the oil price crises in the 1970s, the leading governments again acted. They established the G5 and then the G7 process, with the United States effectively in the chair, as a sort of directorate to manage the process. The system produced half a century of unprecedented global prosperity, though some countries, especially in Africa, never benefited. One important reason for this success was the active stewardship and cooperation of governments.

This model of international cooperation and stewardship has come under challenge in recent years. For the 45 years between 1945 and 1990, there had been a clear division of the world – into Soviet bloc governments and their sympathisers, the NATO alliance and its sympathisers and the truly non-aligned. The collapse of the Soviet Union dissolved the certainties of these old super-power client relationships. There is now a more multilateral world with many more players on the scene, a world without much order and diplomatically a bit of a mess. The political predominance of the United States in the Fund and the Bank, once founded on their Cold War military leadership, is no longer accepted. Furthermore, in the 1990s the influence of the G7 countries to set the agenda for international financial cooperation began to erode as the newly emerging market economies began to translate their economic, especially trade, power into the debates about international economic and financial cooperation. The administration of President George W. Bush provided further evidence of the United States' 'retreat from multilateralism'. The increased availability of cheap private sector capital flows for financing both development projects and balances of payments has reduced the dependence of former borrowing countries on the Bretton Woods institutions. So has the accumulation of massive exchange reserves by some countries which in earlier times were chronic borrowers from the IMF. Countries once significant borrowers from the World Bank are now themselves establishing significant development aid programmes This is the new, and in some ways more difficult, political and economic environment in which the Bank and the Fund have to operate in the first decade of the twenty-first century.

The IMF, the World Bank and Globalisation

The so-called 'globalised world' of fast moving ideas and capital has had four particular consequences for the work of the Fund and the Bank. First, the communication revolution, in the shape of e-mail, fax, cheap telephone calls and air journeys, enables activists, lobbyists and campaigners to seek to influence, criticise and assail, sometimes physically, the institutions. Second, the new forms of communication make it easier too for ministers and officials in national capitals to have deeper and more regular contact with their counterparts, either bilaterally or in groups (G7, G24, G20 and so on), in a way which tends to bypass the Fund and the Bank.

The third consequence of globalisation is the profound effects on the work of the institutions of the power of the financial markets and the mobility of capital flows. This is well captured by the shift of the institutions' attention from the current account to the capital account and the national financial balance sheet. The fourth consequence of globalisation for the Fund also lies in the development of the international capital markets. This has brought about a sharp division between Fund members. It is well over 20 years ago that the Fund last lent to a developed country. Balance of payments crises, once the stuff of IMF business, have, at least for the time being, become a thing of the past for the developed countries. They now rely on the seemingly inexhaustible well of international capital markets for balance of payments finance. A decade or so ago in the 1990s developing countries could not expect such finance from the international capital markets, without the support of the Bank and the Fund. Yet ten years later, such is the abundance of global liquidity chasing after yield that even the more impecunious emerging market borrower can tap the international capital markets, whatever the views of the IMF and the World Bank managements on the merits of the stability of its finances and the aptness of its development programme.

These various forces have altered the relationship between the Fund and its members. Many of the larger emerging market borrowers which regularly featured during the 1990s in the Fund's list of borrowers have repaid loans, either in full or in part, sometimes with capital raised in the private markets. As a result in April 2006 total Fund credit outstanding was only a third of its level two years earlier. One consequence of this fall has been a significant reduction in the Fund's income, which is a cause of some concern and study by those involved with the finances of the Fund. Moreover, these changes have made the Fund's relationship with this group of countries somewhat ambivalent. For the present they are free of Fund tutelage. But their economies do not yet enjoy the distinction of a Triple A rating from the rating agencies and there is still a lurking suspicion that should the pool of private liquidity dry up, the IMF may once again prove to be their lender of last recourse. Typically, the Fund's lending relationships are, by and large, confined to the low income developing countries in support of poverty reduction and debt reduction programmes.

The Fund's main interest in the developed countries lies in the surveillance of their economies and, especially during the last few years, their financial systems. Much has been written about the effectiveness of Fund surveillance of (i.e. examination of and comment on the prospects of) its members' economies, both developed and developing and of the world economy generally.[1] Inevitably surveillance can, and if it is to be effective must, occasionally be a cause of tension

---

1   A comprehensive and up to date treatment is in the *Evaluation Report on Multilateral Surveillance 2006* (IMF 2006), produced by the Independent Evaluation Office of the IMF and available on the Fund's web site, http://www.imf.org, under 'surveillance'. This publication has a list of further references relating to multilateral surveillance on p. 38.

with its member governments, whatever the size of the country concerned. New initiatives for improving surveillance are regularly promulgated. Yet the recurrent reviews of the effectiveness and modalities of surveillance suggest some continuing dissatisfaction with the working of this core IMF responsibility. Typical is the finding of the IMF's Independent Evaluation Office in 2006 that 'the absence of an overall strategy has meant that the IMF's multilateral surveillance as a whole is less than the sum of its parts' (IMF 2006, 1). Undoubtedly, the effectiveness of Fund surveillance relies heavily on the continued ability of Fund management and staff to make independent and unbiased judgements of the economic prospects of its members and of the world economy. Increasingly, and rightly, these judgements are being published. The Fund's Managing Director has a big responsibility here in resisting pressures from member states for the Fund to blunt the edge of the message in its surveillance judgements. One change canvassed in recent years has been to give Fund management and staff greater independence in their multilateral surveillance role. So far such efforts have not borne fruit, though probably more will be heard of them.

This brief discussion of the impact of globalisation on the work of the IMF and on its relationships with its members illustrates the difference in interests that its varied groups of members have in its work. To some extent, this is not new. But the degree and nature of the differences has increased the challenge in managing the Fund. That the world economy has, fortunately, escaped crises in the early 2000s has paradoxically weakened the cohesion of the Fund. There has been no event to persuade the disparate Fund members of their essential unity of interest. Long may the economic-crisis-free world continue. But Fund members need to recognise that when the storm clouds gather again, as one day they surely will, a functioning and effective Fund will once again be needed.

The impact of globalised capital markets has had a similar effect on the World Bank. Many of the traditional borrowers of the Bank now finance their development programmes, wholly or very largely, from the capital markets. The Bank's power to influence the development programmes of its former middle income borrowing members has thereby declined. The Bank's attention has therefore, rightly in the views of many, focussed on poverty reduction, notably, but not solely, in Africa, the continent that has the most intractable economic problems. The globalisation of ideas, of lobbyists and of pressure groups too has made the Bank's task more challenging. Through the power of the internet, lobbyists across the world can mobilise opinion, and sometimes physical force, against Bank projects. The fight against corruption, again rightly in the view of many, has moved to the centre of the development debate. But how best to pursue this objective, necessary as it might be, has proved controversial within the World Bank.

The Governance of the IMF and the World Bank

There are five actors on the IMF's stage: the management, the staff, the Board of Executive Directors, the Board of Governors and the International Monetary and

Finance Committee, formerly the Interim Committee. Besides these five, there is another set of actors lurking in the wings, but more of them later.[2]

The IMF Management

The Fund's management comprises the Managing Director and three Deputy Managing Directors, one of whom is the First Deputy. Until 1994, the Fund had only one Deputy Managing Director and his main responsibility was the Fund's internal administrative management. Managing Director Michel Camdessus appointed three Deputy Managing Directors. One of the new arrivals took over the functions formerly held by the single Deputy Managing Director, leaving the senior Deputy, called the First Deputy, free to act, to all intents and purposes, as the Fund's Chief Operations Officer. That proved to be a significant move. Hitherto power below the Managing Director had been dispersed among the Fund's many staff departmental heads and their senior subordinates. Under Camdessus it became centred, to a greater or lesser extent, on one person. This subtly altered the balance of power between staff and management, the Executive Board and the Fund's shareholders, the national governments. For the first time it was possible to talk to one official in the Fund responsible for most lending decisions below the (rightly) Olympian figure of the Managing Director. In latter years, the influence of the First Deputy has waned somewhat with the role being more of primus inter pares.

The Fund's management runs the Fund's day-to-day operations and for those operations the buck stops with the Managing Director. The management decides whether to recommend the Executive Board to lend or not to lend. By convention, the Executive Board of Directors always endorses the Management's recommendations. This approach may appear supine. In fact, it is essential to the smooth operation of the Fund. The government of a borrowing member would be in an untenable position if it publicly committed itself to a highly politically sensitive programme of economic reform, only for that programme to be subsequently overturned by the Executive Board. Even so, individual governments occasionally cast negative or abstaining votes against Fund management recommendations. While such votes are not successful in overturning the management's recommendations, they are not nugatory. They send signals to management about the content of subsequent programmes, either for the particular borrowing member or for future programmes generally.

Hitherto, by convention stemming from the establishment of the IMF and the World Bank, the Fund's Managing Director has been effectively chosen by a caucus of European states and the Bank's President by the United States. Whatever the justification in years past for such a procedure, it can hardly be justified in the world at the beginning of the twenty-first century. There are increasing calls

---

2   For an excellent history of the IMF, see James 1996, together with more recent references listed at the end of the chapter. Many relevant current papers are to be found on http://www.imf.org.

for the appointments to be made following an open and transparent procedure that draws the world's best talent.

The IMF Staff

Below the four management figures, there is the Fund staff. The professional personnel are overwhelmingly macro-economists. Most do not have direct experience of senior levels of government or of the financial markets. They are dedicated and long suffering, of high quality, and great integrity, and the same can be said of the staff of the World Bank.

Sometimes governments seeking to borrow from the Fund accuse Fund staff of political naivety. Such accusations can usually to be dismissed. Senior Fund officials are often more experienced in the politics of Fund programmes than ministers in the countries to whom they are lending. Such criticisms usually are evidence of unwillingness to accept lending conditions. Yet it would be wrong to deny that Fund staff has great influence and power. When the staff are on mission (that is, when they are visiting a member country to agree a lending programme or conduct an examination – 'surveillance' – of its economy), they operate under mandates approved by Fund management. But it is the staff who draft the negotiating mandates and implement them in the discussions and it is their judgement and advice on which the management relies for the crucial decisions. It is not sufficiently recognised that such judgements by the Fund's staff have often to be taken in a fog of uncertainty about the economic numbers and the ability of ministers with whom the Fund is negotiating to deliver their commitments. Sometimes too, Fund staff are not as well informed as they would wish on the workings of the member's economy, especially when the member has been unwilling over a considerable period to enter into dialogue about the prospects for its economy. Sometimes too, the Fund's involvement is delayed until the financial crisis is well under way, when time is of the essence and prudent due diligence of the economic programme is well nigh impossible. The job of Fund staff is a difficult one.

The Board of Executive Directors

The Executive Board is the third actor on the Fund's stage. The Board is composed of the Executive Directors (colloquially known as EDs). The Fund's articles stipulate that there should be 20 Executive Directors. But there are, in fact, 24. This increase is achieved by a vote every two years. This vote requires an 85 per cent majority and that majority requires the participation of the United States. This gives the United States a considerable contingent power over the Fund, though a power somewhat in the nature of an atomic bomb in its potential destructiveness. Blocking the periodic increases in Executive Directors would provoke an enormous crisis in the Fund, potentially uniting virtually the whole of the Fund membership against the United States.

The Executive Directors have a dual function. They represent national governments. Yet at the same time they owe loyalty to the Fund. This dichotomy need not cause problems in practice. Every Fund member, from the biggest to the smallest, shares a common interest in the maintenance of the Fund as an institution, for example in ensuring that its finances are solvent, loans are repaid on time and that salaries are adequate to retain staff.

The Executive Director is the principal link between his or her government and the Fund. Normally, but not invariably, Executive Directors come from finance ministries or central banks. This reflects the important fact, effectively endorsed in the Fund's Articles, that governments maintain their relationships with the Fund through those two institutions.[3] This is true for big and small members. This exclusive relationship is jealously prized by finance ministries, central banks and by the Fund itself. Foreign ministries are not formally involved, though it would be a foolish Executive Director from a major country who did not keep his foreign ministry broadly aware of developments. The Executive Director chooses his or her staff. They too usually come from national central banks and finance ministries. Finance ministries and central banks protect their exclusive role with the Fund partly for reasons of turf (which, unfortunately, is often a factor in international diplomacy). But the main reason is because it helps to safeguard the portion of their foreign exchange reserves that creditor countries pay over to the Fund to finance their contribution to Fund finances. If foreign ministries were heavily involved, such overt involvement would lead to pressure to adapt lending policies to political rather than economic ends. This could prejudice repayments and thus put at risk the foreign exchange reserves which members paid over to the Fund as their contributions to the Fund.

Because governments' relationships with the Fund are carried out through finance ministries and central banks, the Fund is, for good or ill, an institution that is heavily dominated by economics. There is a long-standing convention within the Executive Board that its language of debate should be the language of economics and finance and not of politics and inter-state relations. This helps to avoid wrangling on the most sensitive issues of international politics. But a skilful Executive Director can make a political point, within the conventions, through the use of economic language. The Chicago-trained Argentinian Alternate Executive Director mounted a skilful and vigorous monetarist attack on British monetary policy during the Board's discussion of the UK economy in the aftermath of the Falklands conflict. In the 1980s, African Executive Directors mounted devastating attacks on 'structural impediments' in the South African labour market, thereby castigating the inefficiencies and inequalities of the apartheid system.

The dominance of economics in the Fund has not kept the lending decisions of the Fund (and the Bank) altogether immune from politics. During the Cold War, the Fund lent to 'clients' of some of its larger members to an extent that was disproportionate with the economic merits. Such egregious treatment is, hopefully, a thing of the past, though there are still occasions when strategically important members receive especial attention. Yet even in the case of these countries,

---

3   'Each member shall deal with the Fund only through its Treasury, central bank, stabilization fund, or other similar fiscal agency, and the Fund shall deal only with or through the same agencies.' See IMF Article V, section 1.

reasons of global stability can be invoked for their treatment. This did not prevent complaints from some Asian countries during the 1997–1998 Asian financial crises that they did not receive the generosity of treatment accorded, for example to Latin American countries. But whatever the merits of this debate, smaller, less strategically situated members with economic programmes deserving of support will receive that support. The hallowed principle of uniformity – the Fund's rules and practices apply equally to all its members – is by and large respected.

Constituencies and Quotas

The Executive Directors are grouped into so-called 'constituencies'. The Articles provide for five appointed one country constituencies, the United States, Japan, Germany, France and the United Kingdom. There are in addition three further one country constituencies for large or rich countries (Saudi Arabia, China and Russia). The rest of the Executive Directors head multi-country constituencies. These constituencies group together disparate countries, often with a regional bias. The constituency leader, the Executive Director, assembles the constituency every two years. Often, this is only after some hard bargaining both to retain and attract new members into the constituency. Each director has a number of votes, comprising the total of the votes for all the countries in the constituency. The Executive Director has to cast his votes as a block. He cannot split them according to the views of the governments of the constituency members.

A Fund member's votes are closely related to, but are not exactly the same as, the sum of its contributions to the finances of the Fund, which are known in Fund jargon as 'the member's quota'. Quotas are calculated, usually every five years, according to an arcane formula broadly related to the wealth of a country and to its position in the world economy. So the wealthier a country, the greater its contribution to Fund finances and the more votes the country has in deciding to how the Fund's resources are used. This system of weighted voting suggests that the Fund is more in the nature of a plutocracy rather than a democracy. This is perhaps inevitable given the fact the Fund in financed from contributions from members' foreign exchange reserves. These contributions would never be forthcoming unless the member could protect them through its voting power.

The same point applies in broad terms to the World Bank. Most of Bank lending is financed by borrowings from the capital market (or in the case of lending to the poorest countries from contributions largely provided from developed countries' aid budgets). This market borrowing is implicitly guaranteed by developed countries' formal undertakings to make further capital subscriptions to the Bank if the Bank's finances so require. These capital subscriptions determine Bank members' voting strength in the Bank. So naturally enough, developed countries in the Bank seek to ensure that Bank policy minimises the risk of calls for further capital subscriptions.

The arcane formula for calculating a Fund member's contribution gives considerable weight to past economic performance. So it was only in the 1990s that Britain surrendered its place as the second biggest shareholder in the Fund. Even that was achieved only as a result of an ad hoc calculation, which overrode the standard calculation and put Britain in fourth place in shareholder rankings, level with France and behind Germany and Japan with the United States as the largest shareholder. In November 2006, the United States had 16.83 per cent of total Fund votes, Japan 6.04 per cent, Germany 5.90 per cent and France and Britain equal with 4.87 per cent. The largest constituency in terms of members is the Francophone African constituency with 24 members, but only 1.96 per cent of Fund votes – the smallest voting share on the Board. This mismatch is due to the poverty, and therefore the low quota, of the constituency members. The constituency's Executive Director carries an enormous load in looking after his often troubled constituency members.

The constituency system is the key to the operation of the Fund's Board. It operates, in a very subtle way, to moderate opposing views in the Board. For example, countries such as Turkey and the new independent states of the former Soviet Union are members of constituencies, which are led by European countries, such as the Netherlands, Belgium and Switzerland. Australia shares a constituency with South Korea and New Zealand as well as some small South Sea islands. The constituency leaders know that they have to assemble a constituency every two years and this sensitively modifies the line, which they take on all matters of Fund business. But they do this in a way that still maintains their essential economic beliefs. This subtle process helps to maintain the balance in the Board and moves extremes to a central consensus.

There are increasing complaints that the system for calculating votes does not properly reflect the balance of global economic power – mainly for the reason that the backward looking quota system reflects past, not present, economic performance. Some critics argue that the system results in too many European Executive Directors – from France, Germany, the United Kingdom, Italy, Scandinavia, Belgium, Netherlands, Russia and Switzerland, over a third of the Executive Board. Many argue that rapidly growing emerging market economies should have a bigger share. And the Monterrey Consensus in 2002 called on the IMF and the World Bank to increase the voice and participation of developing countries and countries with economies in transition.[4]

This debate is, by its very nature, a difficult one. Clearly the voting shares of all countries have to sum to 100 per cent, so any redistribution will create losers as well as winners. Nevertheless some progress has been made. At the 2006 Annual Meetings in Singapore, there was an agreement on initial quota increases for China, Korea, Mexico and Turkey (the most under-represented of the emerging markets), to be followed by a comprehensive programme of quota and voice reform (including a new formula). The intention was to make significant progress in realigning quota shares with members' position in the world economy, and to enhance the participation and voice of low-income countries in the IMF; and to

---

4   The Monterrey Consensus encapsulates the understandings reached by the international community at the UN Conference on the Financing of Development held in Monterrey, Mexico, in 2002. These embody a strategy, whereby sustained pursuit of sound policies and good governance by the low-income countries is to be matched by larger and more effective international support.

complete all this within two years. This is a daunting agenda and success is by no means guaranteed. But it is the first genuine opportunity for many years to overhaul the system.

Another strand to this debate – though one for the medium to long term rather than the next couple of years – is the idea occasionally mooted by some member states of the European Union or eurozone to consolidate their voting shares into a smaller number of constituencies, or even into one jumbo constituency.[5] This would, it is argued, give greater coherence and presence to the views of European Union members, and especially to the views of members of the euro area. It would also provide an opportunity to tidy up some curiosities among the present constituency arrangements, Spain for example being in a South American constituency and Ireland in the Canadian constituency. But constituency change raises issues of national sovereignty and amour propre and is deeply controversial. So change will be neither easy nor quick. The more drastic forms of consolidation would probably require an amendment of the Fund's Articles. Amendments require a vote equivalent to 85 per cent of the votes of the Board of Governors. Such a majority requires the support of the United States, which no doubt would wish to reflect carefully before sanctioning the creation of a constituency with more votes than its own!

In fact, though simple majority votes govern individual lending decisions, the United States has a powerful grip on much, but not all, of the strategy of the Fund and the Bank. The voting arrangements in both the Boards of Governors and in the Executive Boards give the United States a veto on many strategic policy decisions. This, coupled with the geographical proximity of the US Treasury and the Fund and Bank buildings and the resources and expertise of the US Treasury and Federal Reserve, has permitted the United States to dominate the two institutions. While it is possible to take exception to particular decisions of the United States, successive administrations' support for the institutions, often in the face of significant Congressional opposition and public apathy if not hostility, was an important factor in sustaining the global prosperity of the second half of the twentieth century. Some member states of the European Union have found United States' dominance of the Fund particularly irksome. The remedy is, in part, in the European Union's own hands – greater cooperation and cohesion in formulating and implementing Fund policies so as to provide the basis for a more equal partnership with the United States!

An effective Executive Board is crucial for the successful operation of the Fund. But the Board needs to be brought up to date. The IMF Board was once the place where policies were thrashed out and where contacts were made between governments. This is hardly the case today. Modern communications, e-mails, fax, easy and cheap telephone calls and air travel, have strengthened direct links between national capitals and senior officials resident in national capitals. Increasingly therefore, Fund policy, direction and decisions are discussed between

---

5   This idea is discussed further in Kenen and others 2004, p. 93. This publication also contains further references relating to international economic and financial cooperation, pp. 145–6.

national capitals or in groups of 'deputies' (that is, senior officials from capitals), such as the Group of Seven and Group of Twenty (G7 Deputies and G20 Deputies respectively), with the Executive Board left to filling out the details.

The authority of the Fund would be strengthened if this reality were recognised in the operation of the Executive Board. This could be accomplished if the Executive Director was the senior official responsible for Fund issues in national capitals (Kenen and others 2004, 92). He, or she, would attend Washington, say once every six weeks, for two days for the major discussions, with the Alternate Executive Director, the Executive Director's second in command and resident in Washington, dealing with the day to day business. Such a change would be unpopular with many Executive Directors. But it would return power to the Board table in 19th Street in Washington.

The Board of Governors

The fourth actor in the International Monetary Fund is the Board of Governors. The Board comprises a representative from the governments of the 185 Fund members. The Fund's articles give the Board power, among other matters, to amend the Articles, to change quotas, and to admit new members to the Fund. (Montenegro became the 185th member in 2007.) The Fund's (and Bank's) Board of Governors is not an effective policy-making body. It meets once a year in the early autumn at the so-called Annual Meetings. But its meetings are an empty shell. The national Governor reads his speech into a cavernous hall of aircraft hangar proportions, which for most of the time is at best a third full. This aspect of the Annual Meetings could be abolished with no loss.

The IMFC

The fifth actor on the Fund stage is the International Monetary and Financial Committee (IMFC), formerly the Interim Committee. It has, like the Executive Board, 24 members. It comprises a minister or the central banker from each constituency (normally from the country that provides the Executive Director on the IMF Board). It is an informal body with no legal power, but its communiqués effectively set the policy and direction of the Fund. Since 1999 Deputies (Ministers' nominated senior official representatives) have prepared its meetings, much to the chagrin of some of the Executive Directors who perhaps see this as a small step in the direction of the non-resident Board referred to earlier.

The Articles of the IMF provide an option which, if exercised, would effectively convert the International Monetary and Financial Committee into a formal Council of the IMF. This is a proposal dear to French hearts but it has not been much liked by previous US governments who have a veto on its establishment under the Fund's voting rules. Most other countries have not expressed a view. But there does seem to be some value in the idea of a Council. It would give expression to the fundamental belief that the Fund is an instrument of government for which governments should take responsibility.

The G7

The sixth actor lurking in the wings is the G7 group of industrialised countries, meeting either as heads of state or government, or as G7 finance ministers and central bank governors.[6] The G7 finance ministers and governors always meet, and usually issue a communiqué, before meetings of the IMFC. Their statements effectively set the agenda for discussion in the IMFC and provide the substance for its communiqué. This intensely annoys non-G7 countries, from the smaller Europeans to the larger Latin Americans. But like it or not, for the last quarter of the twentieth century the G7 set the international financial agenda and sought to have that agenda implemented. In particular, the G7 often provided the lead for the development of IMF policies setting the substance of measures to improve the functioning of the international financial system. This covered, for example, the management of the Latin American (and other country) debt crises of the 1980s, exchange rate crises of the 1990s, the transition of the countries of the former Soviet Union into the international financial system, poor country debt relief and reform of the so-called international financial architecture. By the early part of the twenty-first century, this pre-eminence of the G7 came under challenge as new actors came on the international financial scene, notably the middle income emerging countries in general and China in particular. As a consequence the Group of Twenty countries (G20) was established with a membership drawn from across the globe. It is fair to say that while the G20 has successfully established itself, it has not yet assumed the pre-eminence of the G7, which still continues to meet regularly and to some extent still sets the agenda.

The World Bank

The governance of the World Bank is radically different from that of the Fund.[7] It is modelled on the governance of an American corporation. Its top man is called a President and his immediate subordinates are Managing Directors, Senior Vice Presidents and Vice Presidents. There is no distinction in the Bank equivalent to that in the Fund between management and staff. The Bank's Board appears as if it was intended to function rather like a US corporate board, keeping broad oversight over policy and leaving the direction to management. But it has never worked like that. This is not surprising given that the Executive Directors are hardly likely to be content with the non-executive status of a typical US corporate board member. Moreover, the Bank's work in a member country impact on sometimes sensitive domestic policies and interest groups. Pressures from the home country are unlikely to allow the Executive Director, the Government's resident

---

6   The heads of state or government have not met as G7 since 2002, but always as G8, including Russia – see Chapter 15 above. The finance ministers and central bank governors have continued to meet in G7 format but from time to time invite Chinese representatives to attend informally.

7   The basic reference work on the World Bank is Kapur, Lewis and Webb 1997. Many relevant recent reports are on the Bank's website, http://www.worldbank.org.

representative in Washington, to act in non-executive mode and to divorce him or herself from day to day operations of the institution. So it is not surprising that there have been periods of friction between President and Board.

It is said that Lord Keynes, the British architect of the Bretton Woods settlement, was aware of this potential conflict. He sought, according to the folk history, to deal with the conflict by making the Executive Directors 'non-resident'. But he lost the argument in the face of US opposition (Gardner 1980, 257–60). So he insisted that for Britain the same person should hold the posts of British Executive Director at the Fund and at the Bank and of Economic Minister at the British Embassy. It is recounted that Keynes thought that this would prevent the Executive Director from succumbing to fussy interventionism in Bank and Fund business. This arrangement still persists in the case of the United Kingdom. France also has a single Executive Director for both Fund and Bank; all other countries have two Executive Directors, one in each institution.

The Bank is a much harder institution to manage than the Fund. The Fund's activity is concentrated on its surveillance and on its lending programmes. Its staff broadly share the same skills. To some extent, its success is observable, if not measurable. Fund surveillance of its members' economies is either effective or not effective and the lending programmes achieve or do not achieve their objectives. The Bank's activities are more varied and are spread over the entirety of a member's development programme, from governance issues to health policy, infrastructure design, financial sector reform and a host of other pressing needs. The results of such activities often appear, and sometimes are, diffuse and can take many years to become apparent. The Bank's activities can raise vociferous objections from, or on behalf of, groups that are geographically or politically concentrated. Bank staff too are drawn from many disciplines and their objectives can appear to conflict. If the Fund staff's leitmotiv is the somewhat austere concept of macro-economic stability, that of Bank staff is the somewhat more sympathetic concept of poverty reduction. It is therefore not surprising that Fund staff recognise the adage, dear to finance ministry officials worldwide, that they did not join their institution to be loved. Nor is it surprising that Bank personnel tend to become uncomfortable if they do not feel loved!

In the Bank, the distinction between developed and developing countries (Part I and Part II countries in Bank parlance) is more accentuated than in the Fund. Nor does the moderating force of the constituency system appear to be so powerful. This is perhaps because for many decades the Bank has lent only to developing countries. It does not exercise a 'universal' function over all its members akin to Fund surveillance. It is therefore unsurprising that in the Bank there is something of the attitude of 'them' and 'us' (the countries who provide the funds and the countries who borrow the funds). Executive Directors in the Bank from the developed countries are sometimes represented by officials from aid or development ministries and sometimes by officials from finance ministries (and occasionally by academics or business people). This can sometimes cause problems of coordination with governments delivering different messages in the Boards of the Bank and the Fund. Governments with joint directors, like the United Kingdom, avoid this problem.

There is considerable overlap between the work of the Fund and the Bank, which has led to perennial problems of coordination and occasional frictions between the two institutions. In 1984 the author proposed a long list of steps to deepen collaboration between the Bank and the Fund and obtained support significantly from the two other joint Fund and Bank directors, from France and (at that time) Belgium (Kapur, Lewis and Webb 1997, vol. 2, 500). But the rest of the Board was at best lukewarm and it took a further two years before there was any progress in the shape of limited joint working on poor country work. Even so, complaints about poor cooperation have continued to surface from time to time. As a result there has been some improvement in particular areas of work, notably work on financial sector reform and poor countries. But it is clear that if the institutions were being designed today, the distribution of functions between the institutions would be different.

The Challenges Ahead

The post-Cold War world, where capital and ideas flow almost instantaneously, presents a paradox for the Fund and the Bank. These forces have to some degree weakened the power of the national state. Yet the attraction of the national state as the basis for governmental organisation has never been so popular, as the burgeoning membership of the Fund and the Bank testifies. Those two institutions, together with the WTO and the economic agencies of the United Nations, can play a crucial role in defusing the tensions implicit in this paradox. They can provide the fora for debate, the instruments for rule-making and the political crucible in which the legitimacy and accountability of the system can be fashioned.

If the institutions do not succeed in this endeavour, the risks are clear. They are the establishment of a global economic system without the appearance, let alone the actuality, of accountability, and a world economy that is prone to periodic crises, especially for its smaller and more vulnerable members with open economies. In short, back to the pre-Bretton Woods belief that mankind is subject to the dictates of forces, which are either random or deterministic, according to taste.

If the Bank and the Fund are to rise to the challenge, governments, at least in democratic societies, must have political backing in their own countries for their relationships with the institutions. Until recently, that political backing could be taken for granted in most developed countries, except perhaps in the United States where an active lobby has always been critical of the two institutions.[8] But in recent years, the institutions have been subject to much wider attack, and not only in the United States. This attack comes from environmentalists, anti-globalisation campaigners, human rights activists, and labour organisations, those campaigning for debt relief and from some sections of the academic economic community.

Lurking beneath many of these criticisms are protectionist forces which run counter to the Fund's and the Bank's core beliefs. But some criticisms have

---

8   See, for example, Meltzer 2000, with the reply in Gurria and Volcker 2000.

force and the Fund and the Bank must respond to them. For example, they must provide stronger action to shield the poor from the rigours of economic adjustment programmes and give more help for the poor so that they can benefit from globalisation. They must acknowledge the need for greater openness, accountability and transparency, concentrate on their core tasks and avoid mission creep. Most senior officials in the Fund and the Bank would agree with these precepts and the institutions are working hard to respond to their critics.

Whatever the success of the two institutions in responding to their individual critics, they cannot by themselves meet the criticism that the governance of the international economy lacks coherence. The Fund, the Bank and the other international institutions active in the global economy, notably the World Trade Organization and various organs of the United Nations, are all effectively in the same business. They are helping to create a stable framework for the world economy and in particular are seeking to help the developing world prosper in that economy. The institutions have (mostly) the same shareholders, though the voting weight of the shareholders differs between the institutions. Yet each institution is perceived as ploughing its own furrow. Their chief executives, the Fund's Managing Director and the Bank's President, may meet from to time, but such meetings are ad hoc and informal. This may have been tolerable in the compartmentalised, pre-globalisation world of a decade or so ago. But it is not well suited to today's integrated international economy. It appears to many that the system is without governance and is at the mercy of massive, impersonal economic forces. It is therefore not surprising that some again are coming to believe that man is no longer master of his economic fate, but is subject to the dictates of fundamental, blind deterministic laws and forces.

One way of tackling this perception of lack of coherence and of governance of the international economy is to establish an overarching council – a World Economic Council (Kenen and others 2004, 96–101). The council's role would be to seek to give coherence to often disparate initiatives – ensuring that the institutions are in fact cooperating towards common objectives – and to ensure that all that needs to be done to ensure the stability of the system is being done. It would not interfere with the governance of the individual institutions. Its membership would consist of nominees of representative countries, perhaps based on the membership of the International Monetary and Financial Council, the Managing Director of the IMF, the President of the World Bank, the Director General of the WTO, the General Manager of the Bank for International Settlements (BIS) and the Secretary General of the United Nations. Properly presented and structured such an overarching council could be an important step in establishing confidence in the governance of the global economy.

The effectiveness of the IMF and the World Bank will be undermined if they are subject to constant attacks. If that happened on a large scale, we would have abandoned essential instruments that enable us to demonstrate that we are masters of our economic fate and are not subject to the dictates of some fundamental, blind deterministic laws and forces. That would set the world back more than sixty years.

References

Blustein, P. (2001), *The Chastening: Inside the Crisis that Rocked the Global Financial System and Humbled the IMF*, Public Affairs, New York.

Blustein, P. (2005), *And the Money Kept Rolling In (and Out): Wall Street, the IMF and the Bankruptcy of Argentina*, Public Affairs, New York.

Crockett, A. (Chairman) (2007), *Report of the Committee to Study Sustainable Long-Term Financing of the IMF*, accessible at http://www.imf.org.

Gardner, R. (1980), *Sterling-Dollar Diplomacy in Current Perspective*, Columbia University Press, New York.

Gurria, R. and Volcker, P. (2000), *The Role of the Multilateral Development Banks in Emerging Market Economies*, accessible at the website of the Carnegie Endowment for International Peace, http://www.ceip.org.

IMF (1999), *External Surveillance of Fund Surveillance: Report by a Group of Independent Experts*, accessible at http://www.imf.org under 'surveillance'.

IMF (2003), *The IMF and Recent Capital Account Crises: Indonesia, Korea and Brazil*, Independent Evaluation Office of the IMF, accessible at http://www.imf.org.

IMF (2006), *Evaluation Report, Multilateral Surveillance, 2006*, Independent Evaluation Office of the IMF, accessible at http://www.imf.org.

James, H. (1996), *International Monetary Cooperation since Bretton Woods*, International Monetary Fund, Washington.

Kapur, R., Lewis, J. and Webb, S. (1997), *The World Bank: Its First Half Century*, Brookings Institution, Washington.

Kenen, P., Shafer, J., Wicks, N. and Wyplosz, C. (2004), *International Economic and Financial Cooperation: New Issues, New Actors, New Responses*, Geneva Reports on the World Economy, No. 6, International Centre for Monetary and Banking Studies, Geneva.

Malan, P. (Chairman) (2007), *Report of the External Review Committee on Bank-Fund Collaboration*, accessible at http://www.worldbank.org and http://www.imf.org.

Mallaby, S. (2004), *The World's Banker*, Yale University Press, New Haven, CN.

Meltzer, A. (Chairman) (2000), Report of the International Financial Institutions Advisory Commission, United States Congress, Washington.

Woods, N. (2006), *The Globalizers: the IMF, the World Bank and their Borrowers*, Cornell University Press, Ithaca, NY.

Useful Websites

International Monetary Fund: http://www.imf.org.
World Bank Group: http://www.worldbank.org.

Chapter 18

The World Trade Organization

Roderick Abbott

This chapter analyses the management structures within the World Trade Organization (WTO) for negotiation and decision-making.[1] It begins with a short account of the history of the Organization and especially its forerunner, the General Agreement on Tariffs and Trade (GATT), with a summary of their basic principles. The main body of the chapter explains how the WTO is organised and how it works, commenting on the effectiveness of this process and on the problems that have arisen. The conclusions review the current state of the multilateral trading system and draw some lessons for the future.

The Origins of the GATT[2]

Although trade as well as monetary issues had been discussed in planning for the post-war economic regime, trade matters were not in fact on the agenda for the Bretton Woods Conference (1944) where the structure of post-war economic organisations was designed. The conference focused on financial, monetary and banking issues and agreed to set up two post-war bodies, the International Monetary Fund (IMF) and the World Bank. However, the general recognition that trade policies would also need to be regulated led later to the concept of an International Trade Organisation (ITO).

In 1946 the United Nations set up a Preparatory Committee to discuss a draft ITO Charter submitted by the United States and this Committee met four times: in London in late 1946, in the US and in Geneva in 1947, and finally in Havana in 1948. In parallel with negotiation of the Charter, tariff negotiations were held in Geneva to agree on reciprocal cuts in import duties and to draft general clauses for a treaty designed to give effect to, and protect the value of, such concessions. This was the genesis of the GATT.

This agreement was accepted by the 23 original Contracting Parties and entered into force as a provisional arrangement pending the full acceptance of the ITO which was submitted to the US Congress in 1949. However it was destined to be rejected by Congress and the legislation was withdrawn in 1950.

---

1 The chapter draws on the personal recollections of the author as a participant in GATT and WTO activities, 1973–2005.

2 The sources for this account include Gardner 1980, Jackson 1997and Woolcock 2003.

Thus the GATT, the only element to survive, became the basis for international regulation of trade.[3]

The French have a saying: 'Rien ne dure que le provisoire'. In formal terms, the GATT was never considered to be an international organization, since that would have been outside US negotiating authority in 1947, which was limited to securing reciprocal tariff cuts. The institutional title of the GATT was 'the Interim Committee of the ITO' or ICITO. Since the entry into force of the WTO, the original Treaty has been referred to as GATT 1947 and its successor, incorporated into the WTO, as GATT 1994. The difference is that amendments to the 1947 text, protocols of accession and tariff schedules adopted, and other decisions taken by the Contracting Parties up to 1994 are included, while the protocol of provisional application is omitted.

The Evolution of the GATT, 1947–1994

For evident reasons, given this background, the GATT was not part of the UN family, and the scope of its rules was reduced in comparison to the draft ITO. Thus provisions designed to support policies for full employment, rules to regulate competition and investment issues were eliminated. The GATT was limited to trade matters *stricto sensu*, such as tariffs, quantitative restrictions and other barriers closely related to border measures, such as customs valuation, licensing, subsidy issues, anti-dumping. As the tariffs of developed countries were significantly reduced and import restrictions were lifted through the 1950s and 1960s, the emphasis moved gradually towards broader kinds of trade regulation, like public procurement, standards and technical barriers.

This led to some important differences with other international organisations. The GATT was designed as a set of binding rules for the conduct of international trade. In themselves, such rules are not so different from the principles that underlie the UN Charter, or the IMF or World Bank Articles. The difference comes from the attitudes of the participating governments, who considered GATT rules to be contractual in nature and effectively binding, largely because of their negotiating experience of writing a treaty among the parties. This also meant that new countries wishing to join at a later date were obliged to negotiate their accession, a feature which was absent in the UN.

Is this in fact a valid distinction? There are of course elements of decisions in the UN and elsewhere (for example in the Security Council) which are intended to be executive rather than simple recommendations. But, arguably, the GATT and later the WTO have gone further in the direction of supranational rules than most, especially in the area of dispute settlement. From the earliest days GATT obligations were taken seriously. The requirements to notify and then discuss trade measures with other members and the decisions of the Council were scrupulously respected. More recently, questions have been raised about loss of sovereignty due

---

3   One American Senator is reported to have said: 'Anyone who reads the GATT is likely to have his sanity impaired'. Some of us hope that we have avoided that fate.

to the acceptance by governments to manage their trade policies in accordance with international rules – and not only by NGOs and other critics in civil society. This needs to be compared with the way that governments behave in foreign policy matters (the 2003 invasion of Iraq being a good example) and more generally in attitudes towards the United Nations, which nobody would accuse of having taken over the sovereign powers of its members. An interesting comparison is to see how the same policy matters are handled within the European Union – see Chapter 13 above. In economic policy areas with an international aspect, such as trade and agriculture, and in competition matters more generally, EU Member States have agreed to respect common rules and policies and to pool their sovereignty to a large degree. In foreign policy the situation remains very different.[4]

Major Developments of the GATT Years

There was a general elimination by industrial members of the quantitative restrictions in place from the war years, with liberalisation effected through the programme of the Organisation for European Economic Cooperation (OEEC) during the 1960s. Japan acceded in the 1950s after difficult negotiations, but for some years many other members used GATT Article XXXV (the opt-out clause) and Japanese trade was subject to discrimination. Some Central European countries with Soviet-style planned economies acceded in the 1960s (Poland, Hungary, Romania). Part IV of GATT was added in the early 1960s to introduce agreed principles and objectives, as well as some limited commitments, in favour of developing countries.

During these years the practice of negotiating rounds also developed, from 1949 through 1956 in Annecy, Torquay and Geneva; later during the 1960s and 1970s the Dillon, Kennedy and Tokyo Rounds; and finally the Uruguay Round from 1986 onwards, which led to the institution of the WTO. The early negotiations were entirely focussed on customs tariffs, but non-tariff elements began to appear in the Kennedy Round, such as anti-dumping and the US valuation system for chemicals – the American Selling Price (ASP). Later, in the Tokyo Round, nine specific side agreements (often called 'Codes') were concluded, together with four important 'understandings' in areas such as differential treatment for developing countries, balance of payments and safeguard measures for development purposes, and the procedures for dispute settlement.

Basic Principles of the GATT and WTO

Two fundamental principles are essential to an understanding of the international trade rules, as they exist today. The first of these is non-discrimination, usually expressed as *most-favoured-nation treatment.* This means that that every WTO member is to be treated strictly in accordance with the rules and in the same

---

4   Another difference between the GATT (and later the WTO) and other international organisations is in how such rules are enforced. This will be examined later in the chapter.

manner as every other WTO member. The striking thing about this principle, as it was drafted in 1947 and as it is still expressed in GATT 1994, is that it is unconditional. There are no stated exceptions to the rule, save some pre-existing preferential regimes which are explicitly covered in the relevant Article.[5]

It has to be admitted, however, that there can be, and there are, exceptions de facto to most-favoured-nation treatment. One, which was built in at the start in Havana, is the rule that permits a customs union or a free trade area to eliminate import duties among its members without extending the same treatment to other members. Another is the provision for discrimination to be permitted where the member has secured a waiver of its obligations (Art XXV.5). Yet another situation, admitted in the 1970s, is the existence of general preference schemes (GSP) in favour of developing members, and later the special treatment accorded to least developed countries.

The second broad principle is usually called *national treatment* and expresses the idea that there should be no difference in treatment in the way that trade rules are applied to national or foreign companies and situations. This rule is not of general application in all circumstances (its full title is 'National Treatment on Internal Taxation and Regulation') although the situations covered are extensive enough.[6]

There are in addition some principles which apply mainly to rule-making, as opposed to the application of tariffs and regulations. These include: consensus as the basis for decisions; the Single Undertaking (expressing the idea of the same rules and obligations for all); the binding nature of WTO rulings in dispute settlement; and the acceptance of non-reciprocity in negotiations with developing countries.

The Decision-Making Structure of the WTO

The hierarchy of decision-making bodies is set out in the Marrakesh Agreement establishing the WTO (GATT 1994). This provides, in Article IV:

- 'There shall be a Ministerial Conference, composed of representatives of all the members, which shall meet at least once every two years.'
- 'There shall be a General Council composed of representatives of all members, which shall meet as appropriate.'

These bodies correspond to the UN General Assembly or other similar bodies open to all members of an organisation. In practical terms, a ministerial body that meets rather infrequently is not an executive body. So these tasks fall to the *General Council,* which is explicitly mandated to carry out the functions of the

---

5   See GATT 1947, Article I, paragraph 1. The limited exceptions for former colonial regimes and some between neighbouring countries are found in paragraphs 2 and 3 and in Annexes.

6   See GATT 1947, Article III, mainly paragraphs 1–5.

ministers 'in the intervals between the meetings of the Conference' (Art IV. 2). The General Council meets at ambassador level about six to eight times a year. Although ministers are of course only in Geneva occasionally, more recently they have started to meet in smaller groups for negotiating purposes and can thus exercise some degree of oversight of the Council.

The WTO's decision-making process is set out in Article IX (emphasis added):

- Art IX. 1 is clear: 'The WTO shall continue the practice of *decision-making by consensus* followed under GATT 1947. Except as otherwise provided, where a decision cannot be arrived at by consensus, the matter at issue shall be decided by voting'.
- 'At meetings of the Ministerial Conference and the General Council each member shall have one vote ... Decisions ... shall be taken by *a majority of the votes cast,* unless otherwise provided in this Agreement ....'

Consensus and Voting

A first point which emerges from this text is that the General Council is explicitly instructed to take decisions by consensus, in line with previous practice. In perhaps an implicit recognition that this may create difficulties for the smooth operation of the WTO, a footnote was added to the Article to simplify matters and to help define what a consensus is in some situations.

This footnote reads (emphasis added): 'The body concerned shall be deemed to have decided by consensus on a matter submitted for its consideration, *if no Member, present at the meeting when the decision is taken, formally objects to the proposed decision*'. This leaves slightly open what is meant by a formal objection. But it is clearly enough of an encouragement to members to abstain rather than vote negatively.

Voting by the 'one member, one vote' principle is quite normal in democratic, international institutions. However, the language about voting is in contradiction with the language about consensus and must therefore be considered to be an exception of last resort. In fact voting has become a dead letter, in terms of the actual practice followed within the organisation. Other than when new members join or when waiver decisions are proposed, votes have *never* been part of GATT/ WTO practice. Even in those contexts, in more recent years decisions have been based upon consensus and thus unanimity.

Accessions have sometimes been the occasion of political disputes, for example, between China and Taiwan, Armenia and Azerbaijan, Georgia and Russia. But they are considered 'ordinary' decisions with no special provisions. Waivers also can be occasions for political pressure, as in the case of EU banana imports. As exceptions to the rules, they are subject to a special voting procedure if no consensus is agreed. This adds to the pressure on the member seeking such a waiver.

Consensus is undoubtedly a very democratic method of taking decisions (even if no single legislature anywhere in the world operates on this basis).[7] Unfortunately it carries with it a sharp double-edged weapon, the reverse side of the coin, and that is a veto. This has led to the general perception that any delegation that feels disgruntled with the way a discussion has evolved, or is opposed to the views of the majority, or which stands to gain by insisting on modifications to a waiver, can easily block a decision. The empirical evidence suggests that such 'threats' have not been realised, especially not by any country in isolation, and indications of strong opposition have normally led to further informal debate; but the threat per se and the implicit idea that the country could seek support from 'natural allies' is an effective means to secure delays or text changes.

Absence of Executive Bodies

The second key point is that there is, below the General Council, no body of a broad executive character. No other committee, group, or body can take any decision for all members. I make a distinction here between decisions that members take and those which the Director General can take by delegation of powers from the Council. These latter are executive in character, once a general policy line has been agreed, and include many elements of staff management and administration of the work of the Secretariat.

This point needs to be underlined since it has led to much time-consuming and probably wasteful discussion in the plenary meetings, in an effort to prepare and achieve consensus. This requirement has also led to endless informal discussions on even relatively minor issues. (This point is elaborated later in the chapter.) Informal discussion was a well-established GATT practice, among many fewer and more like-minded delegations. In the WTO context different opinions have become more contentious, thus consensus is more difficult. It is certainly not an effective decision-making process, but then most international organisations suffer from this failure to work effectively.

The General Council and its Associated Bodies

The functions explicitly reserved to the General Council are to take decisions about interpretations of WTO Agreements (Art IX. 2) and to decide on waiver requests from the members (Art IX. 3–4). The General Council meets also as the Dispute Settlement Body (DSB) – of which more later – and the Trade Policy Review Body (TPRB). It is assisted by three other Councils – for Goods, for Services and for Trade Related Intellectual Property Rights (TRIPS). These Councils can take 'operational' decisions, for example, about their work and agenda and how issues are to be discussed. But policy matters relating to the WTO agreements and to negotiations have to be referred to the General Council.

---

7   I should not however fail to mention the decision-making practices of some Swiss cantons which are much attached to direct democracy.

Reporting to the Councils are a number of Committees whose primary function is to oversee the functioning of each WTO agreement and to carry out the Work Programme. These bodies therefore reflect the main policy areas that were subject to negotiation in the Uruguay Round.

In addition to these 'functional' committees that report to the three main Councils, there are other Committees, Working Parties and Groups of a more traditional character, largely inherited from the GATT. Their functions reflect the mandates that members have given to the Secretariat to monitor basic obligations and debate other policy issues of interest to them, for example, trade and development, trade and environment, regional trade agreements, and budget, finance and administration matters.[8] Working Parties for individual accessions are created on an ad hoc basis, as required.

In parallel with the General Council, the practice has been to establish a Trade Negotiations Committee (TNC) whenever a negotiating round is initiated. The present TNC was established after the 2001 Doha conference, with the task of overseeing the negotiating mandate as agreed by ministers there, and with the Director General as Chairman. The TNC Chairman reports to the General Council which can and does also debate these issues. In practical terms, the day-to-day responsibility for the management of negotiations lies with the TNC, but the ultimate authority and the division of responsibility for negotiations is a matter left deliberately vague. Some of the above-mentioned Committees also meet in special sessions when negotiating issues that are part of the Doha round are discussed (for example, on Agriculture, Services or Dispute Settlement). In other cases specific Negotiating Groups have been established, for example, on Non-Agricultural Market Access (NAMA) or Rules, and since Cancun on Trade Facilitation. These groups report to the TNC.

The structure of the various bodies within the Organisation is shown in Figure 18.1 below.

The Director General and the Secretariat

The central Secretariat role is commonly agreed to be one of support to the members (in organising regular meetings and servicing negotiations) and of management of the Agreements. In these areas its tasks are not contested, and the dispute settlement system is effective in ensuring a high level of surveillance and respect for agreed disciplines. The work of preparing a negotiation in detail and providing background information on matters likely to be raised is of course infinitely elastic and variable.

Beyond that, an additional role as a spokesman for the 'common good' – to represent the interests of members collectively – and as a voice to promote the benefits of the multilateral trading system is also recognised to some extent. This recognition has varied over time, with the open issue focused on the relative efforts of the members as well as of the Secretariat in this crucial area. Clearly, both

---

8   There is also a Committee on Balance of Payments Restrictions, but it is largely obsolete as few members now invoke the relevant Articles.

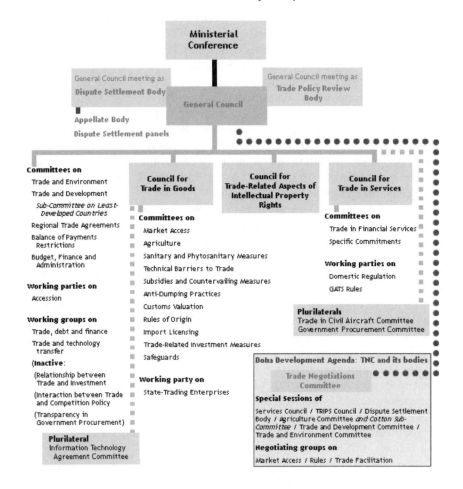

Figure 18.1 The organisational structure of the WTO

Source: WTO.

are needed; and the issue is currently under sporadic discussion (in the follow-up, for example, to the report issued in 2005 by the Eminent Persons Group chaired by Peter Sutherland).[9] This report made important recommendations in the sense of giving more flexibility to the Director General and the Secretariat to speak in defence of the multilateral system and to issue publications on their own responsibility.

What is clear is that the Director General, personally, has a role to represent the Organization around the world and to maintain close contacts at ministerial level with all the members. In recent years, as the selection process has become

---

9   This report, called *The Future of the WTO*, was issued in January 2005 and published by the WTO (WTO 2005b).

more open and transparent, it has become an explicit part of the job description. In any case, it is a matter of record that holders of this office past and present have visited every continent regularly and attend a wide range of regional and informal ministerial gatherings (for example, APEC, ASEAN, the G20, the African Union and ACP meetings, as well as events in Central and South America and the Caribbean).

The Director General also has a role to play in the process of the negotiations themselves. Since the 1960s, these have become increasingly wide ranging in the issues covered and thus long drawn out. What is always needed is a balanced, objective assessment by a neutral party of the central ground where the final compromises will need to be found. In the current Doha round, for example, much effort has been expended by the Director General in identifying the core issues around which a deal needs to be found (market access, agricultural support and liberalisation of trade in services).[10]

This analysis has been based on the broad consensus that the distortions of trade inherent in systems of agricultural support must be corrected. This in turn was due to pioneer work in the measurement of subsidies, and their impact on trade flows, by the staffs of the OECD and WTO which has contributed significantly to the development of policy thinking in the management of agriculture. It would be fair to add that NGOs, in more recent times, have also contributed to the general public awareness of the importance of these issues by the campaign in favour of 'trade justice' and by their forceful advocacy of pro-development issues – a role which is difficult for a 'policy neutral' Secretariat.

The Secretariat is organised in about 20 Divisions, each headed by a Director. About half of these are essentially engaged in the core areas of negotiation, while the others deal with more traditional trade policy matters or provide the support and management functions which are a necessary part of any international organisation.[11] In the WTO case, it would not be an exaggeration to call it a 'document factory'. It produces (and translates) tens of thousands of pages of internal documents, including the lengthy dispute settlement reports; as well as publishing books, annual reviews and trade statistics, trade policy reviews and other glossy brochures.

---

10 Earlier examples of the central role of the Director General in steering a negotiation towards final success can be found in the role of Eric Wyndham White in the Kennedy Round (1967); and in the initiative by Arthur Dunkel to issue a draft set of final agreements in 1991 after the Uruguay Round had virtually collapsed at the Brussels Ministerial Conference of December 1990.

11 This includes press and media and external relations (with civil society and other organisations); economic research and statistics; and language services, informatics, human resources, budget and general administration. More traditional subject areas are technical assistance and training for developing country members, trade policy reviews, and work related to new accessions. A full list can be seen on the WTO website at http://www.wto.org.

It is important to remember that this is a small secretariat: a total of 600 staff including those on temporary posts – not to be compared with the very much larger numbers at the OECD, the IMF or the World Bank.

Commentary on the Decision-Making Structures

As time has passed since 1995, the role of the Chair of the General Council as a player alongside the Director General and his staff has grown. Other Chairs of Councils and Committees have also played an increasing role in informal consultations, thus reflecting the often quoted maxim: 'the WTO is a member-driven Organisation'.

In reality the WTO is no *more* driven by its members than other organisations, since they all exist to serve the interests of their membership, and this is certainly equally true of the UN. But one does have the impression that the secretariats of the IMF and World Bank, and to some extent the OECD, have a greater liberty of action than the WTO has, especially to analyse matters related to their core functions and to publish such studies. In addition the Fund and the Bank have over the years accumulated their own funds and sources of revenue. They are therefore less dependent on the formal budget which provides the members (who contribute to it) with their main leverage over the activities of the organisation.

There is a case for arguing that the General Council has been unable to carry out its functions in some areas where decisions have been required (interpreting Agreements) and that it has failed to adapt efficiently. What is sure is that it has not conducted its business very efficiently. The following examples illustrate the point:

- The General Council was unable to agree in 1999 upon a successor to Renato Ruggiero as Director General, and the recommendations of the Chair were openly contested.
- The Council was asked in 1999 to consider making an interpretation of certain Articles of the Dispute Settlement Understanding, following acrimonious exchanges between the US and the EU over the correct procedure to be followed in the banana dispute. This was widely seen as a 'two elephants' spat', and the Council took no action although the textual contradictions were evident.
- The inability to secure consensus on this and other matters of interpretation (a virtual abdication of role) meant that the pieces had to be picked up elsewhere, through litigation in dispute panels and in appeals. Examples relate to export subsidy commitments, certain tariff preferences, whose application was discriminatory, and safeguard measures.
- The Council has been embroiled in long, repetitive debates about the implementation of the Uruguay Round, and about special and differential provisions and their 'mandatory' quality, without any solution being found.

The Evolution of the WTO

Well before the start of the Uruguay Round in 1986, Professor John Jackson, author of some of the most penetrating books about GATT and the WTO, and the leading authority in legal analysis of GATT, had proposed a new organisation to promote world trade. He had this to say about the evolution of this idea during the negotiations (emphasis added):

> [I have] flagged a number of institutional and legal problems of the GATT, with its various 'birth defects'. With the Uruguay Round Agreement (in 1995) establishing a new institution – the WTO – one can report that most of these problems have been corrected or at least improved. Yet no institution is perfect, nor for that matter complete and final. *The WTO ... will have to adapt and evolve to meet the rapidly changing circumstances of international economic relations. A key question in that context is whether the new charter for the WTO will allow the organisation to adapt efficiently.*[12]

The remainder of this chapter will consider whether this challenge, to adapt and to evolve, has been satisfactorily met or whether the institution has fallen short. There are, it has to be admitted, proponents of both sides of this argument and perhaps, as a famous saying goes, 'it is too soon to tell'.[13]

The first major change in the WTO scenery occurred immediately, on 1 January 1995, with the explosive increase in active membership which took place at that time. The conditions attached to becoming a member are part of what is called the *Single Undertaking*. This is a multi-faceted concept, which in this context means that a would-be member has to accept *without reservation* all the agreements incorporated into the WTO corpus of rules governing international trade. These consist of the Marrakesh Agreement, with three Annexes: Annex 1 contains GATT 1994 and the agreements on trade in goods, on trade in services (GATS) and on trade-related intellectual property matters (TRIPS); Annex 2 is the Dispute Settlement Understanding; and Annex 3, which is the Trade Policy Review Mechanism. Annex 4 contains the plurilateral agreements, binding on those that have accepted them. This seemingly tough approach was however somewhat softened for those that had been previously GATT members (called Contracting Parties). They were able to sign up without having to add much to previous tariff commitments and in particular without making new commitments in the services area after negotiations with other members.

In consequence the WTO started off with 76 members, and soon grew to 123. Large numbers of these now faced WTO obligations which they had escaped hitherto, leading to a natural desire to give more attention to the Organization and its activities and to participate more fully in its work. There had long been a majority of developing countries in GATT, but since decisions had never been

---

12 The quotation is from Jackson 1997, 342. Professor Jackson is also the author of *World Trade and the Law of GATT* (Jackson 1969), which is an essential companion to understanding the GATT texts and their interpretation.

13 This is the response attributed to Chou En Lai, when asked to comment whether the French Revolution had been a good thing.

taken by voting this had not made much of an impact on the organisation. With the larger membership in WTO, and greater participation by more active members, the task of reaching a consensus was to become more complicated and above all much more time-consuming.

Two particular areas tend to be controversial. The first concerns all development matters, where many members intervene in debates on entirely predictable and often repetitive lines. The second covers such issues as requests for waivers or for interpretations of the Agreements. Article IX above mentioned contains specific provisions on these matters, in paragraph 2 as regards interpretations and in paragraphs 3 and 4 as regards waivers. In practice no decision on any new interpretation has ever been taken in the last ten years. It has been left largely to panels and the Appellate Body in the context of WTO dispute settlement to clarify the meaning of certain parts of the texts. On the other hand, some waivers have been granted, on occasions at major political cost.

In some cases one might ask oneself whether the controversial element has come from the labyrinthine procedures and pattern of decision-making, or whether it has depended on the subject matter. The EU's waiver requests related to its banana import regime are an example of this. This issue was of concern to a large number of members, who held widely divergent views, and in addition involved a set of widely divergent developmental arguments.

Current Problems in WTO Decision-Making

It will immediately be obvious from the earlier description that a meeting with 100 or more countries in the room is not the ideal way to take any kind of decision. (There are at present 150 WTO members, but some of these have no representation in Geneva, while others do not always attend, even at this top level.) Most other UN bodies have an *intermediate level body* – a steering committee or governing body – on which a selected number of members serve and which constitutes the real forum for debate on the pros and cons of policy decisions. The WTO has never gone that way, and when the idea has been mooted, opinion has tended to be hostile to it.[14]

Hence the practice has developed of lengthy *informal discussions in smaller groups*. Some of these are convened by the Director General in the now notorious 'Green Room'; others are based upon regional groupings. Yet others are derived from Committees in the Organisation and are therefore functional in character. The composition of these groupings is variable and depends upon who convenes the meeting, but their common characteristic is that they do not take decisions. Rather, they provide a platform for transparency. As the membership of WTO has grown, and more and more members take an active interest in its business, these problems of maintaining transparency in the preparation of a consensus

---

14 The reasons for this attitude are not always clear or rationally expressed. But it would be a major distraction to explore this here. Some observers might think that the Consultative Group of 18 which was established in the late 1970s was an intermediate level committee of this kind. But its functions were not at all operational.

have become more and more acute. Loud complaints on the lack of transparency have become a 'shibboleth' in the WTO. But in fact the percentage of developing countries present in the Ministerial Green Room during the WTO conferences from 1999 to 2004 was above 70 per cent.[15]

There are of course critics of this process, especially among the NGOs and civil society. Many such critics believe that, even if decisions are not taken, certain general approaches to issues are developed which makes it more difficult for individual members to disagree at a later stage. This of course is implicitly a criticism that those present do not sufficiently report to their colleagues in regional groups, and a new intermediate level body might improve on that. At any rate critics do not usually explain how sensible debates and decisions can be managed with over 100 delegates in the same room.

In reality, total transparency can never be achieved. Meetings for transparency purposes will always fail to reach the 20–30 delegations that are not present in Geneva, and another group of countries have such limited resources available that they will not be able to attend. Further, if the delegates that do attend will not share the details of the discussions with others, then the whole purpose of the mechanism will fail. You can make as much information and documentation available as you like, but you cannot force others to obtain or use it, especially where there are resource constraints.

Shifts in Power within the WTO and Impact on Trade Negotiations

These changes have proceeded in parallel with other shifts in power among major participants, while significant regroupings of the members that provide leadership and initiatives have occurred within the organisation.

Looking back, one should have seen the signs of these shifts already in Seattle (1999). So much else went wrong there – the street battles due to over-muscled police tactics, the US Chairman conducting the conference in a highly partisan way, President Clinton flying in and telling the press that he wanted the WTO to agree on new rules to prevent 'social dumping' – that they were camouflaged. But the fact remains that the Ministerial Green Room process was done exactly as in Singapore (1996) and therefore left out large numbers of developing members whose ministers got bored and angry. These members with others more or less walked out – and that was the end of the conference.

The next conference, in Doha in late 2001, was taking place shortly after 9/11 and there were major concerns before the meeting whether it was 'security-wise' to have a major multilateral conference in the Arab world. Although there was much disagreement on many matters, the divergences were finally swept under the carpet by the slogan (invented during the conference, and not a planned agenda item) that this was going to be the Doha *Development* Agenda, with potential benefits for all members. This process was possibly helped by a desire to show that terrorism could not kill cooperation within the multilateral economic system.

---

15 This emerges from the excellent description of the Green Room and other informal processes in Pedersen 2006.

Thus the WTO ship sailed on towards the shoals and rocks of Cancun (2003) where it duly ran aground and was wrecked. There, even a short-sighted observer could not miss the realignment of power: the emergence of an opposition group (the so-called G20) to stand against the EU and US and industrial countries generally. Even more telling were the whoops of joy of NGO and civil society representatives, working closely with third world delegates, when the Mexican Chairman announced that it was all over without any agreed text. The fact that several different Directors General handled different WTO conferences (with changing Ministerial Chairmen also) did not help lessons to be learned. Thus for Singapore the Director General was Renato Ruggiero, Seattle and Doha were Mike Moore, Cancun was Supachai Panitchpakdi, and most recently Hong Kong (2005) was Pascal Lamy.

So what has happened and why? The general theme for the World Economic Forum in Davos in January 2007 was 'the shifting power equation' and this phrase is fully applicable to the evolving situation within the WTO. As a thoughtful press article expressed it (emphasis added):

> An increasingly global world has exacerbated the need for multilateral action, but it has also shaken the foundations of the multilateral system. *Authority is leaking away from international institutions and from the Western powers that have traditionally led them*, leaving the world short on leadership ...[16]

One common *leitmotif* is that America has lost its power to dominate but is too strong to be ignored. Another is that the old EU-US tug-of-war for leadership has been replaced by a cacophony of voices from New Delhi to Brasilia, from Beijing to Canberra.

Conclusions: Reflections on the WTO and Lessons to be Drawn

Trade negotiations had in the past been 'steered' by the major participants, on the assumption that they had most at stake and would be making most of the new commitments (policy or tariff levels), whereas others who would be mainly beneficiaries would in the end accept the results. Through the Kennedy, Tokyo and Uruguay Rounds (1964–1967, 1973–1979 and 1987–1993) the Quad group of US, EU, Japan, Canada had provided leadership, with other OECD countries in support. After the Uruguay Round the Quad rapidly lost much of its force, and nothing has been found to take its place. Limited groupings existed for specific purposes, such as the Cairns Group of agricultural exporters, or the Least Developed Group, but a vacuum developed at the centre.

As the WTO came into being with, as we have seen, an explosion of members both more active and more aware of new obligations, the old scenarios no longer met the needs. Tariffs in the OECD countries were now pretty low (except in

---

16 See Bennhold 2007. The *Financial Times* Survey, 'The World in 2007', also of 24 January 2007 develops the same theme.

agriculture), while quantitative restrictions and 'voluntary restraints' were things of the past. The main source of concern became the distortions affecting agricultural trade, a sector where liberalisation had lagged badly behind the trends in other areas. The massive growth in participation of developing members meant also that the issue of development – or the special and differential treatment to be enjoyed by such members – needed to be moved into the centre of WTO discussions.

In Singapore and Seattle the process seemed little changed. Even in Doha developing countries were working together, informally, but without creating specific groups. An alliance developed against the so-called Singapore issues. After Cancun the G20 became the opposition alliance on agriculture. Significantly, the immediate cause of the G20 group was a joint EU-US proposal, which was interpreted to be an effort to steer the outcome in a direction that suited them but failed (as others saw it) to meet the members' needs. In fact Cancun broke down for other reasons in the end, but the seed of new groupings had been sown.

Gradually other groupings have been created, mainly alliances directed at specific negotiating interests. The G10 takes defensive positions on agriculture. The G33 comprises developing countries that are net food importers and fear the effect on world prices of the abolition of subsidies. There is a Group for the ACP countries, in favour of preferences, and so on. These groups have become a permanent part of the WTO scenery and add to the process of informal consultations, which was already onerous enough. At the overall policy level a bridging group, the G6, brought the leaders of developing countries (Brazil and India, supported by others) together with EU, US, Japan and Australia to encourage dialogue. But this has clearly not provided the leadership required to make the Doha negotiations progress towards a conclusion.

Dispute Settlement

In contrast to the problems described so far, the dispute settlement system in the WTO has worked efficiently and well. In this area there is a completely different paradigm for reaching decisions where a member's actions are alleged to be incompatible with the rules and a ruling is required.

This is perhaps not the place for a detailed explanation of how the Dispute Settlement Understanding (DSU) works. It is enough to say that the emphasis has totally changed from the practice of considering a complaint in terms of changes that were 'politically feasible' towards a much more juridical approach, what is 'legally required'. In procedural terms, the progress from complaint to consultation, to setting up a panel, to issuing a report, to managing an appeal, to adoption of a ruling has become automatic. This in turn means, as a practical matter, that vetoes do not apply and all members, large or small, will face judgment without excessive delay. The speed of proceedings contrasts favourably with other International Tribunals which tend to last a long time, in some cases many years.

In political terms, the aim of the new system is to offer fair and equitable opportunities to all members. This has been expressed as 'every member has an equal right to have his day in court'. Further, while there are still possibilities to exercise political muscle at the bilateral consultation stage, the formal panel and appeal processes are almost entirely immune from such pressures. Therefore, the small are as well able to make complaints against the large as vice versa, and power politics have been neutralised, compared with what occurred in the days of the GATT.

The system has clearly a supranational character. Panel and Appellate Body reports based on legal analysis of the rights and obligations of the parties, state unequivocally that a country's actions or measures are inconsistent with WTO rules, where that is the case. Once adopted by the DSB, the rulings put pressure on the losing party to 'bring itself into conformity' within a reasonable period of time, which is itself subject to negotiation. It is hard to think of other dispute scenarios which have such effects. Although the International Criminal Court in The Hague has a similar mandate to pass judgment on individuals that have been indicted, it does not directly condemn a country's policy or practices.

Lessons to be Drawn

As I have tried to show in this chapter, the WTO since 1995 has faced major challenges in the composition and trade policy interests of its members, in the way it works and takes decisions, and in securing the necessary leadership to pursue its goals. All these elements have generated criticisms inside and outside the Organization – and the wider hostility of NGOs and of civil society to the WTO, perceived as an agent of globalisation, has not even been mentioned.

Some lessons might be drawn from the events of 1995 to 2006. First, it is unhelpful to set too short a term for the Director General, even if this solves another political problem; this only results in discontinuity of policy and management. Second, the clear tendency to limit – and even reduce – the powers of the Director General may well have contributed to current difficulties in leadership within the Organization. There is a need for a personality to speak for and promote the common good, in the interests of the multilateral trading system. The Director General and the Secretariat should resume a greater role in this context as they have done in the past. Finally, ways need to be found to ensure that a degree of freedom to pursue development aims can be combined with respect for basic trading principles, in a more harmonious framework than exists at present.

References

Bayne, N. and Woolcock, S. (2003), *The New Economic Diplomacy: Decision-Making and Negotiation in International Economic Relations*, 1st edition, Ashgate, Aldershot.
Bennhold, K. (2007), 'At the World Economic Forum: A Look at the Dangers of a Shifting Power Equation', *International Herald Tribune*, 24 January.

Evenett, S. (2006), '"Global Europe": An Initial Assessment', *Swiss Review of International Economic Relations*, Special Issue, available at http://www.unisg.ch/org/siaw/web.nsf/w wwPubInhalteEng/97C9C24CCB7863A4C125728E004EFF79?opendocument.

Gardner, R. (1980), *Sterling-Dollar Diplomacy in Current Perspective*, revised edition, Columbia University Press, New York.

GATT (1994), *The Results of the Uruguay Round of Multilateral Trade Negotiations*, General Agreement on Tariffs and Trade, Geneva.

Jackson, J.H. (1969) *World Trade and the Law of the GATT*, Bobbs-Merrill Company, New York.

Jackson, J.H. (1997), *The World Trading System*, MIT Press, Cambridge, MA.

Hoekman, B.M. and Kostecki, M.M. (2001), *The Political Economy of the World Trading System: the WTO and Beyond*, Oxford University Press, Oxford.

Meunier, S. (2005), *Trading Voices: the European Union in International Commercial Negotiations*, Princeton University Press, Princeton, NJ.

Pedersen, P. (2006), 'The WTO Decision-Making Process and Internal Transparency', *World Trade Review*, Vol. 5, No. 1, pp. 103–31.

Rollo, J. (2006), 'Global Europe: Old Mercantilist Wine in New Bottles?', *Swiss Review of International Economic Relations*, Special Issue, available at http://www.unisg.ch/ org/siaw/web.nsf/wwwPubInhalteEng/97C9C24CCB7863A4C125728E004EFF79? opendocument.

Woolcock, S. (2003), 'The ITO, the GATT and the WTO', in Bayne, N. and Woolcock, S. (eds), *The New Economic Diplomacy: Decision-Making and Negotiation in International Economic Relations*, 1st edition, Ashgate, Aldershot, pp. 103–20.

WTO (2001a), Doha Ministerial Declaration, Document WTO/WT/MIN(01)/DEC1 of 20 November 2001.

WTO (2005b), *The Future of the WTO*, Report of the Eminent Persons Group chaired by Peter Sutherland, World Trade Organization, Geneva.

Useful Websites

World Trade Organization: http://www.wto.org.

Chapter 19

The Future of Economic Diplomacy

Nicholas Bayne and Stephen Woolcock

This final chapter is intended to pull together the record of economic diplomacy, as expounded in this book. It will not offer detailed predictions about future developments. Economic diplomacy constantly changes in unforeseen ways – it is very much a moving target. The aim is rather to pick out some of the dominant trends in the new economic diplomacy which have emerged in the 1990s and the early 2000s and appear to be durable. These trends will be illustrated from the case studies set out in the practitioner chapters.

The chapter will return to many of the features of economic diplomacy identified in Chapter 1: the analytical framework based on three tensions; the challenges posed by advancing globalisation; and the new strategies adopted in response to those challenges. In brief, as the 2000s advance, economic diplomacy seems set to continue to grow in importance. The original challenges persist: economic diplomacy has become more complex, with more issues now subject to negotiation; more state and non-state actors engaged in domestic decision-making; and more countries actively participating in the international system. The new strategies – involving ministers, bringing in non-state actors, greater transparency and using international institutions – have all been modified in the early 2000s. For example, summitry has expanded, but without becoming more effective; rule-making has lost ground to voluntary co-operation, with greater use of multi-level diplomacy; transparency and engaging non-state actors is giving the process more legitimacy; and institutions are wrestling with the problem of inclusiveness.

These trends indicate greater progress in reconciling the first and third tensions of economic diplomacy – between politics and economics and between government and other forces – than the second. Governments are often failing to resolve the inherent tensions between domestic and international pressures. Paradoxically, they have been encouraged to do so by the buoyancy and resilience of the world economy during the 2000s. There has been strong and steady growth in many industrial and developing countries, with inflation under control despite surging oil prices. These achievements build on the advances in economic diplomacy of the previous decade and future projections are encouraging. But in such easy times, governments shy away from difficult decisions and economic diplomacy is less fruitful

The First Tension: Economics and Politics

Reconciling international economics and international politics is a constant objective of economic diplomacy. It is often overshadowed by the other two objectives, which involve domestic pressures. The international incentives for economic cooperation are frequently held in check by domestic constraints, both economic and political. But on occasion the demands of international politics reinforce the arguments for economic cooperation so as to enable advances to be made.

The classic example of successful interaction between international economics and politics occurred in the years following World War II. The political objectives of avoiding future wars and containing the spread of communism stimulated the creation of ambitious and durable economic institutions, as Nigel Wicks noted in Chapter 17. But though the United States was the dominant, 'hegemonic' power, it did not impose its ideas on the rest of the world. In the Marshall Plan, the United States made the Europeans take responsibility – 'ownership' in current usage – for cooperation among themselves and accepted a degree of discrimination against its own interests. When the institutions were being created after World War II, there were relatively few states involved. The US was predominant and led in the creation of a multilateral order by making concessions to weaker developed economies. As US relative power declined, a 'club model' emerged, in which the major industrialised countries cooperated closely to ensure stability in the international financial system, after the Bretton Woods system collapsed in the 1970s, and to keep protectionist pressures of in check.

Globalisation and Inclusiveness

The end of the Cold War and the advance of globalisation created a new set of international political pressures at the start of the 1990s. This contributed to some striking achievements in economic diplomacy: the conclusion of the Uruguay Round and the creation of the WTO; and the harvest of environmental agreements associated with the UNCED conference at Rio. But there was too much of a tendency for the industrial West to impose its own ideas. Western industrial countries still expected international institutions like the IMF, World Bank and WTO to operate for their own benefit, rather than for the entire worldwide membership. This approach received a rude shock at the Seattle meeting of the WTO in 1999. It became brutally clear that developing countries did not see the Uruguay Round and the WTO in the same positive light as the rich countries did.

The need for genuinely worldwide institutions is one of the consequences of advancing globalisation. The 'club model' is looking worn out, as it does not include the growing number of developing countries, led by Brazil, China, India and South Africa, that play a much more active role in international negotiations. The biggest challenge is to make the international system more inclusive of emerging economic powers, while retaining effectiveness in reaching agreed solutions to global problems.

In a range of different policy areas the new emerging leaders are too important not to be included in negotiations. This is increasingly the case in international finance, given the volumes of foreign reserves held by China and other Asian economies. It is the case in trade and investment, where progress on the multilateral level cannot be achieved without the explicit agreement of these countries. It is the case with regard to the environment, since most of the growth in CO_2 emissions will come from large developing countries. It is also the case for energy supply and consumption, which cannot be addressed without including the major oil and gas producers. The rhetoric should not get too overblown. The US, the European Union and Japan are still major powers and sources of initiative, while the OECD provides an effective means of cooperation with other industrial countries. But the trend is clearly towards a more multi-polar world in economic diplomacy.

In response to the rise of major developing countries, all international organisations have engaged in outreach, that is, the informal inclusion of more countries, without modifying their formal decision-making structures. For example, the G8 summits now have regular consultations with non-G8 countries, in particular the 'Plus-5' (Brazil, China, India, Mexico and South Africa) as explained in Martin Donnelly's chapter. In the context of the IMF and World Bank the G20 finance ministers have emerged alongside the G7. In the WTO the infamous 'Green Room' is now called the 'Consultation Process', and is somewhat more inclusive, as shown by Roderick Abbott in Chapter 18. The OECD has for many years been engaged in outreach to developing countries and emerging markets and has also expanded its membership to include newly industrialised countries and countries that have undergone transition.

But while the debate on reform has been engaged, there has been little in the way of formal innovation or structural reshaping in any of the international economic institutions. The G8's membership has not changed since Russia was admitted in 1998. Canadian Prime Minister Paul Martin proposed the idea of a L20 to complement or replace the G8 with a larger group of 20 leaders including China, India, Brazil and South Africa as well as representation of other developing countries; but this remains on the drawing board. The IMF and World Bank have essentially retained the structure that was created to fit the balance of economic power in 1944. There is a renewed awareness of the need to reform, but considerable difficulties in changing the constituency system. Greater voting powers for the new leading developing countries, whose weight in the IMF is increasingly out of line with their growing economies, will mean other countries having to give up some of their powers. Creating a single voice for the Eurozone countries must overcome obstacles from both inside and outside the EU.

After the Seattle Ministerial meeting and again after the failure of the Cancun Ministerial there has been debate about institutional reform in the WTO. With formal equality but practical inequality of influence, the WTO faces different problems. The challenge in the IMF and World Bank is to allow greater formal representation of developing countries. The issue in the WTO is how to retain effectiveness when the organisation has nearly global membership and the practice is consensus among members having equal voting rights. Despite the Sutherland Report and various proposals for formal changes, the reform debate has not produced much. On the one hand developing country WTO members wish to see a greater codification of processes that ensure their inclusion in all key decisions. On the other hand, there is the view that what is needed is flexibility and a will to ensure effective involvement of all. So far those favouring flexibility seem to have the upper hand. In the meantime, the response has been a proliferation of different groups. These can represent different regions (the EU and the Africa group), levels of development (the G20, G90 and Least Developed Countries) or sectoral interests (the Cairns Group, the G10 and the G33, all concerned with agriculture).[1]

Naturally, the mature industrial countries have been reluctant to give up the advantages they enjoy from the existing regimes. But leading developing countries have also been cautious in taking on new responsibilities for managing the international system. In trade, for example, Brazil has taken the lead as spokesman for the G20 and accepted the responsibility this involves. But India is active mainly in defending its own national interests, while China keeps a low profile. In the global environment, none of the large developing countries have been prepared to accept international limits on their greenhouse gas emissions. China is not pressing to become a permanent member of the G8 summit or the G7 finance ministers, preferring to keep its options open. Yet all these leading countries want to make the institutions work better, not to replace or abandon them. These organisational problems have made the institutions less efficient. But they are not the principal cause of failures to agree in international negotiations in the early 2000s. The failures are due instead to the domestic obstacles preventing international cooperation, to be treated later in this chapter.

Policy towards Poor Countries

Meanwhile, it has become clear that globalisation's undoubted benefits are not equally spread. Many middle-income countries are using globalisation to catch up on the rich ones; but many of the poorest are falling further behind. Since the poorest countries in general pose no threat to the economic system and offer few economic attractions, policy towards them must be politically motivated. Such motivation was largely lacking during the 1990s. For most poor countries, aid receipts went down, private capital went elsewhere and their share of world trade shrank.

The 2000s opened, however, with a growing recognition of the need for change: more had to be done to ensure that the poorest countries also benefit from globalisation; but the poor countries should have 'ownership' of their own development – it could not be imposed from outside. Development issues, especially in Africa, became the top priority for the annual G8 summits. Measures to reduce the debts of poor countries agreed at Cologne (1999) were linked with moves to give these countries ownership of the poverty reduction strategies they agreed with the IMF and World Bank. The Africa Action Plan issued at

---

1　The G20 contains large or middle-income developing countries, the G90 small or poor ones. The Cairns Group are agricultural exporters, the G10 want to protect agriculture and the G33 are poor importers. See Chapter 18 above.

Kananaskis (2002) promised G8 support for the measures the African leaders had themselves agreed to take as part of the New Partnership for Africa's Development (NEPAD). The African countries promoting NEPAD believed that by improving their standards of political and economic governance they would attract more foreign aid and investment.

The Fight against Terrorism

A further political impetus was provided by the terrorist attacks on the United States on 11 September 2001. Initially the United States mobilised an impressive international coalition to fight against terrorism. It recognised that this must attack not just the symptoms of terrorism, but also its causes – which include poverty, disease and economic marginalisation. The political campaign against terrorism could thus be used to promote economic measures to ensure that even the poorest countries share in the benefits of globalisation. In March 2002 the US promised an extra $5 billion in official aid annually over five years and this pledge has been met. The EU members made comparable undertakings and in 2005 set a target date for giving 0.7 per cent of their GDP in aid. This impetus enabled the 2005 Gleneagles summit to promise a doubling of aid to Africa by 2010, together with the complete forgiveness of debt for many countries. These economic undertakings are linked with clear commitments to help Africans restore peace and security in troubled areas, recognising the danger of persistent conflict in states like Congo, Somalia and Sudan.

But the political impulses to economic cooperation generated by the fight against terrorism have also met serious obstacles, of two kinds. The first are provoked by domestic resistance and will be considered in the next part of this chapter. The second has arisen from the change in the political climate brought about by the US invasion of Iraq. This has provoked widespread hostility, not only among other Middle Eastern countries but from many of the United States' allies in Europe. There is no direct impact on international economic relations, whose institutions have continued to function as normal, but there are indirect effects. The US has become less inclined to pursue multilateral initiatives, reinforcing its disposition to act bilaterally or on its own. Where the US has launched wider programmes, other countries are less inclined to react favourably. Thus the Broader Middle East initiative introduced at the 2004 Sea Island summit soon ran into the sand. In addition, persistent unrest in this major oil-producing region has caused energy prices to rise, shifting power towards oil exporters and making oil importers more concerned about their sources of supply. But the instruments of economic diplomacy concerned with energy are still limited in scope, as Joan MacNaughton's chapter shows.

The Second Tension: International and Domestic Pressures

The interaction of international and domestic pressures, already a standard feature of economic diplomacy, has greatly intensified in the 1990s and 2000s.

This emerges from many of the practitioner chapters, for example those by Matthew Goodman, Matthias Buck and Kishan Rana on the United States, the EU and developing countries. The number of issues on the economic diplomacy agenda has greatly increased and become more intrusive into domestic policy. International trade relations now include a range of issues that were previous considered to be of national concern, such as services, intellectual property and investment. Environment policy has become a major preoccupation of economic diplomacy and has intimate links with economic growth and energy policy in particular. The increase in the number of issues and their greater intrusiveness has resulted in more departments of government becoming involved. It is not longer just foreign, finance, trade and development ministries that engage in economic diplomacy. Virtually all departments now have some role to play, in line with the growth of issues. Ministries responsible for the environment, energy and health, for example, all now have active roles in international negotiations, acting as the lead departments.

Privatisation and the growth of the regulatory state have also been associated with an increase in the number of independent or quasi independent regulatory bodies that now engage in economic diplomacy. There are international links between the regulators that supervise financial services, transport, communications and the media, as well as the autonomous bodies that set standards for accounting, the environment and the quality of food and industrial products. Independent central banks and competition authorities play their part in international negotiations and rule-making. This all means a greater need for effective consultation processes within national governments and a much more complex network of links between countries. The rise of the independent regulators can make economic diplomacy harder. Because they are jealous of their autonomy and have tightly drawn mandates, they often resist suggestions from other parts of the government that they should take wider issues into account.

The impact of the growth in issues and in state actors can be assessed by examining the balance between rule-making and voluntary cooperation in the 1990s and 2000s.

The Rise and Decline of Rule-Making

The economic institutions created after World War II – the IMF, World Bank and GATT – were rule-based bodies, even if the detailed rules of the ITO were never adopted. By the 1970s, however, economic interdependence was well advanced, at least among industrial countries, while the post-war institutions were under severe strain. Governments reacted to the strains of interdependence by strengthening voluntary cooperation.[2]

With the globalisation of the 1990s, however, the balance shifted back to rule-making again. The WTO introduced rules for trade in agriculture and services, as well as legally binding dispute settlement. International commitments on climate

---

2   Professor Robert Putnam's analysis of the Bonn G7 summit of 1978 was intended to show how much voluntary cooperation could achieve (Putnam and Henning 1989).

change, biodiversity and protecting the ozone layer were embodied in formal UN treaties. As late as 1996 Harold James, the IMF's historian, could still write:

> The general evolution of the international monetary system has been away from rules and towards cooperation. Increased information has played the role previously occupied by a legal or quasi-legal framework. (James 1996, 586)

But the IMF and World Bank responded to the financial crises of 1997–1998 by tightening its rules for supplying economic data, for conducting monetary and fiscal policy and for regulating financial institutions.

International rules have four clear advantages over voluntary cooperation, in conditions of globalisation:

- First, they are more *durable*. Voluntary cooperation will work while conditions favour it, but may well collapse under pressure. Rule-based systems are better able to survive bad times as well as good. It is like the difference between cohabitation and marriage.
- Second, rule-based systems are more *equitable*, since all are subject to the same rules and this protects the weaker members against the strong. Systems of voluntary cooperation are too easily dominated by the large and powerful.
- Third, voluntary cooperation can easily become elitist and non-transparent. Rule-based systems have to be *transparent* to some degree; otherwise no one will understand what the rules are.
- Fourth, as governments' relative power shrinks, they are prone to make voluntary commitments that they cannot deliver. There is much less risk of this with international rules.

These arguments carried much weight during the 1990s. But as the 2000s arrived, rule-making everywhere has come under attack. Both developed and developing countries became discontented with the results of the Uruguay Round, so that the WTO meeting in Seattle failed to launch a new rule-making round of trade negotiations. In the subsequent Doha Development Agenda (DDA), the proposals for rule-making covering investment, competition and other issues were taken off the table before negotiations on them could begin. The DDA seems likely to produce very little in terms of new rules on trade, but even so it has struggled to make progress. Meetings to agree new commitments under environmental agreements failed as often as they succeeded. On climate change, the most prominent issue, deep transatlantic differences emerged and the United States declined to accept any formal commitment to reduce greenhouse gases. The OECD's attempt to set new rules for investment came to nothing, while its efforts to discipline tax havens were bitterly resisted.

The trouble arose because the new international rules adopted in the 1990s went far beyond determining what happened *between* countries and began to dictate what happened *inside* countries. The WTO's agreements, for example, went much further than the GATT. The increased interdependence of the world economy meant that international rules had to reach much deeper into domestic arrangements if open markets were to be guaranteed. This deeper penetration created tensions between emerging international rules and domestic regimes. Some of these regimes were long established; others were just being reformed in response to privatisation and technological change. So the issue was whether the domestic regulatory regimes would be compatible with those being negotiated internationally. For example, popular demands for greater environmental protection resulted in the introduction of domestic regulatory regimes in many developed countries. The strengthening of trade rules in the WTO was then perceived as threatening hard fought environmental regulation.

It has thus become clear that operating a worldwide rules-based system is more demanding than governments expected. During the 1990s the governments of developed countries persuaded themselves that the new rules amounted to no more than extending their existing domestic approaches to the international level. When it emerged that they were going to have to change their domestic policies, for example the EU on food safety or the US on greenhouse gas emissions, this led to dispute or disagreement. Meanwhile developing countries, hoping for changes in their favour in the economic system, soon became disillusioned. If industrial countries, with their greater freedom of action, would not set a good example in accepting that international rules meant structural change, developing countries were reluctant to change domestic policies either. There have been some rare exceptions, however: as Matthew Goodman notes, China used its entry into the WTO as the stimulus for major domestic economic reforms.

Voluntary Cooperation and Multi-Level Diplomacy

Rule-making is a demanding technique of economic diplomacy, not to be pursued without realising the consequences. Failures in rules are worse than failures in voluntary cooperation, just as the break-up of a marriage causes more upheaval than the parting of a cohabiting couple. While the major institutions struggle to agree new international rules or to reform their procedures, simpler and less demanding processes are being revived.

The spread of summitry   The growth of summit meetings on economic subjects has already been noted in Chapter 1. This is a special form of the strategy of involving ministers, which seeks to make progress by moving issues from the bureaucratic to the political level. The expansion is evident in multilateral events, like the UN Summits of 2000 and 2005 to advance the Millennium Goals; and in the plurilateral G8 summit, which not only pursues outreach to non-G8 countries but is underpinned by an expanding network of ministerial meetings. There has also been a growth of regional and bilateral summitry. The US holds bilateral summits with a range of countries, such as China and India, and takes part in annual APEC summits and periodic Summits of the Americas. The EU holds not only its own summits, but meets regularly at head of government level with a growing number of countries. Developing countries follow the same trend, with existing summits like the Arab League being complemented by new groupings like

IBSA (India, Brazil, South Africa) noted by Kishan Rana in Chapter 12. Indeed, most if not all regional groups or potential regional groupings hold summits.

But more meetings have not always meant more effective results. Some bilateral relationships are established but produce little by way of concrete results. They can soon degenerate into a process in which there are just formal presentations of positions rather than genuine dialogue; the EU-US summit illustrates this. These summits have had some successes but rather than facilitate agreement at the top political level on difficult problems, they have focused on detailed regulatory issues. While important, this has meant the summits have not achieved a very high political profile. In addition the US Administration has been reluctant to do anything that might require Congressional approval.

The G8 summit has been more effective in reaching agreement on solid commitments, where other channels have failed. The Gleneagles summit of 2005 engaged the United States in action on climate change, focused on developing new emissions-reducing technology, despite American rejection of the Kyoto Protocol. But summit commitments only amount to voluntary cooperation. They are not binding on the participants, so that they often lose momentum and fail to get implemented when they run into domestic obstacles (Bayne 2005).

The G8's treatment of Africa illustrates this well. After Kananaskis (2002) launched its Africa Action Plan, the Africans hoped the G8 would provide more generous debt relief and more market access for their agricultural exports. Instead, the conditions for debt relief remained unchanged, the United States increased subsidies for its farmers and the European Commission's proposals for reforming the CAP, which would reduce trade distortions, were resisted by many Member States. To restore momentum at the 2005 Gleneagles summit, as Martin Donnelly's chapter explains, the UK successfully pressed for full debt forgiveness, a doubling of aid to Africa by 2010 and better trade access through the WTO. The debt measures were enacted, but the trade promises came to nothing and aid increases so far are falling short of the target.[3] During the Marshall plan the United States accepted some economic damage by allowing European countries to discriminate against it, as the price of its political aims. There is little sign yet of the G8 countries doing this for Africa. So even when international politics and economics reinforce each other, this is often too weak to overcome domestic constraints.

Multi-level diplomacy   While rule-making has declined at the multilateral level, it has continued at simpler levels of economic diplomacy, led by the United States. There has been a clear shift towards a greater emphasis on bilateral agreements across the board, supplemented by a few new regional agreements like CAFTA. The number of Free Trade Agreements (FTAs) notified to the WTO has risen steeply, to reach 300 by early 2007. The US now openly pursues FTAs in line with its multi-level trade strategy, as explained in Matthew Goodman's chapter. The EU is pursuing FTAs with ASEAN, India and Korea to cover the one region

---

3   See Beattie 2007, recording OECD calculations that aid fell in 2006, compared with 2005.

of major economic importance (apart from North America) with which it has no FTA in force or under negotiation. Developing countries in the Asia-Pacific region and the Western Hemisphere are following the trend.

This reflects an increase in the relative importance of the bilateral and regional levels rather than a fundamental shift from multilateralism to regionalism. When faced with difficulties in accepting formal commitments at a multilateral level, it is not surprising that governments have opted for rule-making on a less demanding bilateral basis or for voluntary cooperation through plurilateral institutions.

Preference for unilateral measures   With the retreat from rule-making and multilateral commitments, many countries now prefer to take economic decisions on a wholly national basis. Almost all states are now prepared to welcome foreign direct investment, but every attempt to create a comprehensive international regime has failed. International exchanges in services are expanding strongly, but countries are reluctant even to bind their existing regimes in the WTO. Major developing countries like China and India, whose greenhouse gas emissions are rising fast, refuse commitments under the Kyoto Protocol but are beginning to introduce national measures in their own interest. The new regime of 'multilateral surveillance' introduced in the IMF consists of the juxtaposition of national macroeconomic policies, without any commitment to mutual adjustment.[4] This trend is the strongest sign that economic diplomacy is penetrating deep into domestic policy making and provoking a defensive reaction.

This fragmentation of economic diplomacy into voluntary cooperation and bilateral or unilateral policy-making clearly makes it easier to overcome domestic resistance. But it weakens the foundations for an effective international system, for reasons indicated earlier in this section. Policy becomes less predictable when based on unilateral measures, as it is easily put into reverse. Bilateral agreements can successfully make progress when the multilateral level is blocked, taking advantage of liberal forum shopping in multi-level diplomacy. But without a multilateral umbrella, there is the risk of a tangle of overlapping, inconsistent regimes being created.[5] The big powers gain advantages at the expense of the poor and weak, who are already at risk of marginalisation. Yet even big powers like the United States, as Matthew Goodman testifies, find such a regime laborious.

Democratic Accountability and Legitimacy

Globalisation, by widening the range of actors, increases the pressure on governments to make their economic diplomacy more accountable. While using institutions is intended to increase the *efficiency* of economic diplomacy, the other three new strategies adopted in the 1990s – involving ministers, engaging non-state actors and greater transparency – are meant to improve its *accountability*. This

---

4   See Daneshku 2007. She quotes the US Treasury Secretary as saying: 'These consultations were never intended to produce joint policy commitments'.

5   Jagdish Bhagwati has argued this point vigorously, with his image of the 'spaghetti bowl' (Bhagwati 1995).

brings us to a further issue in the tension between international and domestic pressures in economic diplomacy. Increased interdependence and globalisation calls for greater cooperation between states, in order to ensure open markets and address potential market failures at an international level. But the existing means of providing democratic legitimacy to economic diplomacy remain domestic and national.

In the past, governments used to take the legitimisation of international economic decisions for granted. This made the process of reaching international agreements easier by easing the domestic constraints under which negotiators have had to operate. Policies in the IMF, the GATT and WTO or in terms of other international economic issues were decided within government. Political legitimacy was provided by having officials deal with the uncontroversial issues and ministers decide on the more sensitive questions. But consultation with national parliaments was not very extensive and often took the form of a brief report from ministers on the course of negotiations.

The United States provides an exception to this and Congress has progressively tightened its grip over the policy process and reduced the discretion in the hands of executive branch negotiators or officials. Within the EU the scope for discretion by Commission negotiators is limited by the oversight of the national governments in the Council of Ministers or in specialist committees. But the role of national parliaments in Europe has been very limited and the 'democratic deficit' this represents has not yet been filled by the European Parliament. The same applies in Japan and most developing countries. Economic diplomacy has thus been largely shaped by negotiations between governments, with bureaucratic politics largely determining the scale of concessions that were acceptable in order to reach agreement.

This prevailing model is now being challenged. Civil society does not see the established channels of democratic legitimisation, centred on elected ministers reporting to parliament, as sufficiently accountable and has therefore sought to engage directly in the policy process. Elected representatives have found it difficult to provide effective scrutiny of the negotiating process because of the often technical nature of the negotiations and the fact that they are conducted in different fora, eg in the EU and the WTO for the case of EU Member States. But opening economic diplomacy to the influence of civil society and the views of national parliaments could render the task of finding international agreement much more difficult, if not impossible. The pressure for increased transparency has also reduced the discretion available to negotiators, thus making it harder to find means of reconciling domestic and international objectives or rules. Phil Evans' Chapter 8 illustrates some of the implications of this.

One of the new strategies in economic diplomacy is the greater involvement of ministers and heads of government, who have much greater political accountability than bureaucrats. These politicians, as they become more active in economic diplomacy, should, in their turn, provide for more extensive debates in national parliaments. If national parliaments are to play a positive role in economic diplomacy, as opposed to a blocking negative role, they must be able to contribute to all stages of a negotiation, not just ratification. This will require more resources to enable specialist committees or working parties to monitor negotiations. If governments do not help to develop this form of effective scrutiny, national parliaments are likely to adopt a more negative approach and could end up vetoing the results of negotiations.

The Third Tension: Government and Other Forces

The question of accountability leads naturally to the tension between government and non-state actors. It is by now conventional wisdom that non-state actors are playing a more important role in economic diplomacy, with civil society NGOs gaining, at least in visibility, vis-à-vis the business sector. Parliaments and legislatures, as already noted, make their impact on economic diplomacy overwhelmingly at the domestic level. What is striking about the new trends among business and NGOs is that they now operate at the international level as well.

NGOs

The increase in the role of NGOs can be dated to the early 1990s when environment NGOs, alerted by the NAFTA negotiations, became aware of the potential for trade and investment rules undermining regulation aimed at environmental protection. During the 1990s development NGOs became more visible in economic diplomacy. They came to the view that project based development in developing countries was not sufficient. The international policy framework, in debt, trade and investment, needed to be made more development oriented. Consumer NGOs began to focus more on the international dimension in the wake of various food safety concerns and a growing awareness of how international rules relating to the regulation of biotechnology might affect consumer interests. Organised labour saw its negotiating position vis-à-vis employers undermined by the increased internationalisation of production and outsourcing.

NGOs aim to promote action in areas that they think government is neglecting and they often seek to counter the power of business as well. They have profited from the widespread popular anxiety about globalisation, which makes people feel vulnerable to forces outside their control. The extreme manifestations of anti-globalisation feeling have been the obstructive and often violent demonstrations at international meetings, mounting in intensity from Seattle in 1999 to the Genoa G8 summit in 2001. The terrorist attacks of 11 September 2001 brought this cycle of violence to an abrupt halt. Though obstructive demonstrations still take place, public tolerance of anti-globalisation riots has dropped sharply, while many NGOs have explicitly rejected violence. But that does not mean that popular worries about globalisation have gone away. Responsible NGOs, with dedicated members, well-argued programmes and often substantial resources, continue to gain support in industrial countries. They are having a growing impact on the legislature, the media and the public generally and are trusted as a source of informed opinion that is independent of government. Such NGOs will wish to make clear their broad-based support and distinguish themselves from small protest groups that exploit the internet to disseminate extreme views.

Globalisation and greater awareness of the popular impact of economic diplomacy has been the driving force behind the civil society 'Movement' (Green and Griffiths 2002). The existing formal channels of representation, with ministers reporting on international negotiations to legislatures are seen to be inadequate. Civil society NGOs therefore organise their own campaigns, mobilising public opinion in support of the moral case for debt relief, 'fair trade', poverty alleviation or safeguarding the future of the planet. From the basis of moral positions fortified by popular backing, they engage directly with government officials, as Martin Donnelly explained in his account of preparations for the G8 summit.

NGOs also seek direct involvement with business and international institutions. For example, they are targeting private firms to make them adopt programmes of corporate social responsibility. International firms are thus finding that greater power brings them more responsibility towards public opinion. Governments and institutions often want to make use of NGOs' research capacities, their links with the wider public and their ability to generate new ideas. This confronts NGOs with a delicate choice. Those that are ready to work with others will find that both governments and business are keen to tap their expertise, while they can exert a healthy influence in making international institutions more transparent. But NGOs will not want to forfeit their ability to take an independent position, in order to maintain their links with their grass-roots supporters. So all the parties concerned – NGOs, government and business – will be trying to work together while avoiding being captured by the others.

The picture is rather different in developing countries. One obstacle facing Western-based NGOs at the time of the Seattle WTO Ministerial in 1999 was that they were regarded with suspicion in the developing countries that they professed to help. But that had begun to change by the Doha Ministerial in 2001, especially because of the successful joint campaign by Médécins sans Frontières and Brazil to promote better access to patented drugs and the use of generic alternatives. Developing countries are coming to regard NGOs as more benign, though some scepticism persists, as Kishan Rana records. In addition, many NGOs are building up local chapters and alliances in developing countries that can contribute to poverty-reduction strategies. This enables NGOs to represent themselves as a genuine source of alternative international opinion, which national governments cannot provide and which justifies speaking of NGOs collectively as 'global civil society'.

Private Business

Globalisation is driven by the enterprise and innovation of private business. During the 1980s and early 1990s it was thought, at least in Britain and the United States, that business got things right, while government got things wrong. There was a general belief that the market could adjust to any potential failures and that public intervention to prevent market failures was likely to be flawed. Government surrendered many of its functions to the private sector and adopted business practices for much of what was retained. Business thus became more powerful, as government's relative powers dwindled.

In some areas, the private sector assumed a role as regulator in its own right, in what might be called the partial privatisation of economic diplomacy. The private sector has always played a role in developing standards, for example in the International Standards Organisation (ISO). During the 1990s, however, the growth of new technologies, especially in information technology and telecommunications, and the globalisation of business accelerated this trend. Because of the complexity of many technical areas, governments made greater use of delegation of regulatory authority to private or semi-public standard-setting bodies, which could shape access to markets. For example, governments were willing to let independent professional bodies shape accounting standards, both nationally and internationally.

Sometimes the private sector developed structures to enable firms to regulate themselves. At other times it resisted any form of regulation on the grounds of greater economic efficiency, arguing that the market should act as regulator. Electronic commerce and the internet provided the clearest example of this. In the late 1990s IT firms argued that the rapid development and diffusion of this new technology for economic purposes was due to the absence of regulation; governments should therefore keep out. But by the early 2000s these arguments were being undermined by evidence of the inadequacies of firms as regulators. The Asian financial crisis, the collapse of the 'dot-com' bubble and the Enron and WorldCom scandals have shown that the private sector makes mistakes just as much as government does. In short there remains a role for government and public regulation to anticipate and deal with market failures. Governments have therefore been re-asserting their right to regulate, for example to ensure data protection, fight against fraud, money-laundering and high-tech crime and look after the interests of consumers in general. They are strengthening public regulatory agencies, for example in financial services and food safety.

However, there remains a major constraint on governments in making regulatory policy; they have to think of the impact of their decisions on markets. Markets have become endogenous to the policy process to a far greater extent than had been the case in earlier decades (Odell 2000). The policy areas in which markets impinge most upon policy-making are those which have a direct bearing on financial flows and foreign direct investment. The general liberalisation of capital markets worldwide means government policies that are not seen by markets to be credible in the longer run will lead to adverse market reactions, in which investors move money out of the economy concerned. Governments are now obliged to consider whether the policies they pursue are 'business friendly'. The globalisation of markets has not resulted in the demise of the state, but it has clearly resulted in governments being obliged to consider how policies impact upon the attractiveness of the country concerned to foreign investors.

Meanwhile, private business is as active as ever in lobbying government, as Reinhard Quick's chapter shows. In contrast to civil society's public campaigning, business generally prefers to make its case directly to government. Business firms can best hope to influence policy by persuading government of the more technical merits of their case and will proceed in a much less public fashion than NGOs. They will argue that a particular policy will lead to greater investment, more wealth creation or indeed reduced environmental pollution. The threat of 'exit', such as moving overseas or outsourcing is not seen as very effective.

The Government Response

Governments have sought to reconcile the tensions with NGOs and business in a number of ways, following the strategies of engagement and transparency identified in Chapter 1. First, governments have worked hard to improve the transparency of the decision-making processes and thus defuse the criticism that economic diplomacy was opaque and unaccountable. Governments and international organisations now provide far more information, in the form of agendas and position papers. This has been facilitated by electronic information systems.

Second, governments are making considerable efforts to consult more widely with all 'stakeholders' and engage them more closely. Negotiators and international organisations have sought to co-opt those civil society NGOs willing to be co-opted into the policy process by including them in consultations. As has been the case for the private business sector for many years, the consultation with civil society NGOs has both formal and informal aspects. For example, the EU holds regular consultation meetings and pays for NGOs to attend them; the UN has a well-defined process for associating selected NGOs with its work; national delegations to WTO negotiations often include NGOs. Generally speaking, however, NGOs are involved in preparatory consultations and in disseminating results. They have not been allowed direct access to the decision-making process where deals are struck.

These measures have been reasonably effective in defusing some of the sharp criticism of economic diplomacy in the fields of trade, finance and development. In many respects international environmental policy making was more transparent already. With continued work to ensure that NGO views are heard and that policy-making is transparent, it may be possible to achieve general acceptance of the legitimacy of economic diplomacy. It may be too early to say that the days are past when economic diplomacy served client based or interest based politics, as defined by Phil Evans in Chapter 8. Client based politics is where private lobbies seek to 'capture' the decision-making process for their own benefit. This clearly influences economic diplomacy even in major developed economies, notably in agriculture. Interest based economic diplomacy is still a powerful force, in which specific sector interests compete against each other for economic advantages. But the more open, public nature of economic diplomacy today has increased the importance of 'entrepreneurial politics', in which a group or coalition of actors campaigning for a specific policy or cause can also shape negotiating positions.

Conclusions and a Final Image

In the future, economic diplomacy faces a number of interdependent challenges:

- to make the international system more inclusive, engaging more countries without undermining the ability to deal effectively with the issues;
- to coordinate more state actors in decision-making and improve the capacity of governments to overcome domestic obstacles to international commitments;
- to ensure decision-making is accepted as legitimate and respond to the growth in 'entrepreneurial politics'.

The responses most favoured in the mid-2000s have been an increase in summitry and the use of informal groupings, together with a shift to more overt use of multi-level economic diplomacy and to more voluntary co-operation. These all increase flexibility, which may well be needed to make economic diplomacy more inclusive, but reduce the incentive to reach international agreement.

The essence of the two-level game metaphor is that dynamic interaction between the international and the domestic levels provides an incentive for domestic policy reform and international agreement. The responses identified above indicate not only the systemic difficulties in including more states, but also, more seriously, a reduced willingness to accept domestic reform. The greatest danger for economic diplomacy lies in continued failure to reconcile its second tension, between international and domestic pressures. If this persists, any progress in reconciling the first tension, by greater international inclusiveness, or the third tension, by engaging non-state actors, is likely to be incomplete and short-lived.

In economic diplomacy it no longer makes sense to think of states as impervious entities that can operate internationally while protecting their domestic regime completely. The few remaining countries to try that, like North Korea, are descending ever deeper into poverty. Even the deplorable Taliban movement in Afghanistan relied heavily on revenues from the international drugs trade. But at the same time it makes no sense either to talk about 'a borderless world' or the end of the nation state. Physical borders are being removed, but regulatory borders are still in place. Governments have lost some of their powers, but their responsibilities remain. Only the nation state provides the basis for democratic legitimacy.

The borders that are disappearing, however, are the borders between international and domestic policies. This book about economic diplomacy has tried to show what that means for decision-making and negotiation, within governments, between governments and by governments in international institutions.

Economic diplomacy is like cookery. If the national economic pudding goes into the international steamer for too short a time, it comes out hard and unpalatable, however much brandy and raisins may be in it. But if it is left there too long, it dissolves into a tasteless mush. The skill is in the balance between ingredients, timing and intensity of cooking. There are all sorts of different types of cookery in economic diplomacy, as this book has shown, and Chinese and Indian cuisine is now gaining ground. The authors of the practitioner chapters, like practising chefs, have explained how different dishes are prepared. But in the end, the proof of the pudding is in the eating.

References

Bayne, N. (2005), *Staying Together: the G8 Summit Confronts the Twenty-first Century*, Ashgate, Aldershot.

Beattie, A. (2007), 'G8 Pledge on Aid to Africa Threatened as Spending Falls', *Financial Times*, 4 April.

Bhagwati, J. (1995), 'US Trade Policy: the Infatuation with FTAs', in Bhagwati, J. and Kreuger, A. (eds), *The Dangerous Drift to Preferential Trade,* American Enterprise Institute, Washington.

Daneshku, S. (2007), 'Big Economies Renew Vow on Imbalances', *Financial Times*, 16 April.

Green, D. and Griffith, M. (2002), 'Globalisation and its Discontents', *International Affairs*, Vol. 78, No. 1, pp. 49–68.

James, H. (1996), *International Monetary Cooperation Since Bretton Woods*, International Monetary Fund, Washington.

Odell, J.S. (2000), *Negotiating the World Economy*, Cornell University Press, Ithaca and London.

Putnam, R.D. and Henning, C.R. (1989), 'The Bonn Summit of 1978: A Case Study in Coordination', in Cooper, R.N. and others (eds), *Can Nations Agree? Issues in International Economic Cooperation*, The Brookings Institution, Washington, pp. 12–140.

Bibliography

Note. The main part of this bibliography lists books, articles and papers posted on websites. A list of useful websites is added at the end.

Aberbach, J., Putnam, R.D. and Rockman, B. (1981), *Bureaucrats and Politicians in Western Democracies*, Harvard University Press, Cambridge, MA.

Addison, T., Hansen, H. and Tarp, F. (eds) (2004), *Debt Relief for Poor Countries*, Palgrave Macmillan, Basingstoke.

Aggarwal, V. and Fogerty, E. (2004), *EU Trade Strategies: Regionalism and Globalism*, Palgrave Macmillan, Basingstoke.

Baldwin, D.A. (1985), *Economic Statecraft*, Princeton University Press, Princeton, NJ.

Baldwin, M., Peterson, J. and Stokes, B. (2003), 'Trade and Economic Relations', in Peterson, J. and Pollack, M. (eds), *Europe, America and Bush: Transatlantic Relations after 2000*, Routledge, London, pp. 29–46.

Ball, A. and Millard, F. (1986), *Pressure Politics in Industrial Societies: A Comparative Introduction*, Macmillan Education, Houndmills.

Ball, C., Falkner. R. and Marquand, H. (eds) (2002), *Cartagena Protocol on Biosafety: Reconciling Trade in Biotechnology with Environment and Development*, Earthscan, London.

Bamberger, C.S. (2004), *IEA – the First 30 Years*, Organisation for Economic Cooperation and Development/International Energy Agency, Paris.

Barnsley, I. (2006), 'Dealing with Change: Australia, Canada and the Kyoto Protocol', *The Round Table*, No. 385, pp. 399–410.

Barston, R.P. (2006), *Modern Diplomacy*, 3rd edition, Longmans, London.

Bayliss, J. and Smith, S. (1998), *The Globalization of World Politics: an Introduction to International Relations*, Oxford University Press, Oxford.

Bayne, N. (1987), 'Making Sense of Western Economic Policies: the Role of the OECD', *The World Today*, Vol. 43, No.1, pp. 4–11.

Bayne, N. (1997), 'What Governments Want From International Institutions and How They Get It', *Government and Opposition*, Vol. 32, No. 2, pp. 361–79.

Bayne, N. (1997a), 'Globalization and the Commonwealth: International Economic Relations in the Post-Cold War World', *The Round Table*, No. 344, pp. 473–84.

Bayne, N. (1998), 'Britain, the G8 and the Commonwealth', *The Round Table*, No. 348, pp. 445–57.

Bayne, N. (2000), 'Why Did Seattle Fail: Globalisation and the Politics of Trade', *Government and Opposition*, Vol. 35, No. 2, pp. 131–51.

Bayne, N. (2000a), *Hanging in There: the G7 and G8 Summit in Maturity and Renewal*, Ashgate, Aldershot.

Bayne, N. (2005), *Staying Together: the G8 Summit Confronts the Twenty-first Century*, Ashgate, Aldershot.

Bayne, N. and Woolcock, S. (2003), *The New Economic Diplomacy: Decision-Making and Negotiation in International Economic Relations*, 1st edition, Ashgate, Aldershot.

Bergsten, C.F. (2001), 'America's Two-Front Economic Conflict', *Foreign Affairs*, Vol. 80, No. 2, pp. 16–27.

Bergsten, C.F. (2004), 'Foreign Economic Policy for the Next President', *Foreign Affairs*, Vol. 83, No. 2, pp. 88–101.

Bergsten, C.F. (2005), *The United States and the World Economy: Foreign Economic Policy for the Next Decade*, Institute for International Economics, Washington.

Berridge, G.R., Keens-Soper, M. and Otte, T.G. (2001), *Diplomatic Theory from Machiavelli to Kissinger*, Palgrave, Basingstoke.

Berridge, G.R. and James, A. (2003), *A Dictionary of Diplomacy*, 2nd edition, Palgrave Macmillan, London.

Bhagwati, J. (1995), 'US Trade Policy: The Infatuation with FTAs', in Bhagwati J. and Kreuger A. (eds), *The Dangerous Drift to Preferential Trade*, AEI Press, Washington.

Bhagwati, J. (2001), 'After Seattle: Free Trade and the WTO', *International Affairs*, Vol. 77, No. 1, pp. 15–30.

Bhagwati, J. (2004), *In Defense of Globalization*, Oxford University Press, Oxford.

Bhagwati, J. and Srinvasan, T. (1982), 'The Welfare Consequences of Directly Unproductive Profit-seeking (DUP) Lobbying Activities: Price *Versus* Quality Distortions', *Journal of International Economics*, Vol. 13, No. 1, pp. 33–44.

Blair, D. (1993), *Trade Negotiations in the OECD: Structures, Institutions and States*, Kegan Paul International, London and New York.

Blair, T. (2005), Special Address by Tony Blair at the World Economic Forum in Davos, 27 January 2005, accessible at www.g8.gov.uk.

Blustein, P. (2001), *The Chastening: Inside the Crisis that Rocked the Global Financial System and Humbled the IMF*, Perseus Books Group, Cambridge, MA.

Blustein, P. (2005), *And the Money Kept Rolling in (and out): Wall Street, the IMF and the Bankruptcy of Argentina*, Public Affairs, New York.

Bodensky, D. (2003), 'Transatlantic Environmental Relations', in Peterson, J. and Pollack, M. (eds), *Europe, America and Bush: Transatlantic Relations after 2000*, Routledge, London, pp. 59–68.

Bomberg, E. and Stubb, A. (2003), *The European Union: How Does it Work?*, Oxford University Press, Oxford.

Borowiak, C. (2004), 'Farmers' Rights: Intellectual Property Regimes and the Struggle over Seeds', *Politics & Society*, Vol. 32, No. 4, pp. 511–43.

Breslin, J.W. and Rubin, J.Z. (eds) (1991), *Negotiation Theory and Practice*, PONs Books, Cambridge, MA.

Broad, R. (2002), *Global Backlash: Citizen Initiatives for a Just World Economy*, Rowman and Littlefield Publishers, Lanham, MD.

Budd, C. (2003), 'G8 Summits and Their Preparation', in Bayne, N. and Woolcock, S. (eds), *The New Economic Diplomacy: Decision-Making and Negotiation in International Economic Relations*, 1st edition, Ashgate, Aldershot, pp. 139–146.

Bull, H. (1977/1995), *The Anarchical Society: A Study of Order in World Politics*, 1st edition 1977, 2nd edition 1995, Macmillan, Basingstoke.

BusinessEurope (2006), BusinessEurope *Position on Non-Agricultural Market Access Negotiations* at www.businesseurope.eu/content/default.asp?PageId=435.

Cable, V. (1999), *Globalisation and Global Governance*, Royal Institute for International Affairs, London.

Carius, A. and Lietzmann, K.M. (1999) (eds), *Environmental Change and Security*, Springer, Berlin.

Castells, M. (1994). 'European Cities, the Informational Society and the Global Economy', *New Left Review*, Vol. I/204, pp. 18–32.

CEFIC *Facts and Figures*, accessible at www.cefic.org/factsandfigures.

CEFIC (1999), *CEFIC Comments on a New Multilateral Trade Round*, 15 March 1999, at www.cefic.be/Templates/shwPublications.asp?NID=2&T=3&S=9&P=4.

Chan Chin Bock (2002), *Heart Work: Stories of How EDB Steered the Singapore Economy from 1961 to the Twenty-first Century*, Singapore Economic Development Board, Singapore.

Chandler, J.A. (ed.) (1993), *Local Government in Liberal Democracies: An Introductory Survey*, Routledge, New York.

Christopher, W. (1998), *In the Stream of History*, Stanford University Press, Stanford, CA.

Cigler, A. (1991), 'Organisational Maintenance and Political Activity on the Cheap: the American Agriculture Movement', in Cigler, A. and Loomis, B. (eds), *Interest Group Politics*, Congressional Quarterly Press, Washington.

Cohen, J.E. (2000), *Politics and Economic Policy in the United States*, 2nd edition, Howard Mifflin Co., Boston.

Cohen, S. (1994), *The Making of United States International Economic Policy: Principles, Problems, and Proposals for Reform*, Praeger, Westport, VA.

Cohen, S., Paul, J. et al. (1996), *Fundamentals of US Foreign Trade Policy: Economics, Politics, Laws and Issues*, Westview Press, Boulder, CO.

Cohn, T. (2002), *Governing Global Trade: International Institutions in Conflict and Convergence*, Ashgate, Aldershot.

Commission for Africa (2005), *Our Common Interest: An Argument*, Penguin Books, London.

Compa, L. and Vogt, J. (2001), 'Labor Rights in the Generalized System of Preferences: A 20-Year Review', *Comparative Labor Law and Policy Journal*, Vol. 22, No. 2/3, pp. 199–238.

Cooper, A.F. (1997), *Canadian Foreign Policy: Old Habits and New Directions*, Prentice Hall, Scarborough, Ontario.

Crockett, A. (Chairman) (2007), *Report of the Committee to Study Sustainable Long-Term Financing of the IMF*, accessible at www.imf.org.

Croome, J. (1999), *Reshaping the World Trading System: a History of the Uruguay Round*, 2nd edition, World Trade Organization, Geneva.

Cutler, C. (2003), *Private Power and Global Authority: Transnational Merchant Law in the Global Political Economy*, Cambridge University Press, Cambridge.

Daedalus (1975), 'The Oil Crisis: In Perspective', Special Issue, Vol. 104, No. 4, pp. 1–294.

Destler, I.M. (2005), *American Trade Politics*, 4th edition, Institute for International Economics, Washington.

Diamond, J. (2005), *Collapse: How Societies Choose to Fail or Succeed*, Penguin Books, London.

Diebold, W. (1952), 'The End of the ITO', *Essays in International Finance No. 16*, Princeton University Press, Princeton, NJ.

DFID (2000), *Eliminating World Poverty: Making Globalisation Work for the Poor*, White Paper on International Development Presented to Parliament by the Secretary of State for International Development, Stationery Office, London.

Drake, W.J. and Nicolaides, K. (1992), 'Ideas, Interests and Institutionalization: "Trade in Services" and the Uruguay Round', *International Organization*, Vol. 46, No. 1, pp. 37–100.

ECJ (1971), European Court of Justice Judgment of 31 March 1971, Commission/Council – *AETR*, Case 22/70.

ECJ (2006) European Court of Justice Judgment of 30 May 2006, Commission/Ireland - *Mox Plant Sellafield*, Case C-459/03.

ECR (2001), Opinion 2/00 (2001) European Court Reports I-9713.

ECR (2002), Case C-281/01 (2002) European Court Reports I-12049.

ECR (2006), Case C-94/03 (2006) European Court Reports I-1.

Eichengreen, B. (1998) 'Dental Hygiene and Nuclear War', *International Organization*, Vol. 52, No. 4, pp. 993–1012.

Eichengreen, B. (1999), *Towards a New International Financial Architecture*, Institute for International Economics, Washington.

Ellings, R. and others (eds) (2003), *Strategic Asia 2003–04*, National Bureau of Asian Research, Seattle.

European Commission (1994), Directorate General for External Economic Relations, Unit of Analysis and Policy Planning, *Trade and Investment*, Discussion Paper, December 1994.

European Commission (1999), Submission from the European Communities 'EC Approach to Trade and Investment' to the World Trade Organization, Document WT/GC/W/245 of 9 July 1999.

European Community (2002), Treaty establishing the European Community, Official Journal C325 of 24 December 2002.

European Union (2006), REACH Regulation, EU Official Journal, L 396 of 30 December 2006.

Evans, H. (2000), *Plumbers and Architects*, FSA Occasional Papers, Financial Services Authority, London.

Evans, P., Jacobsen, H.K. and Putnam, R.D. (eds) (1993), *Double-Edged Diplomacy: International Bargaining and Domestic Politics*, University of California Press, Berkeley, CA.

Evenett, S. (2006), '"Global Europe": An Initial Assessment', *Swiss Review of International Economic Relations*, Special Issue, available at http://www.unisg. ch/org/siaw/web.nsf/wwwPubInhalteEng/97C9C24CCB7863A4C125728 E004EFF79?opendocument.

Evenett, S.J. and Meier, M. (2007), 'An Interim Assessment of the US Trade Policy of "Competitive Liberalisation"' accessible at www.evenett.com.

Fasan, O. (2006), 'Compliance with WTO Law in Developing Countries: A Study of South Africa and Nigeria', PhD Dissertation, LSE.

Fisher, R., Ury, W. and Patton, B. (1991) *Getting to Yes*, Houghton Mifflin and Co., Boston, MA.

Frankel, J. (2001), 'The Crusade for Free Trade: Evaluating Clinton's International Economic Policy', *Foreign Affairs*, Vol. 80, No. 2, pp. 155–61.

Gardner, R. (1980), *Sterling-Dollar Diplomacy in Current Perspective*, revised edition, Columbia University Press, New York.

Garrett, G. (1998), *Partisan Politics in the Global Economy*, Cambridge University Press, Cambridge.

Garten, J.E. (2005), 'The Global Economic Challenge', *Foreign Affairs*, Vol. 84, No. 1, pp. 37–48.

GATT (1994), *The Results of the Uruguay Round of Multilateral Trade Negotiations*, General Agreement on Tariffs and Trade, Geneva.

Gilardi, F. (2001), *Principal-Agent Models Go to Europe: Independent Regulatory Agencies as Ultimate Step of Delegation*, paper presented at the ECPR General Conference, Canterbury, UK, accessible at www.leidenuniv.nl/fsw/ ecpr/pubchoice/gilardi.pdf.

Gilardi, F. (2002), 'Policy Credibility and Delegation to Independent Regulatory Agencies: a Comparative Empirical Analysis', *Journal of European Public Policy*, Vol. 9, No. 6, pp. 873–93.

Gilpin, R. (1987), *The Political Economy of International Relations*, Princeton University Press, Princeton, NJ.

Goldstein, J. (1988), 'Ideas, Interests and American Trade Policy', *International Organization*, Vol. 42, No. 1, pp. 179–217.

Goldstein, J. and Martin, L. (2000), 'Legalization, Trade Liberalization, and Domestic Politics: A Cautionary Note', *International Organization*, Vol. 54, No. 3, pp. 603–32.

Goodman, M. (2003), 'An Overview of US-Japanese Economic Relations', in Bayne, N. and Woolcock, S. (eds), *The New Economic Diplomacy: Decision-Making and Negotiation in International Economic Relations*, 1st edition, Ashgate, Aldershot, pp. 181–96.

Goodwin, M. and Painter, J. (1996), 'Local Governance, the Crises of Fordism and the Changing Geographies of Regulation', *Transactions, Institute of British Geographers*, Vol. 21, pp. 635–648.

Green, D. and Griffith, M. (2002), 'Globalisation and its Discontents', *International Affairs*, Vol. 78, No. 1, pp. 49–68.

Greenwood, J. and Wilson, D. (1990), *Public Administration in Britain Today*, Unwin Hyman, London.

Grieco, J. (1990) *Cooperation Among Nations; Europe, America and Non-Tariff Barriers to Trade*, Cornell University Press, Ithaca, NY.

Grubb, M., Koch, M., Thomson, K., Minson, A. and Sullivan, F. (1993), *The 'Earth Summit' Agreements – a Guide and Assessment: an Analysis of the Rio 1992 UN Conference on Environment and Development*, Earthscan, London.

Grubb, M. with Vrolijk, C. and Brack, D. (1999), *The Kyoto Protocol: a Guide and Assessment*, Royal Institute of International Affairs, London.

Grubb, M. and Neuhoff, K. (eds) (2006), *Emissions Trading and Competitiveness: Alllocations, Incentives and Industrial Competitiveness under the EU Emissions Trading Scheme*, Earthscan, London.

Gurria, R. and Volcker, P. (2000), *The Role of the Multilateral Development Banks in Emerging Market Economies*, accessible at the website of the Carnegie Endowment for International Peace, www.ceip.org.

Haas, P. (1992), 'Epistemic Communities and International Policy Coordination: Introduction', *International Organization*, Vol. 46, No. 1, pp. 1–35.

Hajnal, P. (2007), *The G8 System and the G20*, Ashgate, Aldershot.

Halpin, D. (ed.) (2005), *Surviving Global Change? Agricultural Interest Groups in Comparative Perspective*, Ashgate, Aldershot.

Hanson, P. (1988), *Western Economic Statecraft in East-West Relations: Embargoes, Sanctions, Linkage, Economic Warfare and Détente*, Royal Institute of International Affairs, London.

Hart, J.A. (2004), *Technology, Television and Competition: The Politics of Digital TV*, Cambridge University Press, Cambridge.

Hart, J.A. (2005), 'The G8 and the Governance of Cyberspace', in Fratianni, M., Kirton, J.J., Rugman, A.M. and Savona, P. (eds), *New Perspectives on Global Governance: Why America Needs the G8*, Ashgate, Aldershot, pp. 137–52.

Haufler, V. (2001), *A Public Role for the Private Sector: Industry Self-Regulation in a Global Economy*, Carnegie Endowment for International Peace, Washington.

Held, D., McGrew, A., Goldblatt, D. and Perraton, J. (1999), *Global Transformations: Politics, Economics and Culture*, Polity Press, Cambridge.

Henderson, D. (1993), 'International Economic Cooperation Revisited', *Government and Opposition*, Vol. 28, No. 1, pp. 11–35.

Henderson, D. (1999), *The MAI Affair: A Story and Its Lessons*, Royal Institute for International Affairs, London.

Hirst, P. and Thompson, G. (1999), *Globalisation in Question*, 2nd edition, Polity Press, Cambridge.

Hocking, B. (2000), *Diplomacy of Image & Memory: Swiss Bankers and Nazi Gold*, Diplomatic Studies Program Discussion Paper No. 64, University of Leicester.

Hoekman, B.M. and Kostecki, M.M. (2001), *The Political Economy of the World Trading System: the WTO and Beyond*, Oxford University Press, Oxford.

Howe, G. (1994), *Conflict of Loyalty*, Macmillan, London.

Hufbauer, G.C., Wong, Y., and Sheth, K. (2006), *US-China Trade Disputes: Rising Tide, Rising Stakes*, Institute for International Economics, Washington.

Hughes, N.C. (2005) 'A Trade War with China?' *Foreign Affairs*, Vol. 84, No. 4, pp. 94–106.

ICCA (1991), *ICCA Position on the Joint Framework Agreement for Tariff Harmonization in the Uruguay Round*, 28 October 1991, see www.icca-chem.org/section06e.html.

ICCA (2005), ICCA *Market Access for the Doha Development Agenda*, May 2005, at www.icca-chem.org/section06e.html.

ICCA (2005a), ICCA *Position Paper on SAICM* of 9 June 2005, accessible at www.icca-chem.org/section06.html.

IEA (1974), Agreement on an International Energy Program, accessible at www.iea.org/textbase/about/iep.pdf.

IEA (1993), Shared Goals of Energy Policy, accessible at www.iea.org/textbase/about/sharedgoals.htm.

IEA (2005), *World Energy Outlook 2005*, accessible at www.worldenergyoutlook.org.

IEA (2005a), Communiqué from Meeting of Governing Board at Ministerial Level, 2005, accessible at www.iea.org/textbase/press/pressdetail.asp?PRESS_REL_ID=147.

IEA (2006), *Energy Technology Perspective Scenario Analysis*, accessible at www.iea.org/textbase/papers/2006/scenario.pdf.

Ikenberry, G.J., Lake, D.A. and Mastandano, M. (eds) (1988), *The State and American Foreign Economic Diplomacy*, Cornell University Press, Ithaca, NY.

IMF (1999), *External Surveillance of Fund Surveillance: Report by a Group of Independent Experts*, accessible at www.imf.org under 'surveillance'.

IMF (2003), *The IMF and Recent Capital Account Crises: Indonesia, Korea and Brazil*, Independent Evaluation Office of the IMF, accessible at www.imf.org.

IMF (2006), *Evaluation Report, Multilateral Surveillance, 2006*, Independent Evaluation Office of the IMF, accessible at www.imf.org.

IPCC (2007), The Fourth Assessment Reports of the Intergovernmental Panel on Climate Change, accessible at <http://www.ipcc.ch/>.

Jackson, J.H. (1969) *World Trade and the Law of the GATT*, Bobbs-Merrill Company, New York.

Jackson, J.H. (1990), *Restructuring the GATT System*, Royal Institute of International Affairs, London.

Jackson, J.H. (1997), *The World Trading System*, Massachusetts Institute of Technology Press, Cambridge, MA.

James, H. (1996), *International Monetary Cooperation Since Bretton Woods*, International Monetary Fund, Washington.

Johnson, P. (1991), 'Organised Labor in an Era of Blue Collar Decline', in Cigler, A. and Loomis, B. (eds), *Interest Group Politics*, Congressional Quarterly Press, Washington.

Jones, M. (1998), 'Restructuring the Local State: Economic Governance or Social Regulation?', *Political Geography*, pp. 959–88.

Kagan, R. (2006), *Dangerous Nation: America's Place in the World from its Earliest Days to the Dawn of the Twentieth Century*, Atlantic Books, London.

Kantha, S. (2006), *Building India with Partnership: The Story of CII 1885–2005*, Penguin, New Delhi.

Kaplan, R.D. (1996), *The Ends of the Earth. From Togo to Turkmenistan, from Iran to Cambodia – a Journey to the Frontiers of Anarchy*, Vintage, New York.

Kapur, R., Lewis, J. and Webb, S. (1997), *The World Bank: Its First Half Century*, The Brookings Institution, Washington.

Keck, M.E. and Sikkink, K. (1998), *Activists Beyond Borders : Advocacy Networks in International Politics*, Cornell University Press, Ithaca, NY.

Kenen, P.B. (ed.) (1994), *Managing the World Economy: Fifty Years after Bretton Woods*, Institute of International Economics, Washington.

Kenen, P.B. (2001), *The International Financial Architecture: What's New? What's Missing?*, Institute for International Economics, Washington.

Kenen, P.B., Shafer, J., Wicks, N. and Wyplosz, C. (2004), *International Economic and Financial Cooperation: New Issues, New Actors, New Responses*, Geneva Reports on the World Economy, No. 6, International Centre for Monetary and Banking Studies, Geneva.

Keohane, R.O. (1984), *After Hegemony. Cooperation and Discord in the World Political Economy*, Princeton University Press, Princeton, NJ.

Keohane, R.O. and Nye, J.S. (2001), 'Between Centralization and Fragmentation: The Club Model of Multilateral Cooperation and Problems of Democratic Legitimacy', *Kennedy School of Government Working Paper No. 01–004*, available at SSRN: http://ssrn.com/abstract=262175.

Kindleberger, C. (1973), *International Economics*, R.D. Irwin, Homewood, IL.

Klein, N. (2000), *No Logo*, Vintage Canada, Toronto.

Korten, D. (1995), *When Corporations Rule the World*, Kumarian Press and Berrett-Koehler Publishers, San Francisco.

Laird, S. (2002), 'A Round by Any Other Name', *Development Policy Review*, Vol. 20, No. 1, pp. 41–62.

Lalumière Report (1998), *Report by Catherine Lalumière and Jean-Pierre Landau on the Multilateral Investment Agreement*, English translation available at www. geocities.com/w_trouble_o/lumiere.htm.

Lampreia, L.F. and da Cruz, A.S. (2005), 'Brazil: Coping with Structural Constraints', in Robertson, J. and M.A. East (eds) *Diplomacy and Developing Nations*, Routledge, London.

Lampton, D.M. (ed.) (2001), *The Making of China's Foreign and Security Policy in the Era of Economic Reforms*, Stanford University, Stanford, CA.

Landau, A. (2000), 'Analyzing International Economic Negotiations: Towards a Synthesis of Approaches', *International Negotiation*, Vol. 5, pp. 1–19.

Lantzke, U. (1975), 'The OECD and its International Energy Agency', *Daedalus*, Vol. 104, No. 4, pp. 217–28.

Lehne, R. (1993), *Industry and Politics: United States in Comparative Perspective*, Prentice Hall, New Jersey.

Leifer, M. (2000), *Singapore's Foreign Policy: Coping with Vulnerability*, Routledge, London.

Lempereur, A.P. and Colson, A. (2004), *Méthode de Négociation*, Dunod, Paris.

Lincoln, E. (1999), *Troubled Times: US-Japan Trade Relations in the 1990s*, The Brookings Institution, Washington.

Lovelock, J. (1995), *Ages of Gaia*, 2nd edition, Oxford University Press, Oxford.

Lovelock, J. (2006), *The Revenge of Gaia*, Penguin Books, London.

McNamara, K. (2005), 'Economic and Monetary Union', in Wallace, H., Wallace, W. and Pollack, M.A. (eds), *Policy-Making in the European Union*, 5th edition, Oxford University Press, Oxford, pp. 141–60.

McNamara, K. and Meunier, S. (2002), 'Between National Sovereignty and International Power: What External Voice for the Euro?', *International Affairs*, Vol. 78, No. 4, pp. 849–68.

Mahler, G. (1992), *Comparative Politics: An Institutional and Cross-National Approach*, Prentice Hall, New Jersey.

Majone, G. (1994), 'The Rise of the Regulatory State in Europe', *West European Politics*, Vol. 17, No. 3, pp. 77–101.

Majone, G. (1997), *The Agency Model: The Growth of Regulation and Regulatory Institutions in the European Union*, http://aei.pitt.edu/786/01/scop97_3_2.pdf.

Malan, P. (Chairman) (2007), *Report of the External Review Committee on Bank-Fund Collaboration*, accessible at www.worldbank.org, and www.imf.org.

Mallaby, S. (2004), *The World's Banker*, Yale University Press, New Haven and London.

Malloy, M. (2001), *US Economic Sanctions: Theory and Practice*, Aspen Publishers, New York.

Mandelbaum, M. (2002) 'The Inadequacy of American Power', *Foreign Affairs*, Vol. 81, No. 5, pp. 61–73.

Mansfield, E. and Milner, H. (1997), *The Political Economy of Regionalism*, Columbia University Press, New York.

Marjolin, R. (1989), *Architect of European Unity: Memoirs 1911–1986*, Weidenfield and Nicholson, London, translated by William Hall from *Le Travail d'une Vie*, Robert Laffont, Paris 1986.

Marshall, P. (1999), *Positive Diplomacy*, Palgrave, Basingstoke.

Mbirimi, I., Chilala, B. and Grynberg, R. (2003), *From Doha to Cancun: Delivering a Development Round*, Commonwealth Secretariat, London.

McIntyre, W.D., Mole, S., Ashworth, L.M., Shaw, T.M. and May, A. (2007), 'Whose Commonwealth? Responses to Krishnan Srinavasan's *The Rise, Decline and Future of the British Commonwealth*', *The Round Table*, No. 388, pp. 57–70.

Meltzer, A. (Chairman) (2000), *Report of the International Financial Institutions Advisory Commission*, United States Congress, Washington.

Meunier, S. (2005) *Trading Voices: The European Union in International Commercial Negotiations*, Princeton University Press, Princeton, NJ.

Meunier, S. and Nicholaidis, K. (1999) 'Who Speaks for Europe? The Delegation of Trade Authority in the EU', *Journal of Common Market Studies*, Vol. 37, No. 3, pp. 477–501.

Milner, H. (1988), *Resisting Protectionism: Global Industries and the Politics of International Trade*, Princeton University Press, Princeton, NJ.

Milner, H. (1997) *Interests, Institutions and Information: Domestic Politics and International Relations*, Princeton University Press, Princeton, NJ.

Milner, H. (1998) 'Rationalizing Politics: The Emerging Synthesis of International, American and Comparative Politics', *International Organization*, Vol. 52, No. 4, pp. 759–86.

Misquitta, L. (1991). *Pressure Groups and Democracy in India*, Sterling Publishers Private Limited, New Delhi.

Moran, M. (2003), *The British Regulatory State: High Modernism and Hyper-Innovation*, Oxford University Press, Oxford.

Munck, R. and Waterman, P. (1999), *Labour Worldwide in the Era of Globalization*, Macmillan Press, Houndmills.

Murphy, R.T. (1996), *The Weight of the Yen: How Denial Imperils America's Future and Ruins an Alliance*, W.W. Norton & Co., Inc., New York.

Narlikar, A. and Tussie, D. (2004), 'The G20 at the Cancun Ministerial: Developing Countries and their Evolving Coalitions in the WTO', *World Economy*, Vol. 27, No. 7, pp. 947–66.

NFTC Report (2005), *Making the Case for Ambitious Tariff Cuts in the WTO's Non-agricultural Market Access Negotiations*, National Foreign Trade Council WTO Tariff Analysis Project, May 2005, see www.nftc.com.

Nordström, H. (2005), 'The World Trade Organization Secretariat in a Changing World', *Journal of World Trade*, Vol. 39, No. 5, pp. 819–53.

Nye, J. (2003), *The Paradox of American Power: Why the World's Only Super-power Can't Go it Alone*, Oxford University Press, Oxford.

Oberthür, S. and Ott, H. (1999), *The Kyoto Protocol: International Climate Policy for the Twenty-first Century*, Springer, Berlin.

O'Brien, R., Goetz, A.M., Scholte, J.A. and Williams, M. (2000), *Contesting Global Governance: Multilateral Economic Institutions and Global Social Movements*, Cambridge University Press, Cambridge.

Odell, J.S. (2000), *Negotiating the World Economy*, Cornell University Press, Ithaca, NY.

Odell, J.S. (ed.) (2006), *Negotiating Trade: Developing Countries in the WTO and NAFTA*, Cambridge University Press, Cambridge.

OECD (1987), *Introduction to the OECD Codes of Liberalisation*, Organisation for Economic Cooperation and Development, Paris.

OECD (1992), *The OECD Declaration and Decisions on International investment and Multinational Enterprises*, 1991 Review, Organisation for Economic Cooperation and Development, Paris.

OECD (1993), *Foreign Direct Investment: Policies and Trends in the OECD Area During the 1980s*, Organisation for Economic Cooperation and Development, Paris.

OECD (1995), *A Multilateral Agreement on Investment*: Report by the Committee on International Investment and Multinational Enterprises (CIME) and the Committee on Capital Movements and Invisible Transactions (CMIT), Document OECD/GD(95)65, Paris.

Ohmae, K. (1992), *The Borderless World: Power and Strategy in the Interlinked Economy*, Routledge, London.

Ohmae, K. (1995), *The End of the Nation State*, HarperCollins, London.

Olins, W. (1999), *Trading Identities: Why Countries and Companies are Taking on Each Others' Roles*, Foreign Policy Centre, London.

Olson, M. (1965), *The Logic of Collective Action*, Harvard University Press, Cambridge, MA.

O'Neill, J. and Hormats, R. (2004), *The G8: Time for a Change*, Global Economics Paper 112, Goldman Sachs, accessible at www.gs.com.

Ostry, S. (1997), *The Post-Cold War Trading System: Who's On First?*, University of Chicago Press, Chicago.

Paarlberg, R. (1995), *Leadership Begins at Home: US Foreign Economic Policy after the Cold War*, The Brookings Institution, Washington.

Padoa-Schioppa, T. (2004), *The Euro and its Central Bank: Getting United after the Union*, MIT Press, Cambridge, MA.

Page, S. (2003), *Developing Countries – Victims or Participants: Their Changing Roles in International Negotiations*, Overseas Development Institute, London, accessible at www.odi.org.uk.

Pedersen, P. (2006), 'The WTO Decision-Making Process and Internal Transparency', *World Trade Review*, Vol. 5, No. 1, pp. 103–31.

Persaud, B. (2001), 'OECD Curbs on Offshore Financial Centres: A Major Issue for Small States', *The Round Table*, No. 359, pp. 199–212.

Peterson, J. and Pollack, M. (eds), *Europe, America and Bush: Transatlantic Relations after 2000*, Routledge, London.

Porter, M.E. (2000), 'Location, Competition, and Economic Development: Local Clusters in a Global Economy', *Economic Development Quarterly*, Vol. 14, No. 1, pp. 15–34.

Preeg, E. (1970), *Traders and Diplomats: An Analysis of the Kennedy Round of Negotiations under the GATT*, The Brookings Institution, Washington.

Preeg, E. (1995), *Traders in a Brave New World*, Chicago University Press, Chicago.

Princen, S. (2005), 'Governing through Multiple Forums: The Global Safety Regulation of Genetically Modified Crops and Foods', in Koenig-Archibugi, M. and Zürn, M. (eds), *New Modes of Governance in the Global System*, Palgrave, Basingstoke.

Putnam, R.D. (1988), 'Diplomacy and Domestic Politics: the Logic of Two-Level Games', *International Organization*, Vol. 42, No. 4, pp. 427–60.

Putnam, R.D. and Bayne, N. (1987), *Hanging Together: Cooperation and Conflict in the Seven-Power Summits*, SAGE, London.

Putnam, R.D. and Henning, C.R. (1989), 'The Bonn Summit of 1978: A Case Study in Coordination', in Cooper, R.N. and others (eds), *Can Nations Agree?*

Issues in International Economic Cooperation, The Brookings Institution, Washington, pp. 12–140.

Rana, K.S. (2000), *Inside Diplomacy*, Manas, New Delhi.

Rana, K.S. (2002), *Bilateral Diplomacy*, DiploFoundation, Malta, and Manas Publications, New Delhi.

Rana, K.S. (2004), 'Economic Diplomacy in India: A Practitioner's Perspective', *International Studies Perspectives*, Vol. 5, pp. 66–70.

Rana, K.S. (2004/5), *The Twenty-first Century Ambassador*, DiploFoundation, Malta and Geneva, and Oxford University Press India, New Delhi.

Rana, K.S. (2006), 'Singapore's Diplomacy: Vulnerability into Strength', *The Hague Journal of Diplomacy*, Vol. 1 No. 1, pp. 81–106.

Rana, K.S. (2007), *Asian Diplomacy: The Foreign Ministries of China, India, Japan, Singapore and Thailand*, DiploFoundation, Malta and Geneva.

Ray, J.E. (1995), *Managing Official Export Credit: The Quest for a Global Regime*, Institute for International Economics, Washington.

Reinalda, B. and Verbeek, B. (eds) (1998), *Autonomous Policy Making by International Organisations*, Routledge, London.

Reiter, J. (2006), 'International Investment Rules', in Woolcock, S. (ed.), *Trade and Investment Rule-making: The Role of Regional and Bilateral Agreements*, UN University Press, Tokyo, pp. 208–40.

Rollo, J. (2006), 'Global Europe: Old Mercantilist Wine in New Bottles?', *Swiss Review of International Economic Relations*, Special Issue, available at http://www.unisg.ch/org/siaw/web.nsf/wwwPubInhalteEng/97C9C24CCB7863A4C125728E004EFF79?opendocument.

Ruggie, J.G. (1982), 'International Regimes, Transactions and Change; Embedded Liberalism in the Postwar Economic Order', *International Organization*, Vol. 36, pp. 379–415.

Sachs, J.D. (2005), 'The Development Challenge', *Foreign Affairs*, Vol. 84, No. 2, pp. 78–90.

Saner, R. and Yiu, L. (2003), *International Economic Diplomacy: Mutations in Modern Times*, Studies in Diplomacy No. 84, Clingendael, The Hague.

Sassen, S. (2001), *The Global City: New York, London, Tokyo*, Princeton University Press, Princeton, NJ.

Schanz, K.-U. (1995), 'Der Marktzugang im WTO-Welthandelssystem: Zollsenkungen auf Industrieprodukten und Neuerungen bei den Ausgleichsmassnahmen für Dumping und Subventionen', in Cottier, T. (ed.), *GATT-Uruguay Round*, Verlag Stämpfli & Cie, Berne.

Scholte, J. A. (2000), 'Global Civil Society', in N. Woods (ed.), *The Political Economy of Globalisation*, Macmillan Press, London.

Scholte, J.A. and O'Brien, R. (1999), 'The WTO and Civil Society', *Journal of World Trade*, Vol. 33, No. 1, pp. 107–24.

Schoppa, L. (1997), *Bargaining with Japan: What American Pressure Can and Cannot Do*, Columbia University Press, New York.

Schott, J. (ed.) (2003) *Free Trade Agreements: US Strategies and Priorities*, Institute of International Economics, Washington.

Scott, R. (1994), *IEA – the First 20 Years*, Organisation for Economic Cooperation and Development/ International Energy Agency, Paris.

Sebenius, J.K. (1983), 'Negotiation Arithmetic: Adding and Subtracting Issues and Parties', *International Organization*, Vol. 37, pp. 281–316.

Sell, S. (2003), *Private Power, Public Law: The Globalization of Intellectual Property Rights*, Cambridge University Press, Cambridge.

Slaughter, A.-M. (2000), 'Governing the Global Economy through Government Networks', in Byers, M. (ed.), *The Role of Law in International Politics: Essays in International Relations and International Law*, Oxford University Press, Oxford.

Slaughter, A.-M. (2005), 'Disaggregated Sovereignty: Towards the Public Accountability of Global Government Networks', in Held, D. and Koenig-Archibugi, M. (eds), *Global Governance and Public Accountability*, Blackwell, Oxford.

Snyder, E. (1963), 'Foreign Investment Protection: a Reasoned Approach', *Michigan Law Review*, Vol. 61, No. 6, pp. 1087–124.

Spero, J. and Hart, M. (2003), *The Politics of International Economic Relations*, 6th edition, Thompson/Wadsworth, Belmont, CA.

Srinavasan, K. (2005), *The Rise, Decline and Future of the British Commonwealth*, Palgrave Macmillan, Basingstoke.

Stern, N. (2006), *Stern Review on the Economics of Climate Change*, Cambridge University Press, Cambridge.

Stiglitz, J. (2006), *Making Globalization Work*, Penguin/Allen Lane, London.

Stockholm Declaration (1972) of the Stockholm Conference on the Human Environment, accessible at www.unep.org/Law/PDF/Stockholm_Declaration.pdf.

Strange, S. (1988), *States and Markets: an Introduction to Political Economy*, Pinter, London.

Strange, S. (1996), *The Retreat of the State: the Diffusion of Power in the World Economy*, Cambridge University Press, Cambridge.

Tarrow, S. (2005), *The New Transnational Activism*, Cambridge University Press, Cambridge.

Thatcher, M. (1993), *The Downing Street Years*, HarperCollins, London.

Thatcher, M. (2002), 'Delegation to Independent Regulatory Agencies: Pressures, Functions and Contextual Mediation', *West European Politics*, Vol. 25, No. 1, pp. 125–47.

Truman, D. (1981), *The Governmental Process: Political Interests and Public Opinion*, Greenwood Press.

Ulbert, C. and Risse, T. (2005), 'Deliberately Changing the Discourse: What Does Make Arguing Effective?', *Acta Politica*, Vol. 40, No. 3, pp. 351–67.

UNCED (1992), Agenda 21 adopted at UN Conference on Environment and Development, accessible at www.un.org/esa/sustdev/documents/agenda21/english/agenda21toc.htm.

UNCTAD (2000), *Bilateral Investment Treaties 1959–1999*, United Nations, New York.

UNCTAD (2004), International Investment Agreements: Key Issues, Volume I, Document UNCTAD/IIE/IIT/2004/10 of 10 December 2004.

UNEP (2002), Enhancing Civil Society Engagement in the Work of the United Nations Environment Programme, Document UNEP/GD.22/INF/13 of 21 November 2002.

US Council for International Business (1995), *The Multilateral Agreement on Investment; the Next Challenge for Global Interdependence*, United States Council for International Business, New York.

US Senate (1982), US-Panama Bilateral Investment Treaty, Senate Treaty Document 99–14, 99th Congress, 2nd Session, 27 October 1982.

Vandevelde, K. (1998), 'The Political Economy of a Bilateral Investment Treaty', *American Journal of International Law*, Vol. 92, no 4, pp. 621–41.

Van den Bosche, P. (2005), *The Law and Policy of the World Trade Organization*, Cambridge University Press, Cambridge.

Wallace, H., Wallace, W. and Pollack, M.A. (eds) (2005), *Policy-Making in the European Union*, 5th edition, Oxford University Press, Oxford.

Walter, A. (2000), 'Unravelling the Faustian Bargain: Non-State Actors and the Multilateral Agreement on Investment', in Josselin, D. and Wallace, W. (eds), *Non-State Actors in World Politics*, Palgrave, Basingstoke.

Waterman, P. (1999), 'The New Social Unionism: A New Union Model for a New World Order', in Munck, R. and Waterman, P. (eds), *Labour Worldwide in the Era of Globalization*, Macmillan Press, Houndmills.

Watts, R. (1970), *Administration in Federal Systems*, Hutchinson Educational Ltd, London.

Wechsler, W. (2001), 'Follow the Money', *Foreign Affairs*, Vol. 80, No. 4, pp. 40–57.

Wilson, E.O. (2006), *The Creation: An Appeal to Save Life on Earth*, W.W. Norton, New York.

Wilson, G. (1981), *Interest Groups in the United States*, Clarendon Press, Oxford.

Wilson, J.Q. (ed.) (1980), *The Politics of Regulation*, Basic Books, London.

Wilton Park (2005), 'Diplomacy Today: Delivering Results in a World of Changing Priorities', www.wiltonpark.org.uk/documents/conferences/WP505–4/pdfs/WP505–4.pdf.

Winham, G.R. (1986), *International Trade and the Tokyo Round Negotiations*, Princeton University Press, Princeton, NJ.

Winham, G.R. (1992), *The Evolution of International Trade Agreements*, University of Toronto Press, Toronto.

Wolf, M. (2004), *Why Globalisation Works*, Yale University Press, New Haven and London.

Wolfe, R. (1998), *Farm Wars: The Political Economy of Agriculture and the International Trade Regime*, Macmillan, London.

Wolfe, R. (2007 forthcoming), 'From Reconstructing Europe to Constructive Globalisation: the OECD in Historical Perspective', in Mahon, R. and McBride, S. (eds), *The OECD in Global Governance*, University of British Columbia Press, Vancouver.

Woods, N. (2006), *The Globalizers: The IMF, the World Bank and their Borrowers*, Cornell University Press, Ithaca, NY.

Woodward, R. (2006), 'Age Concern: the Future of the OECD', *The World Today*, Vol. 62, No. 8–9, pp. 38–9.

Woolcock, S. (1998), 'European and American Approaches to Regulation: Continuing Divergence?', in Van Scherpenberg, J. and Thiel, E. (eds), *Towards Rival Regionalism? US and EU Economic Integration and the Risk of Transatlantic Regulatory Rift*, Stiftung Wissenschaft und Politik, Eberhausen.

Woolcock, S. (1999), 'The United States and Europe in the Global Economy' in Burwell, F.G. and Daalder, I.H. (eds), *The United States and Europe in the Global Arena*, Macmillan, London, and St Martin's Press, New York, pp. 177–207.

Woolcock, S. (2000), 'European Trade Policy: Global Pressures and Domestic Constraints', in Wallace, H. and Wallace, W. (eds), *Policy Making in the European Union*, 4th edition, Oxford University Press, Oxford.

Woolcock, S. (2003), 'The ITO, the GATT and the WTO', in Bayne, N. and Woolcock, S. (eds), *The New Economic Diplomacy: Decision-Making and Negotiation in International Economic Relations*, 1st edition, Ashgate, Aldershot, pp. 103–20.

Woolcock, S. (2005), 'European Trade Policy', in Wallace, H., Wallace, W. and Pollack, M.A. (eds), *Policy-Making in the European Union*, 5th edition, Oxford University Press, Oxford, pp. 377–400.

Woolcock, S. (ed.) (2006), *Trade and Investment Rule-Making: The Role of Regional and Bilateral Agreements*, UN University Press, Tokyo.

Woolcock, S. and Hodges, M. (1996), 'The European Union in the Uruguay Round: The Story behind the Headlines', in Wallace, H. and Wallace, W. (eds), *Policy-Making in the European Union*, 3rd edition, Oxford University Press, Oxford, pp. 301–24.

World Bank (2006), *World Development Report 2006*, World Bank, Washington.

WSSD (2002), Report of the World Summit on Sustainable Development, UN Document A/CONF/199/20*, accessible at www.un.org/doc/UNDOC/GEN/N02/636/93/PDF/N0263693.pdf?OpenElement.

WTO (1996), Guidelines for Arrangement on Relations with Non-Governmental Organizations, Document WTO/L/62 of 23 July 1996.

WTO (2001), Minutes of the General Council Meeting of 22 November 2000, Document WTO/WT/GC/M/60 of 23 January 2001.

WTO (2001a), Doha Ministerial Declaration, Document WTO/WT/MIN(01)/DEC1 of 20 November 2001.

WTO (2003), Japan's Submission on 'Zero-for-Zero' and 'Harmonisation', Document WTO/TN/MA/W/15/Add.2 of 4 March 2003.

WTO (2003), Ministerial Statement of World Trade Organization Ministerial Conference, 5th Session, Cancun 10–14 September, Document WT/MIN(03)20 of 23 September 2003.

WTO (2004), Decision adopted by the General Council on 1 August 2004 (the July Package), Document WT/L/579 of 2 August 2004.

WTO (2005), Communication on Tariff Liberalization in the Chemicals Sector made by Canada, Japan, Norway, Separate Customs Territory of Taiwan, Penghu, Kinmen and Matsu, Singapore, Switzerland, and the United States, Document WTO/TN/MA/W/58 of 4 July 2005.

WTO (2005a), Hong Kong Ministerial Declaration, Document WTO/WT/MIN(05)/DEC, of 22 December 2005.

WTO (2005b), *The Future of the WTO*, Report of the Eminent Persons Group chaired by Peter Sutherland, World Trade Organization, Geneva.

WTO (2006), Communication by Singapore on an Update on the Negotiations on the Sectoral Tariff Component, Document WTO/TN/MA/W/8/Add.1 of 1 February 2006.

WTO (2006a), Progress Report: Sectoral Discussions on Tariff Elimination in the Chemical Sector, Communication from the United States, Document WTO/TN/MA/W/18/Add. 13 of 4 April 2006.

WTO (2006b), List of Documents, Note by the Secretariat, WTO/TN/MA/S/16/Rev.4 of 5 April 2006.

WTO (2006c), Communication on Tariff Liberalization in the Chemical Sector by Canada, Norway, Singapore, Switzerland, the Separate Customs Territory of Taiwan, Penghu, Kinmen and Matsu, and the United States, Document WTO/MA/W/72 of 15 May 2006.

WTO (2006d), *The Changing Landscape of Regional Trade Agreements*, World Trade Organization, Geneva.

Yergin, D. (1991), *The Prize: the Epic Quest for Oil, Money and Power*, Simon and Schuster, New York.

Zajac, E.E. (1995), *Political Economy of Fairness*, MIT Press, Cambridge, MA.

Useful Websites

American Chemistry Council: www.americanchemistry.com.
Asia-Pacific Economic Cooperation: www.apec.gov.
Bundesverband der Deutschen Industrie, e.V: www.bdi-online.de.
Bureau of Economic Analysis, US Department of Commerce: www.bea.gov.
Business and Industry Advisory Council (OECD): www.biac.org.
BusinessEurope (formerly UNICE): www.businesseurope.eu.
Chemical Industries Association (UK): www.cia.org.uk.
Commonwealth Secretariat: www.thecommonwealth.org.
DiploFoundation: www.diplomacy.edu.
European Central Bank: www.ecb.org.
European Chemical Industry Council: www.cefic.org.
European Commission: www.ec.europa.eu.
European Union: www.europa.eu.
Federchimica (Italy): www2.federchimica.it.
German G8 Presidency (2007): www.g-8.de.
G8 Research Group, University of Toronto: www.g8.utoronto.ca.
Indian Brand Equity Fund: www.ibef.org.

Intergovernmental Forum on Chemical Safety: www.who.int/ifcs/en/.

Intergovernmental Panel on Climate Change: www.ipcc.ch.

International Chamber of Commerce: www.iccwbo.org.

International Council of Chemical Associations: www.icca-chem.org.

International Energy Agency: www.iea.org.

International Energy Forum: www.iefs.org.sa.

International Monetary Fund: www.imf.org.

Inter-Organization Programme for the Sound Management of Chemicals: www.who.int/iomc/en/.

Japan Chemical Industry Association: www.nikkakyo.org.

Joint Oil Data Initiative: www.jodidata.org.

Millennium Ecosystem Assessment: www.maweb.org.

Organisation for Economic Cooperation and Development: www.oecd.org.

Organisation of Petroleum Exporting Countries: www.opec.org.

Professor G.R. Berridge: http://www.grberridge.co.uk.

Russian G8 Presidency (2006): www.g8russia.ru.

Singapore Economic Development Board: http://www.edb.gov.sg.

'Studies in Diplomacy' Papers, Clingendael Institute, The Hague: http://www.clingendael.nl.UK Department for International Development: www.dfid.gov.uk.

UK G8 Presidency (2005): www.g8.gov.uk.

Union des Industries Chimiques (France): www.uic.fr.

United Nations Environment Programme: www.unep.org.

United Nations Millennium Goals: www.un.org/millenniumgoals/.

US Trade Representative's Office: www.ustr.gov.

US Department of State: www.state.gov.

US Treasury Department: www.ustreas.gov.

Verband der Chemischen Industrie, e. V. (Germany): www.vci.de.

World Bank Group: www.worldbank.org.

World Bank 'Education for All' Programme: www1.worldbank.org/education/efafti/.

World Business Council for Sustainable Development: www.wbcsd.org.

World Summit on Sustainable Development: www.un.org/events/wssd/.

World Trade Organization: www.wto.org.

Index